Sports

coaching

Principles

Sports Training Principles

Third edition

Frank W. Dick

A & C Black · London

Published by A & C Black (Publishers) Ltd
35 Bedford Row, London WC1R 4JH

Third edition 1997
Second edition 1989

First edition published 1980 by Lepus Books,
an imprint of Henry Kimpton (Publishers) Ltd

Copyright © by Frank Dick 1980, 1989, 1997

ISBN 0 7136 4149 5

A CIP catalogue record for this book
is available from the British Library

Typeset in 10½ on 12pt Sabon

Printed and bound in Great Britain by
Bell & Bain Limited, Scotland

Contents

Preface

Introduction   1

Part 1 **Rods to levers**   3

1 The working parts   4
Axes   4
Joint actions   6
Basic structure   8
The upper limbs   12
Spine   16
The lower limbs   19
Male/female body
   variations   23
Summary   26

**2 Structural changes in the
growing child**   27
Stages of growth   27
Summary   32

3 Basic mechanics   34
Definitions   34
Laws of motion   40
Summary   42
Summary of part 1   42

Part 2 **The living machine**   45

4 Nutrition   46
Carbohydrates   48
Fats   52
Proteins   57
Mineral elements   60
Vitamins   62
Nutritional intake for
   the athlete   65
Summary   68

**5 The oxygen transporting
system**   69
Definition, functions and
   effects   69
Maximal oxygen uptake   80
Acclimatisation to altitude   81
Summary   82

6 The working muscle   84
The energy pathways   84
The muscle   88
Summary   96

7 The fluid systems   97
Homeostasis   97
Specific fluids: composition
   and function   97
Temperature regulation   101
Summary   106

8 The hormones   107
Local hormones   107
General hormones   110
The secreting glands   113
Summary   121

**9 Physiological differences in
the growing child**   122
Effects of stress   122
Summary   126
Summary of part 2   127

Part 3 **Mission control**   131

**10 *Victor in mente,
victor in corpore***   132
Intellectual preparation of
   the athlete   132
Personality of the athlete   146
Relationship between
   athlete and coach   147
Summary   153

11 Technical training   **154**
Motor learning   154
The learning concept   156
Aims of technical training   162
Summary   172

**12 Psychological changes
and the growing child**   **173**
General patterns   173
Motor learning
   characteristics   175
Summary   178
Summary of part 3   **178**

Part 4 **The language of
training theory**   **183**

13 Fitness   **184**
The general picture   184
Basic principles in training   187
Effect of training   188
Basic physical
   characteristics   189
Points on fitness and
   training   189
Summary   191

**14 Theory and practice of
strength development**   **192**
Strength   192
Strength relative to
   movement   197
Development of strength   198
Summary   214

**15 Theory and practice of
speed development**   **215**
Speed in sport   215
Speed development   216
The annual cycle   224
Summary   225

**16 Theory and practice of
endurance development**   **226**
Training methods   226
Summary   239

**17 Theory and practice of
mobility development**   **240**
Mobility classification   240

Mobility training   244
Summary   246

18 Evaluation in sport   **247**
Status classification   247
Summary   250
Summary of part 4   **250**

Part 5 **Planning the
programme**   **253**

19 Periodising the year   **255**
Preparation period   255
Competition period   258
Transition period   259
Year-round adaptations   260
Summary   260

**20 Variations in
periodisation**   **261**
Setting out the time scale   261
Single and double
   periodisation   264
Summary   265

**21 Units, microcycles and
macrocycles**   **267**
The training unit   267
The microcycle   267
Macrocycles   272
Summary   274

22 Adaptation to loading   **275**
Definition   275
Summary   284

23 Training v straining   **286**
Summary   293

24 Competition period   **294**
Competition   294
Summary   302
Summary of part 5   **303**

Postscript   **305**
Putting the principles into practice

Index   **307**

Preface

It has always fascinated me that athletes whose training plans seem extremely diverse are able to produce almost identical times over their racing distance. This fascination naturally led me to enquiry, the beginning of which is a study of the relevant aspects of anatomy, physiology and psychology. In presenting my interpretation of these aspects, I wish to acknowledge, both with respect and gratitude, the counsel of several authorities:

Dr H. Robson (Loughborough University) and Dr Siggerseth (University of Oregon), who were my lecturers in anatomy and kinesiology; Tom Craig (formerly physiotherapist to Glasgow Rangers Football Club), who wrapped much 'meat around the bones' of part 1. Dr Soderwall (University of Oregon), Dr Clyde Williams (Loughborough University), and Dr Craig Sharp (West London Institute of HE), guided me through the complexities of physiology, which I present as part 2. Professor Miroslav Vanek (Charles University, Prague), Peter Hill and Jean Carroll (both formerly of Dunfermline College of Physical Education), and Pamela F. Murray (Wolverhampton University) provided new insight to the world of psychology, as set out in part 3. Bridging anatomy, physiology and psychology is the theme of applying each science to the growing child, a concept made much clearer for me by Dr Ivan Szmodis (Central School of Sports, Budapest).

The sciences of anatomy, physiology and psychology are essential basics to arriving at the result of the enquiry, but are as far from being an explanation as are bricks to being a house. Part 4 might be thought of as the 'cement', to give these bricks their shape. So many associates have helped me in this area of study that it would be impossible for me to list them all here. However, I would like to record my deep indebtedness to them and to mention especially:

Dr Geoff Gowan, Ron Pickering, Wilf Paish, Friedhelm Endemann, Stewart Togher, Vladimir Kuznyetsov, Peter Radford, Sandy Ewen, Gerard Mach, Carlo Vittori, Wilson Young, Gordon Forster, Denis Watts, Harry Wilson, Alex Naylor, Bill Bowerman, Elio Locatelli, Seppo Nutilla, Peter Coe, Max Jones, Carlton Johnson, John Issacs, Erkki Oikarinen, Rita Englebrecht, Dr Ekkart Arbeit, and Norman Brooke for their thoughts and comments on strength, speed, mobility and endurance.

It would be very difficult to say exactly when I first began to draw together the detail of the final part of this book. Whenever it was, it will coincide with the origins of that fascination referred to above. Part 5 I see as the design or blueprint, and it is my opinion that every coach I have ever met (from several sports) is responsible for its content.

It has also become very clear to me that central to the education and development of any coach, is that unique learning which athletes provide. I owe each one of the athletes I have coached an immense debt in this respect.

Although the book began to grow several years before pen was put to paper in the autumn of 1975 for the first edition, the nature of its contents is such that the subject matter will require regular review. The second edition did, in fact, review certain aspects of strength, speed and endurance training, and, in particular, focussed more tightly on the area of regeneration in the section 'Training v straining'.

In this, the third edition, three colleagues have contributed their specialist knowledge to take the components of training theory as set out here, to a new level. Dr Craig Sharp (West London Institute) has reviewed and edited part 2, whilst Professor Miroslav Vanek (Charles Institute, Prague) and Pamela F. Murray (researcher, Wolverhampton University) have written and introduced new material for part 3. I am very grateful for their professional and authoritative input.

As a student, it was put to me that each one of us is exposed to thousands of facts and opinions and that any ideas we think of as our own are, in fact, simply an interpretation of these facts and opinions. My objective here has been to present my interpretation of principles which may help you establish your interpretation of training theory to the advantage of the athletes in your charge. I hope you discover this to be the case.

Throughout this book athletes and coaches are, in the main, referred to individually as 'he' rather than 'he or she'. This has been agreed with the publisher as an expedient only.

Introduction

'Those who are enamoured of practice without science, are like a pilot who goes into a ship without rudder or compass and never has any certainty of where he is going.' Leonardo da Vinci

Coaching is mainly an art and, like the artist, the coach must have two attributes. The first is creative flair, that marriage of aptitude and passion which enables him to draw an athlete's dream towards realisation. The athlete, moved to express himself within a social mosaic, chooses to do so in pursuit of competitive excellence in sport. The coach creates, for that expression, order and direction.

The second attribute is technical mastery of the instruments and materials used. The athlete is the instrument and the material with which the coach works. Structurally, he is a system of levers, given movement by the pull of muscle, and obedient to the laws of physics. Functionally, he is a dynamic integration of adaptive systems. But more than that, he is a reasoning being.

A gardener who works to create ever greater beauty in a plant, does so on the basis of his knowledge of the plant's behaviour in certain conditions. His art lies in the adjustment of these conditions. The coach may have the advantage over the gardener in that the athlete, unlike the plant, can perceive his total environment, rationalise situations, compare present with past, predict the consequences of actions and rapidly adapt his behaviour within his personal framework of mood, morality and motivation. At first sight, the active involvement of the athlete makes the coach's task seem simpler than that of the gardener. After all, 'two heads are better than one'! Yet the infinitely variable behaviour, which might result from even one simple adjustment to the athlete's environment, confirms the extraordinary complexity of the coach's art. The coach must clearly understand the purpose of each practice and its relevance to the total scheme of preparation, yet comprehend fully the role of sport as but one part of the life of a growing and changing person.

To accept the full weight of this responsibility, the coach, in these the final years of the 20th century, must move towards a deeper appreciation of those sciences which relate to the athlete. This is not to say that pragmatism is dead because there will continue to be situations where the coach 'knows' a practice is correct, according to his 'feel' for coaching athletes. This is, of course, part of the coach's art and it should stimulate

1

rather than inhibit pursuit of explanation. Many established practices may work (and for good reason) but, until underlying principles are defined, what basis do we have for developing further practices or for communicating experience in coaching to *all* sports?

In drawing together the substance of the following pages, it has not been my intention to create an apotheosis of sports-science. The various chapters will, I hope, contribute to the coach's sources of reference, form part of a basis for understanding current coaching research, and offer a framework of training principles for the development of an ever-expanding reservoir of practices designed to help the athlete acquire a fitness for excellence in his sport.

The coach is most certainly not 'enamoured of practice without science', but I would not wish to make of him a bookworm, equipped only with sports-science jargon. His art is to weave his understanding of related sciences into the fabric of coaching an athlete. It is a practical art, based on careful appraisal of all relevant knowledge. I hope that this book will contribute to your interpretation of this fine art.

Part 1

Rods to levers

An athlete may be thought of, structurally, as a series of connected rods. The design of each connection will determine the nature and range of movement between adjacent rods and, consequently, their potential function. These connections are, of course, the joints, and the rods, bones. Combined, they form the *skeletal system*. The movement at any given joint is made possible by the pull of muscle on bone across the joint. The total arrangement of muscle and its attachment to bones forms the *muscular system*. Part 1 looks at these two systems, and the mechanical laws which they must obey, to effect an appreciation of the athlete's aggregate movement potential for the expression of energy.

1
The working parts

Axes

It is easy to understand how a wheel spins, as it does, about an axle and at right angles to that axle. If the athlete had wheels instead of arms and legs, the axles being located at the shoulders and at the hips, it would again be easy to understand why the wheels would rotate or spin at right angles to the body and on the same plane as the direction in which the athlete was moving. If the axles are now faded out in the mind's eye and the arms and legs are considered as rotating like wheels – not round and round, but forwards and backwards like pendulums – one begins to appreciate that the body is equipped with invisible axles, or axes, and that the movement at the joints is rotation. However, whereas the wheel may rotate on one plane only, the body's joints permit greater freedom of movement.

Our bodies are three dimensional. There are three axes of rotation – vertical, transverse and anterio-posterior – for the body as a whole and, in theory, at each joint. We now look at the axes and consider them in the light of the whole body movement and the movement at various joints (fig. 1).

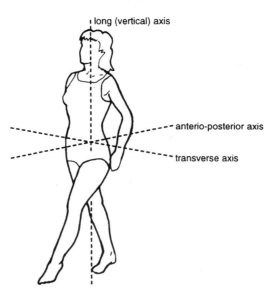

long (vertical) axis

anterio-posterior axis

transverse axis

Fig. 1 *The body's axes*

■ Vertical axis

The vertical axis is the long axis of the body and is best pictured as that about which the figure skater spins, or the ballet dancer pirouettes.

If the body is tilted to lie parallel with the ground, i.e. horizontal, rotation is still possible about the long axis (e.g. the child rolling sideways downhill or the straddle jumper rolling round the bar). However the axis is no longer vertical. In describing rotations, then, it is important to identify clearly the axes under consideration. Very little confusion arises when discussing the whole body in flight, but occasionally problems arise with a particular joint action. For example, just as the long axis of the body is referred to as the vertical axis, so also is the long axis through a joint. Hence the actions of turning out one's feet like Charlie Chaplin, twisting one's head and shoulders to the rear, and turning off a tap (with elbow extended) are all examples of rotation about the long/vertical axis. Taking the last example however, consider the arm held out to the side (abducted) and swung forwards, as in a discus throw. This rotation is about the vertical axis through the shoulder, while long axis rotation would, in this case, be about the transverse axis through the shoulder. The moral of the story is to *be precise in defining axes*.

■ Transverse axis

The transverse axis is that described in the 'wheels for limbs' reference above. These particular axes would apply to shoulder and hip. Examples of rotation about these axes in the athlete are kicking a ball, the pulling action of the arms in swimming, and the piking to extension movements of the gymnast. Returning to the vertical axis situation mentioned above, rotations about the transverse axis become rotations about the vertical axis when the arm is abducted. For example, the actions of underarm bowling and the forehand drive in tennis are similar in terms of movement at the shoulder joint, although different muscles may be involved due to changing angles of pull on levers. Consequently, when considering transverse axis rotations, one must also consider rotations with an abducted limb. These include the pull-through of the hurdler's trail leg into the line of running, and the golfer's swing.

The transverse axis of the body as a whole is that about which the trampolinist or springboard diver rotates in a front or back somersault, similarly the high jumper who uses flop technique.

■ Anterio-posterior axis

The cartwheel somersault of an acrobat gives the best visual image of an athlete rotating about the body's anterio-posterior (A-P) axis. This axis is from front to back and is seen in joint actions where, for example, a rider presses her knees against the flanks of her mount. A soldier standing at ease, then responding to a command to stand to attention (or vice versa), would be rotating the leg on the hip about the A-P axis. Similarly, arms raised sideways or returned to the side are rotating on the shoulder about the A-P axis. Other examples are the hip/spine movements of the sidestep or body swerve in football, the tilting of the pelvis in recovering the hurdler's trail leg, and certain expressions of movement in dance where the body reaches over to one side.

Joint actions

Related to the axes of rotation outlined, there are the specific actions of flexion, extension, adduction, abduction, and rotation. An understanding of these actions will allow fuller appreciation of movement and technique.

Flexion

Flexion is the rotating of one lever about another in such a way that the angle between these levers is reduced. The 'Mr Universe' pose, which looks as if the demonstrator is attempting to crush a melon between forearm and shoulder, is an example of flexion at the elbow. The soccer player who can keep the ball in the air by using his knee only is doing so by flexing his thigh on his hip and, simultaneously, his lower leg on his thigh. The spine too may be considered as a lever or a series of levers. As a guide, any movement which curls the athlete into a tucked shape or round, like a ball, is flexion of the spine.

Two types of flexion which tend to cause confusion are at the shoulder and at the ankle. Flexion at the shoulder is the raising forward of the arm above the head, as in swimming backstroke arm recovery. Flexion at the ankle is turning the toes up towards the knee (as in Aladdin's shoes!) when the foot is bearing weight. A variation of flexion at the shoulder is in actions such as bench press, discus arm, forehand drive in tennis, and shot-put arm. This action is referred to as horizontal flexion.

Extension

Extension might be thought of as the opposite of flexion and is the rotating of one lever away from another. Thus the angle between the levers increases towards 180°, in some instances even greater. When this happens, the action is referred to as hyper-extension. At the moment of delivery in shot-put, the arm is completely extended (straightened) at the elbow; as the basketball player leaves the floor for a jump shot, extension takes place at the hip, knee and ankle; or as the volleyball player jumps to block an opposition spike, then elbows, wrists and fingers are extended. In a hollow-back somersault, the extreme arching of the spine is hyper-extension.

Extension of the arm on the shoulder is the opposite action to that described for flexion and is demonstrated in the overhead smash shots in tennis, squash and badminton, also in javelin arm and in the powerful pull phases of the arm action when swimming butterfly, freestyle or breast-stroke. Extension at the ankle is pointing the toes away from the body so that the line of lower leg/foot is straight, or even convex. Ballet dancers and gymnasts are capable of the latter. Horizontal extension at the shoulder is seen when the athlete, standing in the crucifix position, presses the arms backwards.

The actions of flexion and extension are considered as rotations about the transverse axis of a given joint, and the body's tendency to a total flexion or extension is also about this axis.

■ Adduction

Adduction is the drawing of a lever towards the mid-line of the body, e.g. moving the legs from standing astride to standing with the legs together, or in returning the arms from a position in which they are out from the side back to the side. Thus the action of bringing the legs towards each other in breaststroke leg action is one of adduction, as is gripping the body of a horse with one's knees when riding.

The action of adduction may take a lever past the mid-line, e.g. in crossing one's legs or in sweeping a soccer ball across the body from one side to the other. Obviously, to perform such an action, the leg would have to be either slightly extended or flexed on the hip to permit passage of one leg beyond the obstruction of the other.

■ Abduction

Abduction is the opposite movement to adduction and is therefore the movement of a lever *away* from the mid-line. Raising an arm to the side and moving the legs from being together to legs astride are examples of abduction. The shot-putter emphasises the abduction of his putting arm and the hurdler abducts the trailing leg to ensure clearance of the barrier.

The actions of adduction and abduction are normally considered to take place about the A-P axis.

■ Rotation

All movements of levers are rotations, but the expression 'rotation', when considered with the anatomical actions of flexion, adduction, abduction and extension, is taken to mean long-axis rotation. When Charlie Chaplin turned his feet outwards, the action was outward or lateral rotation. When he turned them inwards, so that he was pigeon-toed, the action was inward or medial rotation. Lateral means 'to the outside or outwards', medial means 'to the inside or inwards'. Abduction, then, could be described as a lateral movement and adduction as a medial movement.

The action of rotation is normally understood to take place about the vertical axis, but care must be taken to define the axes precisely.

Basic structure

Bone

The rods are the athlete's bones and they become levers via the joints. The structure of each joint will dictate its function potential, hence the contrast between the mobility of the shoulder complex of joints and the stability of the hip joint; the difference between cervical intervertebral movement and the lumbar intervertebral movement; and the functional variable available to the elbow as opposed to the knee. While it is not essential that bone names be memorised, it is useful to know their relationship to each other (fig. 2).

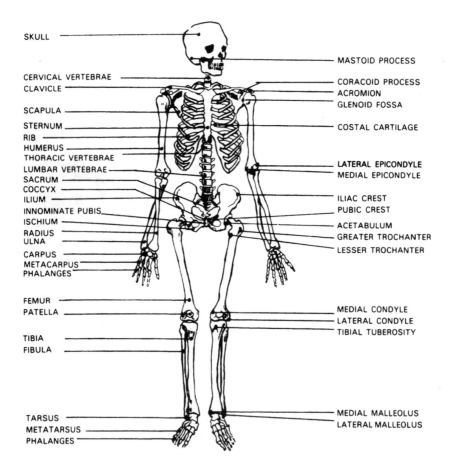

SKULL

MASTOID PROCESS

CERVICAL VERTEBRAE
CLAVICLE

CORACOID PROCESS
ACROMION
GLENOID FOSSA

SCAPULA

STERNUM
RIB
HUMERUS
THORACIC VERTEBRAE
LUMBAR VERTEBRAE
SACRUM
COCCYX
ILIUM
INNOMINATE PUBIS
ISCHIUM
RADIUS
ULNA
CARPUS
METACARPUS
PHALANGES

COSTAL CARTILAGE

LATERAL EPICONDYLE
MEDIAL EPICONDYLE

ILIAC CREST
PUBIC CREST

ACETABULUM
GREATER TROCHANTER
LESSER TROCHANTER

FEMUR
PATELLA

MEDIAL CONDYLE
LATERAL CONDYLE
TIBIAL TUBEROSITY

TIBIA
FIBULA

TARSUS
METATARSUS
PHALANGES

MEDIAL MALLEOLUS
LATERAL MALLEOLUS

Fig. 2 *The skeleton*

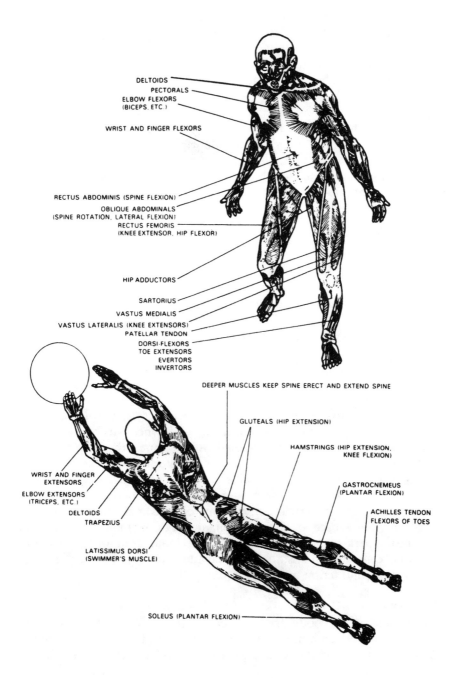

Fig. 3 *The muscles* (from McNaught and Callender, 1963)

■ Muscle

Muscles, by converting chemical energy into mechanical energy, pull on the bones and bring about the actions already described. The specific action of a muscle will be defined by the levers it connects and the position and angle of attachment (fig. 3). In several instances, a muscle crosses two joints and is therefore responsible for two separate actions. The efficiency of each action will be critically affected by the stability status of each joint.

■ Tendon

Tendon attaches muscle to bone. The Achilles tendon, for example, attaches the calf muscles responsible for ankle extension to the large bone at the rear of the heel (the calcaneus). If one grips this particular tendon between forefinger and thumb, the extreme toughness of this tissue is at once apparent. Due to this strength, the tendon itself is seldom injured. However, the connections of tendon to muscle or tendon to bone are very vulnerable to injury.

■ Ligaments

The ligaments are bands of white fibrous tissue connecting bones about a joint. They may be considered as guardians of the joint's stability as they are extremely resistant to distortion and stretch. Certain types of mobility work are geared to passive stretching of ligaments to permit a greater freedom or range of movement. However, it must be borne in mind that such work restricts their role as stabilisers. Once stretched, the ligament will maintain its new length, having plastic rather than elastic properties (fig. 4).

■ Periosteum

The connective tissue surrounding the bone is periosteum. In the grown organism it has a supporting function and when strong tendons or ligaments or muscle are attached to a bone, the periosteum is incorporated with them. This is the final connection of muscle to bone. While it is obviously a strong connection, it is nevertheless vulnerable to injury when strained. Stress may accumulate or occur as a result of fatigue and strong muscle contraction, or maximal contraction when imbalance has caused an unnatural alignment of the joint. In the growing organism, periosteum protects a layer of tissue containing the 'bone-growing' cells. It is an unstable material and extremes of muscular fatigue or force of contraction must be discouraged.

■ Synovia

Most joints of the body are completely surrounded by a capsule lined with a synovial membrane. This membrane lines the whole of the interior of the joint except the actual ends of the bones which meet in that particular joint. The membrane releases a constant small flow of a lubricant called synovia or synovial fluid. Exercise appears to increase the amount of fluid released, while injury to the joint encourages an extremely rapid flow.

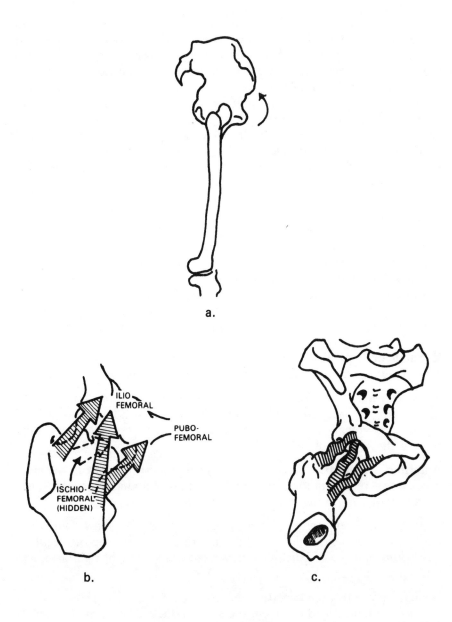

a.

b.

ILIO-
FEMORAL

PUBO-
FEMORAL

ISCHIO-
FEMORAL
(HIDDEN)

c.

Fig. 4 *The ligaments of the hip (from Kapandji, 1970). As the child develops from the quadruped posture to the erect posture, and the pelvis tilts upwards and backwards (a), all ligaments become coiled round the neck of the femur, in the same direction. Extension winds these ligaments tighter (b); flexion unwinds, and slackens them (c). The stretching of these ligaments in the quadruped to upright posture, demonstrates plastic, rather than elastic properties of ligaments*

■ Cartilage

Cartilage may be thought of as a shock-absorbing or reducing agent. In the knee, cartilage discs not only cushion the impact of movement between the two bones, but also serve to ensure perfect contact between them. Fibrocartilage discs act as cushions between the various bones or vertebrae which are stacked one upon the other in the spine. Finally, the ends of each bone meeting at a joint are protected by *articular* cartilage.

It should be remembered that cartilage has no blood supply and consequently cannot repair itself once damaged. However, it would appear that synovia provides cartilage with nutrients and it has been shown that with exercise the amount of available fluid increases. This flow increases the efficiency of joint movement.

▌ The upper limbs

Reflection on the number of movements and actions performed by the upper limb complex will point to its primary characteristic – mobility. Mobility depends on combinations and permutations of actions at four joints. These joints will be considered in order from that nearest the spine to that farthest from the spine. The technical terminology to describe part of an appendage nearest to the spine is proximal, and that more distant is distal.

■ Shoulder

The following shoulder actions are possible about the axes indicated.

Transverse axis: *flexion* – arm raised forwards; *extension* – arm pulled downwards or backwards. These opposing actions can be seen clearly in the arm movements in running. The plane in which these movements take place is the *sagittal* plane (fig. 5a).

Anterio-posterior axis: *abduction* – raising the arm out from the side; *adduction* – returning the arm from a position of abduction to the side. These actions are in the *frontal* plane (fig. 5b).

Vertical axis (arm parallel with spine): *rotation outward (lateral)* – clockwise movement of the straight right arm, e.g. turn a tap off; *rotation inward (medial)* – anti-clockwise movement of the straight right arm, e.g. turn a tap on.

Vertical axis (arm abducted): *horizontal flexion* – starting from a position with arm held out from the side (abducted), the arm is brought forward towards the mid-line. This is seen in the discus arm action, in bench press, or in wrapping the arms about the body to keep warm; *horizontal extension* – the reverse to horizontal flexion. These actions are in the *horizontal* plane (fig. 5c). Combinations of these actions permit immense adaptability, e.g. slipping an arm into a coat sleeve, combing the hair at the back of the head, scratching the opposite shoulder blade from above or below, throwing-in a ball at soccer, and even dislocations on the gymnastic rings.

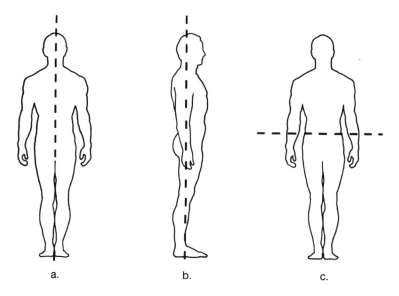

Fig. 5 *The primary planes of the body: (a) separation at the sagittal plane; (b) separation at the frontal plane; (c) separation at the horizontal plane*

Application examples of shoulder mobility

Arm action in high jump: a coaching point often quoted for high jump arm action is 'thumbs in, elbows out'. By turning in the thumbs the arms are medially rotated and this in turn slides the wing-like scapulae (shoulder blades) round the rear wall of the rib (thoracic) cage. As this happens, the joint between the humerus and the part of the scapula which receives it (glenoid fossa), is brought forward allowing greater range of extension.

Discus arm: in discus, the abducted arm must be supported by the powerful abductor muscles and the discus aligned by controlled inward rotation of the arm – yet the action which applies force to the discus is one of fast horizontal flexion over as great a range as possible. The limited degree of inward rotation must cause the scapula to be a restricting agent to a great range of horizontal extension, but is preferable to the outward rotation employed by the beginner who struggles to keep the discus securely gripped by the distal phalanges of his throwing hand at the limit of extension. (It is interesting to note that if the athlete continued this outward rotation, his arm would assume the starting position for javelin throw.) Many top discus throwers hang the discus low and behind the hip as if they were attempting to place the throwing hand in their hip pocket. Here the arm is kept inwardly rotated until the athlete moves into his throwing position, when the discus is then allowed to swing the arm out to an increased range of movement.

Javelin arm: the arm in the javelin throw is withdrawn prior to the actual throw, as in the outward rotation of the arm, the horizontal extension of the shoulder (arm abducted), the backward movement of the shoulder girdle, and rotation about the long axis of the spine. A fundamental adjustment must then be made to allow the thrower to pull along the length of the javelin and forcefully project it. This involves even greater rotation and a consequent sliding of the entire shoulder under the javelin. In fact, what is involved is a rapid positional change from extreme horizontal extension to extreme flexion. There is a clear relationship between this action and that of the tennis serve, the volleyball spike, and the soccer throw-in.

■ Elbow
At the elbow joint, two axes of rotation are evident.

Transverse axis: *flexion* – hand brought to the same shoulder; *extension* – elbow straightened. These opposing actions can be seen clearly in activities such as chinning the bar (flexion) and push-ups (extension).

Vertical axis: *pronation* – forearm is rotated medially to a palm down or overgrasp position; *supination* – forearm is rotated laterally to a palm-up or undergrasp position. These positions are clearly seen if one is using a screwdriver to screw or unscrew with the right hand. The clockwise action of screwing on a nut is supination, whilst the anti-clockwise action of unscrewing a nut is pronation. The right-handed vaulter supinates the right forearm and pronates the left in gripping the pole. The tennis player serves with pronation but supinates for backhand shots.

Elbow mechanics
Flexion efficiency depends on the position of the forearm, i.e. pronation or supination, and on the position of the arm relative to the shoulder. Extension efficiency depends on the position of the arm relative to the shoulder. Note, as an obvious example of relative efficiency, the varying strength measurements in table 1.

Table 1 *Elbow extension and flexion force compared in three different positions (Kapandji, 1970)*

position	extension force	flexion force
Arm stretched above shoulder	43 kg	83 kg
Arm flexed at 90°	37 kg	66 kg
Arm hanging at side of the body	52 kg	51 kg

From this we can deduce man's suitability to climbing and certain implications of limb alignment for vaulters and apparatus gymnasts. Considerable difference can be measured at 90° of flexion when the forearm assumes varying points of rotation between supination and pronation (table 2). The difference has been explained by Provins and Salter (1955) as (1) biceps are stretched but poor leverage, (2) brachioradialis is the same, (3) brachialis is the same, and (4) pronator teres is at greatest length and leverage.

Table 2 *Isometric flexion strength relative to elbow joint position*
(adapted from Rasch, 1968)

position	strength force	standard deviation
Supination	19.64 kg	3.82
Mid-position	21.60 kg	4.05
Pronation	13.41 kg	2.00

This will obviously make a difference in how biceps curls and chinning the bar are performed, also how high bars, poles, etc., are gripped. It should also be pointed out that in gripping a bar in pronation, with the object of performing biceps curls, the weight of the bar will place considerable stress on the extensor muscles of the wrist as the bar is raised. As the stress increases the wrist will be pulled to a position of flexion, thus stretching the extensors of the fingers and forcing the flexors to release their grip on the bar. The total effect is similar to that used in unarmed combat when attempting to disarm an opponent who holds a weapon. The hand containing the weapon is seized and the wrist forced into flexion.

Returning to extension of the elbow, the triceps are at their greatest mechanical advantage and are stretched when the arm is abducted. On the other hand, it must be realised that there is a problem since the action at the elbow and the shoulder are really opposing each other. Immediate connection should be clear with the 'high elbow' in shot. There is another little muscle involved in extension and that is the anconeus. Its main function is to pronate as the elbow extends, e.g. in javelin long-axis spin and in imparting spin to tennis shots.

■ Wrist

The wrist is a very adaptable complex of joints, offering rotation about three axes.

Transverse axis: *flexion* – palm of hand is moved towards the forearm; *extension* – back of hand is moved towards the forearm. These actions are immediately recognisable in the final wrist flick in shot-put (flexion), or the whip-cracking action of a badminton backhand (extension).

Anterio-posterior axis: *adduction* – small finger side of hand is moved towards the forearm; *abduction* – thumb side of the hand is moved towards the forearm. The former is seen when chopping wood with a hand axe, the latter in the final flicking action of the wrist when imparting spin to the discus.

Vertical axis: there is a limited amount of rotation about the long axis which contributes to the total manipulative capacity of the fingers. It must be constantly borne in mind that the force efficiency of this joint is limited, but must be developed if an accumulated force from leg, hip, trunk, shoulder and elbow are to be transferred to an implement held in the hand. This is particularly the case with a heavy implement such as shot, where wrist or finger injury can terminate an athlete's ambitions for an entire season. It is also pertinent for lighter implements such as javelin, racquet or golf club.

■ Fingers

All other joints of the upper limb complex combine to allow the discrete manipulative capacity of the fingers to function efficiently. The grab of a mechanical digger cannot perform its tasks efficiently if the arm has not been driven to the most efficient functioning site. Similarly, the control of shoulder, elbow and wrist are basic to the working of the fingers. These small joint complexes make fine movement possible by rotation about two axes for the four fingers and thumb.

Transverse axis: *flexion* – the beckoning action of curling the finger towards the palm; *extension* – the straightening of the finger to point or indicate. The fingers are flexed in all gripping activities. For example, holding a bar or bat or a throwing implement. Actions of extension are mainly seen as a return from flexion, but static extension may be held as, for example, in karate.

Anterio-posterior axis: *abduction* – spreading the fingers; *adduction* – bringing the fingers and thumb together as in the characteristic 'karate chop' position. The fingers are abducted to grip a discus or give maximum area to present to a basketball or water (swimming). Adduction is used when the talon grip is used in javelin.

In addition, the thumb is capable of *opposition*. This action is the bringing of the thumb across the palm to the small finger.

▌ Spine

The bony axis of the trunk is the spine, or spinal column. The spine is at once a single rigid lever and a series of levers. As a single lever it can sustain great burdens, or accept the powerful extension of the lower limbs to propel an object or the body itself. As a series of levers it is capable of immense mobility and can absorb the shock of impact from above or below. Thus the spine offers the body an extremely wide range of movement by virtue of its adaptability. The spine may be likened to a series of cotton reels joined end to end with a piece of string passing along the central tunnel. Each cotton reel represents a *vertebra*: man is a vertebrate because he has a backbone, a worm is invertebrate because it has none.

■ Vertebrae and discs

The vertebrae gradually increase in size from neck to tail. This is because each vertebra must bear the weight of all parts of the body above it. The farther down the spine, the greater the weight. Through the large part of the vertebra is transmitted the weight, hence its solid structure. Through the hole in the middle passes the spinal cord, like a vast bundle of wires in a telephone cable. This is the communications system linking brain and body. To damage this cable will cut off communications to parts of the body below the level of the damage, hence the terrible consequences of spinal injury and the classification system according to the level of injury in paraplegic sport.

The discs are the cushions between vertebrae. To damage a disc brings considerable pain and discomfort. Such discomfort is not so much due to the pressure of bone on bone, but to pressure on the cord, or branches of the cord, which leave the main cable via the gap between the two vertebrae normally kept free by the disc in question.

■ Shape of the spine

The analogy of a column of cotton reels is slightly inaccurate because the spine is not straight when viewed from the side or behind. The spine has a characteristic series of curves, the evolution of which is interesting.

Babies at birth have only one curve, that which gives the body the appearance of a comma (fig. 6a). The cervical (neck) curve is formed by the strong intermittent pull of the infant's muscles on the spine as he begins to sit up and hold up his head. It is emphasised further in the tilting back of the head to see where he is crawling to, or to look for his next meal (fig. 6b). Once he is on his feet, the pelvis (hip bone) is pulled forward and downward by ligaments attached to the bone of the thigh (fig. 4). This action, combined with the body's weight bearing down on the lower spine as he pulls himself erect, pulls the lower spine forward, completing the final shape of the spine (fig. 6c).

■ Movements in the spine

The tension of ligaments joining vertebrae and the shape of vertebrae at different levels of the spine dictate the movements of which the spine is capable. (Exceptions are the two vertebrae upon which the head rests; the atlas and axis vertebrae.) Rotation is possible about three axes in the spine, rendering a most mobile complex of joints.

Transverse axis: *flexion* – the curling forwards of the head towards the hips. It takes place in all regions of the spine, but is most free at the cervical and lumbar regions. The contribution of head and hip movement to the overall picture of spine flexion is worth noting. Tension of extensor muscles and solid restrictions, such as the ribs or excess weight about the middle, are the main limiting factors to spine flexion. Flexion is seen in front somersault or in the rock-back position in pole vault. The shoulders may readily become rounded, encouraging flexion of the spine at its upper third. This shows in a stoop and can be brought about by tiring or weakening of the extensors, occupational postures, or overconditioning of flexors. The ease with which this may happen creates a problem in weight bearing on the shoulders, where instability is introduced and injury may result due to exceptional pressure for which this part of the lever system is ill-prepared; *extension* – the straightening of the spine. It takes place most freely at the cervical and lumbar spine, but is restricted in the thoracic spine. The expression of hyper-extension is used to describe a degree of extension which moves far beyond normal postural extension. This movement is very evident in the crab position in gymnastics, the hollow-back somersault, and so on.

Anterio-posterior axis: *lateral flexion* – the curving of the spine to either side, as in reaching the right fingers towards the right ankle while looking straight ahead. It is possible at all levels, but is greatest at the junction between thoracic and lumbar spine. The tilting of the pelvis to recover the trail leg in hurdles involves a degree of lateral flexion, as do twisting movements involved in the complex patterns of agility displayed in diving, ball games, etc.

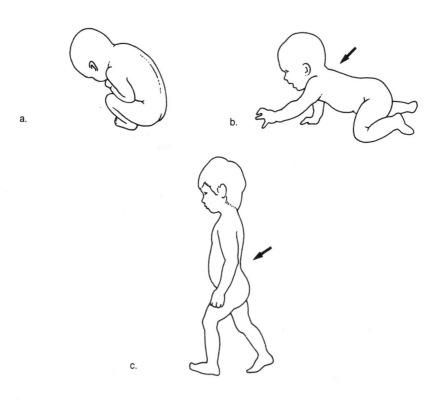

Fig. 6 *The developing spine: (a) the new-born baby has one spinal curve – making the basic shape something similar to a comma. This curve will remain in the thoracic region; (b) the young child has already introduced a second curve in the cervical region; (c) once upright, the third curve is developed in the lumbar region*

Vertical axis: rotation/twisting along the length of the spine is most free in the cervical region and through the thoracic region, but is negligible in the lumbar spine. This particular property of the spine is very important and both strength and mobility must be worked for. The athlete attempts to take the spine to extremes of rotation in order to 'compress the spring' in throws, hence the 'wound-up' position in discus and javelin.

The lower limbs

Although the complex of lower limb joints offer a limited movement potential compared with the upper limbs, they are extremely stable. Indeed, this stability is fundamental to the two basic functions of the lower limbs: support of the body's weight, and locomotion.

Hip

It is very important to remember two details when considering hip joint movement. First, many of the muscles which are involved in joint actions at the hip are also involved in joint actions at the knee (fig. 7). Secondly, the pelvis (hip) is jointed not only with the femur (thigh) but also with the spine.

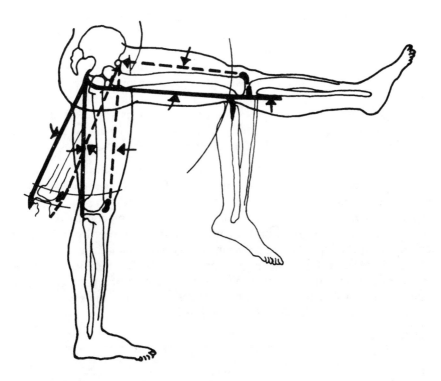

Fig. 7   *Effect of two-joint actions on two-joint muscles: rectus femoris (dotted line) and hamstring group (solid line) (from Kapandji, 1970)*

This suggests the importance of careful analysis of movement in any technical sport. The correct alignment of pelvis and spine is critical if maximum advantage is to be gained from the contribution of muscle actions at the hip joint (with femur), knee, ankle and foot. The following actions are possible about the axes indicated.

Transverse axis: *flexion* – the thigh is raised forward towards the chest. A limiting factor in this action is the state of flexion or extension at the knee. This is due to the 'hamstrings' group of muscles bridging two joints. When both hips are flexed, there is a tilting upwards and backwards of the pelvis, flattening the lumbar curve. Tilting the pelvis in this way aids hip flexion; *extension* – the thigh is pulled backwards. A limiting factor again is the state of flexion or extension at the knee. This is due to the rectus femoris bridging two joints. The forwards and downwards tilting of the pelvis helps extension. Hyper-extension is brought about by exaggerating the lumbar curve. In effect then, this does not alter the degree of extension between femur and pelvis but *does* considerably influence the angle between femur and the erect or extended spine above the lumbar region.

Anterio-posterior axis: *abduction* – the drawing apart of the thighs as in moving to stand with legs astride. The movement is limited by the adductor muscles, the ilio- and pubo-femoral ligaments, and the bony structures themselves. The active maximum is 90°, while passive gives a greater angle only when combined with flexion and the forward tilt of the pelvis; *adduction* – the drawing together of the thighs as in gripping the flanks of a horse. This obviously must be combined with flexion or extension if a thigh is to be adducted past the mid-line of the body. The maximum degree of adduction beyond the mid-line is approximately 30°. The position of greatest instability of this joint is when the hip is well flexed and adducted, e.g. when sitting with the legs crossed.

Vertical axis: *rotation outward (lateral)* – the action of moving towards splayed feet is limited by the ilio- and pubo-femoral ligaments and, consequently, by the state of flexion or extension of femur on pelvis; *rotation inward (medial)* – the action of moving to stand pigeon-toed. This is limited by the ischio-femoral ligament and therefore by flexion or extension at the hip. Inward rotation is the easier, due to the slackness of the ischio-femoral ligament in movements combining flexion/abduction/inward rotation. This particular situation is the root of a problem for the beginner-hurdler, who habitually drops the trailing knee to give an abbreviated first stride away from the hurdle.

outward rotation	hip	inward rotation
60°	flexed	35°–45°
30°	extended	30°–40°

■ Knee

This joint must effect a mechanical compromise to reconcile two mutually exclusive requirements: great stability in extension when body weight and lever lengths impose stress, and great mobility in flexion when the joint must adapt to irregularities of terrain, changes of locomotive speed, direction, and so on.

Satisfying these two requirements completely is almost impossible. Despite the ingenious mechanical devices incorporated in the joint, the poor degree of interlocking of surfaces (an essential for mobility) exposes the joint to immense risk of strain and injury. The following actions are possible about the transverse and vertical axes.

Transverse axis: *extension* – straightening the knee. The knee is considered extended when the thigh and lower leg form what is virtually a straight line. Only a very slight increase (5°–10°) is possible beyond this point and may be produced by passive extension, i.e. when standing on a decline. Extension beyond this is abnormal. Extension of the hip aids extension of the knee by stretching the rectus femoris; *flexion* – the action of bringing the heel towards the buttock. The possible range depends on the state of flexion/extension at the hip joint and also whether the knee flexion is active or passive.

active	hip action	passive
140°	flexed	160°
*120°	extended	†110°–140°

*Due to weakened hamstring and stretched rectus femoris, but follow-through can bring heel to buttock.
†Due to stretch of rectus femoris.

Vertical axis (leg in natural alignment with body): *rotation* – this is only possible when knee is flexed, and the degree of rotation varies with the degree of knee flexion until the knee is flexed at 90°; *outward* – the foot is turned outwards, with knees bent as in commencement of the breast-stroke leg kick; *inward* – the foot is turned inwards with knees bent, as in the initiation of rotation in javelin and discus.

outward rotation	knee flexion	inward rotation
32°	30°	20°
42°	90°	30°

There is also a phenomenon known as automatic rotation. At completion of knee extension the lower leg rotates outwards on the femur. Conversely, if the knee is extended while the foot is anchored on the floor (as in standing) then the first action described is seen as the femur rotating inwards on the lower leg. The injury potential in field games such as football and rugby will be clearly appreciated if one considers the possibility of forced outward rotation of femur on lower leg, while it is naturally rotating inward in extension.

■ Ankle

Several expressions are used uniquely in describing ankle joint actions. These actions are possible about the transverse, anterio-posterior, and vertical axes when the joint is not weight bearing (e.g. when the foot is not in contact with any surface).

Transverse axis: *plantar flexion (flexion)* – this is the action of pointing the toes. To complicate matters, this action is referred to as ankle extension when rising up on the toes (i.e. when the ankle is weight bearing). The main muscles responsible for plantar flexion have greatest efficiency when the knee is extended and the ankle is in dorsi flexion; *dorsi flexion (extension)* – the action of turning the toes up towards the knee. There is less rotation possible in dorsi flexion than in plantar flexion.

Anterio-posterior axis: *inversion* – the action of turning the medial (big toe) side of the foot upwards towards the inside of the knee. Inversion injuries (i.e. where the trauma is sustained on the lateral side) account for 80% of all ankle injuries; *eversion* – the action of turning the lateral (small toe) side of the foot upwards towards the outside of the knee.

Due to the demands for directional change in the majority of games, the latter two actions are extremely important. Lateral changes of direction will ultimately require departure from the running surface via inversion or eversion. Moreover, these actions facilitate adaptation to a terrain.

Vertical axis: as indicated above, rotation is more free in plantar flexion than in dorsi flexion; *outward* – the turning of the foot outwards; *inward* – the turning of the foot inwards. Once again, these actions are critical in changing direction and in adjusting balance in variable terrain.

■ Foot

In discussing the ankle joint actions, especially those of inversion and eversion, the actions of the foot have already been introduced. Man's foot has been the unfortunate victim of the progress of civilisation, and its properties are gradually being lost. Our ancestors may well have been able to oppose their big toes in the same way that we can oppose our thumbs. However, the toes may be flexed, extended, adducted and abducted in much the same way as fingers.

Due to the complex of 26 bones, the foot is well equipped both in strength and mobility to adapt to any type of terrain. This adaptability is obviously fundamental to efficient locomotion. The foot is the first and final contact with the surface of the ground, and a lack of ability to accept loadings of momentum on any given surface will result in dissipation of effort or possible injury.

Kapandji's observations (1970) are worth noting: 'The town dweller always walks on even and firm ground with his feet protected by shoes.

There is therefore little need for the arches of his feet to adapt to new terrains and the supporting muscles eventually atrophy: the flat foot is the price paid for progress and some anthropologists go so far as to forecast that man's feet will be reduced to mere stumps. This thesis is borne out by the fact that in man in contrast to the ape the toes are atrophied and big toe can no longer be opposed'. This stage is still to come and even civilised man can still walk barefoot on a beach or on the rocks. This return to the primitive state is highly beneficial to the plantar vault (*inter alia*), which thus retrieves its adaptive capabilities.

By way of summarising the extraordinary movement potential of the lever system, some of the range of exercises, easily expanded by the thoughtful coach, are portrayed in figure 8.

▋ Male/female body variations

Before leaving this section, male/female variations are worth noting. Due to the extreme width of the female pelvis compared with the male pelvis, the angle between femur and tibia is generally greater for women than for men. This is clearly a disadvantage when force of knee and hip extension is required and highlights the high injury potential not only at knee and hip, but at the junction of sacrum and ilium, and pubic symphysis which are less stable in women than in men.

The female shoulders are also narrower than in men and the lateral angle radius/ulna on humerus is greater, providing a weaker force application potential in 'pulling' activities. The length of the female spine is approximately 86% that of the male spine and this, combined with a greater distribution of weight towards hips/thighs, gives women a relatively lower centre of gravity.

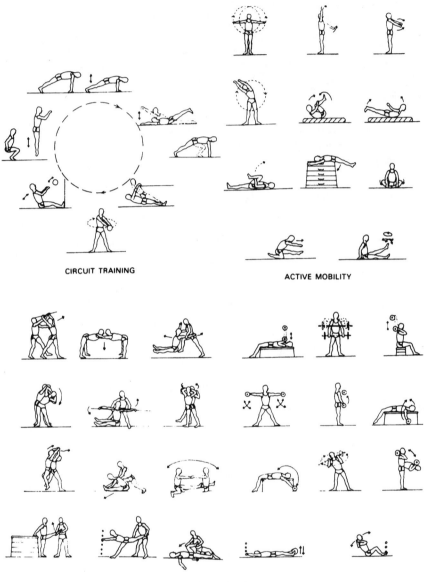

CIRCUIT TRAINING

ACTIVE MOBILITY

PASSIVE MOBILITY

Fig. 8 *Examples of exercises demonstrating the total movement potential of the body's system of levers: circuit training; active mobility; passive mobility; basic weight training; special exercises*

BASIC WEIGHT TRAINING

SPECIAL EXERCISES

Fig. 8 *(continued)*

▌ Summary

Whole body movement, and movement at each joint, can be described in terms of rotations about axes. These movements are classified as actions in specific anatomical terms. In any given activity, several combinations of joint actions, made possible by a specific programme of muscle contractions, will take place. The interplay of these actions will dictate the final efficiency as an expression of energy.

In the first instance, the range of a joint action will be a function of that joint's structure. Secondary limiting factors are imposed by the soft tissue structures bridging and surrounding the joint. A working knowledge of all the body's structures must then be seen as basic to an appreciation of the body's total movement potential and to analysis of technical models. It is convenient to study body movement with reference to three areas.

(1)   The upper limb complex is designed for mobility and is the final link in a force sequence for many activities. By its nature, it is the fastest link in the force sequence and training is aimed at ensuring that the contribution of this link is synchronised in its application of speed, force and range after other joint complexes have provided their contributions.
(2)   The spine is variously a complex of joints providing a remarkable range of movement in some activities and a powerful pillar linking lower and upper limb complexes in others. Both strength and mobility must be developed to ensure that demands of stability and mobility can be met.
(3)   The lower limb complex is the initiator of a force sequence in many activities. Great force must be generated by the complex, frequently with only instantaneous ground contact. Moreover, it must offer sufficient mobility to permit rapid adjustment to any given terrain. Consequently the lower limb must provide mobility, stability and the capacity to express force at speed.

It must be stressed that although the coach considers each joint action in analysis of a given movement, no action should be thought of in isolation, but as part of the total movement.

2
Structural changes in the growing child

Stages of growth

It takes approximately twenty years for all the morphological, physiological and psychological processes of development to bring the newly-born child to maturity. The unfolding of his development is a long but necessary period, during which time growth cannot simply be seen as an increase in height and weight, but as a gentle ebb and flow of differentiating and integrating forms and functions.

The child, in his various stages of growth, is not a mini-adult. It must be clearly understood that from stage to stage in his growth, the child varies in the proportion of individual body parts in terms of length, volume and weight. Each part grows at a different rate, ranging from two-fold expansion (head) to five-fold expansion (legs), between birth and maturity (figs. 9, 10). Implicit in this is that certain skills may require considerable adjustment of the neuromuscular processes from year to year, according to shifting emphasis of growth. Consequently, as the athlete grows, it seems advisable to maintain principal elements of technique training throughout the year.

Several authorities have attempted to classify the stages of development and table 3 may be valuable as a reference.

Table 3 *Stages of growth against age* (adapted from Grimme, 1953)

stage	characteristic growth landmarks	age male	female
Newly-born	Healing of the umbilicus		
Infant	Up to appearance of first milk teeth	0.5	0.5
Crawling age	Up to learning to walk	1–1.5	1–1.5
Small child	Up to appearance of the first permanent tooth	6	6
Early school age (pre-puberty)	Until first signs of maturity. Beginning of growth spurt, rapid genital development, first breast development	11	9
Puberty	Period between appearance of pubic hair and first menarche or development of male sperms	14	14–15
Adolescence	Puberty and end of physical growth	22	18
Age of achievement	Period of optimal capacity	Variations in	
Age of curtailment	Onset and continuing diminution of performance	these stages cover	
Old age	Considerable physical changes accompanied by serious loss of capacity	a great range but are normal	

27

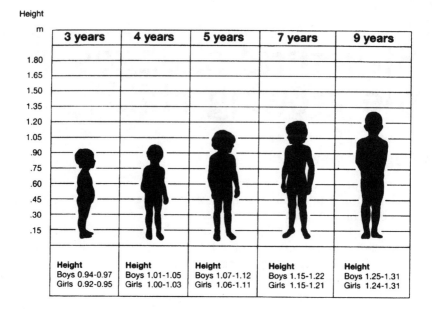

Height m	3 years	4 years	5 years	7 years	9 years
1.80					
1.65					
1.50					
1.35					
1.20					
1.05					
.90					
.75					
.60					
.45					
.30					
.15					
	Height Boys 0.94-0.97 Girls 0.92-0.95	**Height** Boys 1.01-1.05 Girls 1.00-1.03	**Height** Boys 1.07-1.12 Girls 1.06-1.11	**Height** Boys 1.15-1.22 Girls 1.15-1.21	**Height** Boys 1.25-1.31 Girls 1.24-1.31

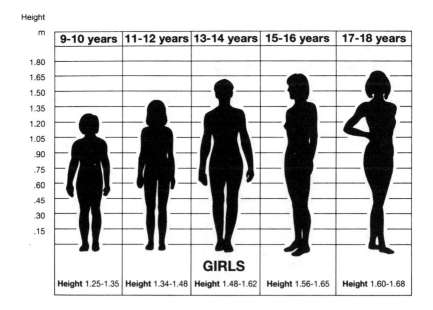

Height m	9-10 years	11-12 years	13-14 years	15-16 years	17-18 years
1.80					
1.65					
1.50					
1.35					
1.20					
1.05					
.90					
.75					
.60					
.45					
.30					
.15					
	Height 1.25-1.35	Height 1.34-1.48	Height 1.48-1.62	Height 1.56-1.65	Height 1.60-1.68

GIRLS

Fig. 9 *Growth of the child. Average height progression, showing the 'parting of the ways' after approximately 9 years, in terms of relative height increase, and absolute height. Modified from Family Health Guide (Reader's Digest, 1972)*

Height
m

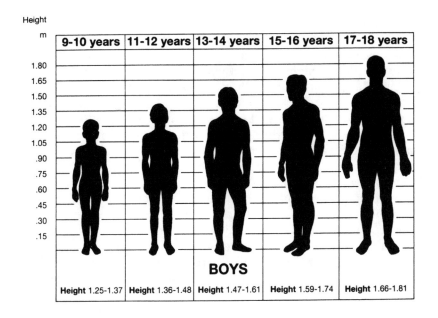

	9-10 years	11-12 years	13-14 years	15-16 years	17-18 years
	Height 1.25-1.37	Height 1.36-1.48	Height 1.47-1.61	Height 1.59-1.74	Height 1.66-1.81

BOYS

Fig. 9 (continued)

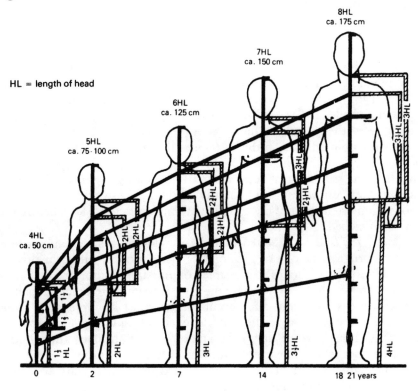

HL = length of head

Fig. 10 Alterations in body proportions during growth (from Bammes, 1964)

■ Skeletal development

With the exception of the skull and collar bone (clavicle), all the bones in the body are formed from cartilage. The process starts from before birth and concludes with final ossification of the skeleton between 18 and 22 years of age. Bone lengthens by growing at the junction between the main shaft and the growing end which is known as the epiphysis. In the long bones (i.e. the arms and legs), most growth takes place at one end only. This is extremely significant when one considers that the thigh bone, for example, grows mostly at the knee end, which is exposed to considerable training loads. Ossification is the destruction and breakdown of cartilage and its replacement with bone tissue. This process is accompanied by the setting down of an increasingly thick layer of bone around the cartilage (perichondral ossification) and from within the cartilage (endochondral ossification).

The growing bone has a greater proportion of softer material in the basic substance, which is essential for compressive and tensile strength. This and the sponge-like nature of immature bone material, which is still in the process of developing adaptability to loading, means that the growing bone is more elastic but has less bending strength. This is a major cause of the reduced load-bearing capacity of the child's skeleton.

Hormones affect the process and rate of skeletal development, but functional loading may also influence the process. Most research has considered the role of hormones, but a considerable volume of research would indicate that controlled loadings will favourably influence skeletal growth. Research in this area has suggested then that: (1) intermittent sub-maximal loading (80–90% maximum) stimulates height growth (Tittel, 1963), (2) excessive loading in quality or quantity inhibits height growth (Schede, 1963), and (3) muscle pull, above all, is the functional stimulus for the growth in thickness of the bone (Harre, 1973).

It is my opinion that, in the early growth stages, working the child to a point where loading cannot be repeated due to fatigue and/or insufficient strength is fundamentally working against the most favourable conditions for healthy growth. However, insufficient motivation on the part of the child may terminate activity long before this point is reached.

Craig (1972) has suggested that, by developing a systematic general training programme of exercise for all muscle groups, sufficient drive is available to relieve bones of possible continuation and/or accumulation of stressors which can exist where the bone is required to accept a loading for which it is not ready. Such accumulation must be avoided, as Craig has noted: 'the cumulative effect of the repetitive trauma of such stressors will cause injury, which may not manifest itself until later athletic life'. Caution, then, should be exercised in encouraging the growing athlete to attempt loadings near his or her 'motivated limit', i.e. limits arrived at through strong external motivation.

■ Tendencies of growth

In figure 11 we can see that height does not increase continuously, but in phases. This can also be seen when other factors such as weight are plotted against age. Consequently there is reference in several papers to phases of extension and phases of abundance (filling out). It should be noted here that *bone growth precedes muscle development*, a factor of importance in the training of athletes. Several attempts have been made to relate these phases to athletic events and performances (table 4).

The changes in relative body dimensions have been mentioned earlier in connection with the possible variations in the development of athletic skill and ability. The amazing complexity of this shift in relative dimension is probably best illustrated in a piece of work conducted on élite swimmers between 8 and 14 years of age in GDR, as figure 12 shows. Looking to the future, tables may be constructed to show indices of age-specific, strength-weight ratios as this might give a clear guide as to which physical characteristics (age-dependent, or specific growth rate dependent) are temporarily regressive (table 4).

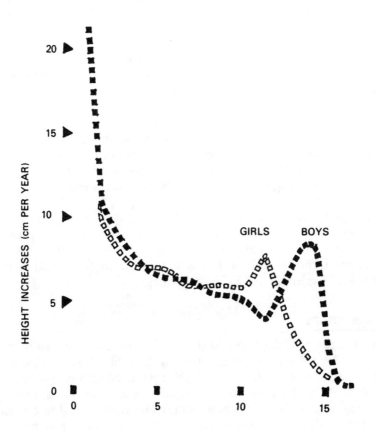

Fig. 11 *Growth increases for average development* (from Bayley in Harre, 1973)

Table 4 *Comparison of body measurements of young middle distance athletes with the average values for German Democratic Republic (adapted from Harre from Marcusson 1973)*

	feature	norm value value	norm value age	mean value value	mean value age	spread	mean of 5 best value	mean of 5 best age
Class 7 $\bar{x}$ = 12.8 yrs	Height cm	151.6	13	159.2	14.5	150.9–167.3	160.3	16
	Weight kg	40.7	13	43.0	13.5	34.4–51.6	54.5	15.5
	Thigh length mm			429		409–447	444	
	Lower leg length mm			358		336–378	380	
Class 8 $\bar{x}$ = 13.8 yrs	Height	157.8	14	167.1	15.5	160.9–173.2	169.3	16
	Weight	45.7	14	50.0	15.0	43.4–56.6	52.2	15.5
	Thigh length			448		430–466	460	
	Lower leg length			376		352–397	386	
Class 9 $\bar{x}$ = 15 yrs	Height	163.6	15	173.0	16	168.1–177.9	175.3	16
	Weight	50.7	15	56.6	16	50.9–62.3	60.1	16
	Thigh length					450–478	469	
	Lower leg length					374–408	400	

One must avoid the temptation to ignore the less proficient in favour of the superior athlete in his early teens. Superiority may well be due to early physical development which frequently leaves an athlete's peers unable to meet him on equal terms. The spread of growth in these years is considerable. Attention must therefore be given to those youngsters who are able to perform skills efficiently and compete with considerable success, but have yet to develop. In short, a judgement of body size based solely on age is unreliable, but can be made reliable if it is seen against the individual's stage of maturity. Early, late and normal developers must be seen in 'performance perspective'.

The total time of pubescent growth lasts longer for boys, although girls start earlier by 1½–2 years. The 14 year old girl is already approximately 97% final height, and at 18 years of age is 96% final leg length. On the other hand, the 14 year old boy is approximately 85% final height, and 80% final leg length at 18–22 years of age.

▌Summary

Whereas the period up to and through adolescence used to be simply a preparation for serious competition in the athlete's early 20s, it is now also a period of preparation for high pressure competition in the years of growth. As a consequence, the coach must understand the athlete's patterns of growth. From these patterns it seems logical to establish the fundamentals of techniques before the pubertal growth spurt, as pubescence and adolescence create disproportionate relationships between body parts. Overload in resistance work is acceptable, but not beyond 80–90% maximum loading. Epiphyses are almost certainly

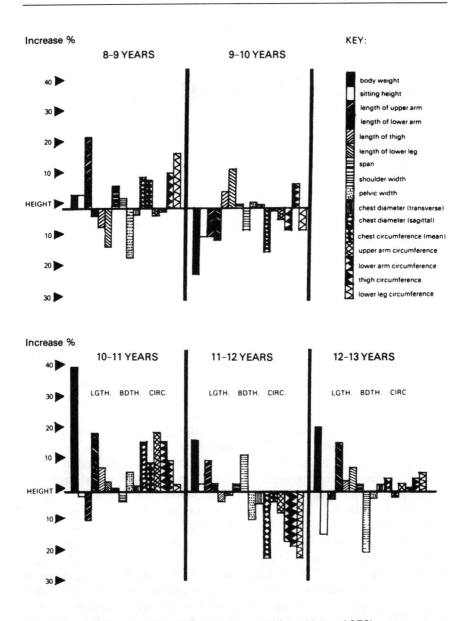

Fig. 12 *Relative rate of growth of body parts* (from Harre, 1973)

damaged if this advice is ignored. Loading of the spine, as in several orthodox weight lifting exercises, must not be considered until the spine has stopped growing and/or has been protected by developed spinal musculature. Prediction of height growth patterns is possible and is used in several countries to select athletes according to anthropometric trends in given disciplines.

3
Basic mechanics

A detailed knowledge of 'laminae and particles' is not required by the student of training theory, but he should attempt to achieve some working knowledge of those terms most frequently used in analyses. To this end, the following is presented.

Definitions

Motion
Motion is simply a change of position, but should be defined as a change relative to another body, a fixed point, etc. For example, the femur flexes on the pelvis; the basketball player breaks past his opposite number, and so on. Some types of motion are not easily observed because they are too slow (e.g. the opening of a flower) or because they are too fast (e.g. the beating of a fly's wing). Cinematographic analysis is often used to study motion in sport. Such study may range from an analysis of team play to the analysis of an athlete's technical efficiency.

Rest is the status of an object when its position, with respect to some point, line, surface, etc., remains unchanged. It is important to know that in any given activity there is no movement at some joints while there is at others. Where there is no movement the muscle activity is referred to as *static* and where there is movement the muscle activity is *dynamic*.

A study of motion and rest, relative to limbs or bodies, etc., forms the basis of mechanical analysis: *linear motion* is motion in a straight line. This is also referred to as translatory motion (e.g. running 60 m); *angular motion* is the motion of rotation. This is also referred to as rotary motion (e.g. a front somersault); *curvilinear motion* is motion which involves linear and angular motion (e.g. a cartwheel or a hammer thrower advancing and turning across the circle).

Centre of gravity
The centre of gravity is a body's centre of weight. In other words, it is that point about which the body is balanced relative to all three axes. When a body is in flight, any rotation takes place about the centre of gravity. When describing rotation in flight, direction of rotation about an axis is defined as clockwise or anti-clockwise.

Vertical axis (long axis of the body): the athlete is standing on the clock face, i.e. a pirouette to the right is a clockwise rotation (fig. 13b).

Transverse axis (axis through the hips, left to right): the athlete has the clock face on his left, i.e. a front somersault is a clockwise rotation (fig. 13a).

Anterio-posterior axis (axis from front to back through hips): the athlete faces the clock, i.e. a cartwheel to the right is clockwise rotation (fig. 13c).

The centre of gravity represents the intersection of these axes, which in the athlete's body is roughly half way between umbilicus and pubic crest and 3cm in front of the spine. Provided the imaginary perpendicular from this point to the ground falls within the athlete's 'base' (e.g. feet), he will not fall over. The relationship of this perpendicular to the body's point(s) of support is critical in the study of sports technique.

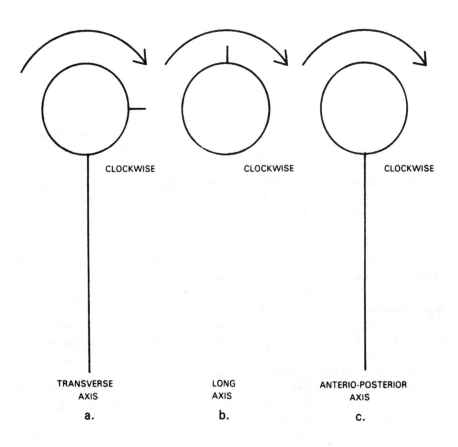

Fig. 13 *Basis for defining rotation about the body's axes*

■ Force

Force is anything which produces motion or changes of motion. It could also be seen as a push or pull, a tendency to distort, and so on. As applied to work or movement analysis, three factors must be considered: (1) magnitude of force, i.e. its size (e.g. 400 joules), (2) direction of the force, i.e. in which direction the force is applied (e.g. vertically), and (3) point of application of force, i.e. where the force is being applied (e.g. at the athlete's foot) as figure 14 shows.

Work is the overcoming of a load or resistance and is measured as the product of force x distance moved. In most cases, the force producing work in moving the athlete's limbs is the contraction of muscle. This usually results in a shortening and thickening of the muscle without a change in volume. The product of the force with which it contracts, and the range through which the force is applied, is the measure of the mechanical work performed by the muscle. Some confusion must arise when the muscle contraction is static (isometric). The force provided by the contracting muscle is applied through 0 range – producing mechanical work of force x 0 = 0. In this case there appears to be no mechanical work performed, but energy has certainly been expressed as physiological work which might be measured in terms of heat energy. It becomes convenient, then, to measure mechanical work according to its energy cost.

■ Energy cost

One joule of work is that performed in raising 1 newton, 1 m. One newton is the force acting on the mass of 1 kg at normal acceleration of gravity. One joule may also be expressed as 0.239 calories. One calorie is the amount of heat required to raise 1 g water, 1°C. The basic unit for most purposes is a kilocalorie (kcal) which is 1000 calories (4186 joules). The energy costs of various activities can be calculated and standardised as an aid to studying the balance of energy input (nutrition) against energy output (work). For example, sitting at ease = 1.6 kcals/minute, whilst walking at 8.8 kph on flat ground = 5.6 kcals/minute. (See also table 6, p. 47.)

The athlete's body weight should remain constant if the calorie input (diet) equals the calorie output (activity).

■ Machines

A machine is a device for performing work. Among the simplest machines are the pulley, the lever, the wheel and axle, the inclined plane, the wedge and the screw. All complex machines are comprised of simple machines, which in the case of the athlete are almost always levers. Machines are concerned with two forces – that put into the machine (effort, or internal force, or force) and that which the machine attempts to overcome (resistance, or external force, or load).

A lever is a rod turning about a fixed point (axis). In the athlete, the levers are bones. The forces are expressed by the contracting muscles pulling on the bones, and the loads vary from other bones or the athlete's

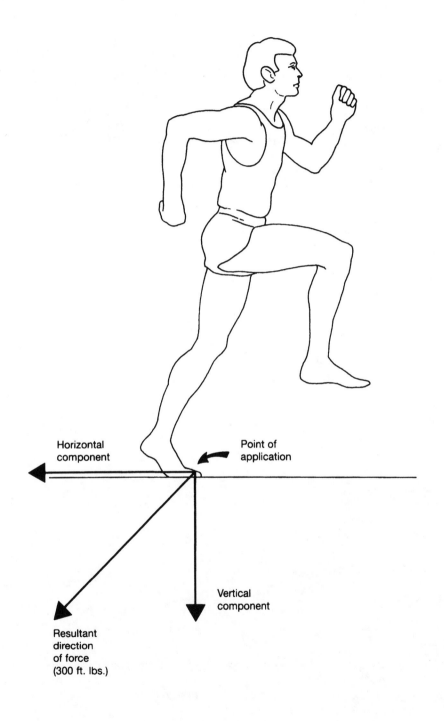

Fig. 14 *Force application in long jump*

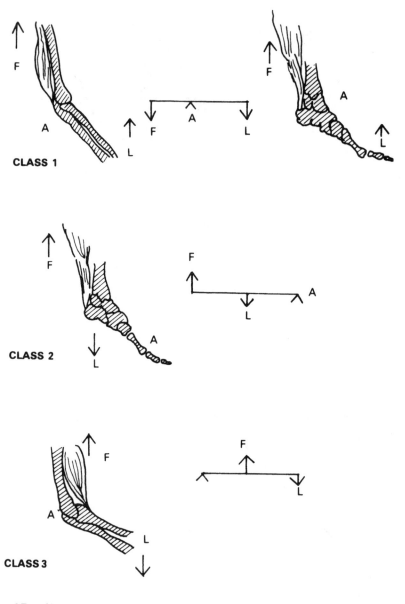

Fig. 15 *Classes of lever*
Class 1 Triceps extending forearm on arm; gastrocnemeus and soleus and plantaris
plantar flexing – when foot is off the ground
Class 2 Gastrocnemeus and soleus and plantaris
plantar flexing – when the foot is on the ground
Class 3 Biceps, brachialis, brachioradialis and pronator teres flexing the forearm on the arm

own body weight, to external loads such as bar-bells, discoi, oars, water, kinetic energies, etc.

The efficiency of the lever depends on certain mechanical factors. Of primary importance are the exact position on the lever of the application of force (F), the location of the load (L), and the axis in question (A). The relative positions of these points dictates the 'class' of lever and, while it is not essential that these are memorised, an understanding of how these levers work may help in technical analysis (fig. 15). Broadly speaking, class 1 is built for equilibrium, class 2 for saving force, and class 3 for speed and range of movement. The distance from F to A is known as the force arm, and the distance from L to A as the load arm. Any lever system will balance when:

$$\text{force} \times \text{force arm} = \text{load} \times \text{load arm}$$

In table 5, what force is required to make each system balance in a class 1 lever system? From the figures in table 5, the following can be seen.

(1)   The force required to move the lever is indirectly proportional to the length of the force arm.
(2)   Only when the two arms are equal in length will the force equal the load.
(3)   By adding to the length of the force arm, the force may be reduced to almost nothing.
(4)   The effect of the load follows the same rules as those which determine the effect of the force.
(5)   The force necessary to operate the class 1 lever depends upon the relative length of the lever arms.

With small adjustments these observations also apply to class 2 and class 3 levers.

Table 5   *Equilibrium exists where force x force arm =*
load (resistance) x load arm

force	x	force arm	=	resistance	x	load arm	answer
F	x	2	=	10	x	18	F = 90
F	x	8	=	10	x	12	F = 15
F	x	16	=	10	x	4	F = 2.5
F	x	8	=	10	x	2	F = 2.5

This brief expansion on the 'mathematics of levers' is not advanced purely for academic interest. It may help, for example, in creating new possibilities for strength training where the total available resistance is relatively low. By thoughtful use of levers, or pulleys, the effect of this low resistance can be increased.

Before leaving levers, the value should be noted of bony devices which provide greater mechanical advantage of muscle pull. They achieve this by increasing the length of the lever arm, changing the direction of force application, and so on. There are several examples, but few illustrate this better than the patella (kneecap). The force of muscle pull may be thought of as having two components. One provides rotation of one lever on another and the other pulls along the length of the levers, and by so doing provides joint stability. If the direction of muscle pull is almost parallel with the levers concerned, the stabilising component is very great and the rotational component small. The converse is true if the direction of muscle pull is more angular. The patella changes the direction of application of force of the knee extensors by providing a greater angle of insertion of the patellar ligament into the tibial tuberosity. This change of direction increases the effective force of the knee extension by increasing the component of rotation and decreasing the stabilising component.

▌ Laws of motion

There are three laws of motion – inertia, acceleration and reaction.

The law of inertia
A resting or moving body will remain in that state until a force alters this situation. By this law, both motion and rest are states of resistance or loading. The amount of resistance to change of state (inertia) is dependent upon the mass of the body concerned and its velocity. Velocity is the relationship of the distance covered to the time taken – *and it has a direction* (45 kph south). Inertia has legion examples in sport, ranging from starting in rowing or sprinting, to raising an opponent in wrestling.

The law of acceleration
Acceleration is directly proportional to the force causing it and inversely proportional to the mass of the body involved. Acceleration is the rate of change of velocity. This implies increase or decrease in the distance covered in a given period of time, but in addition, since velocity has direction, acceleration must also be implied in a rate of change of direction. Thus centripetal acceleration is that continuous change of direction which permits an athlete or cyclist to move round a curve.

The law of reaction
For every action there is an equal and opposite reaction. When stepping onto a chair or box, one is supported by the counterforce offered by the chair or box. If the counterforce is less, one will fall through! When flight is considered, as in jumping, and a body part moves in one direction, then some other part or equivalence of force must act in the opposite direction.

Gravity
One force which will act on the body at all times is that of gravity. When an athlete launches himself or an object into flight, as soon as flight is commenced, there is a force which causes a reduction in upward velocity at a speed of 981.274 cm/sec^2. The centre of gravity of the object or

athlete will be seen to trace a course – a parabola (fig. 16). It should be noted that whether or not the athlete rotates or moves parts of his body whilst in flight, the parabola of the athlete's centre of gravity is dictated by the angle and speed of take-off. Should the implement have aerodynamic properties then of course the flight path will not be a parabola.

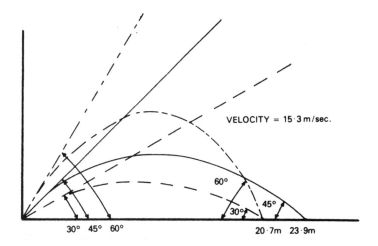

Fig. 16 *Once launched, the centre of gravity of athlete or implement must follow a parabolic path in flight. Here, this is seen in the path of the object projected at various angles at 15.3 m/sec*

■ Momentum
Momentum is the quantity of motion and is therefore the product of mass x velocity. The body is frequently put in motion, or assisted in motion by transfer of momentum from part of the body to the whole body. For example, the free leg and arms in the high jump. Momentum may be linear or angular.

Mass
Mass is the quantity of matter. It is given dimension from weight/gravity.

Moment of inertia
Moment of inertia is the distribution of a body's mass, i.e. its size. If a gymnast tucks himself into a ball, his moment of inertia is small about the transverse axis. If he extends into a star shape, his moment of inertia is large about the transverse axis. Moment of inertia might well be thought of as the rotating body's radius.

Angular momentum
Angular momentum is the product of moment of inertia x angular velocity, i.e. revolutions per minute. The importance of understanding angular momentum should not be underestimated because it has a

considerable number of applications in sport. This concept may be illustrated by assuming that an imaginary gymnast is rotating at 5 revs/minute with a radius of 3 units. His angular momentum is (3 x 5) = 15 units. Now, assuming there is no deceleration due to friction, air resistance, and so on, the momentum will remain at 15 units. If the athlete now reduces the radius to 1 unit, the momentum remaining the same, his angular velocity is now 15 revs/minute. An understanding of this may enable sophisticated control of rotation in flight.

Related in part to this is that the reaction of the body to a long lever will be greater than to a short one. In throwing movements involving rotation of the body, the longer the lever, the less will be the force but the greater will be the instantaneous linear speed at the end of the lever. This is also relevant in all striking activities, ranging from golf to soccer.

▌ Summary

There has been no intention here to present an exhaustive review of mechanics, but more realistically to establish some understanding of basic terminology used in mechanical analysis. What must be remembered is that in dealing with mechanical laws, the athlete is biomechanical and flexible. He is not a machine, but a man. The excellent and detailed mechanical information available to students of physical education and coaches must always be interpreted with this in mind.

▌ Summary of part 1

When analysing movement or investigating new possibilities of technique, it is tempting to focus one's attention on a single joint action or on one mechanical principle. However, it is basic to all study of movement that it is the most efficient compromise which must be sought. Moreover, one must be constantly aware of a joint action relative to other joint actions, a joint action relative to whole body movement, and all actions relative to mechanical laws. Consequently it is suggested that the student of techniques in sport should establish a technical model for a given event or sport. This technical model will represent the most efficient compromise. It will embrace broad principles of movement, such as upward tilting of the pelvis for all activities where vigorous extension of the leg(s) is required to give vertical force (e.g. in most lifts, throws and jumps), or the sequence of joint action and force direction in all arm strike activities. These broad principles are, in the main, based on common sense and a knowledge of anatomy and mechanics. However, many principles have grown simply from experience and observation. For example, it is debatable whether coaching points such as 'keep your eye on the ball' in racquet games, cricket, volleyball, baseball, and so on, or 'keep your head down' when playing a golf shot, kicking a ball, and so on, grew from a knowledge of anatomy or mechanics!

Whether principles grow from theory or from experience, one is always drawn to the same conclusion that our system of levers *must* be considered in its entirety when creating technical models and, thereafter, suggesting coaching advice. The sciences of kinesiology and biomechanics have grown from applied anatomy and mechanics. It is recommended that the coach, who wishes to create a deeper reservoir of information as a basis for establishing technical models and for studying their development, should take time to study these sciences.

References for part 1

Collective Authors (1972) *The Family Health Guide.* Reader's Digest, London

Craig, T. (1972) *Prevention is the Only Cure.* 3rd Coaches' Convention Report

Harre, D. (1973) *Trainingslehre.* Sportverlag, Berlin

Kapandji, I. A. (1970) *The Physiology of the Joints.* 2nd Edn. Vols 1 & 2. Churchill-Livingstone, London

Marcusson, H. (1961) *Das Wachstrum von Kindern und Jugendlichen in der Deutschen Demokratischen Republic.* Akademie Verlag, Berlin

McNaught, A. B. & Callender, R. (1963) *Illustrated Physiology.* Churchill Livingstone, Edinburgh

Provins, K. & Salter, N. (1955) Maximum torque exerted about the elbow joint. *Journal of Applied Physiology* 7, pp 393–398

Rasch, P. J. & Burke, R. K. (1968) *Kinesiology and Applied Anatomy.* 3rd Edn. Lea & Febiger, Philadelphia

Tittel, K. (1963) *Beschreibende und Funktionelle Anatomie Des Menschen.* Jena, Fischer (Hueter, Volkmann, Jores)

Bibliography

Clarke, H. H. (1967) *Application of Measurement to Health and Physical Education.* 4th Edn. Prentice-Hall Inc., New Jersey

Collective Authors (1975) *Abstracts of the 5th International Congress of Biomechanics.* S.V.U.L., Helsinki

Cooper, J. M. & Glassow, R. B. (1972) *Kinesiology.* C. V. Mosby, St. Louis

Dyson, G. H. G. (1977) *The Mechanics of Athletics.* 7th Edn. University of London Press

Fleishman, I. E. (1964) *The Structure and Measurement of Physical Fitness.* Prentice-Hall Inc., New Jersey

Hay, J. G. (1973) *The Biomechanics of Sports Techniques.* Prentice-Hall Inc., New Jersey

Hopper, B. J. (1973) *The Mechanics of Human Movement.* Crosby, Lockwood, Staples, London

Jeffries, M. (1976) *Know Your Body.* BBC Publications, London

Kelley, D. L. (1971) *Kinesiology: Fundamentals of Motion Description.* Prentice-Hall Inc., New Jersey

MacConaill, M. A. & Basmajian, J. V. (1969) *Muscles and Movements: A Basis for Human Kinesiology.* Williams & Wilkins Co., Baltimore

Margaria, R. (1976) *Biomechanics and Energetics of Muscular Exercise.* Clarendon Press, Oxford

Nourse, A. E. (1972) *The Body.* 3rd Edn. Time-Life International, Amsterdam

Scott, M. G. (1963) *Analysis of Human Motion*. 2nd Edn. Appleton-Century-Crofts, New York

Spence, D. W. (1975) *Essentials of Kinesiology: A Laboratory Manual*. Lea & Febiger, Philadelphia

Tricker, R. A. R. & Tricker, B. J. L. (1968) *The Science of Movement*. Mills & Boon, London

Part 2

The living machine

The analogy is often made of athlete and machine. The 'machine' in this case must develop increased efficiency of *energy expression* and *energy production* in the athlete's pursuit of competitive advantage.

In part 1, the *skeletal* and *muscular systems* were seen as the basic structures which give final expression of energy when programmed to do so via the *central nervous system* (discussed in part 3).

In part 2, the production of energy to give those structures movement is considered in detail, as are the collective involvement of several other systems. The *digestive system* processes the nutritional content of the athlete's diet to produce not only energy for bodily function, but also the various materials necessary to maintenance, repair and growth. The *oxygen transporting system* combines the *respiratory* and *circulatory* systems in its role of carrying oxygen and fuel to the working muscle where chemical energy is converted to mechanical energy. To permit all systems to function with least possible embarrassment, there must be a dynamic stability of the body's internal environment. This is afforded by the *fluid systems* and *endocrine system*.

Part 2 is edited by Dr Craig Sharp.

4
Nutrition

The connection between the food we eat and our functional capacity has been the subject of considerable interest for at least 3000 years. Biblical injunctions concerning the diet are numerous and, in other religions and cultures, food taboos and rituals may often be traced to this connection. One of the first accounts of how meat might influence muscular work was recorded in Greece around the 5th century BC. The normal diet of the time was vegetarian, but two athletes turned carnivorous and the result was evidently an increase in body bulk and weight. Thereafter, the belief that meat would make up for loss of muscular substance during heavy work gained considerable ground. Even today, the intrusion of scientific half-truths has reinforced this belief and many athletes will not go without meat during preparation for competition. The reason for the popularity of such half-truths and beliefs may be summed up by Astrand (1967): 'The fact that muscles are built of protein makes it tempting to conclude that ingestion of excess protein stimulates muscle growth and strength'. While lack of certain foodstuffs may bring about a decrease in functional capacity, or even illness, it has yet to be proved that excessive consumption of foodstuffs will increase functional capacity.

The energy value of food is measured in kilocalories (kcal) (see chapter 3). Foods vary in their calorie content: 1 g carbohydrate yields 4 kcal, 1 g fat yields 9 kcal, 1 g protein yields 4 kcal. A detailed account of the day's activities can help establish the athlete's daily kilocalorie expenditure. For quick reference, the energy cost of various activities is often standardised (table 6). Yakovlev, in a detailed work in 1961, suggested not only the daily kilocalorie intake for various events and sports, but also the quantity of protein, carbohydrate and fat (table 7).

Energy needs depend on activity, age, sex and body build. Most energy is used when the muscles are working during breathing, digestion, circulation, exercise, etc. A balanced diet should provide correct nutrition and, ideally, the same amount of energy that is expended in activity. Foods are classified according to their nutritional value:

- carbohydrates provide the body with energy
- fats provide stored energy
- proteins supply material for growth and repair of body tissues
- mineral elements contribute towards growth and repair and essential body chemistry

Table 6 *Energy expenditure of different activities.* From Astrand and Rodahl (1970)

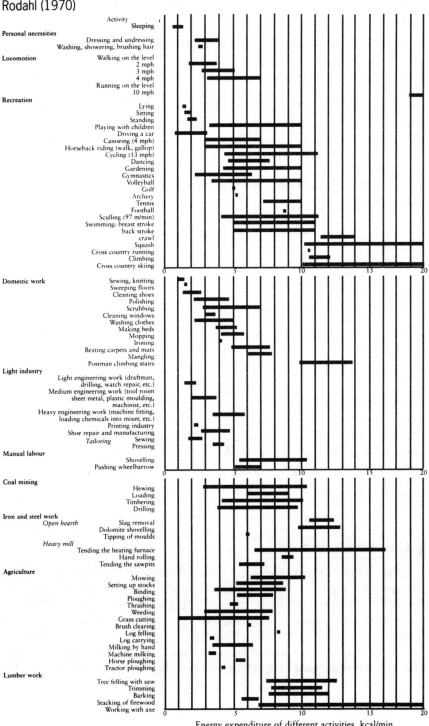

Energy expenditure of different activities, kcal/min

- vitamins regulate the body mechanisms
- water is essential in all body functions (57% of total body weight is water).

The majority of foods only become usable after their complex structure has been broken down into simpler forms. This process begins in the mouth when food is cut and ground up by the teeth and mixed with saliva. Digestion of most foods begins at this stage, due to the presence of enzymes. The stomach, a muscular bag which contracts rhythmically, continues the churning and digestive process by adding its own enzymes in the juices it secretes, and others later in the digestive corridor in the duodenum (part of the small intestine).

Table 7 *Diets for different types of sport/g/kg body weight* (from Yakovlev 1961)

	protein	fats	carbohydrate	calories
Gymnastics	2.1–2.4	1.5–1.6	9.5–9.6	60–65
Fencing / Short/middle distance	2–2.3	1.5–1.6	9–10	60–65
Jumping/throwing	2.4–2.5	1.7–1.8	9.5–10	65–70
Long distance/race walking	2–2.3	2–2.1	10.5–11.5	70–76
Very long distance running	2.4–2.5	2.1–2.3	11–13	75–85
Swimming	2.1–2.3	2–2.1	8–9	60–65
Heavy athletics	2.4–2.5	2–2.3	10–11	70–75
Wrestling/boxing	2.4–2.5	2–2.1	9–10	65–70
Rowing	2.1–2.3	2–2.1	10–11	68–74
Soccer	2.3–2.4	1.8–1.9	9–10	63–67
Basketball/volleyball	2.1–2.3	1.7–1.8	9–10	62–64
Track cycling	2.1–2.3	1.9–2.0	10–11	67–76
Equestrian sports	2.1–2.3	2.1–2.3	8–9	61–67
Road racing	2.6–2.8	2.3–2.4	11–13	80–87
Skating / Skiing (slalom/jumping)	2–2.1	1.9–2.0	9.5–10.5	65–70
Skiing (long distance)	2.1–2.3	2–2.1	10.5–11.0	70–73

Carbohydrates

As their name suggests these are compounds of carbon, hydrogen and oxygen. Carbohydrate is the principal constituent of the normal diet and, generally speaking, it meets most of the body's energy requirement. Carbohydrates occur in several forms – the simple sugars or monosaccharides, and the complex sugars, i.e. disaccharides, trisaccharides, etc. Simple sugars are often regarded as 'empty calories' and the recommended balance in the diet should be 60–65% complex sugars to 40–35% simple sugars.

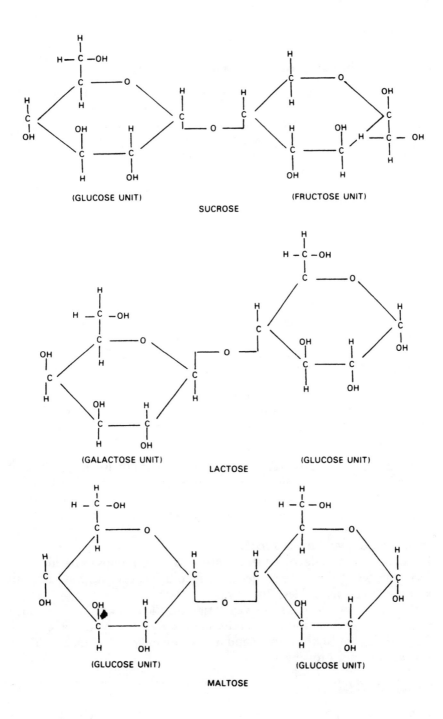

Fig. 17 *Disaccharides*

■ Simple sugars

Major monosaccharides

Glucose: as the end product of carbohydrate digestion, glucose is the main form of carbohydrate used by the body. It occurs naturally in sweet fruits.

Fructose: similar to glucose in terms of its carbon, hydrogen and oxygen composition, fructose is apparently absorbed more readily than glucose and, being independent of insulin, is not associated with the 'rebound hypoglycaemia' sometimes caused by too rich sugar foods, such as sweets and chocolate. Its value as a fuel, then, might be countered by its implications for coronary heart disease and the possibility of acidosis caused by increased blood lactate when consumed in large quantities. It is found in honey and sweet fruits.

Galactose: though similar to glucose, galactose is found in different sources, mainly yeast and liver.

■ Complex sugars

Disaccharides (fig. 17)

Sucrose: this sugar is found most commonly in the diet. It is found in white, brown and demerara sugar. Digestion breaks it down to glucose and fructose. Sucrose is a most valuable energy source, but unfortunately it encourages the activity of oral bacteria responsible for tooth decay.

Lactose: during digestion lactose, which is the starch found in milk, is broken down to glucose and galactose. Milk has a very high nutritional value, although recent research has indicated an apparent 'lactose intolerance' in some individuals.

Maltose: this sugar is found in malt extract. Malt is the product of heating and drying germinated barley (a necessary link in the brewing and distilling processes). Digestion breaks maltose down to glucose only. Malt extract is a most valuable source of energy for the athlete.

Trisaccharides and tetrasaccharides

These sugars occur less frequently in foods than monosaccharides and disaccharides. The trisaccharides are found in peas, beans, and in both root and green vegetables. The tetrasaccharides are found in such foods as the meat substitutes used by vegetarians. Little importance is attached to the trisaccharides and tetrasaccharides as energy suppliers and, since they are difficult to breakdown and may cause indigestion, their intake is not recommended for the athlete.

Polysaccharides

Starch: as the principal source of nourishment from which one derives energy, starch is the product of cereals and might be thought of as the stored energy of vegetables. The digestive system breaks down the starches to maltose, which itself is broken down to glucose. Sources of starch are legion, ranging from bread to rice to spaghetti. Heating breaks down the starch molecules to smaller compounds called dextrins.

Glycogen: this sugar is to animals as starch is to vegetables. It might also be referred to as 'stored glucose' in the athlete, and is found in liver and muscle. It is a readily available fuel source as glucose in muscle, and it assists the liver in its vital function of maintaining blood glucose, which is the *only* fuel for the brain.

Cellulose: though of very little food value to the body, cellulose gives plants their rigid structure and provides roughage in the diet. Western diets tend to lack cellulose, a fact that is of some concern to nutritionists for it is a most vital part of the diet. Intestinal health is promoted by a regular through-flow of nutrients and exodus of waste, and roughage in the diet assures this. Bran-type cereals for every breakfast are very strongly recommended.

The body is well equipped with regulatory mechanisms which discourage the immediate absorption of food substances once saturation level has been reached. However, this mechanism can be by-passed according to Saltin and Hermansen (1967) who advanced the 'glycogen overshoot' theory. It is believed that this has considerable significance for the long duration endurance athletes who must have high reserves of energy. Applying this theory one week before a major competition, the

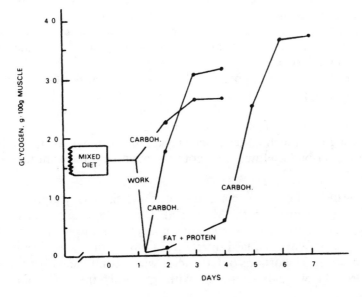

Fig. 18 *Glycogen 'overshoot'. Different possibilities of increasing the muscle glycogen content. For further explanation see text (from Saltin and Hermansen, 1967)*

athlete depletes glycogen stores by hard training and then is deprived of carbohydrate for four or five days. On the final days before the major competition, the athlete takes a very rich carbohydrate diet. The result is that the amount of available glycogen in the body is much higher than would normally be the case (fig. 18). This may not, however, be an ideal situation for the long endurance athlete (see p. 57). Such 'carbo loading' still has an important place in distance running, but now it is programmed as a 'non-stop' boost, i.e: during the final three days of the taper, the carbohydrate intake is much increased (but not the total calories).

▌Fats

Fats, like carbohydrates, are composed of carbon, hydrogen and oxygen, but the quantity of oxygen is considerably less in fats. Fats are certainly the most concentrated source of energy of all foodstuffs, yielding twice as many kilocalories, weight for weight, compared with carbohydrates. Consequently the provision of stored energy is probably their most important role in nutrition. However, they also have important roles to play in maintaining body temperature, for example the subcutaneous fat layer in sea or loch swimmers, and protecting vital organs (e.g. kidneys) with layers of fat or adipose tissue, as well as in the provision of those fatty acids essential to health and in providing a transport medium for the fat-soluble vitamins.

Fats and oils are broken up into tiny globules by bile salts secreted by the liver. These act on fats like a detergent on an oil slick and in this form they may more readily react with chemicals similar to those involved in carbohydrate digestion. Even the incomplete breakdown substances of fat digestion may pass through the gut wall to be carried in lymph along the lymphatic system to a point in the region of the chest where they are emptied into the blood.

The liver plays a most important role in the metabolism of fats. It may convert available glucose into fat and then into other usable substances in the body. Our fat stores, then, may be derived from excessive carbohydrate intake, or from fats and oils (figs. 19 and 20).

Fats belong to a much larger biochemical family known as lipids. The family is described below, but not all members have nutritional significance.

Acyl glycerols: the most common of these is triacylglycerol, or triglyceride or 'neutral fat'. Most edible fats and oils consist of compounds of glycerol (commonly known as glycerine) plus fatty acids. The main reason why, say, lard differs from nut oil or cream, lies in the different types or proportions of fatty acids which combine with glycerol. When three fatty acids combine with glycerol, the compound is triglyceride (fig. 21).

Fatty acids may consist of long chains of carbon atoms which have two hydrogen atoms attached to each carbon atom (fig. 22). This is referred

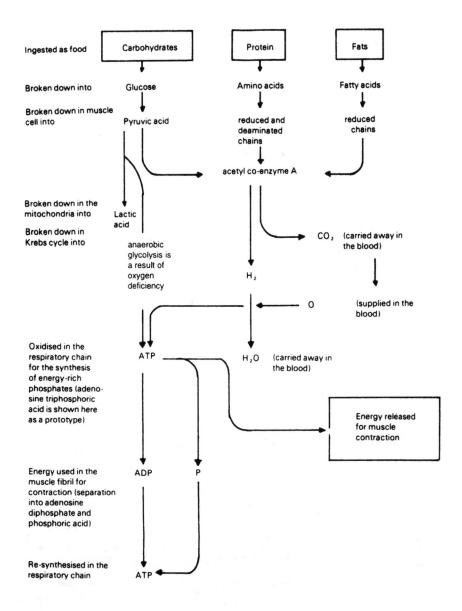

Fig. 19 *Metabolism of nutrients and their conversion into ATP, which when broken down to ADP provides energy for muscle contraction (the conversion of food into energy).*
H₂ – hydrogen; O – oxygen; CO₂ – carbon dioxide; P – phosphate; ADP – adenosine diphosphate; ATP – adenosine triphosphate

to as a *saturated* fatty acid (i.e. it is saturated with hydrogen). On the other hand, a fatty acid may not have all carbon atoms linked to two hydrogen atoms (fig. 23) and in this case it would be referred to as an *unsaturated* fatty acid.

Triglycerides occur in vegetable fats and oils, animal fats, fish oils and dairy fats. The main difference between animal fats and dairy fats, on the one hand, and vegetable fats and oils and fish oils on the other, is that, except for palm oil and coconut oil, the latter have a much higher proportion of unsaturated fatty acids. This is of considerable interest to heart specialists. It is well known that high blood cholesterol levels are associated with coronary heart disease and that the cholesterol level can be reduced by eating foods rich in unsaturated fatty acids. Table 8 illustrates the saturated/unsaturated fatty acid situation in several fats and oils.

Phospholipids: again the glycerol 'backbone' is present in this compound but only two fatty acids are attached, plus phosphate and a nitrogen-containing base. The latter situation bridges the worlds of fats and proteins and as a rule the fatty acids are unsaturated. The phospholipids have important functions to perform in the body, ranging

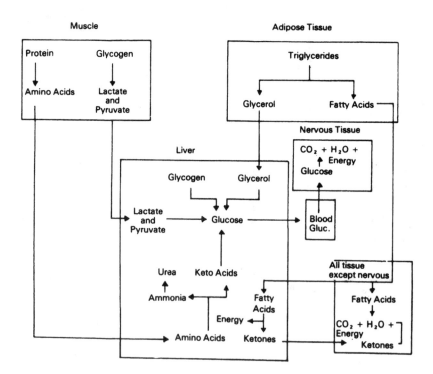

Fig. 20 *Summary of metabolism of stored foods as a source of energy (i.e. in fasting) (from Vander, Sherman and Luciano, 1970)*

from fat absorption to the insulation of nervous tissue with the myelin sheath. They are not only manufactured by and exist in the body itself, but are also in the foods we eat. For example, lecithin is present in egg yolk and soya beans. Yakovlev (1961) has emphasised the inclusion of lecithin in the post competition diet to aid recovery.

Sphingolipids: these compounds contain fatty acid, phosphate, choline, a complex base (sphingosine), but no glycerol. The sphingolipids are closely associated with tissues and animal membranes.

Glycolipids: there is neither glycerol nor phosphate in this compound. Instead there is a monosaccharide galactose, plus fatty acid and sphingosine. The glycolipids are found primarily in photosynthetic tissue (i.e. the leaves of plants).

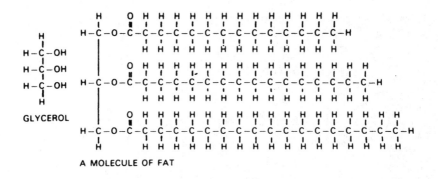

A MOLECULE OF FAT

Fig. 21 *Triglycerides. Such fats are called triglycerides because the compound glycerol in each molecule is attached to three fatty acid units*

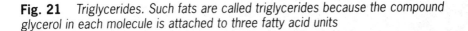

PALMITIC ACID

STEARIC ACID

Fig. 22 *Chemists refer to such fatty acids as saturated due to the presence of pairs of hydrogen atoms along the whole length of the chain. The two saturated fatty acids here are present in the harder fats, such as lard*

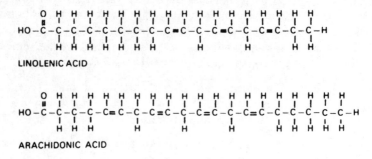

LINOLENIC ACID

ARACHIDONIC ACID

Fig. 23 *The existence of 'gaps' in the pairs of hydrogen atoms characterise the unsaturated fatty acids. The two unsaturated fatty acids shown here are present in fish oils*

Table 8 *Saturated v unsaturated fatty acids in foods expressed in %* (from Pyke, M. 1975)

	saturated fatty acids				unsaturated fatty acids			
	lauric (C_{12})	myristic (C_{14})	palmitic (C_{16})	stearic (C_{18})	oleic	linoleic	lino-lenic	arachi-donic
Vegetable fats								
Coconut oil	48	17	9	2	6	3		
Cottonseed oil		1	29	4	24	40		
Linseed oil			6	4	22	16	52	
Maize oil			13	4	29	54		
Olive oil			16	2	65	15		
Palm oil		1	48	4	38	9		
Peanut oil			6	5	61	22		
Sunflower oil		8		3	13	75	1	
Sesame oil		10		5	40	43		
Soya-bean oil		11		4	25	51	9	
Sunflower-seed oil		11		6	29	52		
Wheatgerm oil		13		4	20	55	7	
Animal fats								
Beef fat		3	25	24	42	2		
Butterfat (cow)	4	12	29	11	25	2		
(goat)	6	12	28	6	21	4		
Lard		3	24	18	42	9		
Mutton fat		5	25	30	36	4		
Fat in egg yolk*			32	4	43	8		
Marine fats								
Cod-liver oil		6	8	1	20	29	25	10
Herring oil		7	12	1	12	20	26	22
Menhaden oil		6	16	1	15	30	19	12
Pilchard oil		5	14	3	12	18	18	14
Sardine oil		6	10	2	13	14	26	29
Whale oil		9	16	2	14	37	12	7

*Fat in egg yolk also contains 13% of a C_{22} saturated fatty acid.

Terpenoids: this is a very large group of compounds made up of a simple repeating chemical unit – the isoprene unit. Due to the number of permutations and combinations of such repetition, and the body's ability to modify these, the terpenoids embrace compounds ranging from rubber to the steroids. The steroids play a vital part in nutrition and in general physiology. Vitamin A, cholesterol, testosterone and oestrogen are all steroids whose values in nutrition and physiology are well established.

Waxes: this class of lipid would appear to have little nutritional value for humans, but may well hold considerable value for marine life. The waxes act as a water barrier for insects, birds and animals, while in plants the waxes protect leaf surfaces against water loss and damage due to abrasion.

Fats in foodstuffs are primarily triglycerides, combined with small amounts of free fatty acids, phospholipids (such as lecithin) and the salts of cholesterol. Eating animal fats may cause problems associated with saturated fatty acids, but they do provide one of the most valuable sources of vitamins A and D. If margarine is therefore used in place of butter, it must be composed of vegetable oils only and enriched with vitamins A and D.

The final breakdown products of fat metabolism are free fatty acids which, like glucose, are fuel for muscular activity. Recent research shows these fatty acids are the preferred fuel for the long duration endurance athletes (fig. 24). Williams (1975) has pointed out that since this is the case, the application of the glycogen overshoot theory may not be in the athlete's interest in training. It may be better to 'train' the free fatty acid energy pathway by training in a 'fasting' state, therefore encouraging the use of free fatty acids as a fuel. However, before competition, glycogen loading is good sense even for the 5000 m (Newsholme, 1994).

Proteins

It has been pointed out that carbohydrates and fats consist mainly of carbon, hydrogen and oxygen. Protein differs in that nitrogen is an essential part of its structure and neither carbohydrate nor fats can replace protein in the diet without eventual damage to the organism.

The end product of protein digestion is a group of chemicals known as amino acids (fig. 19). There are 25 amino acids, 20 of biochemical import and, of these, 10 are known as essential amino acids. They are 'essential' because the body cannot normally manufacture these amino acids at the rate required for proper functioning. The 10 essential amino acids are *arginine, histidine, isoleucine, leucine, lysine, methionine, phenylalanine, threonine, tryptophan* and *valine.*

The amino acids go via the blood from gut to liver to general circulation. The liver again has an important regulatory function in that it acts as a 'buffer' for amino acids, just as it does for glucose and fats. That is, if the concentration is high in the blood, the liver absorbs a large

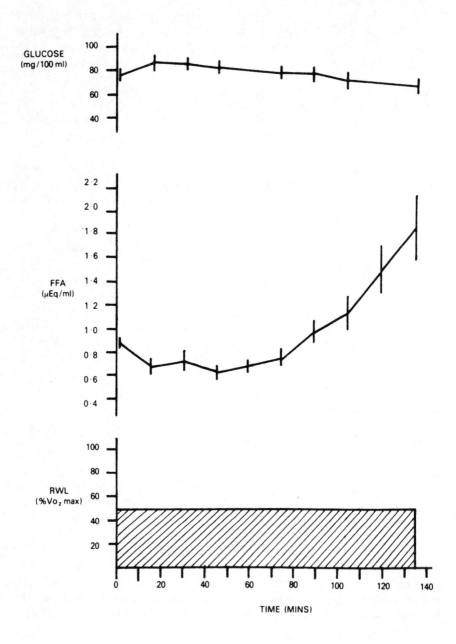

Fig. 24 *Free fatty acids appear to become the preferred fuel with increasing duration of exercise* (from Williams, 1975)

quantity into its cells. Conversely, in times of shortage, the liver releases its store. It would appear that there is a peak of circulating amino acids approximately 2 hours after a protein meal. Apparently then it is helpful, both for maintenance and repair of muscle tissue, to train at this time. It certainly does not seem advisable to train within the 2 hour period, or so late afterwards that the body has begun to starve, except of course in the case of the long duration endurance athletes as previously suggested. The liver is also responsible for preparing amino acids for use as an alternative energy source. However, this is a 'last gasp' mechanism and other sources of energy must be favoured.

The protein value of different foods varies quite remarkably. The disadvantages of the fat associated with meat, as pointed out by heart specialists, must be most carefully weighed against the high quality of animal protein and supply of certain vitamins and minerals. When assessing the protein value of the athlete's diet, quality as well as quantity must be taken into account. Some athletes may eat most of their daily protein in the form of potato chips rather than eggs or milk. Nevertheless, in terms of quality, the egg is the most complete protein food (table 9).

Table 9   *The amounts of essential amino acids in certain proteins (mg per g of nitrogen) (from Pyke, M. 1975)*

	isoleu-cine	leucine	lysine	phenyl-alanine	methio-nine	threo-nine	trypto-phan	valine	protein score as measure of excellence
Amino acid combination estimated as ideal for man	270	306	270	180	144	180	90	270	100
Egg protein	428	565	396	368	196	310	106	460	100
Beef	332	515	540	256	154	275	75*	345	83
Milk protein	402	628	497	334	190	272	85*	448	80
Fish	317	474	549	231	178	283	62*	327	70
Oat protein	302	436	212*	309	84*	192	74*	348	79
Rice protein	322	535	236*	307	142*	241	65*	415	72
Flour protein	262*	442	126*	322	78*	174	69*	262	47
Maize protein	293	827	179*	284	117*	249	38*	327	42
Soya protein	333	484	395	309	86*	247	86*	328	73
Pea protein	336	504	438	290	77*	230	74*	317	58
Potato protein	260*	304	326	285	87*	237	72*	339	56
Cassava	118*	184*	310	133*	22*	136*	131	144	22

*Less than the estimated ideal proportion.

Not all nutritionists agree with the recommended protein intake suggested by Yakovlev (1966) in table 7. In fact, his suggestions are high compared to theoretical requirements which indicate approximately 0.6g/kg/day, a level recommended for sedentary people. For the athlete in heavy endurance training about 2g/kg/day is satisfactory, with 3g/kg/day for power/strength competitors (Wootton, 1988). Durnin (1975) has suggested that an intake of around 1g/kg body weight/day would be quite adequate. Obviously this confusion must be resolved if sportsmen are to justify appeals for protein supplements in training.

Mineral elements

Iron: the element of iron is essential for production of haemoglobin carried in red blood cells (erythrocytes). If there is insufficient haemoglobin, the oxygen carrying capacity of the blood is reduced and it is reasonable to assume that the athlete's functioning capacity is also depleted. This condition is known as anaemia and by far the most common (but not the only) cause is lack of dietary iron. In these circumstances, ferrous compounds may be taken as dietary additives. However, the body will only absorb what it needs and reject the surplus. Many endurance athletes have suffered from so-called Sports-Pseudo-Anaemia, which is a condition where the total quantity of haemoglobin in the blood is high but the concentration is lower than normal, due to a relatively greater increase in blood plasma. The reduced concentration will, however, keep blood viscosity low and consequently aid the rate of flow to and from muscle (Williams, 1975). Although, generally speaking, athletes, women and growing children have greater iron requirements than other members of the population, it is inadvisable to supplement normal dietary iron without medical advice. Regular blood counts for athletes are recommended. Vitamin C aids iron absorption and it is thought that protein may also assist. However, where diets are very high in bran cereals content, the phytic acid found in the outer husks of the cereals may prevent iron absorption by forming an insoluble compound. Iron content is high in green vegetables such as spinach, watercress and cabbage, in liver, black pudding, red meat, kidney, and in yeast.

Sodium chloride (table salt): this is the most important soluble mineral of the diet, and is the main component of the extracellular fluid. Consequently it is very important that the sodium concentration of the extracellular fluid is closely monitored. Athletes losing more salt than usual, due to increased perspiration when in a hot environment, must increase salt intake above that provided by the normal diet. Thus preparations such as 'slow sodium' and various electrolyte drinks are included in special diets for athletes exposed to this situation. Ham, corned beef and cheese all have a high salt content.

Potassium: like salt, potassium is a key mineral in the maintenance of the body's internal environment, but its role is mainly within the cell, whereas salt works outside the cell. While most diets offer an ample supply of potassium to meet the body's needs, it would appear that when training is so severe and prolonged that cellular proteins are beginning to break down, then the potassium levels in the body are reduced. However, like so many of the areas under discussion here, the body is well equipped to increase potassium absorption from foodstuffs in order to restore status quo. Soya flour, dried milk, dried fruit and nuts are high in potassium.

Calcium: this performs several very important functions in the body, namely:

- the formation of bones and teeth
- the initiation of muscle contraction
- blood clotting
- as part of the composition of blood
- certain enzyme activity.

Vitamin D and protein aid calcium absorption, while phytic acid (see Iron), oxalic acid (as in rhubarb and spinach) and fats inhibit calcium absorption. While the well balanced average diet should supply sufficient calcium, and the body will readily adapt to reduced supplies, the athlete is often advised to drink an extra daily pint of (skimmed) milk or to take calcium tablets in order to ensure that calcium levels do not become too depleted due to strenuous training, especially in the case of women endurance competitors who may suffer from osteoporosis. Calcium content is high in foods such as dried skimmed milk, whitebait and hard cheese.

Phosphorus: this is found in foodstuffs and in the body as phosphate. It has many functions in the body, chiefly:

- formation of bones and teeth
- energy production (ATP and ADP)
- as an essential component of blood
- as an essential inclusion of certain enzymes and hormones.

The average well balanced diet will provide ample phosphate for the body's needs. Phosphorus content is high in cheese, brains, meat and fish.

Iodine: vital to the efficient production of the hormone thyroxine by which the thyroid gland controls the body's metabolic rate. Consequently, any lack of iodine in the diet must have serious and far-reaching effects. Where soils are rich in iodine, the plants nourished by that soil are rich in it too. In regions where soils have poor levels of iodine, potassium iodide is added to cooking salts to make up for this deficiency. Iodine content is normally highest in foods such as salt-water fish, vegetables and milk.

Fluorine: serving a most vital role in the healthy growth of bones and teeth, fluorine, like its fellow-halogen iodine, is involved in the functioning of the thyroid gland. Furthermore it is now well established that fluorine protects teeth from decay. Fluoridised drinking water, tea and salt-water fish contain quantities of fluorine.

Trace metals: some minerals are required in minute quantities by the body and are normally supplied adequately by the normal well balanced diet. For example:

- cobalt is vital to the formation of Vitamin B_{12}
- copper is essential to the healthy development of the nervous system, especially in the composition of the protective myelin sheath. It is also a component of certain metabolic enzymes
- magnesium, like calcium and phosphorus, is involved in the development of bones and teeth. However, the role of magnesium is very varied within the body. For example, in certain types of nerve impulse transmission, calcium 'switches on' while magnesium 'switches off'
- manganese is again involved in bone growth, forms part of certain enzymes and is found in the blood and liver
- zinc is essential to tissue growth and is present in certain enzymes. It is also an important agent in the removal of carbon dioxide from the body.

There are other trace elements, such as chromium, molybdenum, selenium, and so on, all of which are involved in the body processes.

Vitamins

The vitamins have somehow assumed a magical quality in the minds of athletes. How much this has been due to excessive advertising or to genuine misunderstanding is debatable. It is true that these must be present in our food at a certain minimal level to enable normal growth, health and life to proceed. However, that their excessive introduction to the diet will increase athletic performance is yet to be proved, and in over-dosage some vitamins, especially A, D and K are toxic enough to cause death. The vitamins are classified as water or fat soluble.

Water soluble

These are the B-complex vitamins and vitamin C.

Thiamine (vitamin B_1): this forms part of the enzyme responsible for the breakdown of pyruvic acid in the process of releasing energy from carbohydrates. Its presence in the diet is therefore essential. Increased intake is required where there is a high energy requirement, when carbohydrate is excessive in the diet, when the diet is high in white sugar or white flour (when there is no thiamine already added), when foods relied upon to supply thiamine are heated in alkaline or neutral solutions, and when raw fish constitutes part of the regular diet. Thiamine is water soluble and so some of it will be lost to the water in which the food is cooked. This applies, of course, to all water soluble vitamins. Thiamine content is high in foods such as brewer's yeast and wheatgerm.

Riboflavin (vitamin B_2): like thiamine, riboflavin is a component of an enzyme in the metabolism of carbohydrates, but there would appear to be no correlation between energy requirements and riboflavin. Research into the relative merits of riboflavin as a dietary supplement is inconclusive. Brewer's yeast, liver and meat extract have a high riboflavin content.

Niacin: this again is involved in enzyme activity in the metabolism of carbohydrates. However, unlike thiamine and riboflavin, niacin may be synthesised within the body through micro-organism activity in the large intestine. High quality protein, such as eggs, which are high in content of the amino acid tryptophan, provide the basis for such synthesis. Supplementing the diet with very high quantities of niacin (2–5 g) reduces the concentration of free fatty acids in the blood. Niacin content is high in meat extract, yeast extract and bran.

Pyridoxine (vitamin B_6): this is involved in enzyme activity in protein metabolism, but little has been revealed in research vis–à–vis the effects of excess or deficiency. Pyridoxine content is high in liver, green vegetables and wheatgerm.

Pantothenic acid: as a principal component of coenzyme A, pantothenic acid is involved in energy production from organic acids. Liver, egg yolk and fresh vegetables contain high levels of pantothenic acid.

Folic acid (pteroylglutamic acid): this is a key substance in the formation of red blood cells and consequently is associated with vitamin B_{12}. However, this relationship is not yet fully understood. It is also, like pyridoxine, involved in protein metabolism. Folic acid content is high in foods such as liver, oysters and spinach.

Cyanocobalamin (vitamin B_{12}): this is essential to the maturation of red blood cells and is also involved in white cell and platelet formation. Some athletes involved in high energy demand sports boost B_{12} levels by injecting large quantities of the vitamin. The athletes concerned claim certain benefits, but there is no research evidence to support these claims at present. Cyanocobalamin content is high in uncooked liver, kidney, meat, yeast extracts, dairy products and eggs. B_{12} is not found in any plants, so vegans have to take it in tablet form.

Ascorbic acid (vitamin C): this cannot be synthesised or stored by the body and therefore must be supplied by the diet. It performs several roles, e.g. it aids repair of damaged tissue and absorption of iron, it maintains healthy gums and decreases susceptibility to minor infections, and it is concentrated in some quantity in the adrenal cortex, although its exact function there is at present unknown. It has been shown that the body's ascorbic acid content falls during periods of intensive training. Moreover, when an athlete is sweating heavily, or is losing body fluids (e.g. during a common cold), ascorbic acid status in the body drops severely. Clearly, steps must be made to maintain this level, but it is not always easy. The normal diet may well supply sufficient ascorbic acid for the athlete's needs, but this is not always the case because vitamin C is easily destroyed or lost. As it is water soluble, it is often washed out of food or dissolved in cooking. Heat, processing and lengthy storage often destroy the vitamin, as does exposure to air and light (e.g. cutting an apple). All of this would appear to suggest some supplement of vitamin C to the diet. During intensive training, athletes have been known to take between 1–10 g per day. The lower end of this range seems reasonable but is nevertheless high compared with UK recommendations of 0.03 g per day and USA recommendations of 0.06 g per day. Ascorbic acid content is high in blackcurrants, green vegetables and citrus fruits.

It should be noted that due to their nature, water-soluble vitamins will simply be passed out in the urine if taken in excess and, since the athlete's needs are almost certainly greater than the recommended minimum for the general public, little harm can come of taking supplementary vitamin B complex and vitamin C, though this is not the case with the fat-soluble vitamins which can accumulate in the body.

■ Fat soluble
These are the vitamins A, D, E and K.

Retinol (vitamin A):   this is only found in animal products. However, some vegetables, including carrots and the leafy green vegetables, contain substances called carotenoids which are converted to retinol during absorption through the small intestine. Being fat soluble and stable in heat, it is not exposed to the same danger of destruction by cooking as are B-complex and C vitamins. However, exposure to oxygen and ultraviolet light can reduce retinol status in foods. Retinol is involved in vision efficiency, carotenoids being found in both rods and cones. It also would appear that bone growth, the health of alimentary and respiratory tracts, and local resistance to infection are all vitamin A dependent. High dosage of vitamin A taken regularly is toxic. Fish liver oils, ox liver and sheep liver all have a high retinol content.

Cholecalciferol (vitamin D):   essential to calcium and phosphorus absorption, cholecalciferol has a key role in development of bone and those physiological areas influenced by calcium, phosphorus and parathyroid gland activity. There are two main types of vitamin D:

- calciferol (vitamin D_2), which is formed by the ultraviolet radiation of ergosterol (a steroid found in plants such as yeast and fungi)
- cholecalciferol (vitamin D_3), which occurs naturally in substances such as egg yolk, butter and the oils of fish liver. It is also formed by the action of ultraviolet radiation on the oils present on the surface of our skins (i.e. when the skin is exposed to sunlight).

Like retinol, vitamin D in excess is toxic. Vitamin D content is high in foods such as egg yolks and vitamin enriched produce such as margarine.

Tocopherols (vitamin E): the role of vitamin E in our nutrition is far from clear. However, due to its antioxidant activity it may help coronary heart disease by preventing the oxidation of unsaturated fatty acids. It may also be involved in the oxygen uptake of muscle, but this could be a secondary effect due to its antioxidant properties. Claims that the vitamin aids athletic performance are very difficult to substantiate. Vitamin E is present in foods such as wheatgerm oil and eggs.

Vitamin K: while the role of vitamin K is clearly involved in blood clotting, no obvious role is played by the vitamin in enzyme systems. It is very difficult to assess whether or not we require vitamin K in our food or whether sufficient is manufactured within our own bodies. Vitamin K is readily inactivated on exposure to light. Of the vitamin K derivatives, vitamin K_1 is found in green vegetables, and vitamin K_2 in bacteria.

Oxygen and water are dealt with in chapters 5 and 7 respectively.

■ Nutritional intake for the athlete

■ Basic nutrient guide

Speed and elastic strength, e.g. sprinting, jumping, tennis, basketball
Biologically high-grade protein (approx. 1.5–2 g per kg body weight) for strengthening muscle tissue, increasing speed of reaction and concentration. Readily digestible carbohydrates (approx. 8 g per kg body weight) to provide reserve energy (glycogen reserve) for longer periods of training or competition. Little fat (if possible not more than 30% of the calorie intake) for formation of fatty acids.

Examples: protein intake from fish, meat, 2 eggs, yoghurt; carbohydrates from dark bread, honey, muesli, rice, noodles, vegetables, potatoes; fat is present in adequate amounts in the normal diet in margarine, vegetable oil, milk, cheese, soups.

Average energy requirement, depending on type of sport: 3500–5000 cal.

Strength endurance, e.g. middle distance, swimming, rowing
Biologically high-grade protein (approx. 1.5–2.5 g per kg body weight), to build up strength reserves for the muscle tissue (endurance training – small requirement; strength training – increased requirement). Readily digestible carbohydrates (8–10 g per kg body weight) to top up glycogen reserve. Little fat (25% of the calorie intake) for formation of fatty acids.

Examples: high protein intake from chicken, meat, fish, cheese, ham, lean sausage, milk; carbohydrates from dark bread, rolls, honey, muesli, vegetables, noodles, rice, potatoes; fat is present in the normal diet in adequate quantities in milk, lean sausage, cheese, meat.

Average energy requirement, depending on type of sport: 4000–6000 cal.

Strength, e.g. throws, wrestling, weight lifting

Large amounts of biologically high-grade protein (approx. 3 g per kg body weight) for strengthening the growth of muscle tissue and increasing strength in the particular muscles involved. The protein should be taken immediately before and as soon after the training exertion as possible. Readily digestible carbohydrates (5–8 g per kg body weight). Little fat (about 30% of the total calories) to ensure formation of the essential fatty acids.

Examples: particularly large amounts of protein from veal and beef, ham, low-fat cheese, yoghurt and milk; carbohydrates from fruit juices, cheese, puddings, dark bread, beans, peas, fruit; fat is present in the normal diet in adequate quantities in cheese, milk, meat, sausages.

Average energy requirement, max: 8000 cal.

Endurance, e.g. long distance, langlauf

Especially large amounts of readily digestible carbohydrates (about 10 g per kg body weight) for optimum topping up of glycogen reserve, as energy reserves with long-term effect, for increased endurance capacity. Biologically high-grade protein (at least 1.2 g per kg body weight) for the necessary muscle performance in prolonged exertion. For prolonged high performance, fat is of major importance as a source of energy, but uneconomical. In extremely prolonged exertion with high calorie consumption therefore, the fat deposits become depleted.

Examples: high carbohydrate intake from fruit juices, porridge, bread, crisp-bread, honey, fruit, semolina, rice, potatoes, pasta, malt; protein intake from milk, eggs, cheese, ham, lean sausage, meat; fat is present in the normal diet in adequate amounts in cheese, milk, sausage, eggs.

Average energy requirement, depending on type of sport: 4000–7000 cal.

■ Before competition or training

Allow 2–2½ hours to elapse after eating a light meal before starting competition or training. The meal should consist of those foods which the athlete knows from experience are acceptable. Large quantities of carbohydrate are not advised in this period. Carbonated drinks, alcohol, iced products, tri/tetrasaccharides and those foods (especially fatty foods), which require long periods of time to digest must be avoided. Foods should be warm and easily digested. Caffeine in the form of coffee is sometimes taken by marathon runners 20–30 minutes before the start to increase blood fatty acid levels, thus helping to conserve muscle glycogen. The endurance athlete will also ensure that ascorbic acid, mineral salts (including phosphoric acid), ample liquid and easily assimilated glucose products are included. Finally, boiled or stewed foods are infinitely preferable to fried or roasted foods.

■ After competition or training

Allow 30–60 minutes to elapse before eating after competition or training. Glucose drinks should be taken to help restore the carbohydrate reservoir during this period. The post-training meal will be as normal as appetite suggests and it is advised that ascorbic acid and B-complex supplements are taken at this time. The post-competition meal requires careful thought, especially if the competition has been hard or of special significance. Carbohydrate intake should be increased and animal fats decreased for 2–3 days. Yakovlev (1961) suggests 20–25% of the normal fat intake should be vegetable oils. Foods such as eggs, milk, brewer's yeast, fish, meat and liver should be included for their contribution to recovery, while the poorer proteins in foods such as rice, soya and jelly should be avoided. Should competition or training have involved considerable loss of body fluids through sweat, the lost fluid *must* be replaced, until the urine is back to its normal pale straw colour.

It should be added here that, provided an athlete's particular 'food fad' is not known to be harmful, then his belief in it may be of greater advantage to him than physiological evidence might suggest. Diets to lose or gain weight for competitive advantage must be discussed with the athlete's doctor.

Internationally agreed doping laws were devised in the first instance for the protection of athletes, and secondly for the protection of sport. The coach should see to it that both athlete and sport are given that protection.

Space does not permit lengthy discussion on smoking and drinking, but evidence is now irrefutable that smoking is incompatible with high athletic performance and sound health, while drinking (the effects of which are traceable 48 hours after ingestion) impairs coordination and disturbs fluid balance and temperature regulation. Alcohol in moderation – a beer or two – as a relaxant is not without its advantages, however, and should be considered if and when a relaxant is required.

Finally, following an extensive review of the diets of athletes, it is perfectly clear that the vast majority overestimate their requirements. This error is a little more serious than it may seem at first sight. It is part of a general tendency in the western population to overeat in the belief that if something is good for you, more of it is better still! Recent work has shown that overeating causes more rapid ageing than a well balanced diet. In fact, periods of fasting apparently prolong the life of certain animals and give them a younger biological age, however this can be overdone in weight-categorised sports including light-weight rowing, and gymnastics.

▌Summary

With the exception of the days preceding and succeeding a competition, a regular well balanced diet should amply supply the nutrition required by the athlete. The rule of thumb of 1 g of protein per kg of body weight per day might well be modified to a range of 1–1.5 g of protein per kg of body weight per day for most athletes, and perhaps even higher (1.5–3.0 kg) for strength athletes during periods of heavy weight training. Several light meals rather than the occasional heavy meal would appear to be more helpful in the pursuit of maximal performance. At least three per day is recommended. Due to the inevitable loss of certain nutrients through cooking, preserving, storing, etc., athletes may require dietary supplements. Reinforcements are most likely to be necessary for the water-soluble vitamins (recommended intake 1–2 g vitamin C, and 0.5 g vitamin B complex per day) and the mineral elements, especially iron and calcium. Many proprietary brands of vitamin pills include several vitamins and minerals. However, other dietary supplements (containing substances such as pollen extract) should be taken 'with a pinch of salt'! Their exact role or importance is not always clear. Care also should be taken to avoid foods which may have an adverse effect on the absorption of other nutrients (e.g. raw fish, raw egg white). Substances such as caffeine, alcohol, and so on, like so many areas of nutrition, are acceptable in the moderation that is implied by a well balanced diet.

5
The oxygen transporting system

Definition, functions and effects

The various nutrients available to the body by the metabolism of foodstuffs must be transported to the sites where they are used or stored. This transport is provided by a remarkable fluid which also carries oxygen, hormones and chemicals, is a buffer solution, removes waste products from the tissues, aids temperature control, and helps maintain fluid balance. This fluid is the blood.

Blood

The volume of blood in the body varies from person to person and will increase with training, but it is approximately as follows: *men* 75 ml/kg body weight; *women* 65 ml/kg body weight; *children* 60 ml/kg body weight.

The composition of blood is quite complex, but is summarised by fig. 25.

Erythrocytes (red blood cells)

Erythrocytes (red blood cells) are formed in the bone marrow at an equal rate to their destruction (haemolysis). This means approximately 2–3 million cells per second. Red cell formation is stimulated by *anoxia* (oxygen deficiency – see p. 81) and *erythropoietin*, a glycoprotein also known as haemopoietin or erythrocyte stimulating factor (ESF) which is produced in the kidneys. Intravenous injections of renal extracts or glucocorticoids stimulate red cell formation and it has been suggested that testosterone derivatives increase erythropoietin formation.

The average erythrocyte count in men is 5.7 million/mm^3 and in women and children is 4.8 million/mm^3. The red colouring is due to its haemoglobin content, which is a combination of a protein (globin) and a red pigment (haematin). Muscle haemoglobin is called myoglobin. The red pigment contains iron, which readily combines with oxygen. This combination is a very loose affair and the oxygen can be just as easily 'disconnected' or cast free. Herein lies the oxygen transporting property of blood and obvious importance of dietary iron. However, excessive iron will not increase the oxygen carrying capacity of the blood. Iron absorption is tightly controlled by the body's requirements. When these are met, absorption through the intestine wall ceases and the excess iron is expelled in the faeces.

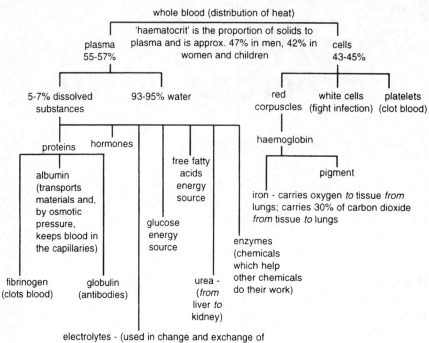

Fig. 25 *Summary of blood composition and function*

In men, the average haemoglobin (Hb) content is 15.8/100 ml blood, while in women it is 13.9/100 ml blood. To be more precise, normal values may be found within the range 14–18 g/100 ml blood for men and 11.5–16 g/100 ml for women. 1 g of fully saturated haemoglobin combines with 1.34 ml oxygen, so haemoglobin may be used as an index of the oxygen carrying capacity of the blood. Occasionally haemoglobin content is expressed as a percentage, but this can be a little confusing since 100% may be normal for one investigator but not for another. Moreover, there appears to be different 'normal' values according to age, sex, nationality, geographic location, and so on. Consequently, one must check the meaning of 100% before evaluating the Hb count of an athlete.

The idea of a normal range seems much less problematic. Information on haemoglobin status is presented in the Edinburgh Royal Infirmary Bioprofile, as in table 10. Reading the haemoglobin line, the athlete appears to be relatively low in the range and consequently we can assume that the oxygen carrying capacity of the blood is also low. The second line tells us why it is low. The Mean Corpuscular Haemoglobin Concentration (MCHC) is an index of the iron status of haemoglobin and here it is clear that the athlete requires some kind of iron therapy suggested by a doctor.

Table 10 *Information sent to an Edinburgh girl who ran 800 m and 1500 m*

	normal range	you
Haemoglobin	Men (14–18): Women (11.5–16)	12.9
*MCHC	32–36	32.2

*Mean Corpuscular Haemoglobin Concentration

Training increases the total amount of haemoglobin in the body and this can be assessed by evaluating the red cell volume and haemoglobin count. Periodically the red cell count may rise by 5–10% with sustained work, but this is normally temporary and due to an imbalance of body fluids. However, training has a more variable effect on MCHC and it has been shown that many top endurance athletes have a tendency to iron-deficiency (anaemia). This may be due to dietary deficiency, iron loss in sweat, damaged red cells, etc., but may also be part of the adaptive process to ensure a higher speed of oxygen provision to the muscle. Endurance training will increase the blood *volume* by 15 to 30%, but this hypervolaemia is usually accompanied by a 5 to 10% fall in red cell and haemoglobin concentration.

Finally, haemoglobin plays an essential part in the removal of carbon dioxide from the tissues to the lungs.

Leucocytes (white blood cells)

The leucocytes (white blood cells) are comprised of the following.

Granulocytes: *neutrophils* – involved in resistance to infection and multiply when there is an infection in the body or when there is local inflammatory reaction brought about by dead or dying tissue. The glucocorticoids increase the number of circulating neutrophils but their ability to migrate into the tissues is reduced, with consequent loss of resistance to infection. The destruction of bacteria by neutrophils is possible because the neutrophils are capable of phagocytosis ('cell eating'); *eosinophils* – collect at sites of allergic reaction and it has been suggested that they limit the effects of substances such as histamine. The level of circulating eosinophils is reduced by the glucocorticoids; *basophils* – have a much smaller share of the leucocyte population (table 11), and relatively little is known of their physiological function. They contain heparin and histamine and may be connected with preventing clotting. Glucocorticoids lower the number of circulating basophils.

Monocytes: like the neutrophils they help remove bacteria and debris by active phagocytosis in the battle against infection. They act against bacteria after the neutrophils, thus forming a second line of defence. The corticosteroids have a similar effect on monocytes and neutrophils.

Lymphocytes: involved in the processes of immunity. They are formed principally from lymphoid tissue. The glucocorticoids decrease the number of circulating lymphocytes and the size of the lymph nodes.

Table 11 *Composition of the blood's cell volume*

type of cells	average number of cells per micro litre of blood
neutrophils	5400
eosinophils	160
basophils	40
lymphocytes	2750
monocytes	540
erythrocytes (male)	4.8×10^6
(female)	5.4×10^6
platelets	300,000

It is worth bearing in mind that these defence manoeuvres require an expenditure of energy in addition to the weakness caused when the 'enemy' infection has gained ground. Training is never recommended during this battle unless the infection is very slight. The problem does not end here, however, because even when the battle has been won, the reserves have been depleted and must be allowed to recoup. Consequently the coach must scale down all training until the athlete feels that things are back to normal.

Thrombocytes (platelets)

The thrombocytes (platelets) are very small bodies which are fragments of giant cells called megakaryocytes. When the walls of blood vessels are damaged, platelets adhere to the injury site and secrete materials contained in their granules. This adhesion and secretion is the action of clotting. The number of circulating platelets is increased by glucocorticoids.

The role of the glucocorticoids has been previously mentioned to draw attention to some of the micro-physical effects of stressors. Stress increases ACTH (adrenocorticotrophic hormone) activity (see chapter 8), which in turn raises the amount of circulating glucocorticoids. Why this occurs is still unexplained, but these micro-physical effects may ultimately cause the major physical problems of high blood pressure, coronary disease, etc. (fig. 26). Hence concern for the health of 30–45 year old males constantly exposed to stressors of business, professional life, and so on.

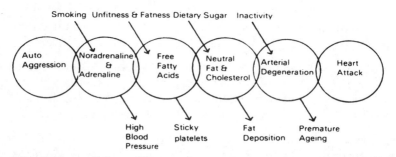

Fig. 26 *Factors which contribute to the possibility of a heart attack. Carruthers referred to this situation as 'knitting a heart attack' (from Carruthers, 1971)*

Plasma

Approximately 55% of the blood volume is a straw-coloured fluid called plasma. It is made up of over 90% water, and under 10% solids. The solids are as follows.

Proteins (comprised of): *albumin* – carries materials to sites of need or elimination (e.g. minerals, ions, fatty acids, amino acids, bilirubin, enzymes, drugs); *globulin* – the gamma globulins are antibodies which help in defence against infection. The globulins are classified into α_1, α_2, β_1, β_2, and λ globulins. Immunoglobins and some lipoproteins are included in this category; *fibrinogen* – aids blood clotting. (The fluid 'squeezed' from a clot is serum.)

Glucose: carried in plasma, and is the body's principal fuel source along with fatty acids.

Electrolytes: break down to electrically charged particles called ions. These are vital for conducting signals along the communications system of the nerves and they allow polarity changes between cells (and tissues) and the fluids which surround them. These can be acids, alkalies or salts. The most common are Sodium (Na^+), Chlorine (Cl^-), Calcium (Ca^{++}), Potassium (K^+), Magnesium (Mg^{++}), Sulphate (SO_4^-), and Carbonate (CO_3^-).

Free fatty acids (see chapter 4).

Amino acids (see chapter 4).

Hormones (see chapter 8).

Urea: waste by-product of used protein, carried by plasma from the liver to the kidneys where this nitrogen compound is processed and eliminated from the body.

Lactic acid: the end product of the lactic anaerobic energy pathway. Normal levels are 1 to 2 mmol/litre, but in violent exercise this can rise to 20 mmol/litre. Due to its ease of diffusion, blood lactate gives a reasonable picture of lactate concentration in muscle. Peak lactic acid concentration in the blood is not achieved till several minutes after activity.

Other substances are present in minute amounts in plasma, but are not listed here in detail. Among the properties of blood already listed is its function as a 'buffer solution'. A buffer solution contains a weak acid or alkali and a highly ionized salt of the same acid or alkali. The presence of the highly ionized salt maintains the pH balance of the solution when it is exposed to an influx of acid or alkali substance.

The pH of a solution is its measure of acidity or alkalinity and neutral pH = 7.0. A pH figure of 7.0+ is in the direction of alkalinity and 7.0– is in the direction of acidity. At rest, the pH of arterial blood is 7.40 and of mixed venous blood is 7.37. The shift towards acidity is due to the formation of carbon dioxide, the formation of substances such as phosphoric and sulphuric acid, and the generally acid nature of metabolites. In severe exercise, although lactic acid is partially buffered by the blood, an arterial pH as low as 7.0 has been recorded (Astrand, 1970). Specific endurance training for those sports where lactic anaerobic activity is involved is partly geared to the improved efficiency of blood as a buffer solution.

Biochemical analysis of blood can probably give the clearest picture of the status of an athlete's body chemistry, short of biopsy techniques. Equipment such as the Technicon Autoanalyzer can carry out over 40 tests on a given sample of blood in 60 seconds. Within a minute one can have a clear picture of haemoglobin concentration, MCHC, erythrocyte count, white cell count, blood glucose, lactates, lipids, etc.

To fulfil its tasks, the blood must be:

- pumped around the body (heart)
- contained in tubes/vessels through which it is pumped (blood vessels)
- taken to a source of oxygen (lungs)
- taken to a source of fuel (gut, liver)
- taken to areas where oxygen and fuel are used (tissues)
- loaded with waste (tissues)
- unloaded of waste (lungs, kidneys).

Astrand's and Rodahl's (1970) diagram of circulation helps to give the overall picture (fig. 27).

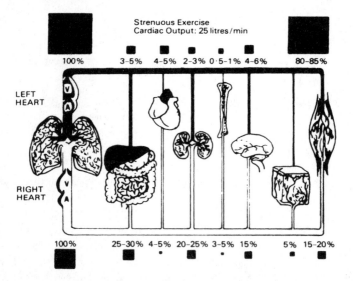

Fig. 27 *Astrand and Rodahl illustrate the circulation 'picture' with great clarity in this extract from* A Textbook of Work Physiology *(1970). The figures indicate the relative distribution of the blood to the various organs at rest (lower scale) and during exercise (upper scale). During exercise the circulating blood is primarily diverted to the muscles. The area of the black squares is proportional to the minute volume of blood flow*

■ The heart

The heart is a muscle which, by its contraction, pumps blood round the body to all areas to meet the needs of the moment. For example, at rest, the gut has a lot of blood to cope with digestion and the acceptance of nutrients for transporting to storage or circulation. During exercise the blood is directed to the particular agents who require it, i.e. the muscle for mechanical and physiological work and the skin for temperature control.

The continuous pumping of the heart also returns 'used' blood, carrying increased carbon dioxide back to the lungs, where the excess carbon dioxide is unloaded and oxygen supplies are replenished. ECGs (electro-cardiograms) are frequently used to assess the status of the heart's contractile mechanisms, but may also be used in laboratory testing work to provide an accurate heart rate assessment. Figure 28 shows the relationship between the ECG, blood pressure, heart sound, and ventricular pressure. The ECG is recorded on a write-out form or on an oscilloscope. Changes in the T-wave have been noted when the athlete is experiencing high level stressors in training or competition (Carlile, 1960).

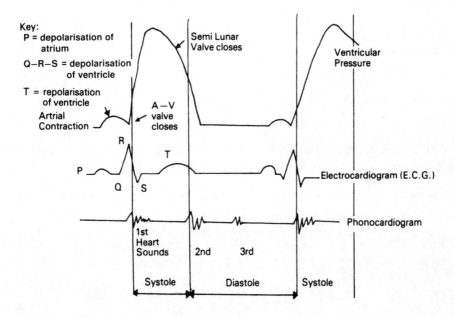

Fig. 28   *The relationship between the contraction patterns and mechanisms of the heart, the ECG and the heart sounds* (from Guyton, 1966)

■ Blood pressure

Blood pressure is also used as a guide to the efficiency of the heart and blood vessels. Normal values are 120 mm/80 mm. This means at systole (i.e. when the heart thrusts its contents from the left ventricle into the aorta which takes the oxygen rich blood to the tissues) the pressure is 120 mm, and at diastole (i.e. when the left ventricle is being refilled) the pressure is 80 mm. These pressures, especially the systole, rise in the first few minutes of exercise, but gradually fall over the following 30 to 45 minutes. Other blood pressures of interest are those of systole and diastole at the right ventricle which send oxygen depleted blood along the pulmonary artery to the lungs. These pressures are 25 mm and 7 mm, to avoid damaging the lungs.

When the blood reaches the tissues, the pressure has dropped considerably but is still sufficient to squeeze the fluids through the capillary walls into the tissue. This is because the *hydrostatic* pressure is lower in the tissue than in the capillaries. The return of the fluid to the capillaries is due to *osmotic* pressure generated by albumen in the blood. This may be thought of as a 'thirst' for fluid. The fluid returns to the capillaries and is pressed back towards the heart by hydrostatic pressure. The oxygen required by the tissues is removed from the blood at capillary level and the carbon dioxide formed by the working tissues passes into the capillary to be carried back to the right heart, then on to the lungs. The cycle is then repeated. Any 'spill-over' of fluid between capillary and tissue goes into the lymphatic system to be drained off into circulation at another point, or into the body's extracellular fluids.

The volume of blood pumped out with each contraction of the heart muscle is known as the stroke volume. The number of heart beats per minute is called the heart rate. Compared with untrained persons, training of the oxygen transporting system at a given workload lowers the athlete's heart rate on recovery from that workload, as well as at rest. The highly trained endurance athlete may have a range from approximately 40 beats per minute to 200 per minute. At the latter rate, the heart is apparently 'failing' because there is insufficient time to fill the volume of the ventricles. As a consequence, the stroke volume is reduced to much less than maximum. (In top male endurance athletes maximum is approximately 220 ml; resting = 80 ml.) As we grow older, maximum heart rate reduces. Astrand and Christensen (1964) suggest 210/minute at the age of 10, 180/minute at 35 years of age and 165/minute at 65 years of age.

Cardiac output is the total volume of blood pumped out by the heart per minute. This is the product of heart rate x stroke volume. Astrand (1970) states that 'cardiac output during standard exercise repeated during a course of training . . . is maintained at the same level'. This implies that stroke volume increases with training (since heart rate decreases).

■ The blood vessels
The blood vessels are best presented in diagram form, as illustrated in figure 29 showing the complete 'circuit'.

■ The lungs
The lungs provide the large surface area necessary for the exchange of oxygen (passing into the blood) and carbon dioxide (passing out of the

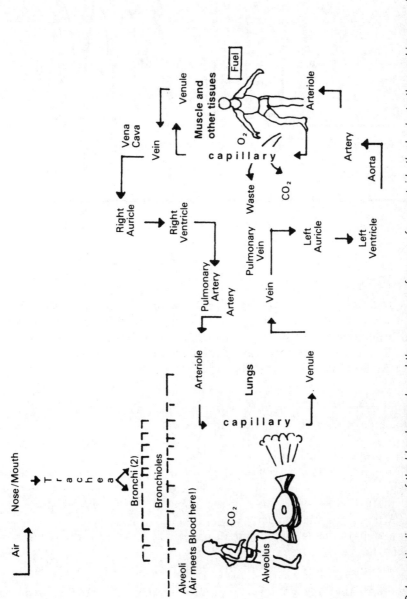

Fig. 29 Schematic diagram of the blood vessels and the passage of oxygen from outside the body, to the working muscle

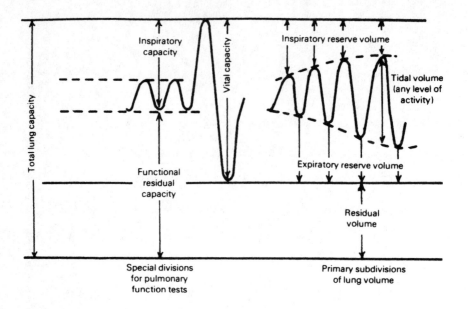

Special divisions
for pulmonary
function tests

Primary subdivisions
of lung volume

Fig. 30 *Diagram of lung volumes and capacities* (from Pappenheimer et al, 1950)

blood). Before it reaches the tiny alveoli the air is warmed, moistened and cleansed as it passes via the nose and mouth through the trachea, bronchi and bronchioles. Finally, the exchange of gases takes place between the alveoli and the pulmonary capillaries. Certain measures of lung capacity are frequently used to assess the efficiency of the breathing mechanisms (fig. 30):

- vital capacity is the maximal volume of gas that can be expelled from the lungs following a maximal inspiration
- inspiratory capacity is the maximal volume of gas inspired from the functional residual capacity
- functional residual capacity is the volume of gas remaining in the lungs when the respiratory muscles are relaxed
- expiratory reserve volume is the volume of gas expired from the functional residual capacity
- residual volume is the volume of gas which remains in the lungs even after forced expiration
- total lung capacity is the sum of the vital capacity and residual volume.

In women, the lung volumes are approximately 10% smaller than for men of the same age and size. Training for aerobic endurance may increase vital capacity. Vital capacity decreases with age. Although this is clear in the over 40s, the exact commencement of this decline is normally in the early 30s, but is variable according to the individual concerned.

Vital capacity is greatest amongst endurance athletes – in Stockholm an Olympic medallist in cross-country skiing recorded 8.1 litres.

■ Gut and liver

It has been pointed out that many of the end products of digestion are absorbed from the intestine into the blood, which carries these products to storage or further processing and then carries required nutrients into general circulation. Concentration of blood flow in this area of the circulatory system is much greater at rest than it is during exercise (fig. 27). Prior to competition, emotional excitement causes an increased flow of adrenaline, an arresting of the digestive process, and a very obvious problem if a meal has been eaten too recently.

The liver performs a number of functions:

- it maintains a supply of glucose to the blood
- it is the most vital organ of metabolism
- it is a storage organ, holding glycogen, fat, proteins, some vitamins, and other substances involved in blood formation, and blood itself. These substances are released and reserves replenished as the need arises
- it synthesizes plasma proteins and heparin
- it secretes bile which is necessary for the absorption of fats and the fat soluble vitamins A, D, E and K
- it is involved in the formation and destruction of erythrocytes, and in the protection of the body against toxic invaders (e.g. through oxidation of alcohol and nicotine).

The liver has the responsibility for making potential energy available to the tissues in the form of glucose. Its efficiency in this role *must* be maximum in exercise. Consequently it is wrong to make demands of the liver to oxidise, say, alcohol, while energy provision is required.

■ The tissues

The main tissues of interest to those involved in training theory are the muscles, which are dealt with in detail in chapter 6.

■ Elimination of the waste products of exercise

The principal waste products of exercise are urea, carbon dioxide, water, metabolites other than lactate, and lactic acid itself. The main fate of urea and water is to be filtered through the kidneys and expelled from the body. Carbon dioxide is carried in the blood to the lungs, where it passes into the alveoli and is then expelled from the body. Metabolites other than lactate are disposed of first by oxidation. The oxygen required for this purpose is referred to as that which repays the alactic oxygen debt. Lactic acid is eliminated as follows.

(1) The muscle lactate is disposed of first by oxidation to pyruvate, and then by dissimilation to carbon dioxide and water.
(2) Some of the blood lactate is then taken up by the liver which reconstructs it to glycogen, via the 'cori cycle'.
(3) The remaining blood lactate diffuses back into the muscle, or other

organs, to be oxidised then dissimilated. Such oxidation of lactate causes formation of carbon dioxide, the fate of which is mostly the reconstitution of blood bicarbonate, before being excreted by the lungs. It should be noted that lactate cannot be oxidised in the blood stream itself. Moreover, it appears that the reconstruction of glycogen from lactic acid is not possible in human muscle.

Maximal oxygen uptake

Maximal oxygen uptake (VO_2 maximum) is the body's maximal aerobic power and is defined as 'the highest oxygen uptake the individual can attain during physical work breathing air at sea level' (Astrand, 1970). Oxygen uptake is the difference in oxygen content between the air inspired and the air expired, expressed in ml/kg body weight/minute. In other words it is the amount of oxygen required by the body to fulfil its functions at a given time. Obviously more oxygen will be required in severe exercise and so oxygen uptake will increase. However, a point is eventually reached where the body can take up no more oxygen. At this point the value is referred to as the maximal oxygen uptake.

Evaluation of the athlete's VO_2 maximum is the best criterion of his status of aerobic efficiency. In table 12, Swedish statistics give the ranges for certain groups of athletes.

Table 12 *VO_2 max. ranges for Swedish athletes according to competition distance (ml/kg body wt/min)*

	male	female
400m	63–69	52–58
800m–1500m	74–77	52–58
3000m	77–82	
Cross country	72–83	55–61
Normals	38–46	30–46

The highest recorded improvements of VO_2 maximum are between 15% and 20%. Improvement is made possible by increasing the efficiency of the oxygen transporting system. The principal areas for its possible improvement are as follows.

(1) The heart. Stroke volume can be increased by specific endurance training, as can the capacity to raise the maximum heart rate.
(2) The blood. The oxygen-carrying capacity of the blood can again be increased by specific training. Both total mass of erythrocytes and total haemoglobin may be increased. Ekblom's (1972) 'blood doping' demonstrated the artificial increase of the blood's oxygen-carrying capacity.
(3) The muscle. The difference between the oxygen content of artery and vein (e.g. before and after the muscle accepts fuel and oxygen from the capillaries) is known as the arterio-venous oxygen difference (a-$\bar{v}O_2$).

Increasing the size and number of mitochondria (the oxygen users) of muscle, and the density of capillaries in muscle by specific endurance exercise, will increase the value of a-v̄O$_2$, as will the increase in myoglobin, the muscles' own internal oxygen transport system.

A relationship between heart rate, % VO$_2$ maximum, and blood lactate concentration is suggested by table 13.

Table 13   *Relationship of blood lactate concentration, % VO$_2$ max. and heart rate* (adapted from Suslov, 1972)

lactic acid mg/100ml blood	% VO$_2$ max.	heart rate	scale of intensity
25	50	130	low
30	60	150	light
70	75	165	high
90	90	180/190	sub-maximum
100	100	190+	maximum

■ Acclimatisation to altitude

In the mid 1960s the problems of competing at altitude raised questions about the possible advantages of training at altitude. At altitudes, such as that of Mexico City (2.3 km, 7500 ft), there is a reduced partial pressure of oxygen (pO$_2$) due to reduced barometric pressure, thus there is a lower pressure forcing oxygen into the blood in the lungs. The partial pressure at any point is obtained from the formula:

pO$_2$ = % oxygen concentration of dry air x barometric pressure–47*

*(47 = partial pressure of water vapour)

Thus, with a constant oxygen concentration of 20.94% dry air, table 14 shows the pO$_2$ at different altitudes.

Table 14   *Relationship of altitude, barometric pressure and partial pressure of oxygen* (abbreviated from Astrand and Rodahl, 1970)

altitude (metres–sea level)	barometric pressure (mm mercury)	tracheal pO$_2$
	760	149
1000	674	131
2000	596	115
19,215	47	0*

*There would only be water in the trachea.

The so-called 'oxygen lack' at altitude is something of a misnomer because the chemical composition of the atmosphere is almost uniform up to an altitude of over 20,000 ft. Also, at altitude, with the reduced barometric pressure, there is a reduced air resistance, implying an advantage to speed activities. The force of gravity is also reduced, suggesting an advantage where relative strength or maximum strength is critical. Air temperature and humidity are on the whole lower and this increases the loss of water via respiration, causing problems in endurance sports, intermittent but long duration team games, and so on. Finally, ultraviolet radiation is more intense so competition or training during hours when the sun is high should be avoided. The immediate effects of exposure to altitude are:

- increased breathing rate, even at rest
- increased heart rate (tachycardia)
- giddiness
- nausea
- headache
- sleeplessness
- greater arterio-venous oxygen difference
- decreased VO₂ maximum
- rapid increase of haemoglobin concentration in first few days.

The total effect of these adjustments is a reduction of work capacity, but the degree of reduction can vary between individuals.

The long-term effects of continued exposure to altitude are:

- increased erythrocyte volume (increased erythropoietin secretion due to oxygen lack)
- increased haemoglobin volume and concentration
- increased blood viscosity
- continued lower VO₂ maximum
- decreased tolerance of lactic acid
- reduced stroke volume of the heart
- increased capillarisation in the muscle.

It is clear that training at altitude is sound preparation for competing at altitude and that altitude performances will improve as adaptation continues. However, there is divergence of opinion that altitude training will improve performance on return to sea level.

Summary

Although blood is referred to as the oxygen transporting system, it is also the principal means of transporting to the tissues the fuel and materials essential for maintenance, repair and growth, and of transporting waste from the tissues to disposal sites. The system may be improved by increased functional capacity of heart, lungs, blood vessels and blood, combined with more efficient use of oxygen, fuel and various materials at the sites where they are required. Blood transports heat from muscle to skin.

Increased efficiency implies increased working capacity, which itself implies more value from training units for the athlete and more life in the years of the non-athlete. Specific training will increase efficiency of the system and it is therefore self evident that both athletes and non-athletes should adopt such training.

Periodic blood analyses are acknowledged to be valuable aids to evaluate body chemistry and are recommended for athlete and non-athlete alike. In addition, it is suggested that VO_2 maximum, blood pressure and blood lactate (for a given workload) be similarly tested to establish a broad picture of oxygen transporting system efficiency, relative to the physiological demands of a sport.

The 'anaerobic threshold', or OBLA point (onset of blood lactate accumulation) is also a very useful measure. The OBLA point gives an indication of the workload (on cycle, canoe or rowing ergometers, or on a treadmill) at which the body just starts to seriously use anaerobic energy with the probability of a rapid build-up of lactic acid in the blood. Knowing the heart rate at which this happens can help a competitor to optimise aerobic training by working appropriately just under the OBLA point, i.e. just below the anaerobic threshold. The anaerobic threshold may sometimes be determined without blood sampling – by noting alterations in breathing patterns during a maximum aerobic test.

|6
The working muscle

On arrival at the muscle, the fuel is combusted with or without oxygen as the muscle converts chemical energy to mechanical energy. Before examining the working parts of the muscle, the various 'energy pathways' should be explained.

▌The energy pathways

The energy pathways are each designed to reform (or reconstitute) the compound ATP (adenosine triphosphate). It is the breaking down of this compound which provides energy for cell function. This breakdown may be expressed as an equation (fig. 31), in full, or diagrammatically as the symbolic removal of P from ATP to produce ADP + P.

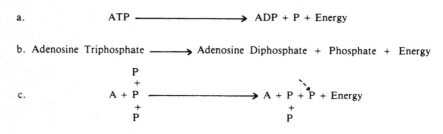

a. ATP   ⟶   ADP + P + Energy

b. Adenosine Triphosphate ⟶ Adenosine Diphosphate + Phosphate + Energy

c. A + P ⟶ A + P + P + Energy
(with P + / P above and below A + P on each side)

Fig. 31 *Breakdown of ATP*

The production of this vital compound, which has been referred to as 'the energy currency of life', may be effected by one of three pathways – alactic anaerobic, lactic anaerobic and aerobic.

Alactic anaerobic energy pathway

In the muscle there is a store of a compound, creatine phosphate, which consists of creatine plus a large number of phosphates. If, after ATP is broken down to ADP, a phosphate was added to ADP, thereby reconstituting ATP, then the process of energy production could be continued. A store of phosphates would be required for this, and that is where creatine phosphate comes in. As ATP breaks down to ADP, a phosphate may be drawn from the creatine phosphate store to make ATP. This process may be continued until the creatine phosphate store is exhausted.

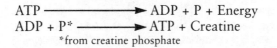

$$\text{ATP} \longrightarrow \text{ADP} + \text{P} + \text{Energy}$$
$$\text{ADP} + \text{P*} \longrightarrow \text{ATP} + \text{Creatine}$$
*from creatine phosphate

There is approximately 3–4 times the amount of creatine phosphate as ATP in the muscle. It permits athletes to work at high intensity for 10–15 seconds without lactic acid production. Hence its title as the *alactic* (without lactate) *anaerobic* (without oxygen) *energy pathway*. Some 25–30 seconds recovery is required for resynthesis of approximately half of the creatine phosphate – ATP energy stores. These energy compounds in the muscle are sometimes known as phosphagen stores and this refers to creatine phosphate plus ATP. Short, intermittent bursts of activity will call upon this pathway. Training can develop alactic anaerobic capacity to some extent. This would involve short intervals of maximum effort (5–10 secs) with long rests (1 minute).

Lactic anaerobic energy pathway

This energy pathway involves the breakdown of glycogen (glycolysis) in the absence of oxygen, with the resultant formation of ATP plus lactate (lactic acid and associated products). This pathway is therefore referred to as the lactic anaerobic energy pathway. The chemical reaction may be summarised as follows:

$$\text{Glycogen} + \text{P} + \text{ADP} \longrightarrow \text{ATP} + + \text{Lactate}$$
(1 Unit) (3 Units)

The accumulation of lactate will terminate use of this energy pathway after 40–50 seconds maximum effort. Consequently it is the pathway called upon principally by athletes whose sports demand high energy expenditure for up to approximately 60 seconds, and those in 'multiple sprint sports' such as squash, soccer, rugby, hockey, lacrosse and hurling. Thereafter, there must be a progressive recruitment of an alternative energy pathway. It is known that exposure to lactic anaerobic stressors in training will increase the athlete's ability to utilise this pathway. It should be said that such training must be based on the sound foundation of training to develop the aerobic energy pathway.

Aerobic energy pathway

This pathway involves the oxygen transporting system and the use of oxygen in the mitochondria of the working muscle for the oxidation of glycogen or fatty acids. Due to this pathway's dependence upon oxygen, it is referred to as the aerobic energy pathway. This is involved in prolonged work of relatively low intensity and is of increasing importance the longer the sport's duration. Taken to its logical conclusion, only lack of fuel (together with overheating and dehydration) will end an exercise of several hours duration involving this pathway. The chemical reaction may be summarised as:

1 unit glycogen $\quad + \text{P} + \text{ADP} + \text{O}_2 = 37$ units $\text{ATP} + \text{CO}_2 + \text{H}_2\text{O}$
1 unit free fatty acids $+ \text{P} + \text{ADP} + \text{O}_2 = 140*$ units $\text{ATP} + \text{CO}_2 + \text{H}_2\text{O}$
*Approx

This pathway may be developed by specific training.

It will be seen from the 'rates of exchange' of free fatty acids and glycogen to ATP, that the free fatty acids appear the most favourable currency. However, about 8% more oxygen per calorie is needed if the energy comes from fat sources. The very poor exchange rate of glycogen in lactic anaerobic exercise is only one factor contributing towards the phenomenon known as 'oxygen debt'. The best way of explaining this is to illustrate the situation with an example:

> 22.4 litres of oxygen are required to remove 180 g lactic acid
> 180 g lactic acid from glycolysis yields 55 kcal
> aerobic glycolysis yielding 55 kcal requires 11.0 litres oxygen.

Thus, if the lactic anaerobic pathway is used, 100% interest must be paid on the debt. This is referred to, naturally, as the lactic oxygen debt. There also exists an alactic oxygen debt. The 'bill' here, looks like this:

refill of oxygen stores (blood, myoglobin)	= 1.0 litres oxygen
elevation of temperature and adrenaline concentration	= 1.0 litres oxygen
increased cardiac and respiratory involvement	= 0.5 litres oxygen
breakdown of ATP and creatine phosphate	= 1.5 litres oxygen
total	= 4.0 litres oxygen

So, in addition to the oxygen debt created by the lactic energy pathway, there is an alactic oxygen debt which must be repaid irrespective of the energy pathway used. Repayment of these debts will, of course, rely on an efficient system to aid recovery, which implies a well developed oxygen transporting system. Consequently it is fundamental to athletes in all sports that the aerobic pathway is trained.

It would appear that the fuelling system for combustion in aerobic exercise varies according to its duration and intensity. In prolonged aerobic exercise the preferred fuel is free fatty acids because the glucose stores (glycogen) are limited compared to the very large fat stores. Unlike glycogen, fatty acids can only be used in the aerobic pathway, whereas in higher intensity exercise involving aerobic and anaerobic pathways, or exclusively anaerobic, the preferred fuel is glycogen. This being the case, Williams (1975) suggests that for those athletes involved in long duration endurance sports the free fatty acid fuelling system should be exposed to conditions in training which will encourage its adaptation to a more ready recruitment and increased efficiency. Furthermore, he suggests that training in a fasting state may well offer the stimulus for such adaptation and that habitual training, when glycogen stores are high, may well discourage such adaptation (see chapter 4, p. 51 – the glycogen overshoot theory).

The contribution of aerobic and anaerobic systems to energy output varies with the duration of the activity concerned. Astrand (1970) has represented this diagrammatically (fig. 32). It must be emphasised,

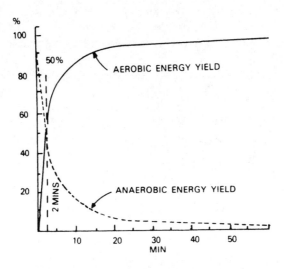

Fig. 32 *Astrand's classic representation of % of total energy yield from aerobic and anaerobic pathways, during maximal efforts of up to 60 mins duration, for an athlete of high maximal power for both types of energy production*

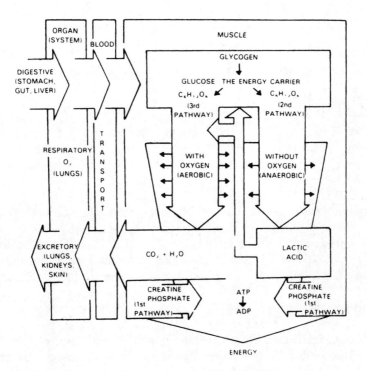

Fig. 33 *Schematic summary of the three pathways* (from Jäger and Oelschlägel, 1974)

however, that it is not sound to deduce from these statistics that the ratio of training time should vary. The aerobic system is the fundamental basis of all endurance sports and there are few sports which do not make demands of endurance capacity. A sound aerobic basis will enable the athlete to be exposed to more frequent specific stressors as stimuli for specific adaptation.

The three energy pathways are summarised diagrammatically in figure 33, but before leaving this area, it might be useful to include a brief glossary of expressions often used concerning energy production.

Glycogenolysis: the conversion of glycogen to glucose, mainly in the liver, for use as a fuel.

Glycolysis: the oxidation of glucose or glycogen to pyruvate or lactate, the latter two substances being intermediate steps in energy production.

Glycogenesis: the synthesis of glycogen from glucose.

Gluconeogenesis: the formation of glucose or glycogen from non-carbohydrate sources (e.g. glycerol, glucogenic amino acids and lactate).

Tricarboxylic acid cycle: also referred to as citric acid cycle, or Krebs cycle, this is the final common pathway of carbohydrate, fats and protein oxidation to carbon dioxide and water.

Hexose-monophosphate shunt: an alternative system to the tricarboxylic acid cycle and glycolysis, this is also known as the direct oxidative pathway or the pentose-phosphate cycle.

Figure 34 gives a general picture of fuel production.

■ The muscle

The breakdown of ATP to ADP supplies the energy that is required to cause the muscle to contract, or shorten. By shortening, the muscle pulls on the tendons which are attached to the bony levers (fig. 35). It now remains to explain the mechanisms involved in muscle contraction and in initiating ATP/ADP breakdown.

The muscle consists of many muscle fibres which, if examined under a light microscope, have a striped or striated appearance (fig. 35b). To each muscle fibre is attached the endplate of a motoneuron. The motoneuron is the nerve cell which finally controls skeletal muscle and the 'endplate' is its attachment to the muscle fibre. A motoneuron and the muscle fibres it supplies is called a motor unit. Occasionally a fibre may be supplied by more than one motoneuron, but as a rule only one motoneuron is involved. Where very fine movement is required, there may be as few as five fibres to one neuron (e.g. the muscles of the eye). On the other hand, when gross movement is required, as in the thigh, the ratio may be one neuron to several thousand fibres. The motoneuron is housed in the anterior (ventral) part of the spinal cord and signals pass from here along

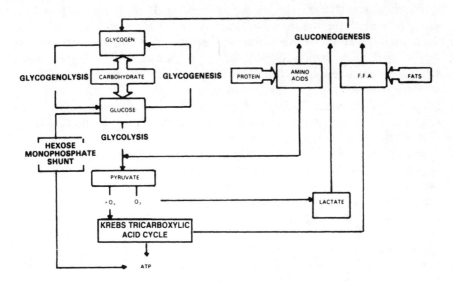

Fig. 34 *Summary of the processing of energy fuel sources in the production of ATP*

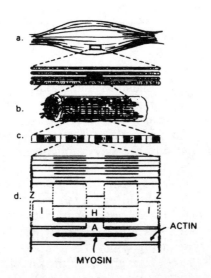

Fig. 35 *The striated muscle (a), is composed of muscle fibres (b), which appear striated (striped) under the light microscope. Each muscle fibre is made up of myofibrils (c), beside which lie cell nuclei and mitochondria. The striated appearance of the myofibril arises from the repeated light and dark bands. A single unit of this 'repetition' is a sarcomere (d). This consists of a Z line, an I band, an A band which is interrupted by an H-zone, another I band – then the next Z line. These bands, in turn, arise from the overlapping of actin and myosin filaments (from H. E. Huxley, 1958). The sarcomere is the actual unit of contraction in the muscle fibre, which contains tens of thousands of both sarcomeres and mitochondria (for aerobic energy)*

a tendril-like arm, the axon, at the end of which are branches to which are attached the endplates (fig. 36). These in turn are attached to a specific number of muscle fibres. The axon is for the most part surrounded by a myelin sheath, which is 'pinched' at intervals like a string of linked sausages (fig. 36). The pinched areas are known as the *nodes of ranvier* and due to their presence the nerve impulses can pass quicker along myelinated axons than non-myelinated axons. It is believed that this is due to a saltatory conduction (jumping) of the impulse from node to node.

Each muscle fibre consists of bundles of myofibrils beside which lie the nuclei of the muscle cells and mitochondria. The striations noted in the fibre are, in fact, striations of the massed myofibrils. If a closer examination is made of the light and dark bands of the myofibril, the actual contractile mechanism is revealed (fig. 35). The contractile unit, bound by the Z lines, is the sarcomere. As the actin filaments attached to opposing Z lines slide past the myosin filaments towards each other, the Z lines are drawn closer together. The sarcomeres of a single myofibril are joined end to end and all sarcomeres in that myofibril will contract at one time giving a total shortening of that myofibril. Moreover, the 'signal' to contract, which arrives via the axon and endplate at the muscle fibre, causes the whole fibre to contract. Thus, when the signal is sent, contraction of the fibre is brought about by the contraction of all its myofibrils and the myofibrils contract as a result of the shortening of their sarcomeres.

It should be pointed out that the 'all or none law' applies to muscle fibre contraction. When the signal to contract arrives at the endplate, the whole muscle fibre contracts to the limit of its capacity. On the other hand, when there is no signal the muscle fibre assumes its resting length. Thus, there are no gradations of contractile force at the muscle fibre level. Contractile force is graded by the selective involvement of an appropriate number of motor units. The selective involvement is controlled by the central nervous system. This system brings a directive from the cerebrum and this directive is modified or qualified by the proprioceptor mechanisms (fig. 37). Thus, recruitment of the appropriate number of selected motor units for a given task is learned and the muscle concerned is programmed to contract (fig. 37).

When the impulse to contract arrives at the sarcolemma of the muscle fibre, it passes rapidly to every sarcomere. Within each sarcomere, running longitudinally, there exists a system of tubules known as the sarcoplasmic reticulum. The sarcoplasmic reticulum contains calcium ions and when the impulse arrives the calcium ions are released. This initiates an enzyme reaction with myosin, which causes the breakdown of ATP to ADP, thus releasing the energy to slide the actin and myosin past each other and bring about contraction of the myofibril. The calcium ions are returned to the sarcoplasmic reticulum by active pumping of its membranes. In the meantime, ADP is reconstituted to ATP via the creatine phosphate stores. Here then, amongst the small

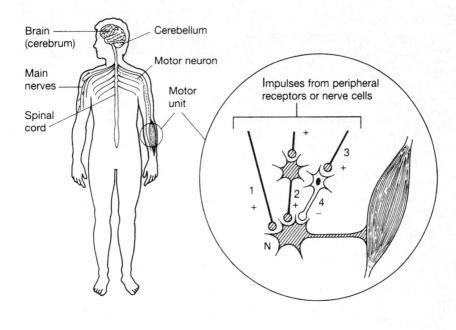

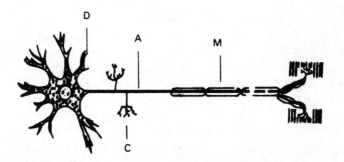

Fig. 36 *(top) The motoneuron N, in the spinal cord can be excited (+) directly (1) or via an interneuron (2). Thus, an impulse is propagated in the nerve fibre, and the muscle is stimulated – causing muscular activity. Other nerve terminals can prevent the motoneuron from being stimulated. Schematically, nerve end (3) stimulates interneuron nerve cell (4) which is inhibitory. (lower) Motor neuron: A, axon; C, collateral; D, dendrite; M, myelin (from Schreiner and Schreiner)*

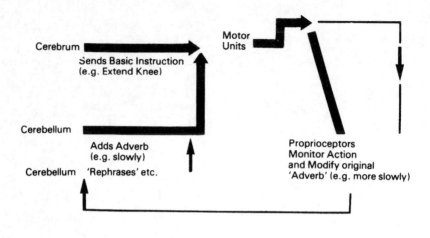

Fig. 37 *Control of muscular action*

pockets of glycogen and scattered mitochondria, is the final product of that process which was started by eating and digesting a meal.

■ Types of muscular activity

Having gone into such detail in order to explain the mechanism of contraction, it should be said that the researcher rather than the coach is concerned with the microstructure of the muscle. It has become fashionable for the coach to consider the complex detail, described above, under the umbrella term 'the contractile component' of muscle. In popular terminology then, the contractile component is joined both in parallel and in series with 'the elastic component' (fig. 38). That part of the elastic component in parallel comprises such elements as connective sheaths and structural proteins, while that part of the elastic component in series comprises the tendons. The elastic component can be stretched and consequently develop tension due to its elastic resistance to that stretch. This in effect is the second mechanism in the muscle's contribution to contractile force. It is effective in those activities which involve voluntary muscle contraction and elastic recoil (e.g. running jumps, hopping, rapid agilities).

There is one other mechanism which may add to the efficiency of the overall force expression of contractile and elastic components. This is the myotonic reflex. Both muscle and tendon are equipped with reflex systems. Approximately 90% of the tendon receptors are accommodated in the musculotendinous junction, while the remainder are in the tendon itself. The stimulus of stretch in this system effects the reflex response of inhibiting the contractile mechanism, thus allowing the muscle to lengthen and therefore relieving the degree of stretch in the tendon and musculotendinous junction. The muscle fibres are equipped with muscle

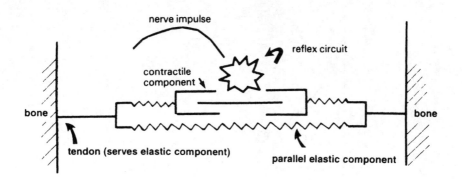

Fig. 38 *Schematic representation of the contractile and elastic components plus reflex mechanisms in muscle*

spindle receptors. Their stimulus is the lengthening of the muscle fibre, the response being a stimulus to the muscle to contract, as elicited by the 'knee jerk' reflex.

It is reasonable to assume that in physical activity the reflex response to contract has an overall lower threshold than that to lengthen. The net result of this reflex activity is a more vigorous contraction of a given muscle when it is forcefully stretched (e.g. in the take-off leg in long jump). This 'net reflex' is the myotonic reflex and its existence now provides the athlete with a third contribution to a summated contractile force, although its activation can be harmful, e.g. in too vigorous bouncy dynamic stretching exercises (as opposed to safer slow stretch). Only when the technical model of an activity is appropriately structured can all three systems (contractile component, elastic component and myotonic reflex) be summated.

The speed of contraction of a muscle will vary inversely with the force opposing it. Thus maximal speed is achieved when the muscle has no force resisting its action and zero speed is achieved when the immovable object is encountered (fig. 39). Maximum strength training is aimed at increasing the quantity of force required before zero speed is reached, while speed training is aimed at acquiring even higher speeds from existing maxima by assisting the movement via motivation, facilitation, learning, etc. If we consider the muscle actions of the athlete in figure 40 it is clear that some muscle actions will be dynamic (cause movement at joints) while others will be static (cause no movement at joints). In any given activity, there is a specific pattern of static and dynamic contraction carefully synchronised to meet the demands of that activity. The specific role of a given muscle within the total scheme of the specific pattern is referred to as auxotonic.

It should be noted that dynamic and static muscle activity may be sub-divided into special classifications. *Dynamic* may be concentric,

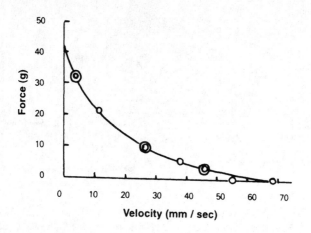

Fig. 39 *Force-velocity curve of tetanized muscle at 0°C. Abscissae: force (g wt). Ordinates: velocity (mm per sec). Small circles: experimental points. Large circles: points 'used up' in fitting the theoretical curve. Agreement between theory and experiment is significant only at other points on the curve* (Wilkie, D. R. 1956 Brit. med. Bull., 12, 177.) (from Samson Wright's Applied Physiology, 1973)

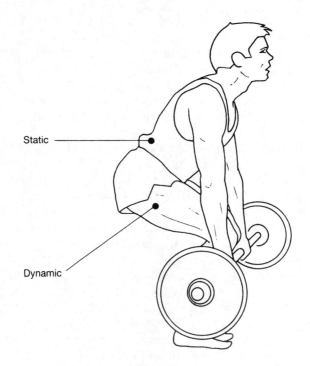

Fig. 40 *Static and dynamic work*

i.e. overcoming a resistance or load (e.g. quads shortening in raising a squat bar); or eccentric, i.e. yielding to a resistance or load (e.g. quads lengthening in lowering a squat bar). *Static* may be maximum, i.e. meeting an immovable object; or sub-maximum, i.e. the role of the postural muscles in holding the spine in position when standing.

In any activity where muscular contraction arrests eccentric contraction prior to concentric contraction (e.g. when muscle contraction stops you yielding to a load before it will allow you to overcome it), the point at which the eccentric movement stops is known as the point of *amortisation* of muscle. In many technical textbooks the phase during which a limb is being forced to yield prior to this point is referred to as the amortisation phase. Examples of this are in the take-off leg in long jump, in the arms in various agilities in gymnastics, etc. The duration of time in the amortisation phase and at the point of amortisation is critical to the efficient contribution of combined force from both contractile and elastic components. It must be emphasised that the eccentric action is *dynamic* in the amortisation phase. If passive, then kinetic energy, which has been derived from an approach run or preparatory movement, will be absorbed and the only force available for the ensuing movement will be from the contractile component alone. This is seen when a trampolinist 'kills' the recoil of a trampoline, when a skier 'damps' the undulations of the ski slope and when the testee in the jump-reach test is not permitted a preliminary movement. This whole area should be clearly understood if the coach is to develop specific training exercises for sports demanding this type of muscle activity. Expressions such as 'pre-tension' have been completely misunderstood because they appeared to connote psychological dilemmas rather than neuromuscular preparation.

■ Types of muscle fibre

The study of muscles' contractile properties usually examines the muscle longitudinally. However, by studying a transverse section, another window is opened on the understanding of muscle function. By working from muscle biopsy techniques and applying appropriate stains to the samples of muscle extracted, it is possible to study two different types of skeletal muscle fibre in greater detail. These are referred to as the slow twitch fibres (red) and the fast twitch fibres (white), and their properties are summarised in table 15. Due to their unique characteristics, their recruitment for specific duration and intensity of activity may provide important evidence of the relative effect of training loads and the suitability of certain athletes to specific sports.

The implications of this fibre differentiation are shown in studies of muscle fibre population and enzyme activity in various groups of athletes. Golnick (1973) showed that specific enzyme activity is involved in speed training (PFK) and endurance training (SDH) (table 16).

Table 15 *Skeletal muscle fibres are broadly classified as red or white. Their properties may be summarised as follows:*

red fibres	white fibres
Slow twitch	Fast twitch (almost twice as fast)
Large proportion in endurance athletes	Large proportion in power athletes
Aerobic capacity higher in trained subjects	Oxidative capacity higher in athletes than in non-athletes
Aerobic (red colour due to presence of myoglobin and more capillaries)	Anaerobic
Greater proportion in extensors	Greater proportion in flexors
Training at 75%–85% VO₂ max. improves aerobic capacity and glycogen activity	Training at 75%–85% VO₂ max. improves aerobic capacity. (This will improve stamina and oxidise FFA and glycogen, which yield greater amounts of ATP than the anaerobic glycolysis of glycogen.) Improves anaerobic capacity and glycogen concentration
Training at 75%–85% VO₂ max. trains these fibres	Training at bursts of 120% VO₂ max. trains these fibres

Table 16 *Relationship of event to % slow twitch fibres and enzyme concentration* (adapted from Golnick, 1973)

athlete	(aerobic) (slow) units of succinic dehydrogenase	% slow twitch fibres	(aerobic) (fast) units of phospho-fructokinase
Distance runner	8.03	75	15.07
Middle distance runner	5.14	65	26.53
Sprinter	3.95	26	28.34

▌Summary

Skeletal muscle converts chemical energy to mechanical energy. The chemical energy, which has its origin in foodstuffs, is provided by one or more of the three energy pathways, each designed to produce the 'energy currency of life' – ATP. When ATP is degraded to ADP, energy is available to slide actin and myosin filaments past each other, thus shortening the contractile element of muscle – the sarcomere. This contraction of muscle may be effected by the contractile component, elastic component, the myotonic reflex, or a combination of the three. The contraction may be either dynamic or static, and represents mechanical energy. Overall control of muscle contraction rests with the cerebrum and its system of communication via motor units and proprioceptive monitoring of events in the two different types of muscle fibre and their tendons.

It is very clear, even from our limited understanding of neuromuscular function, that specific training will make many areas of this complex system more efficient. Greater force of muscle contraction can be developed, sophisticated recruitment of motor units may be learned, and energy systems may be trained to meet the specific demands of sports activities.

|7
The fluid systems

▌Homeostasis

The body is composed of tissues and the tissues are composed of cells. Each cell has fluid in it (intracellular) and outside it (extracellular, mainly interstitial – in-between cells). Provided the various concentrations of substances in the extracellular fluid are controlled, the cells will continue to function efficiently. However, stressors bombard the body and threaten the integrity of the cell-organ fluid cycle within it. 'Stress' is embarrassment of this cycle, evidenced by greater urgency of activity within the cycle. It is therefore essential that the body maintains a certain constancy of internal environment to ensure that the composition of extracellular fluid is not threatened. This process is called *homeostasis*. The functions of all organs in the body, with the exception of the reproductive organs, are directed towards the goal of homeostasis. Should the various tissues which comprise each organ fail in their highly specialised contribution towards homeostasis, the cells bathing in the extracellular fluid will be damaged and reduce the organic functioning capacity. The situation may be summarised:

- total body function relies on the efficient functioning of the organs
- the organs' function relies on the efficient functioning of their tissue cells
- the cells' function relies on the constancy of composition of the extra-cellular fluid
- the extracellular fluid is given constancy (homeostasis) by the efficient functioning of the organs.

Figure 41 illustrates the total fluid in the body, as well as indicating its relationship to blood composition and volume.

▌Specific fluids: composition and function

Blood

This has already been discussed in some detail (see chapter 5). Approximately 97% of the blood is fluid, most intracellular (e.g. within the blood cells), some extracellular (e.g. the plasma). The latter has a higher amino acid concentration than other extracellular fluid, especially albumin, which is an important factor in keeping plasma inside the capillary blood vessels.

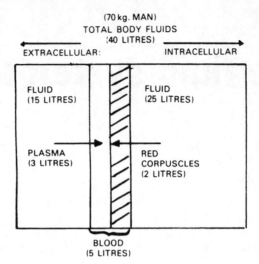

Fig. 41 *Distribution of body fluids*

Interstitial fluid

This is that portion of the extracellular fluid outside the blood vessels (e.g. total extracellular fluid, excluding plasma). This fluid includes that in which the cerebrum and spinal cord bathes (cerebro-spinal fluid), that in the abdominal cavity, the joint capsules (synovial fluid), the pleural envelope about the lungs, and in the eyes.

Intracellular fluid

This is the fluid inside each cell containing many chemicals and electrolytes responsible for functional efficiency of the cell. Various mechanisms are 'built in' to the cell membrane. The mechanisms allow movement of sodium *out* of the cell and potassium and phosphates *into* the cell. Also found in this fluid are glucose, oxygen, carbon dioxide, amino acids and lipids. From previous discussion (see chapter 5), it will be recalled that fuel is combusted with or without oxygen to provide energy for cellular function, leaving substances such as carbon dioxide and lactate which pass through the cell membrane with the assistance of one of the membrane mechanisms already mentioned. These products are then carried in the intra- or extracellular fluids of the blood, to be 'blown-off' or oxidised as the case may be. Oxygen travels the reverse route.

Extracellular fluid

This fluid differs from intracellular principally in its electrolyte concentration. These differences of concentration are responsible for electrical potentials across the membrane of the cell. If these electrical potentials did not exist, it would be impossible for nerve fibres to conduct impulses or for muscle to contract. In addition, the extracellular fluid provides a system for the transport of nutrients and other substances. It may help to recall that plasma and lymph are both extracellular fluids.

Lymph

This has already been discussed with reference to the body's system of immunity (p. 71). The walls of the lymphatic capillaries are freely permeable to protein and approximately 95% of protein, lost from the oxygen transporting system each day, is returned via the lymphatic vessels. If these plasma proteins were not returned, death would result in 12–24 hours. Consequently it has been suggested that the single most important function of lymph is its role in returning plasma protein to circulation.

■ Fluid accumulation

Occasionally fluid collects at certain sites in the body. A fluid collection is known as an *oedema*. If this occurs in a potential space (e.g. joint space) it is known as an *effusion*. Several things may cause this. For example, infection can cause a blockage of the lymphatics (drainage system) in a potential space through the accumulation of dead white cells. Trauma caused by a knock or strain may also cause an effusion, which may be reduced by applying ice packs or cold water to the affected region. Again, hormonal factors can elicit so-called fluid retention. This is the case with the female hormone oestradiol which appears to cause salt-water retention. Fluctuation in body weight in the course of the female menstrual cycle is mainly attributable to degrees of fluid retention. Oedema, effusion, or fluid retention, may lead to discomfort, e.g. swollen ankles, and possible influence on relative strength, as well as reduction of functioning capacity. Consequently, medical advice should be sought to discover the cause.

■ Fluid loss

The kidneys, in addition to filtering approximately 1700 litres of blood in 24 hours and rejecting the blood's waste products in soluble form in the urine, are the key agents in controlling expulsion or retention of body fluid. In other words, they are the principal regulators of the body's fluid volume and concentration. If the body's salt-water balance is disrupted, water must be retained in the body or a greater concentration of salts must be expelled (or both) to restore equilibrium. This imbalance can be caused by internal or external conditions, for example, the high sweat rate required to cool the body by evaporation in a hot environment or the considerable loss of fluid via sweat, urine, 'running nose', etc., which accompany upper respiratory tract infections such as the common cold. Since a greater proportion of water than salts and electrolytes is lost in the first instance, intracellular and extracellular fluid concentration, and ultimately blood concentration, increases. The consequent increased osmotic pressure causes (1) release of anti-diuretic hormone (ADH) from the posterior pituitary which *increases reabsorption of water* by the tubules of the kidney, and (2) withdrawal from circulation of the hormone aldosterone which is secreted by the cortex of the suprarenal gland and this *decreases absorption of salt* by the tubules of the kidney (fig. 42).

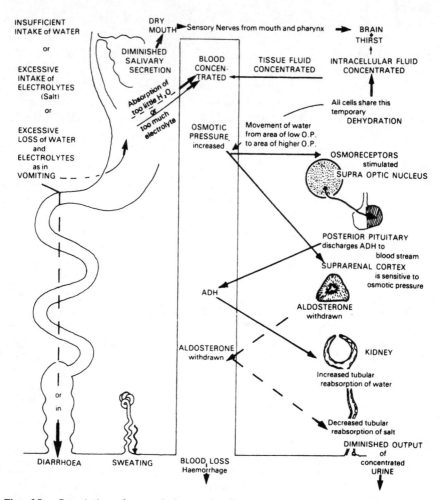

Fig. 42 *Regulation of water balance showing measures that restore blood volume and restore body fluids to normal osmotic pressure* (from McNaught and Callender, Illustrated Physiology, 1963)

When there is excessive water intake, ADH levels are lowered, another hormone angiotensin is formed locally, and aldosterone levels are raised thus diluting and increasing the volume of urine expelled. When body fluids are being reduced, it is self evident that athletes must increase fluid intake to replace that lost and to relieve the body of the increased burden on its regulatory mechanisms. Moreover, where periods of sweating are prolonged, not only must fluids be replaced but also electrolytes and salts. Fortunately there are several electrolyte solutions commercially available to the athlete.

The athlete should be aware of those substances which will increase fluid loss and therefore reduce his ability to combat the stressor of heat. These substances include xanthines such as coffee (caffeine) and tea (theophylline), excess sucrose, alcohol, and drugs involving mercurial compounds, chlorothiazide, Diamox, etc. Certain antibiotics require that the athlete drinks more water. Penicillin for example is actively excreted by the tubules of the kidney and athletes are normally advised to increase fluid intake when taking it.

Intentional dehydration has been attempted by athletes to reduce body weight and therefore increase relative strength. This practice is fraught with dangers, not least of which is the impairment of function due to electrolyte imbalance. If weight must be reduced for some reason, then medical advice must be taken. Of course 'dieting' has been pursued, often very successfully, with the view to reducing weight while maintaining or even increasing normal body function. The following observations on the subject should be noted.

(1)   Dehydration techniques, using diuretic drugs, are most certainly not recommended for athletes.
(2)   Dehydration techniques, via reduction in fluid intake, may only be considered valid if under medical supervision and then only for short periods.
(3)   'Slimming diets' must be considered over an extended period, rather than for rapid weight decrease.
(4)   Initial rapid weight loss in dieting is largely due to loss of that water previously required to store the glycogen now liberated to provide energy (3 g water for each 1 g glycogen). When the stored glycogen is called upon to provide energy, it releases its water which is expelled from the body. Unfortunately, when the 'slimmer' returns to the normal diet, this weight is replaced.
(5)   Any diet *must* include all essential nutrients to support the high metabolic demands of the athlete or the relevant metabolic demands of the non-athlete. While an increase in protein intake will increase metabolic rate (to the slimmer's advantage), and a reduction in carbohydrate intake will certainly effect weight loss, it would be fundamentally wrong to avoid carbohydrate completely since muscle and nerve cells rely on carbohydrate for their metabolism. A return to a balanced diet, but scaled down, is the moral of the story.
(6)   Some athletes, such as crew members in sailing, of course, wish to increase weight. The ingestion of certain drugs can do this, but it is mainly achieved by water retention. It must be said, however, that such practices are not recommended for athletes. In the medium term, body fat can be increased. In the longer term, muscle may be increased.

▌Temperature regulation

The athlete's problem is maintaining body temperature within the limits which permit him to function efficiently. In certain conditions the problem is to avoid overheating (hyperthermia). This can be avoided by the loss of body heat to the external environment and the reduction of heat gain from that environment. This will occur when training or competition takes place in a very hot/dry or hot/humid climate. On the other hand, the problem may lie at the other extreme where the athlete must avoid losing body temperature to the external environment and insulate against the low temperature of that environment. This will occur when, for example, sailors are exposed to dampness and extremely low temperatures for long periods of time. This may lead to the condition of exposure or hypothermia.

The balance between heat production and heat loss will be maintained when the sum of the factors to the left of figure 43 equal the sum of the factors to the right.

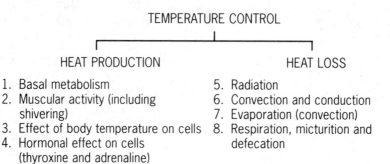

TEMPERATURE CONTROL

HEAT PRODUCTION	HEAT LOSS
1. Basal metabolism	5. Radiation
2. Muscular activity (including shivering)	6. Convection and conduction
	7. Evaporation (convection)
3. Effect of body temperature on cells	8. Respiration, micturition and defecation
4. Hormonal effect on cells (thyroxine and adrenaline)	

Fig. 43 *Factors contributing to the balance between heat production and loss at rest (see below)*

(1) Basal metabolism

The metabolic rate is the measure of the rate at which energy is released from foods. It is therefore the rate of heat production by the body, which is measured in kilocalories. Basal metabolic rate is this measurement when the athlete is at his most rested state, i.e. without temperature stressors, etc. It is determined by the inherent rates of chemical reactions in the cell and the amount of thyroid hormone activity in the cells. The basal metabolic rate is generally expressed in terms of kilocalories per square metre body surface per hour. Several factors influence metabolic rate, which is most closely related to the surface area of the skin:

• the basal metabolism of children is greater than that of adults because they are growing as well as living
• fasting or starvation would appear to decelerate metabolic rate. It has even been suggested that by reducing metabolic rate in this way the ageing process will be slowed down
• protein causes a greater increase in metabolic rate than fats or carbohydrate. On comparing diets of equal calorific value, protein can raise the metabolic rate by 20% over a period of 4–6 hours, while carbohydrate and fats will effect only 5–10% increase.

(2) Muscular activity

Heat production of muscles accounts for 40% of all the body's heat production, even at rest. During severe exercise this can rise to as much as 20 times that provided by all the other tissues put together. This is due to the oxidation of foodstuffs to meet the fuel demands necessary for ATP/ADP breakdown. The metabolic rate, in work of only a few seconds duration, may be over 40 times greater than at rest.

(3) Effect of body temperature on cells

The immediate effect of exposure to high temperature is to increase heat loss via sweating, etc. However, metabolism is not greatly affected. If continued exposure elevates body temperature, basal metabolism increases by 7% for every 0.5°C. This would have the net result of further increasing temperature. The immediate effect of exposure to low temperature is an increase in metabolic rate, and heat production is further increased by shivering. It has been suggested that the metabolic rate can be doubled with the involvement of shivering and that metabolic changes occurring in cold exposure may be hormonally influenced. It is possible to acclimatise both to cold and heat. Should exposure to extremes of temperature continue at a rate incompatible with adaptation to the specific stressor, and without the benefits of acclimatisation, there is a very real risk of hyperthermia or hypothermia.

(4) Hormones

Thyroxine increases the rate of functioning of cell enzymes, thus increasing metabolic rate and heat production. This increase in metabolic rate may also be elicited by adrenaline and noradrenaline. The anterior pituitary gland also influences the metabolic rate indirectly via the thyrotrophic hormone which stimulates the thyroid gland.

(5) Radiation

Radiation is the transfer of heat from one object to another with which it is *not in contact*. Normally, the athlete radiates more heat towards objects cooler than himself, and vice versa. The closer the two temperatures, the less will be the athlete's heat loss. Frequently, athletes express concern that heat is coming from artificial playing areas on which they are training or competing. In many cases this is not really true. What is happening is that the athlete cannot lose all the heat he wishes to that particular playing area. Often, women athletes lose more heat than men by radiation.

(6) Convection and conduction

Heat may also be lost to air and objects with which the body has contact. The cooler the air or object the greater the heat loss. If air is continually moving past the body, warmed air (from the body's heat) is moved away to be replaced by 'unwarmed' air. The more rapidly the air moves the greater is the quantity of heat conducted from the body. Thus, there exists a combined conduction/convection heat loss due to passage of air over the body surface. Where there is a cool wind and body temperature is to be maintained, athletes should be sheltered or wear wet suits (waterproof oversuit). In water, heat is lost directly by conduction.

(7)   Evaporation (convection)

In addition to the small amount of extracellular fluid which continually diffuses through the skin and evaporates, the sweat glands produce large quantities of sweat when the body becomes very hot; up to two litres per hour. This process obviously increases the rate of heat loss through evaporation. As in conduction, air currents play a major role in the removal of heat by evaporation. As the air close to the body becomes saturated, new air arrives to accept the evaporating sweat. Should the air fail to be replaced, then conduction and evaporation avenues of heat loss will be seriously reduced. The situation is even more alarming when air is humid because the sweat will not evaporate. Williams (1975) summarises the situation: 'In hot, dry environments, the limiting factor for heat dissipation is the rate of sweat production, whereas in hot, humid environments it is the capacity of the environment to receive water vapour, i.e. the relative humidity. In the shade outdoors the athlete will therefore be cooler than in the shade indoors, provided the air is moving. On the other hand, when temperature loss is to be avoided, the athlete should keep out of the wind and keep the body surface dry'. Men tend to sweat at higher proportionate rates than women.

(8)   Respiration and expulsion of wastes

Approximately 3% of heat lost at 21°C is via these avenues.

■ Clothing and temperature regulation

Clothing should be considered in light of the foregoing discussion. In a hot environment, cottons, linens and wide mesh (such as string vests) are recommended instead of synthetic fabrics. The latter are less effective in reducing body temperature, being non-absorbent, while the former allow absorption of body moisture and support the evaporation and conduction systems for loss of body heat. It should also be mentioned that where competition is to be held in hot/dry or hot/humid environments, dry kit should not replace sweat-soaked kit. Wet suits are recommended where the competition environment is cold and, where appropriate, these should be worn between rounds of competitions and during warm-up. In field games and/or winter sports, thought should be given to maintaining a comfortable temperature for continued efficient activity. Above all, both skin and kit must be kept as dry as the occasion permits.

Maintaining body temperature should not be confused with the problems of exposure to strong sunlight. In the latter case, athletes should be as conscious of the need to shelter from the weakening effects of the sun as they are to maintain a body temperature compatible with efficient physical activity.

■ Acclimatisation to temperature

The body can adapt to the stressors of dry and wet heat. The stressor of high temperature causes a decrease in endurance capacity. Should athletes be required to compete in such conditions they must therefore be exposed to a stimulus for adaptation if performance capacity is to be maintained. The adaptation to external environments, such as altitude, time shift, heat, etc., is known as acclimatisation. The practical aspects of acclimatisation to heat have been enumerated by Buskirk and Bass (1974).

(1) Acclimatisation begins with the first exposure, progresses rapidly, and is well developed in 4–7 days.

(2) Acclimatisation can be introduced by short, intermittent exercise periods in the heat, e.g. 2–4 hours daily. Inactivity in the heat results in only slight acclimatisation.

(3) Subjects in good physical condition acclimatise more rapidly and are capable of more work in the heat. However, good physical fitness alone does not automatically confer acclimatisation.

(4) The ability to perform 'maximal' work in the heat is attained more quickly by progressively increasing the daily workload. Strenuous exertion on first exposure may result in disability which will impair performance for several days. Care should be taken to stay within the capacity of the athlete until acclimatisation is well advanced.

(5) Acclimatisation to severe conditions will facilitate performance at lesser conditions.

(6) The general pattern of acclimatisation is the same for short, severe exertion as for moderate work of longer duration.

(7) Acclimatisation in hot/dry climates increases performance ability in hot/wet climates and vice versa.

(8) Inadequate water and salt replacement can retard the acclimatisation process.

(9) Acclimatisation to heat is well retained during periods of non-exposure for about 2 weeks; thereafter it is lost, at a rate that varies among individuals. Most people lose a portion of their acclimatisation in 2 months. Those who stay in good physical condition retain their acclimatisation best of all.

(10) If it is desirable to retain acclimatisation, periodic exposures at frequent intervals are recommended and heat exposures should not be separated by more than 2 weeks.

Acclimatisation to cold is rather more difficult to study than acclimatisation to heat. This is because man normally protects himself against cold by creating his own miniature sub-tropical climate with increased and insulated clothing, heated accommodation, etc. 'Local acclimatisation' is known to be possible. For example, when the hands are exposed to cold for short periods over a number of weeks there is an increased blood-flow through the hands, enabling them to perform their normal functions without impairment due to cold-induced numbness. While heat will be lost from the body due to local acclimatisation, at least the athlete's functioning capacity will be maintained. This type of acclimatisation is invaluable to sailors, climbers and athletes involved in outdoor winter games or games played in a cold environment. Having said this, the athlete may simply learn how to avoid becoming extremely cold through experience or advice from the technical authorities concerned in the given sport.

■ Warm-up

Unfortunately there is an astonishing lack of consistency in research conclusions on the physiological value of warm-up. Possible advantages might include:

- increased local muscle blood flow
- increased metabolic rate (7% for 0.5°C increase)
- increased speed of oxygen and fuel transfer to tissues
- increased speed of nerve impulse conduction
- increased speed of contraction and relaxation of muscle
- decreased viscous resistance in the muscle.

Perhaps most of the advantage derived from warm-up is mainly psychological, due to the blend of ritual rehearsal and psychophysiological preparation unique to each athlete. Even if this is the only advantage of warm-up, it seems ample justification for its inclusion. Pending more conclusive support for the value of warm-up, athletes should be encouraged to pursue the preparation which coach and athlete know to be relevant to the forthcoming competition or training unit.

At the conclusion of a competition or training unit, athletes are frequently encouraged to 'warm down'. This normally involves light but continuous activity where the heart rate is in the range of 120–140/minute. In pursuit of recovery from exercise-induced stress, the object is principally to raise the metabolic rate and encourage the removal of waste products from muscle through maintaining local blood flow.

■ Summary

The body's fluid systems comprise blood, interstitial fluid, intracellular fluid, and lymph. Together, they serve two vital purposes. The first is to offer a medium for the transportation about the body of substances essential to normal function. To meet this, a relative stability of fluid volume and concentration must be maintained and this is primarily achieved by a balance between the kidneys and the thirst mechanism. High temperatures, infection and certain dietary inclusions are examples of threats to such stability. The second purpose is temperature control, which is seen as the balance of heat production and loss. A relative stability of body temperature is critical to physical performance. The athlete uses warm-up to attain an optimal temperature for physical performance, using the capacity to adapt to the stressors of dry and wet heat to prepare for competition in climates where such stressors will be evident.

8
The hormones

Hormones are highly specific chemical compounds produced in the specialised cells of the endocrine glands. Unlike, for example, the lymph system, these glands have no ducts and tubes and their secretions are transported normally in the blood. The hormones may exert both generalised and specialised effects on other tissues and organs – functions implied by the word endocrine (*endo*: within, *krinen*: to separate).

Hormones may be divided into two groups – local and general. All general hormones and the most important local hormones are reviewed here. Some general hormones affect all cells, e.g. growth hormone secreted by the pituitary and thyroxine secreted by the thyroid. Other general hormones affect specific cells, e.g. gonadotrophic hormones secreted by the pituitary affect the sex organs. These substances perform a global function of regulation within the context of homeostasis via the fluid systems.

Local hormones

Local hormones affect cells in the immediate vicinity of the organ secreting the hormone.

Acetylcholine: acts locally to promote rhythmic activity in smooth muscle (which has no nerve supply), in heart muscle, and in certain epithelial tissue (e.g. oesophagus and trachea). However, this hormone is probably best known in another capacity: acetylcholine occurs in the motor nerves which run from the spinal cord to skeletal muscles. It is the 'transmitter' substance of the skeletal system. Synthesis of acetylcholine occurs in the cytoplasm of the nerve-muscle junction, but is quickly stored in about 300,000 synaptic vesicles and secreted to effect transmission of nerve impulses across a given synapse (fig. 44). Where chemical transmission of nerve impulses is effected by acetylcholine, these fibres are known as cholinergic. Such fibres are found in parts of the sympathetic and parasympathetic systems and in the motor fibres to skeletal muscle.

Histamine: found in higher concentration in lung, intestine and skin, and those tissues which are exposed to the external environment. It would appear that histamine occurs in the tissue mast cells, the basophil cells and platelets of the blood. The exact form in which it is held in these

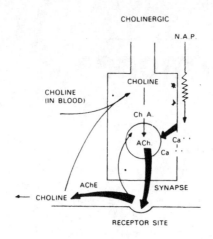

Fig. 44 *Diagram showing processes involved in synthesis release and disposal of acetylcholine at cholinergic nerve terminal and receptor site.*

ACh	*= Acetylcholine*	*NAP*	*= Nerve action potential*
ChA	*= Choline acetyltransferase*	** →*	*= Sites of active transport*
AChe	*= Acetylcholinesterase*		

by Dr P. F. Heffron, Middlesex Hospital Medical School (from Samson Wright, 1973)

cells is not yet known. Secretion by damaged cells anywhere in the body causes the walls of local capillaries to allow more fluid to pass through them, resulting in oedema. Histamine is released in conditions such as hay fever, and anti-histamine drugs are taken to counter the unhappy effects of histamine release. One antihistamine drug, periactin, has been used for its peculiar side effect of increased appetite to promote weight gain. However, research in this particular area is limited.

Prostaglandins: act principally on smooth muscle which contracts or relaxes according to the location, quantity and nature of the prostaglandin involved. They may cause dilation of certain blood vessels and increased heart rate through increased sympathetic nervous action. They may also stimulate or inhibit the release of free fatty acids according to whether the quantity of prostaglandins involved is low or high respectively. The prostaglandins would appear to number approximately 20 and these are divided into two categories: E-Prostaglandins (PGE, or E), and F-Prostaglandins (PGF, or F). Both of these groups occur in the central nervous system where their actions are stimulatory or inhibitory on individual neurons, within or without the central nervous system. The prostaglandins also appear to exert a modulatory role in nerve endings and in hormone secretion. Despite the relative infancy of research, the prostaglandins are noted here because they appear to have a role of considerable importance in the regulation of body function. They were independently identified in 1933–34 by

Goldblatt and Euler, but still the world of prostaglandins is far from being completely understood.

Angiotensin: stimulates the secretion of aldosterone from the adrenal cortex, thereby promoting sodium reabsorption by the kidney. Angiotensin is also the most powerful pressor substance known, causing general constriction of the arterioles, and increasing blood pressure. This hormone also promotes secretion of the catecholamines – adrenaline (epinephrin) and noradrenaline (norepinephrin) – from the adrenal medulla. Angiotensin is formed in two parts:

- by the action of renin, secreted by the kidneys of the α_2 globulin fraction of the plasma proteins, angiotensin I is formed
- by the action of a converting enzyme on angiotensin I, angiotensin II is formed.

The majority of the 'conversion' takes place as the blood passes through the lungs. The α_2 globulin is synthesised in the liver and referred to as *angiotensinogen*. Circulation of angiotensinogen is increased by the glucocorticoids and oestrogen. Angiotensin highlights the interdependence of chemicals in such complex bodily processes as homeostasis. It clearly has a key role in salt-water balance.

Kinins: cause contraction of most smooth muscle. In small quantities they reduce arterial blood pressure due primarily to dilation of blood vessels. By increasing the permeability of the blood vessels, plasma proteins are offered ease of egress. In increased quantities, the kinins facilitate the movement of leucocytes from blood to the surrounding tissues. Finally, it has been shown that the kinins stimulate the sensory nerve endings. It would appear that the plasma kinins are formed by antigen-antibody interplay.

5–HT: (serotonin, 5–hydroxytryptamine) is present in the mucosa of the digestive tract, in approximately 90% of blood platelets, and in the central nervous system. 5–HT is a derivative of the essential amino acid tryptophan. The process is stimulated by an enzyme found in the digestive tract, nervous system, kidney and liver. There does not appear to be any evidence that blood platelets can synthesise 5–HT, so it is presumed that they 'collect' this hormone while passing through the digestive tract. 5–HT is a cardiac stimulant and constricts the blood vessels, especially the large veins. Associated with the latter is the raising of both systolic and diastolic blood pressure. It also increases the respiratory rate, acts as an antidiuretic, and stimulates smooth muscle and pain nerve endings in the skin. It is possible that the release of 5–HT from the blood platelets, following injury, causes pain and associated reflex actions in the circulo-respiratory system. Serotonin is a neurotransmitter in the brain which may be involved in 'central fatigue' in exercise and possibly in the 'overtraining syndrome'.

Due to their proximity in the brain, it is difficult to separate the roles of those nerve terminals whose transmitter substance is noradrenaline or adrenaline (adrenergic) from those whose transmitter substance is 5–HT (serotoninergic). Consequently there is still some question over their respective physiological effects on mood and behaviour.

The adenosine group (ATP, ADP and AMP): found in all cells and the role of ATP in energy production has already been discussed (see chapter 6). The compounds decelerate heart rate and dilate blood vessels, lowering blood pressure. They also relax smooth muscle. The *cytokines* form a group of about 20 which have important effects on the immune system among other functions.

General hormones

The general hormones are associated with specific glands of origin (fig. 45), and are emptied into the blood to be carried all round the body.

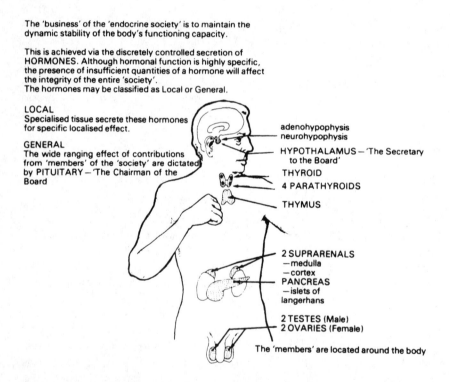

The 'business' of the 'endocrine society' is to maintain the dynamic stability of the body's functioning capacity.

This is achieved via the discretely controlled secretion of HORMONES. Although hormonal function is highly specific, the presence of insufficient quantities of a hormone will affect the integrity of the entire 'society'.
The hormones may be classified as Local or General.

LOCAL
Specialised tissue secrete these hormones for specific localised effect.

GENERAL
The wide ranging effect of contributions from 'members' of the 'society' are dictated by PITUITARY – 'The Chairman of the Board

adenohypophysis
neurohypophysis

HYPOTHALAMUS – 'The Secretary to the Board'
THYROID
4 PARATHYROIDS

THYMUS

2 SUPRARENALS
—medulla
—cortex
PANCREAS
—islets of langerhans

2 TESTES (Male)
2 OVARIES (Female)

The 'members' are located around the body

Fig. 45 *The endocrine system* (from McNaught and Callender, 1963)

■ The pituitary gland

The pituitary gland consists of two parts: *neural* (the posterior pituitary or neurohypophysis), and *glandular* (the anterior pituitary or adeno-hypophysis).

Although the pituitary exerts a 'chairman's' influence over the endocrine system, its role is carefully controlled by a most diligent 'secretary' – the hypothalamus (see p. 113), which in turn is influenced by the cerebrum.

The neural part of the pituitary gland appears to be the 'store house' for hormones manufactured in the hypothalamus.

ADH (antidiuretic hormone or vasopressin): key role in salt-water balance has already been discussed (see chapter 7).

Oxytocin: produces ejection of milk from the lactating breast.

The posterior pituitary secretes these hormones from storage as required.

The glandular part of the pituitary gland has many functions which may be broadly categorised as:

- control of growth (e.g. bones, muscle)
- control of other areas of the endocrine system (e.g. thyroid, adrenal cortex)
- regulation of metabolism of carbohydrates, proteins and fats.

These functions are fulfilled by six hormones secreted by the adenohypophysis, which are as follows.

Growth hormone (somatotrophic hormone, STH, or human growth hormone, HGH): acts directly on the tissues. The following are some effects of growth hormone secretion:

- increases the mass of skeletal muscle
- increases lipolysis (breakdown of lipids) and increases circulating free fatty acids, offering the latter as a source of energy
- increases bone growth
- promotes transfer of amino acids from extracellular fluid to cells
- increases the size of the thymus.

Secretion of growth hormone is increased by:

- exercise, especially in women because oestrogen increases secretion of growth hormone
- lowered glycogen in the blood (hypoglycaemia), or starvation
- circulating amino acids (especially arginine)
- extreme cold and even emotional excitement or stress
- sleep.

Growth itself is primarily affected by heredity, nutrition, good health and the contribution of other hormones in addition to growth hormone, principally the androgens, thyroid hormones and insulin.

ACTH (adrenocorticotrophic hormone or corticotrophin): causes the rapid secretion of glucocorticoids from the adrenal cortex; rapid conversion of cholesterol and its salts to pregnenolone and thence along the mineralocorticoid, or 17-hydroxycorticoid, or androgen and oestrogen pathways; a fall in adrenal cortex ascorbic acid concentrations (though its role in the adrenal cortex is not clear); and stimulation of growth. The secretion of glucocorticoids under normal conditions and stress are both dependent upon ACTH secretion (fig. 46).

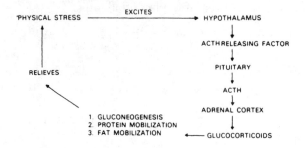

Fig. 46 *Stress and the glucocorticoids*

ACTH is secreted according to a basic rhythm during the course of the day. The peak secretion would appear to occur during sleep before awakening, whereas the trough would appear to occur towards evening. This rhythm of ACTH secretion is reflected in plasma cortisol (fig. 47) and is referred to as the diurnal or circadian rhythm. There is considerable evidence to support the theory that rhythmic control is spread over even longer periods. The rate of ACTH secretion is accelerated by disruption of homeostasis (i.e. stress).

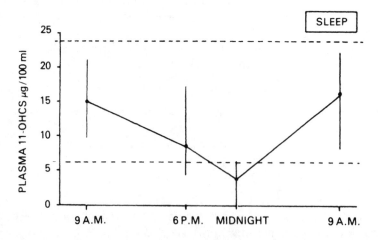

Fig. 47 *Mean diurnal variation of plasma 11-hydroxycorticoid levels in 24 normal subjects. The vertical lines indicate the range of observations. The horizontal dashed lines show the normal range between 9 am and 10 am. (After Mattingly, D. (1968) in Recent Advances in Medicine, 15th ed., ed. Baron, D. N., Compston, N. D., and Dawson, A. M., J. & A. Churchill, London) (from Samson Wright, Applied Physiology, 1973)*

Thyrotrophin (thyroid stimulating hormone TSH, thyrotrophic hormone): stimulates growth and acts directly on the thyroid gland to stimulate thyroid secretions. In children increases in thyrotrophin secretion are produced by cold temperatures, but this effect is slight in adults. Normally the hypothalamus is a controller of thyrotrophin secretion and a decrease in thyroid hormone status also effects an increase in thyrotrophin secretion. Consequently this system is one of negative feedback and is effective both at pituitary and hypothalamus levels. It should also be added that it is thought that stress stimulates secretion of thyrotrophin.

Follicle stimulating hormone (FSH):   stimulates ovarian follicle growth in the female and spermatogenesis in the male.

Luteinising hormone (LH or interstitial cell stimulating hormone – ICSH):   stimulates ovulation in the female and testosterone secretion in the male. FSH and LH are the pituitary gonadotrophins and their inter-related role is evident in the female menstrual cycle, the central nervous system, and the hypothalamus. It is yet to be clearly shown that a similar periodicity exists in men vis-à-vis androgen secretion.

Prolactin (luteotrophic hormone LTH, luteotrophin, lactogenic hormone, mamotrophin, galactin):   stimulates secretion of milk and maternal behaviour.

The secreting glands

Hypothalamus
The hypothalamus has already been suggested as assuming the role of a diligent secretary to the pituitary, and has been referred to in discussion of pituitary hormones. It receives a more generous blood supply than any other cerebral structure. It is mainly via this generous blood supply that stimuli promote the hypothalamus to secrete specific releasing agents to the pituitary, which in turn secretes an appropriate hormone from those listed above. It also manufactures the two hormones stored in the neurohypophysis and has a regulatory function in temperature control, thirst, hunger, sexual and emotional behaviour. It also exerts neuro-endocrine control of the catecholamines in response to emotional stimuli via impulses coming down from the cerebrum.

Thyroid gland
The thyroid gland secretes three hormones: thyroxine, triiodothyronine and calcitonin. The main hormone is thyroxine, although triiodothyronine is relatively more active. The function of these two hormones is similar and it has become conventional to base discussion on thyroxine.

Thyroxine performs several functions in the body:

• it is essential to normal metabolism, and the increased metabolic rate brought about by thyroxine increases oxygen consumption and heat production (calorigenesis). Thyroxine also increases dissociation of oxygen from haemoglobin

- it is essential to normal function of the central nervous system, but does not increase oxidative metabolism within this system
- it is essential to normal growth and development of the body when growth hormone is secreted by the adenohypophysis. Growth hormone can only work at maximum efficiency in the presence of thyroxine. Moreover, thyroxine is vital to differentiation and maturation of certain tissues such as the epiphyses in ossification
- the absorption of carbohydrate through the intestine reflects the level of thyroxine activity. High activity increases absorption and utilization of glycogen by the tissues and increases glycogenolysis in the liver, muscle and heart, as well as increasing gluconeogenesis and insulin breakdown
- it is involved in the regulation of lipid metabolism and is known to reduce cholesterol in the blood by encouraging its metabolism by the liver and by increasing the quantity excreted in bile
- excessive thyroxine causes excessive protein breakdown
- heart rate, blood pressure and cutaneous circulation may increase with an increase in thyroxine secretion
- the gonads (sexual organs) function normally only when thyroxine secretion is normal. Thyroxine levels are important factors in lactation
- the equilibrium of thyroxine secretion is also critical to normal function of the digestive tract.

Thyrotrophin (secreted by the pituitary gland) and the availability of dietary iodine determine the amount of thyroxine secreted by the thyroid.

Calcitonin (thyrocalcitonin): inhibits the process of resorption of bone, and consequently calcitonin is secreted in response to increased concentration of calcium in the blood. Calcitonin should be considered as one of the three main guardians of calcium equilibrium in the body. The others are parathyroid hormone and vitamin D. Magnesium and phosphate are also linked with the body's calcium profile.

■ Parathyroid glands
The parathyroid glands, unlike the thyroid, are essential to life. They secrete a hormone which promotes calcium resorption in the body.

Parathyroid hormone secreted when there is a decrease in calcium concentration in the blood. When magnesium concentration is high, there is a decrease in parathyroid hormone secretion. Although phosphate concentration does not directly affect secretion, it is possible that it does so indirectly when, for example, high phosphate leads to lowered blood calcium levels. Parathyroid hormone acts directly on bone and kidney and it would appear that it also may have a direct effect on the intestine. Vitamin D is essential to the direct actions on bone and probably on intestine. This vitamin also increases calcium and phosphate absorption from the intestine.

■ Adrenal glands

The adrenal glands each lie above one kidney, hence their other title – the suprarenal glands. These glands comprise an inner medulla and an outer cortex, which are, in fact, two distinct organs.

The adrenal cortex

The adrenal cortex is involved in the stress response and regulates carbohydrate, fat and protein metabolism, and also salt-water balance. The hormones secreted by the adrenal cortex fall into three main categories, but two smaller groups of progesterone and oestradiol should also be considered (not known to have any significant feminising activity). The main groups are as follows.

The glucocorticoids *cortisol* (hydrocortisone) and *corticosterone*: promote glucose formation, hence their name. Corticosterone has little importance in man and comprises roughly a third of the glucocorticoids in blood. Consequently it is reasonable to follow convention by discussing only cortisol here. Cortisol has several functions to fulfil:

- it is essential to normal carbohydrate metabolism
- it promotes gluconeogenesis in the liver
- it is essential to breakdown of glycogen to glucose, by adrenaline or glucagon
- it promotes catabolism of proteins
- it brings about redistribution of fats via lipolysis and lipogenesis
- in excess it reduces the response of tissue to bacterial infection
- it mimics but is less effective than aldosterone in salt-water balance and also plays an important role in maintaining blood pressure
- it increases the blood platelet count and shortens blood clotting time
- in excess, cortisol raises blood lipid and cholesterol levels
- it increases acidity in the stomach and when combined with a slight increase in release of pepsin (an enzyme involved in protein digestion) it is possible that peptic ulcer formation may result
- it promotes absorption from the intestine of those fats which are insoluble in water
- in excess it interferes with cartilage development and the reduction of epiphysial plates. This may lead to interrupted growth in children. Also in this connection, it decreases calcium absorption from the intestine and increases calcium loss in the urine.

Finally, it is well known that cortisol is used in the treatment of certain injuries. The injury site is infiltrated with a quantity of cortisol in excess of the normal physiological level. The cortisol protects the site from damage and prevents the normal response to tissue trauma, such as histamine release, or migration and infiltration of leucocytes at the injury site. Cortisol does not actively heal the injury, but creates a favourable environment for healing. However it will be appreciated, from what has been said above, that cortisol infiltration is not without considerable risk and it is hardly surprising that sport authorities in medicine are extremely cautious in suggesting its use. For example, it has a weakening effect on collagen, as in tendons.

The mineralocorticoids *aldosterone* and *11-deoxycorticosterone* (cortexolone): cause retention of sodium and increased excretion of potassium in the urine. Consequently they are key agents in salt-water balance. Aldosterone is approximately 30 times as powerful as 11-deoxycorticosterone in terms of sodium retention, but is less efficient as an agent in potassium excretion.

Androgen secreted by the adrenal cortex has a less masculinising effect than testosterone. It is necessary for the growth of body hair in women. The principal adrenal androgen is dehydro-epi-androsterone. As stated the hormones of the adrenal cortex follow a circadian rhythm, but their secretion is increased by stressful stimuli. The various compounds involved are all steroids and derived from cholesterol (fig. 48). It will be clear that several results of excess secretion of these corticosteroids are not compatible with good health and consequently the continued exposure of man to stressful stimuli is not to be encouraged. In this respect, sport and physical recreation may be considered therapeutic.

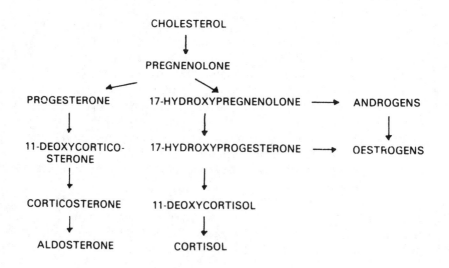

Fig. 48 *Possible pathways in the synthesis of steroid hormones from cholesterol* (from Samson Wright, 1973)

The adrenal medulla

The adrenal medulla secretes the catecholamines adrenaline and noradrenaline. The actions of adrenaline and noradrenaline are very similar, but the latter is more efficient in raising blood pressure and less efficient in metabolic actions and in relaxing smooth muscle. Their secretion is stimulated by: physical and emotional stressors, cold exposure, decreased blood pressure, low blood glycogen, certain drugs (e.g. anaesthetics), and afferent nerve stimulation.

Involvement of the catecholamines and the sympathetic nervous system in the 'flight and fright mechanism' is well known. These two independent systems provide a most efficient means of meeting emergency situations. Such means might be summarised as:

- increase in heart rate and cardiac output and rise in blood pressure
- mobilisation of muscle and liver glycogen, which leads to increased blood sugar
- increase in metabolic rate
- skeletal muscle fatigues less readily
- relaxation of smooth muscle in the wall of the bronchioles, which leads to a better supply of air to alveoli
- respiration rate is raised
- dilation of coronary blood vessels and those of skeletal muscle, thus providing increased blood supply to those organs urgently requiring it
- constriction of blood vessels of abdomen; contraction of sphincters of digestive tract, ureters and sphincters of urinary bladder; inhibition of digestive tract movement and wall of urinary bladder ('butterflies' and increased micturition in pre-competition)
- dilation of pupils of eye
- constriction of smooth muscle of skin and cutaneous blood vessels ('goose flesh' and pallor)
- increased ability of blood to coagulate
- affect on reticular formation of brain to increase memory recall, and to increase attention and concentration.

While the value of catecholamines is clearly of advantage in the flight and fright mechanism, the value is much less clear in the face of psychological and emotional stress. In fact, Carruthers (1971) sees such secretion as part of a most undesirable chain of events (fig. 26, p. 72).

■ The pancreas

The pancreas, in addition to its exocrine function of secreting pancreatic juice, also has an endocrine function which it fulfils via the *islets of langerhans*. There are two types of cell involved in its endocrine function:

(**1**) cells secrete *glucagon* which increases blood glucose by glucogenolysis and gluconeogenesis
(**2**) cells secrete *insulin* (table 17) which decreases blood glucose by stimulating reabsorption of glucose in the kidneys, reducing liver glycolysis and increasing glycogen formation from glucose in muscle.

Table 17 *Factors influencing insulin secretion via blood*

stimulation	inhibition
Monosaccharides	Adrenaline
Amino acids	Noradrenaline
*Ketones	Insulin
Glucogen	Fasting
Growth Hormone	

* product of liver metabolism of FFA.

■ The thymus

The thymus increases in size from childhood till adolescence and thereafter progressively atrophies. This gland is responsible for the 'education' of the T-lymphocyte immune cells so that they do not attack one's own proteins. This process of clonal selection by deletion occurs through apoptosis, or induced cell suicide.

■ The testes

The testes have an exocrine function in the manufacture of sperm and an endocrine function in the secretion of testosterone. Testosterone, in addition to its initial role in the foetus of forming the male genitalia, is also responsible for development of the secondary male characteristics at puberty, the maintenance of some of these throughout adult life, and the male emotional profile.

Testosterone causes nitrogen retention in the body and increased synthesis and deposition of protein, especially in skeletal muscle. By this process, there can be little doubt that testosterone derivatives increase strength, given that dietary factors and training regimens are appropriate. In addition, testosterone and its derivatives promote retention of water, sodium, potassium, phosphorus, sulphate and calcium. It is mainly the retention of water which causes the considerable weight gains recorded in studies of the effect of testosterone ingestion.

For several years, some athletes have been known to take testosterone derivatives for their anabolic effect. Anabolism is the formation of energy-rich phosphate compounds, proteins, fats and complex sugars by processes which take up rather than release energy. (Catabolism = releasing energy, and metabolism = energy transformations in the body.) It would appear that the taking of such substances increases strength, promotes formation of erythropoetin, and so on. However, to do so, with or without medical advice, in pursuit of competitive advantage, is, apart from being illegal in the world of sport, also highly irresponsible. By disrupting one part of the endocrine system in this way the equilibrium of the total system is compromised. For example, the following have been advanced as possible, and in some cases are probable, additional effects of taking testosterone derivatives:

• initial enlargement of the testes is followed by shrinkage because the high level of testosterone causes a negative feedback in the system

resulting in no luteinising hormone being sent to the testes
- the long bones mature too rapidly
- an increase in sexual desire is followed by a decrease
- the salt/water imbalance due to fluid and electrolyte retention may lead to kidney, circulatory and coronary disorders
- the probability of cancer of the prostate gland would appear to be increased
- there is a higher incidence of jaundice in those taking these substances
- liver disorders are associated with testosterone ingestion.

Finally, several of these effects may be irreversible.

■ The ovary

The ovary, in addition to discharging ova, secretes two hormones: an oestrogen known as oestradiol and a progestin known as progesterone. These hormones are responsible for the development of female primary and secondary sexual characteristics, the growth and development of the female sex organs at puberty (e.g. enlargement of uterus), the menstrual cycle, the physiological and anatomical changes associated with pregnancy, and changes in the mammary glands (e.g. conversion of pelvic outlet, broadening of hips).

Oestradiol: the involvement of oestradiol is very slight until puberty when the hypothalamus stimulates the adenohypophysis to secrete gonatrophins, which stimulate the ovary to discharge ova and secrete oestradiol and progesterone. Consequently, athletes may find performance fluctuation due to such changes as strength-weight ratio, alignment of femur relative to tibia, and basic metabolism undergoing gross adjustment. Fig. 49 outlines possible weight variations in the course of the cycle. It has been suggested that the cycle should be adjusted to make 'optimum competition weight' days coincide with major competitions. Indeed, this has been achieved by administration of certain drugs. However, it is not clear what long-term effect such adjustment of this most basic rhythm will have on other rhythms. Oestradiol, in addition to its key role in the menstrual cycle and those functions listed above, also effects:

- deposition of fatty tissue on thighs and hips
- growth rate of bones after puberty. It has a 'burning out' effect leading to an early growth spurt but also an early cessation. Looking at it another way, the male child grows longer longer!
- blood cholesterol levels are reduced by oestradiol and possibly this helps in the prevention of development of coronary heart disease
- while testosterone increases sebaceous gland secretion and the possibility of acne, oestradiol increases water content of the skin and decreases sebaceous gland secretion.

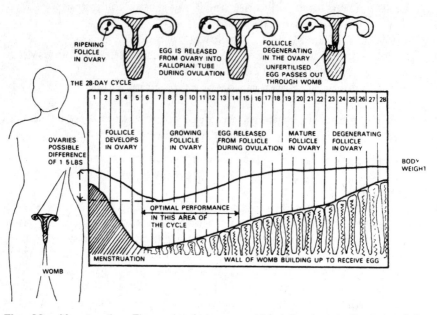

Fig. 49 *Menstruation. The cycle of changes which take place in the tissue lining a woman's womb culminate about every 28 days when the blood-enriched lining comes away as the menstrual flow. The changes in the womb parallel developments in an ovary, where an egg ripens and is released at ovulation, about halfway through the cycle. The egg travels along a Fallopian tube towards the womb. It is fertilised, it becomes implanted in the lining of the womb, and menstruation ceases for the duration of pregnancy* (adapted from Family Health Guide, Reader's Digest, 1972)

Progesterone: increases body temperature and it is thought that its secretion at ovulation is the reason for increased bodily temperature at that time. Combinations of these female steroids have been marketed as oral progestogens (female oral contraceptives). These oral progestogens have been used by some athletes in order to effect control of the menstrual cycle but, again, the general equilibrium of the endocrine system is exposed to the possibility of certain compromises such as weight increase, increase in emotional irritability and feelings of depression, decreased status of vitamin B_6, vitamin B_2, folic acid, vitamin C, vitamin B_{12}, and of trace elements such as zinc. The depression is manageable on trying different types of 'pill', possibly with folic acid supplementation.

▌Summary

The hormones are the supreme guardians of homeostasis. They regulate organic functions through their individual and combined roles. A knowledge of hormone function is essential to a comprehensive understanding of an athlete's status, not only his level of athletic fitness but also his general health. It is possible that an athlete will receive medication in the form of ingested hormone preparations (e.g. oral progestogens), creams rubbed into the skin (e.g. cortisol creams), and so on. Consequently it is important to understand why and how the use of these preparations will affect the integrity of the endocrine system. Medical advice must be sought to establish the implication of exposing the athlete to certain training stressors. In recent years it has been tempting to see the hormones not only as regulators of total body function, but also as possible instruments to advance athletic performance. Indeed, it is not uncommon for hormone preparations to be discussed along with the athlete's nutrition. However, the equilibrium which exists within the body is very delicate and as yet not completely understood. Conservation is as necessary to our internal environment as it is to the external environment and, with or without medical supervision, the pursuit of 'hormonal advantage' in sport is as unwise as it is unethical.

9
Physiological differences in the growing child

It is very easy to see training as the only stressor to which the young athlete's organism is exposed. However, this is most certainly not the case. Training is only one stressor in a complex assault of the organism which must adapt to the demands of growth and maturing function.

Effects of stress

As a result of multi-stressor situations, metabolic functions take place at a higher rate and the stress characteristics of circulation and respiration are quite apparent. One may rightly assume that the resistance or elasticity of the blood vessels contribute to the type of circulo-respiratory adjustments seen in youngsters in training. However, the main focus of attention should be on the heart itself and its ability to pump out blood. The measurements we are looking for, then, are *stroke volume, heart rate* and *blood pressure*. Consequently, considerable attention is also given to cardiac output, which is 4–5 litres at rest and over 20 litres in exercise. The increase can be effected by increasing heart rate and stroke volume. Obviously, the more blood the heart can pump out per unit of time the better it is for the athlete, so endurance training is geared in the first instance to improving cardiac output. Due to the small size of the untrained child's heart, cardiac output increase is brought about almost entirely by increased heart rate. This frequency regulation, in contrast with the volume regulation of adults and trained youths, is a particular feature of the circulation of untrained youngsters.

Research in GDR and Sweden shows a linear relationship between the heart volume and maximum oxygen uptake (VO_2 maximum) with age, from 8–18 years. However, examination of heart size on its own does not give any real indication of the performance capacity of young athletes since the normal size range is very large. The relative size of the heart compared with other morphological and functional values would, however, give some indication of performance (table 18).

According to Hollmann, the greatest increase in heart volume occurs at approximately 11 years of age for girls and approximately 14 years of age for boys. The heart weight is greatest 2–3 years later. Furthermore, as

Table 18 *Heart volumes in ml of untrained and trained 11–15 year olds* (from Harre, 1973)

age	untrained		trained		
	boys	girls	boys	girls	
11	376	349	417	392	
12	440	366	461	448	
13	483	452	508	496	
14–15	549	501	584	539	
*14–15	555.1	469.9	660.6	443.7	sprints
			620.2	498.8	middle distance
			650.9		football

*Entrants to Deutsche Hochschule fur Korperkultur (DHfK), Leipzig, GDR.

young people mature, heart rate decreases while blood pressure and the range between systole and diastole increases. Training adds to these natural growth phenomena, giving greater heart volume, range of blood pressure and maximum heart rate. This provides lower functional values at rest and higher functional values under stress, i.e. an increased range of functional ability.

Muscle biochemistry in pre-puberty does not favour lactic anaerobic activity. This would suggest that 'early teens' success in sprints or endurance events may be due to aerobic and/or alactic anaerobic efficiency, or an early maturity. Attempting to 'force' anaerobesis on the pre-pubertal child is as pointless as it is unwise.

Up to 12 years of age, oxygen intake is approximately equal for boys and girls. Thereafter, girls accelerate to their maximum between 13 and 16 years of age, and boys increase their oxygen intake rather more slowly to reach their maximum at 18–19 years of age. Although it was suggested earlier that cardiac output increase is almost entirely due to heart rate increase in the child, sports physiologists now suggest that a regulation of stroke volume can be seen in trained children and youths. This manifests itself in a greater increase in systolic blood pressure, or in blood pressure range, accompanied by only a slight increase in heart rate. This is illustrated in figure 50 by comparison of trained and untrained boys and girls. It can be seen that heart rate for trained children is lower than for untrained. In recovery, the total time for trained children is shorter (fig. 51).

The peak of biological adaptability in children occurs between 10 and 15 years of age, at a period when physical capacity has by no means reached its maximum. As far as developing physical ability is concerned, youth is the best time for the athlete, bearing in mind that the growing organism is required to expend considerable energy in growing and maturing. Heavy strength work and anaerobic (lactic) work are not to be emphasised in early youth, but mobility, which will almost certainly be on the decline after 8–9 years of age, must be consciously worked for where appropriate. While aerobic endurance training and general training can often be found in simple endurance sports (e.g. orienteering, paarlauf) and field games, care must nevertheless be taken to ensure adequate rest periods, especially where endurance training is taken to the 'controlled' environment of the track or pool. Harre has noted (1973) that 'when there has been a logical choice of training methods and due observation of the basic principles of training, functional disturbances are, as a rule, not the result of loading in training. Much more to blame here are the total stressors put upon the young athlete, and performance-diminishing features such as immoderate amount of stimuli (e.g. excessive TV watching, inadequate sleep, unsuitable diet, etc.)'.

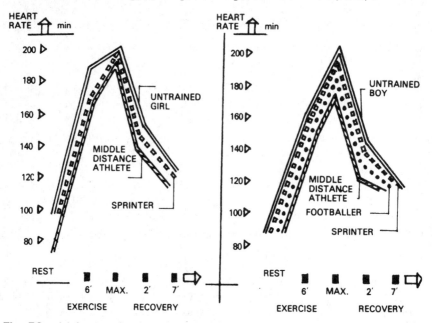

Fig. 50 (a) Average heart rate at rest and in exercise for 12–14 yrs. Trained and untrained girls with standardised exercise loading (Harre, 1973); (b) Average heart rate at rest in exercise for 12–14 yrs. Trained and untrained boys with a standardised exercise loading (Harre, 1973)

Fatigue is a physiological occurrence that affects every form of living substance: due to training it is an important condition for the adaptation of the organism to increasing demands. Muscles, ligaments, joints, nerve cells, bones, etc., are all subject to the process of fatigue, which is a temporary, reversible reduction of function, linked with the disinclination for further loading. The recovery period required to restore normal function following fatigue depends on the size and nature of the preceding stressor. The ability to recover improves as the young athlete grows and as his training load is systematically increased. However, long interruptions to training result in a deterioration of this ability. A regular medical check-up, accompanied by a physiotherapy check-up, will help avoid any functional problems which can arise due to excessive stressor bombardment. This done, training will always, if accompanied by careful thought, be to the athlete's benefit.

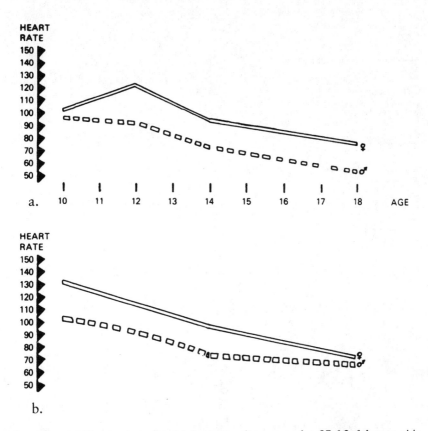

Fig. 51 *(a) Heart rate in the third minute of recovery for 65 10–14 year old athletes in preliminary training for speed sports (Harre, 1973); (b) Heart rate in the third minute of recovery for 43 10–18 year old athletes in preliminary training for endurance sport (Harre, 1973)*

Due to the existence of natural androgenic hormone to an extent never matched elsewhere in their life, girls should be exposed to regular moderate strength training as soon as they finish their adolescent growth spurt, but before sexual maturity. Menstruation is occurring earlier now (13 years 2 months – 13 years 4 months) than in 1890 when 15 years was the age of menarche (it may be earlier or later). The combined stressors of the relatively 'new' phenomenon of menstruation, plus growing itself, suggests avoidance of training loads which produce excessive fatigue in the early teenage athlete.

Finally, although the importance has been stressed of regarding the child as a child and not a mini-adult (because of basic dimensional differences), many measurements and values are, in fact, proportionate to, or 'scaled down versions' of, the adult's. For example, blood volume in terms of ml/kg of body weight is 75 for men, 65 for women and 60 for children (fig. 52).

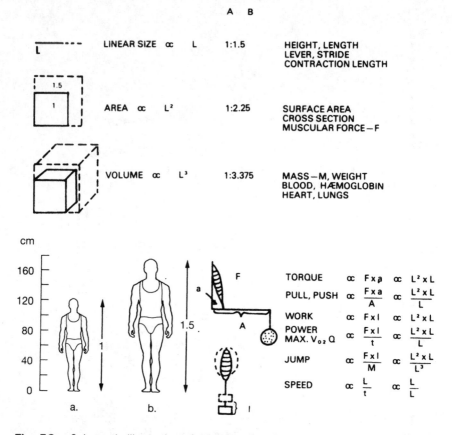

Fig. 52 *Schematic illustration of the influence of dimensions on some static and dynamic functions in geometrically similar individuals. A and B represent two persons with body height 120 and 180 cm respectively (partly modified from Asmussen and Christensen, 1967) (from Astrand and Rodahl, 1970)*

▮ Summary

The process of growing reaches beyond the readily observed anatomical indications. Within the athlete there are proceeding structural and functional changes which are part of the growing process. While these changes in the athlete's physiology are preparation for adult life and the possibility of a progressive intensity and extent of loading consistent with the advanced athlete's training, they also represent high energy expenditure. Moderate exercise reflecting a varied intensity and extent of loading is essential to normal growth. Organised training for boys and girls should be introduced around 10–12 years of age. However, the coach must see the growing athlete's training as characterised by a sound programme of all-round development which does not produce exhaustion of already reduced energy reserves.

Table 19 *Physical, physiological and psychological effects of training*

increase	decrease
Strength of bone	Heart rate at rest
Strength of ligaments	Heart rate at sub-maximal workloads
Thickness of articular cartilage	Oxygen uptake $\Big\}$ for
Cross-section area of muscle	Blood lactate given
Muscle strength and power	Pulmonary ventilation $\Big\}$ workload
Creatine phosphate and ATP in muscle	Triglycerides in blood
Myoglobin	Arterial blood pressure
Capillarisation of muscle (including heart)	Glycogen utilisation
Heart volume	Blood cholesterol
Heart weight	Risk of myocardial infarction
Myocardial contractility	Obesity–adiposity
Blood volume	Platelet stickiness
Total haemoglobin	Stress associated with
2,3, diphosphoglycerate	physical/psychological
Fibrolytic activity	stressors e.g. humidity,
Maximum heart rate	altitude, emotion, etc.
Stroke volume	
a–vO$_2$ difference at maximal workload	
Blood lactate at maximal workload	
Pulmonary ventilation at maximal workload	
Respiratory rate at maximal workload	
Diffusing capacity of lung at maximal workload	
Lean body mass	
Glycogen content of muscle	
Size and number of muscle mitochondria	
Mitochondrial activity (succinic dehydrogenase, phospho-fructokinase)	
Range of joint action	
Speed of limb movement	
Tolerance to stress	

Summary of part 2

Training might be thought of as the practical means of adapting the organism to certain specific demands of a sport. The systems which have been reviewed in these chapters are all involved in the adaptation process or permit adaptation to take place. Some specific effects of training, which illustrate adaptation by the increase or decrease of certain functional capacities, are listed in table 19. It should be said here, however, that no one form of training will affect all of these adaptations.

The athlete trains to compete or participate in physical activity. The demands of each sport and the specific environment of any contest are unique to the individual athlete concerned. Thus, when training for a given sport, the specific adaptation of that athlete's organism to meet the demands of that sport is also unique. Adaptation will also vary according to whether it is a final or a friendly, or at altitude or in high humidity, in pursuit or defence of a title, the location in a circadian or monthly cycle, at home or following lengthy travel, and so on.

Not every problem relating to specific adaptation will be resolved by a study of the human organism. But at least these problems can be more clearly defined and identified even within the limits of our understanding of organic function.

▎References for part 2

Astrand, P. O. (1967) *Federation Proceedings 26*, 1772

Astrand, P. O. & Christensen, E. H. (1964) Aerobic work capacity. In *Oxygen in the Animal Organism* by Dickens, F., Neill, E. & Wicklas, W. F. (eds). Pergamon Press, New York

Astrand, P. O. & Rodahl, K. (1986) *Textbook of Work Physiology*. 3rd Edn. McGraw-Hill

Bloomfield, J., Fricker, P. A. and Fitch, K. D. (1992) *Textbook of Science and Medicine in Sport*. Blackwell Scientific Publications, Melbourne

Brooks, G. A. and Fahey, T. D. (1984) *Exercise Physiology: Human Bioenergetics and its applications*. John Wiley and Sons, New York

Buskirk, E. R. & Bass, D. E. (1974) *Climate and Exercise in Science and Medicine of Exercise and Sports*. Johnson, W. R. & Buskirk, E. R. (eds). Harper and Row, London

Carlile, F. & Carlile, U. (1960) T-wave changes in strenuous exercise. *Track Technique, No. 2*. (From paper to New South Wales, Australia, Sports Medicine Association, 1959)

Carruthers, M. E. (1971) *Biomechanical Effects of Psychological Factors on Physical Performance*. Paper to British Association of Sports Medicine and Scottish Amateur Athletic Joint Coaching Committee Conference on Bio-profiling, Glenrothes

Durnin, J. V. G. A. (1975) *Protein Requirements of Physical Activity*. VIth Coaches' Convention Report

Ekblom, B., Goldbarg, A. N. & Gullbring, B. (1972) Response to exercise after blood loss and reinfusion. *Journal of Applied Physiology, Vol 32*, No. 2

Golnick, P. D., Armstrong, R. B., Saltin, B., Saubert, C. W., Sembrowich, W. K. & Shephard, R. E. (1973) Effect of training on enzyme activities and fibre composition of human skeletal muscle. *Journal of Applied Physiology*, No. 34, pp 107–111

Grisogono, V. (1991) *Children and Sport: fitness, injuries, diet*. John Murray

Guyton, A. C. (1990) *Physiology of the Human Body*. Holt Saunders, Philadelphia

Harre, D. (1973) *Trainingslehre*. Sportverlag, Berlin

Harries, M. (1994) *The Oxford Textbook of Sports Medicine*. Oxford University Press

Huxley, H. E. (1958) The contraction of muscle. *Scientific American*, 19, 3

International Athletic Foundation. (1989) *Too Thin to Win*. IAAF

Jäger, K. & Oelschlägel, G. (1974) *Kleine Trainingslehre*. 2nd Edn. Sportverlag, Berlin

Jones, D. A. and Round, J. (1990) *Skeleta. Muscle in Health and Disease*. Manchester University Press

Keele, C. A. & Neil, E. (1973) *Samson Wright's Applied Physiology*. 12th Edn. Oxford University Press, London

King, J. B. *Sports Medicine*. British Medical Bulletin Publication. Churchill Livingstone, Edinburgh

Komi, P. V. (1992) *Strength and Power in Sport.* Blackwell Scientific Publications, Oxford

Lee, M. (1993) *Coaching Children in Sport: principles and practice.* E & F N Spon

Mackenna, B. R. and Callander, R. (1990) *Illustrated Physiology.* 5th Edn. Churchill Livingstone, Edinburgh

Macleod, D. A. D., Maughan, R. J., Nimmo, M., Reilly, T. and Williams, C. (1991) *Exercise: benefits, limitations and adaptations.* E & F N Spon, London

Macleod, D. A. D., Maughan, R. J., Williams, C., Madeley, C. R., Sharp, J. C. M. and Nutton, R. W. (1993) *Intermittent High Intensity Exercise.* E & F N Spon, London

Maffulif, N. (1993) *Color Atlas and Text of Sports Medicine in Childhood and Adolescence.* Mosby-Wolfe

McArdle, W. O., Katch, F. F. and Katch, V. L. (1991) *Exercise Physiology: energy, nutrition and human performance.* Lea and Febiger, Philadelphia

McArdle, W. O., Katch, F. F. and Katch, V. L. (1994) *Essentials of Exercise Physiology.* Lea and Febiger, Philadelphia

McNaught, A. B. & Callender, R. (1963) *Illustrated Physiology.* Churchill Livingstone, Edinburgh

McNeill, Alexander, R. (1992) *The Human Machine.* Natural History Museum Publications, London

Newsholme, E. A., Leech, T. and Duester, G. (1994) *Keep on Running: The science of training and performance.* John Wiley and Sons, Chichester

Noakes, T. *Lore of Running: Discover the Science and Spirit of Running.* Leisure Press, Champaign, IL.

Pappenheimer, J. R. (1950) Standardisation of definitions and symbols in respiratory physiology. *Fed. Proc.* 9, 602

Pyke, M. (1975) *Success in Nutrition.* John Murray Ltd, London

Saltin, B. & Hermansen, L. (1967) *Glycogen Stores and Prolonged Severe Exercise, Nutrition and Physical Activity.* Almqvist & Wiksell, Uppsala

Schreiner, K. E. & Schreiner, A. (1964) *Menneskeorganismen.* 6th Edn. J. Jansen (ed.). Universitetets Anatomiske Inst., Oslo

Sergeant, A. J. and Kernell, D. (1993) *Neuromuscular Fatigue.* North-Holland, Amsterdam

Sharp, N. C. C. (1995) The Health of the Next Generation: Health through fitness and sport. *J. Royal Soc. Health*, 116, No 1, 48–55

Shepherd, R. J. and Astrand, P. O. (1992) *Endurance in Sport.* Blackwell Scientific Publications, Oxford

Stanton, R. (1988) *Eating for Peak Performance.* Unwin Hyam

Sufte, N. K., Gushiken, T. T. and Zarins, B. (1986) *The Elite Athlete.* SP Medical and Scientific Books, New York

Suslov, F. (1972) Views on middle and long distance training. *Modern Athlete and Coach*, 10, No. 1

Vander, A. J., Sherman, J. H. & Luciano, D. S. (1970) *Human Physiology, The Mechanism of Body Function.* McGraw-Hill, New York

Wells, C. L. (1985) *Women, Sport and Performance: A physiological perspective.* Human Kinetics, Champaign, IL

Williams, C. (1974) *Special Forms and Effects of Endurance Training.* Vth Coaches' Convention Report

Williams, C. (1975) *Adaptation to Stressors of a Changing Environment.* VIth Coaches' Convention Report

Williams, C., Kelman, G. R., Couper, D. C. & Harris, C. G. (1975) Changes in plasma F.F.A. concentrations before and after reduction in high intensity exercise. *Journal of Sports Medicine and Physical Fitness*, Vol 15, 2–12
Wilmore, J. H. and Costill, D. L. (1994) *Physiology of Sport and Exercise*. Human Kinetics, Champaign, IL
Woofton, S. (1988) *Nutrition for Sport*. Simon and Schuster
Yakovlev, N. N. (1961) Nutrition of the athlete. *Track Technique*, Nos 20–26, June 1965

▌ Bibliography

Cohn, E. E. & Stumpf, P. K. (1972) *Outlines of Biochemistry*. 3rd Edn. John Wiley & Sons, New York
De Vries, H. A. & Housh, T. J. (1994) *Physiology of Exercise*. 6th Edn. Brown and Benchmark, Madison Wisconsin
Donath, R. & Schüler, K. P. (1972) *Enharung Der Sportler*. Sportverlag, Berlin
Folk, G. E. (1974) *Textbook of Environmental Physiology (2)*. Lea & Febiger, Philadelphia
Ganong, W. F. (1973) *Review of Medical Physiology*. 6th Edn. Lange Medical Publications, California
Hill, A. V. (1945) *Living Machinery*. G. Bell & Sons Ltd, London
Holmer, I. (1974) Physiology of swimming man. *Acta Physiologica Scandanavica*, Supp 407
Howard, H. & Poortmans, J. R. (1975) *Metabolic Adaptation to Prolonged Physical Exercise*. Birkhauser Verlag, Basel
Jeffries, M. (1976) *Know Your Body*. B.B.C. Publications, London
Karlsson, J. (1971) Lactate and Phosphagen concentrations in the working muscle of man. *Acta Physiologica Scandanavica*, Supp 358
Kelman, G. R., Maughan, R. J. & Williams, C. (1975) The effects of dietary modifications on blood lactate during exercise. *Journal of Physiology*, 251, pp 34–35
Luce, G. G. (1972) *Body Time*. Temple Smith, London
Margaria, R. (1976) *Biomechanics and Energetics of Muscular Exercise*. Clarendon Press, Oxford
McLintic, J. R. (1975) *Basic Anatomy and Physiology of the Human Body*. John Wiley & Sons, New York
Morehouse, L. E. & Miller, A. T. (1967) *Physiology of Exercise*. 5th Edn. C. V. Mosby, St Louis
Pernow, B. & Saltin B. (1971) *Muscle Metabolism During Exercise*. Plenum Press, New York
Richardson, R. G. (1974) Proceedings of the Joint Conference with the British Olympic Committee on Altitude Training. *B.A.S.M.*, Vol 8, No 1
Robson, H. E. (1973) Proceedings of the XVIIIth World Congress of Sports Medicine (1970). Special issue of *The British Journal of Sports Medicine*, *B.A.S.M.*, Vol 7, Nos 1 & 2
Scheuer, J. & Tipton, C. N. (1977) Cardiovascular adaptation to physical training. *Annual Review of Physiology*, 39, pp 221–251
Sperryn, P. (1975) Proceedings of the International Symposium on Anabolic Steroids in Sport. *B.A.S.M.*, Vol 9, No 2
Tanner, J. M. & Taylor, G. R. (1975) *Growth*. 5th Edn. Time-Life International, Amsterdam.

Part 3

Mission control

It has been suggested that coaching is 'more of an art than a science'. Perhaps this idea evolved to explain the existence of several outstanding coaches who have had little or no formal scientific education. They may not have studied biomechanics, physiology, anatomy, and so on, but they will almost certainly claim to be students of human behaviour. Students, moreover, who derive their knowledge from practical experience of working with athletes, rather than from textbooks. This knowledge might include an understanding of teaching methods, individual motivation and the relationships between athletes in a team or squad. In his own way, such a coach is using a scientific approach, for the study of behaviour is the science of psychology. The 'art' of coaching is the ability to relate several sciences to assist an athlete in his pursuit of excellence. Not only is psychology one of these sciences, it is central to equipping the coach to relating them to athlete and sport. This is the framework within which the 'people business' of coaching operates effectively. The most relevant aspects of psychology for coach and athlete are discussed in this section. Chapter 10 has been prepared by Miroslav Vanek and Pamela F. Murray. Chapter 11 is revised (1996) in consultation with Miroslav Vanek and Pamela F. Murray.

10

Victor in mente, victor in corpore
(A mind to conquer, a body to conquer)

Responsibility for the preparation of the athlete has traditionally rested with the coach. The coach-athlete partnership is the long-term aim of any coach wishing to develop his athlete and guide him through the sport. However, the education of the athlete by the coach and supporting team of specialists, and the self-education thereafter, is an underoptimised if not underestimated aspect of training.

Intellectual preparation of the athlete

To maximise performance achievement, the athlete needs to develop his intellectual capacity. Access to knowledge relevant to performance success is a fundamental part of the preparation of the athlete. Each sporting event and discipline requires technical understanding and the beginner generally embarks on a process of gradual accumulation of information pertinent to his activity. The coaching continuum (Dick, 1992) consists of four coaching styles which follow the developmental needs of the athlete: directing, coaching, supporting and counselling.

The directing style of coaching provides the necessary input which the learner accepts and takes on-board. There is little negotiation given the lack of experience and knowledge on the part of the athlete. With more time and experience the coaching style is employed; the athlete may now participate in decision-making during this more interactive style. Psychological preparation can shadow this process and the athlete is encouraged to make independent assessments and begin to reflect on the results of given actions. Outsiders to the coach-athlete relationship, such as specialists dealing with aspects of sport science support, may offer input. This is taken one stage further when the development of the athlete is planned by role exchange and the coaching role assumes functional interchangeability. The athlete may, for example, report on given nutritional advice to other athletes and so maintain athlete motivation for learning while other suitable coaching responsibilities may be passed over to the athlete. The following style along the continuum is that of supporting, where the athlete is more independent in sharing plans and ideas with the coach. The athlete contributes to training programme design and the planning of competitive activity. Continued role interchange encourages the development of the athlete through the style spectrum. The counselling style is used with an accomplished athlete able to manage a lifestyle compatible with training and performance demands. Sufficient input from outside specialists has enabled the athlete to combine personal experience with systematic support. Whilst described as a progression, an athlete may well respond best to one coaching style when concentrating on technical form, but prefer another when handling another aspect of training.

The intellectual preparation of the athlete is designed to develop the ability to accumulate a relevant reservoir of knowledge necessary for successful participation in sport. Decision-making ability and cognitive creativity in part determine how efficiently the athlete will compete. The athlete must be independent, not vulnerable to manipulation by the coach or any other administrator within the sport, and be able to control himself in the chosen competitive arena. Such development of thought capacity requires years, and a patient coach who strategically plans the individual's preparation through integrated inputs. Sport science support is necessary to give an objective foundation to the development of athlete cognition. Such universal preparation is now a basic requirement for the athlete competing against organised coaching systems operating in other countries, which emphasise overall development. The terminology should not put coaches off making use of specialist input; a cognitive strategy is simply needed for a thinking competitor. Given that competition implies adaptation to changing variables, the athlete should not be limited through lack of intellectual preparation.

■ Sensory motor training (SMT), and modelling

The most highly developed form of training for stressful experiences, such as experienced by the athlete under competitive conditions, is that of the senses. SMT, if adequately handled, will give the athlete the opportunity to develop event-specific sensory perception. As a leading sense from the sensory complex will inform the athlete of actual happenings during performance, the coach can rehearse competitive conditions with the aim of developing sensory reception and the ability to read and respond. Modelling is a form of SMT that seeks to reproduce aspects of competitive performance, giving competition specific sensory motor training. It must be said that some competitive characteristics cannot be reproduced, such as the atmosphere. The use of noise or music will not elicit the same response in the athlete as on the day of the event, as was previously thought possible, and the coach is better advised to replicate environmental conditions such as altitude, humidity, time and temperature. Other techniques such as giving a leading or trailing handicap of 10 metres will let the athlete practise the feeling of running from in front or behind and reproduce psychological situations. Team sports, similarly, can make use of tactical advantages and disadvantages during rehearsal activity, such as playing with the restricted use of a particular shot or space.

Role playing has proven to be a most effective technique within modelling, where the role of the opposition can be taken on by some of the potential competitors. Prior to a major championship, the Czechoslovakian artistic gymnastic team were divided into two groups; one group played the role of the then Soviet team, and the other group retained home-nation identity. So realistic were the accompanying conditions, with the roles of dressed officials also being played, that a strong emotional element was created within the model competition. Coaches and gymnasts were thus effectively guided in the refinement of individual preparation strategies. Therefore it is more important for the coach to consider factors which directly affect the performer within competitively induced situations when creating a situational model, than to pay attention to indirect conditions.

Successful models have been created in soccer for goal practice for striker and keeper using an overcrowded goal area, reducing decision-making time and thereby imitating real-game characteristics. Decisions to be taken by striker and keeper are left open to continually rehearse spontaneous situational coping. Such practices without the inclusion of real-game conditions are underoptimised in terms of SMT. The coach can produce innovative practices, taxing the player through the combination of technical and tactical demands. Overloading can also be used to enhance resistance. Very occasionally, the coach may suddenly change a previously agreed session thereby surprising the athlete. For example, if a track athlete is coming to the end of a 300m run and the coach shouts instructions to carry on for a further 150m, the athlete will be forced to mobilise his reserves. Whilst immediately unpopular, the coach has in fact used a technique which will help the athlete when moving into stressful conditions!

Modelling takes many forms. The sensory motor training involved will teach the athlete how to make appropriate adjustments conducive to success-related activity under varying conditions. However, successful training models used by one athlete or team, may not be suitable for use by others. Models are a result of coaching experience, careful observation (perhaps using technological means), and subjective measurement using esteem and self-esteem scales.

■ Esteem scales and self-esteem scales

Esteem scales, used by the coach to evaluate the athlete, and self-esteem scales, used by the athlete to rate himself, are examples of psycho-diagnostic tools at the disposal of the coach. The coach can compare the information revealed through other observational techniques such as video performance and training observations, to either reinforce facilitating aspects or identify existing discrepancies. The construction of esteem and self-esteem scales depends on the coaching style used by the coach, the event, and the personality-determined needs of the athlete. Each coach can design his own scales to provide relevant training design and preparation planning guidance. Flexible designs which alter according to the information required will give both coach and athlete the opportunity to reflect on aspects related to training and competing, which either assist the athlete or detract from optimum conditions.

Figures 53 & 54 show flexible designs which are changed in accordance with the information required.

Overuse is not encouraged but certainly use pre-, mid- and post-season is beneficial, with occasional use when the coach wishes to identify specific pre-determined characteristics, whether positive for reinforcement, or negative for eradication.

This type of design is part of a scale appropriate for a coach wishing the athlete to evaluate his training management. For example, if the athlete is seen to be constantly distracted, the design will allow for the consideration of lifestyle management giving an insight into the broader aspects of the athlete's activities:

training	rating	perception
Training organisation		
Session organisation	1 2 3 4 5	-3 -2 -1 0 1 2 3
Enthusiasm whilst training	1 2 3 4 5	-3 -2 -1 0 1 2 3
Ability to give maximum effort	1 2 3 4 5	-3 -2 -1 0 1 2 3
Communication with coach	1 2 3 4 5	-3 -2 -1 0 1 2 3
Commitment to programme	1 2 3 4 5	-3 -2 -1 0 1 2 3
Interaction with other athletes	1 2 3 4 5	-3 -2 -1 0 1 2 3
Technical support		
Technical expertise of coach	1 2 3 4 5	-3 -2 -1 0 1 2 3
Technical understanding of own event	1 2 3 4 5	-3 -2 -1 0 1 2 3
Sport science support	1 2 3 4 5	-3 -2 -1 0 1 2 3
Personal input to technical programme	1 2 3 4 5	-3 -2 -1 0 1 2 3
Support of other coaches	1 2 3 4 5	-3 -2 -1 0 1 2 3
Recovery		
Recovery within session	1 2 3 4 5	-3 -2 -1 0 1 2 3
Recovery between sessions	1 2 3 4 5	-3 -2 -1 0 1 2 3
Effectiveness of active regeneration	1 2 3 4 5	-3 -2 -1 0 1 2 3
Nutritional care	1 2 3 4 5	-3 -2 -1 0 1 2 3
Sleep pattern	1 2 3 4 5	-3 -2 -1 0 1 2 3
Out of training worries	1 2 3 4 5	-3 -2 -1 0 1 2 3

Please comment on the following aspects of your training management on a scale of 1–5 where 1 = not good and 5 = excellent. The second scale from –3 to 3 is a perception scale by which you can indicate to what extent you feel that this is facilitative or detrimental. –3 represents a very negative response whilst +3 represents an item which you find very positive.

Fig. 53 *Self-esteem scale – to be used by the athlete in a self-rating style*

Competition specific scales may be constructed to include aspects which are thought to influence the athlete at this time. Areas to be covered may well include emotions such as excitement, fear, anxiety, enjoyment; feelings prior to the start of the event; control over self at this time; interference of concentration by others; reaction to opposition; delivery of coach instructions whether unclear or clearly understood; ability to regain focus if interrupted; goal focus; or use of competition plans. The items included are then indirectly athlete initiated.

The scale construction of figure 54 allows the coach an insight into how the athlete approaches training and competition using his personal judgement to assess the athlete:

training and competition behaviour	perception
Training	
Athlete gives maximum effort	–3 –2 –1 0 1 2 3
Responds well to informative feedback	–3 –2 –1 0 1 2 3
Communicates feelings	–3 –2 –1 0 1 2 3
Follows the agreed programme	–3 –2 –1 0 1 2 3
Fatigue	
Loses motivation when tired	–3 –2 –1 0 1 2 3
Gives greater effort when fatigued	–3 –2 –1 0 1 2 3
Loses concentration easily	–3 –2 –1 0 1 2 3
Can mobilise reserves	–3 –2 –1 0 1 2 3
Is prone to negative feelings	–3 –2 –1 0 1 2 3
Competition	
Pre-game/event plan organisation	–3 –2 –1 0 1 2 3
Confidence approaching event	–3 –2 –1 0 1 2 3
Reliance on coach/other	–3 –2 –1 0 1 2 3
Use of performance plan	–3 –2 –1 0 1 2 3
Distraction	
Ability to focus	–3 –2 –1 0 1 2 3
Ability to recover from loss of focus	–3 –2 –1 0 1 2 3
Tendency to relax following score	–3 –2 –1 0 1 2 3
Easily distracted when under pressure	–3 –2 –1 0 1 2 3
Post competition	
Accepts +ve or –ve result	–3 –2 –1 0 1 2 3
Accepts himself as worthy individual	–3 –2 –1 0 1 2 3
Ability to analyse objectively	–3 –2 –1 0 1 2 3
Overly self-critical	–3 –2 –1 0 1 2 3
Return to training following competition	–3 –2 –1 0 1 2 3

Fig. 54   *Esteem scale – for use by the coach evaluating the athlete*

■ Motivation

A highly researched area with many schools of thought, motivation continues to elude coaches and researchers alike, given that there is no finite nor precise list of motives, and also due to the fact that motives cannot be identified through experiment. The development of theories remains an important task. Many current theories are based on the concept of perceived competence such as attributions, goal orientations and intrinsic motivation (Biddle, 1995). Achievement motivation and motivation in the form of competitive stress are also considered by sport psychologists (Weinberg & Gould, 1995). Thus we have to accept some operational theories which fit the competitive basis of sport. In this case we refer to motivation as considered by the McClelland-Atkinson model (McClelland, Atkinson, Clark & Lowell, 1953; Arkes and Garske, 1982) where two factors determine whether an athlete will engage in competition: the motive to achieve success and the motive to avoid failure. Often referred to as competitiveness, achievement motivation has been considered by sport psychologists as a personality factor, where personality traits influence the athlete's need for achievement. An interactional view accounts for more changeable goals, identifying how these affect the situation and the influence the goals themselves exert over the situation.

The motive to achieve success, regarded as the athletes' self-confidence or efficacy, is believed to represent an athlete's intrinsic motivation when approaching a competitive situation. The motive to avoid failure is represented by the individual's personality disposition for anxiety. Motivation consists of a cluster of motives which are inner needs (urges or tendencies), plus external stimulus; *motivation = motive + external stimulus (actual or signal).* Inner and external stimuli create the motive, however the final behaviour will depend on the mental capacity of the athlete. A motive is the basis for energy and direction of behaviour where the athlete requires both movement and mental skill to reach a goal. Singer (1968) proposed that performance is a function of motivation and skill, $p = f(m+s)$. The specific cluster of motives is important given that some combinations may be incompatible: *do not like training* (negative), with *have to compete* (negative); *want to go out with friends* (negative), with *look forward to training* (positive); *want to win* (positive), with *want to train* (positive). Achievement motivation can be described as the predisposition of the athlete to win. Athletes motives are not static. Emotions such as fear, joy or anger are also regarded as motives. The athlete will respond at every moment to the dominant motive according to his intellectual capacity.

Intrinsic and extrinsic motivation should be combined to establish an optimum motivatory effect. Whilst a balance exists, intrinsic motivation should prevail as the goal-centred athlete has greater motivation. If we take the example of the professional footballer anticipating payment, he must first win, and so attend to the actual performance goal before considering the financial bonus following success. Risk-taking behaviour describes a situation where the athlete seeks challenging achievement situations where there is a fifty percent probability of failure. A situation with a low or very high chance of failure would depict an athlete low in the motive to achieve success, as the athlete will either win easily, or be excused for losing against such tough opposition. In this way his self-esteem is not threatened.

Motivation does not operate in isolation. Coupling with cognition, it is thought to form the motivation for the next goal. In terms of goal setting, dealing with success and coping with failure should be approached from mid-term and long-term perspectives; the athlete who performs poorly at a home international or commonwealth games should review the performance in terms of Olympic preparation. Fuoss and Troppmann (1981) used the acronym SCRAM to describe the properties of effective goals: specific, challenging, realistic, and measurable. The coach and athlete should be able to establish appropriate values for these in the knowledge that the stress of competition infers change to such parameters (Beggs, 1993).

All performances are interpreted according to the mid- or long-term goal. This would be impossible to do without first, the motivation, and secondly, the cognition. There is then a relationship between the actual state and expected state (Vanek, Hosek & Man, 1982).

The effect of goal setting is not in itself unlike competition, as challenging goals can be perceived as stressors (Huber, 1985). Proximity, difficulty and specificity have been shown crucial goal-setting characteristics. Proximal goals in training, those which are closer to the athlete rather than distant future goals, are reported to increase the athlete's confidence, strength, stamina and skill, reducing the likelihood of being adversely affected by competitive stress (Beggs, 1993). In conjunction with this input, the operational coaching style will influence the commitment from the athlete, in that a supportive style will allow the athlete to play an active part in goal setting. It is more than likely that assigning goals for the performer using a directive style will not result in optimum conditions for goal achievement. Acceptance of the goal, commitment to the goal, and the responsibility for the goal are encouraged by athlete participation. The coach can provide the athlete with many opportunities to rehearse anxiety-management skills during such times. A goal-setting programme utilising appropriate sub-goals to manipulate the goal type will expose the athlete to various strategies.

■ Emotions and arousal effect

There exists a biology to basic emotions in which certain points in the brain house emotions such as fear, aggression and pleasure. One point of stimulation can be continually aroused, as with the drug abuser becoming addicted, and the individual will behave in a certain way to bring about that specific emotion. Sport is one such stimulus, a need to be fulfilled by the athlete. Participation in competitive sport is related to pleasure whether through the movement itself, or through the accompanying money, glory, or effort and pain accompanying training. Educating the athlete to behave according to an appropriate value system can change such behaviour. New emotions and needs come from the external environment, and so the athlete will internalise emotions related to the fulfilment of these needs. The level of the athlete's needs is then raised. With further internalisation the athlete will have greater influence over the external environment, and be in a position to give others new values, skills and approaches to society. This process is called externalisation. The coaching continuum provides a useful analogy, and indeed mirrors, the process. Directing activity sees the athlete receiving information and knowledge which is internalised allowing the athlete to develop a little and move on to the next style, coaching, where the athlete now becomes more involved with training decisions. Again the role interchangeability raises the needs of the athlete who progresses to supporting style. The coach adjusts the style according to the developing needs of the athlete. The athlete externalises information setting an example for other athletes. With more experience and competence the athletes evolving needs require a different style of coaching; from a counselling style the athlete independently manages training and competition activity although the coach can assist with the overall planning.

The autonomous athlete, having reached an élite level, should not divorce himself from those values which underpinned his early career, nor the emotions and behaviours of that period. A higher complex of values now influence the athlete, and this in turn provides others with 'messages' due to the process of externalisation. It is vital that replacement emotions are guided by ethical values. Ethical behaviour does not simply arrive with the rise to élite performance level, and yet performers at this level carry a great responsibility to ensure that behaviour is commendable. Behaviours can be changed through education, a responsibility of both coach and athlete. Coaching systems should be based on the process of athlete internalisation-externalisation, ensuring the necessary progressive development.

Extreme positive or negative emotion can detract from an appropriate mental state for performance, as arousal may increase quite dramatically blocking movement co-ordination and mental processes such as cognition. Under such conditions, the athlete is unable to produce a normal performance. The personality of the athlete will determine how the stresses are coped with. For those individuals who perform better when external pressures cause inner tension, performance in competition exceeds that of training. Such athletes have frustration tolerance, a higher level of resistance, whereas those who perform better in training than in competition have a very low frustration tolerance. From the coaching point of view it is important to realise that mental resistance, sometimes referred to as mental toughness, is either inborn, influenced by the type of education received by the athlete, or influenced by experiences under stressful conditions. It is advisable to create a system of athlete education leading to the independence of the athlete, involving complete knowledge of the self, and optimal risk-taking. The resistance level and frustration tolerance of the athlete can be established through athlete observation whilst training and competing, self-esteem scales carried out by the athlete, and esteem scales used by the coach. Competitive stress has been approached by both emotion-focused and task-centred methods: emotion-focused coping methods, such as relaxation techniques and self-talk, attempt to address anxiety and other non-facilitative emotions. Task-centred coping methods, such as goal setting, aim to remove the cause of unwanted emotions (Cohen and Lazarus, 1979).

■ **Psychological management of the opposition, and self-management**
It is important to teach the athlete how to handle the opponent
psychologically, as he will not be looking out for the best interests of fellow
competitors. There are many behaviour patterns which will assist the
athlete prior to the event, at the competition site and in other areas such as
the athlete village.

As with event favourites, Danek, a Czech discus thrower and world
record holder of the time, received much media attention and support prior
to the Tokyo Games. His main opposition came from the American, Oerter,
who also proceeded to confirm Danek as firm favourite, sure to win the
competition in his absence as he was too injured to throw. On the day of the
competition, Oerter turned up with a bandaged shoulder, visibly distracting
Danek. Danek started with a throw of 59m, short of normal performances.
Oerter's first throw was 62m. At this moment Danek was crushed, his
arousal was so high that further attempts were not completely co-ordinated.

Pre-performance and performance routines should cover a range of
potential incidents as risk-management for the athlete. Every athlete must
learn how to handle the opposition psychologically. This is not unethical
but more along the lines of self-preservation and quite pragmatic. Every
activity must feed the athlete's performance, and not detract from it in any
way. To reduce pressure as event favourite, he must think of challenging for
the medal rather than defending himself against challenges. If he has a high
performance expectation, it is easier to achieve this goal from the position
of the outsider than from the lime-light. Competition strategy involves
learning about self-portrayal; focus on goal fulfilment should be cleared of
distractions. Each athlete will create his own recipe establishing flexible
successful ingredients. The athlete must also exert complete self-control
learning to adapt to a range of situations. A British international high
jumper reported that he liked to feel 'bouncy' before competing. When
asked how this was achieved, the athlete stated that running round a 400m
track and jumping the occasional hurdle was necessary. This same athlete
was about to compete in an indoor arena with a 200m track. Suffice to say
that the performance was certainly not supported by this rigid performance
plan. Competitive experience will assist in the design of such plans, and
various should be devised and rehearsed in light of changing conditions.
The mental plan will direct energy and effort carefully in light of familiar
experience. Contingency for the unknown is not as difficult as it may sound
– the athlete will have a range of mental skills at his disposal which provide
tools with which to approach adversity. Confidence is instilled by the very
fact that the performer can call upon internal resources to help deal with
the unexpected. Central to the success of a plan is athlete control. No
athlete can afford to wait for the opposition to impose competitive
conditions. If the athlete allows this to happen, he is abdicating the
responsibility for the performance.

Table 20   *Race focus plan for international 800m runner*

600–800m	trigger 'squeeze'; kick hard
600m	get ready to kick
500m	trigger 'stay up'; work onto the back straight
200m	in position, stay relaxed
Start	trigger 'get out fast'
Pre-start	alone, ignore people around me, avoid eye contact. Attention on breath control, relaxation routine

Plan development I

The plan is followed from the lower sections upwards, as the athlete visualises the ascent to victory within the structure of the plan. The performer was shadowed in training and competition to establish relevant plan ingredients. A loose structure was implemented to guide the acquisition of relevant mental training skills. Warm-up races, such as club commitments and national championships, were used to refine the flexible framework.

Table 21   *Refocusing plan for rugby international*

KEY: when you pass the ball, you don't give away responsibility.

1. *Loss of concentration through mistakes*

Attention lost on missed kick	park it
Use gear box	select a gear, 1st to recover, 2nd gear up to playing speed
Concentration 1	use movement pattern – still loss of focus
5-point kick plan	visualise, successful imagery
Concentration 2	use trigger word 'precise'
Return to game pace	change gear, 3rd for aggressive acceleration. 4th gear – in control, smooth play

2. *Loss of concentration through fatigue*

Reinforce gearbox	keep changing gear
Positive self-talk	use triggers 'big hit'; 'safe hands'
Team energy	talk to team-mates, remember 'the hill'
Energise	energy-ball imagery
Be aware of roles: attack, support.	

3. *Heads are down*

4 points down	we need 5 to win
Team energy	keep recycling
Basics	simple moves
Time	use every second

Plan development II

This player established a range of plans reflecting his individual needs throughout the game. Training camp venues were used to introduce and practice mental training techniques in controlled and modified conditions. Personal reserves such as emotional and physical commitment were necessary throughout the intense training activities. Individual and collective strategies were implemented, where the player could call upon internal reserves and the accumulated willpower of the group. During match play, associated emotions are recalled by the player which help elicit a similar response. Complete control is assumed. The player, with a specific route in mind, thus remains the driver and does not become a passenger throughout the game. Cues relevant to the immediate game can be attended to in the secure knowledge that the problem will be effectively handled. Technical training sessions were used to rehearse the different techniques, where conditions reflected the real game demands more closely. Non-league games theoretically provided the next step in plan refinement, however due to the vast difference in the approach of the player to this type of game as opposed to a league game, and the difference in the level of performance arousal, it rarely provided a sequential progression.

The player must realise that such plans do not fall into place on their own. He is actively involved in making them happen. The mental plan can be reviewed through post-game analysis one or two days following the event, in addition to a short self-esteem scale designed for this purpose. Practice is essential. Confidence in mental plans is fundamental and therefore supporting staff should be careful to refer to aspects of the player's plan so as to publicly reinforce its practical value. The integration of mental training with the physical preparation of the player is vital.

There are also potential problems away from the competition site which the athlete can address. The athlete village at any major championships plays host to many potential stressors which may affect the athlete: distractions from social activity, continued presence of the opposition, and the constant intensity which distinguishes the site from the home environment. Experience reveals that it can be a testing ground for athletes wishing to psyche-out opposition. The athlete must live amongst failures, those with great aspirations, and those with unethical values. To be polite, calm and live in comfortable isolation may then suit those wishing to conserve performance energy. Carl Lewis did not stay at any Olympic village, preferring to stay away from that type of environment and successfully minimising his exposure to other variables, which he perceived as potentially distracting. Refraining from other athletes' psychological handles can be difficult, and so the athlete can be comfortable in the knowledge that predetermined routines will look after his respective interests.

Performance support should also be aware of the potential downfalls associated with athlete deprivation at competition sites. For instance, athletes competing abroad may experience taste deprivation, a desire for food that satisfies their specific requirement. Whilst competition hosts may offer excellent facilities, it is important for the athlete to operate within a comfortable zone, in touch with aspects typical of the home environment. It is worth sending a cook from home with any travelling team, as did Nestlé sponsoring the Swiss team during the 1980 Moscow Olympics. The athlete should not spend too much energy adapting to constant change.

Pre-performance routines within the long pre-start conditions (fig. 56) provide familiar structures and flexible, but controlled, patterns. The performance routine, within the competition itself, will facilitate consistency. Boutcher (1993) reports further advantages: attention control is increased, helping the athlete to concentrate more efficiently; the warm-up decrement is addressed, concerned with a loss in motor performance following a short break by giving psychological and physiological warm-ups in stop-start activities; and automatic skill execution is encouraged.

Despite the use of naive, so-called non-scientific, techniques designed to harmonise bodily and mental states, there are occasions when the desired result is not achieved. Therefore the athlete should have an operational understanding of mental training techniques with a scientific basis such as Jacobson's progressive relaxation (1929), which involves a systematically ordered tensing and relaxing of muscle groups; or autogenic training, similar to progressive relaxation with an emphasis on how the body parts feel (Schultz and Luthe, 1959; Harris and Harris, 1984; Nideffer, 1985; Orlick, 1986).

It is possible to identify which mental training techniques and cognitive strategies successful performers use. Weinberg and Gould (1995) report a qualitative approach to the investigation of differences between successful and less successful athletes, using in-depth interviews with the 1988 U.S. Olympic wrestling teams. Medal winners used more positive self-talk, had a narrower and more immediate focus of attention, had better mental preparation for unforeseen negative circumstances, and had more extensive mental practice.

Many procedures have been developed, but not all are as effective as they are claimed to be. Whilst the athlete should learn to relax the body as a basis for intervention strategies, he must also learn reactivation, depending on the athlete and sport. Players in English first division rugby are currently making effective use of a combination of pre-game relaxation followed by individually designed reactivation strategies. Individual programming is crucial for both team and individual sports where blanket strategies may even serve to distract some players, and certainly not produce a viable ideal performance state for all within the

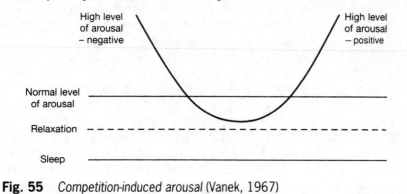

Fig. 55 *Competition-induced arousal* (Vanek, 1967)

team. The relaxation-reactivation is rehearsed for competition-type whether for home and away games, or national and international events. Competition-induced arousal is given a new direction.

Theoretically, arousal can be very low such as sleep, or higher for normal daily activities. It is described as physiological and psychological activation (Gould & Krane, 1992). A high level of arousal results in mental activation which can manifest itself in sweating, increased heart rate, and respiration. Some individuals may experience overarousal to the extent that they lose control over their actions. Arousal does not infer either negative or positive reactions. However, anxiety is a negative emotional state characterised by feelings of apprehension associated with the activation or the arousal of the body (Weinberg & Gould, 1995).

Figure 55 shows the arousal level prior to competition (on the left), which is negatively affecting the individual. Using a mental training technique, this is reduced to a relaxed level, but not sleep. From there, reactivation occurs with the use of an appropriate follow-on technique. The arousal again increases but this time with a new direction, positively affecting the athlete (to the right of the figure). The performer has controlled pre-competition anxiety avoiding, for example, loss of energy leading to a feeling of flatness. In addition, an indirect consequence is that of increasing self-confidence. The athlete, in the knowledge that self-management techniques have been learned and rehearsed, will approach competition with self-assurance. Risk management activity is a fundamental part of performance preparation.

Many arousal models exist, describing the anxiety of the athlete and subsequent behaviour; Hardy and Fazey's (1987) catastrophe model assumes that anxiety is made up of cognitive anxiety and a physiological response. When physiological arousal is high, such as on competition day, this model predicts that a negative correlation between cognitive anxiety and performance exists, although moderately high levels of physiological arousal are necessary for peak performance. Reversal theory (Apter, 1982) asserts that a high arousal level occurring within an evaluative state will be negatively interpreted as anxiety, whereas the same level of arousal occurring when the athlete is within a non-evaluative state will be interpreted positively.

The category and perception of anxiety determines the athlete's responses and coping strategies; identified differences between cognitive and somatic anxiety influence stress management models (Davidson and Schwartz, 1976). The mental component of anxiety, referred to as cognitive anxiety, is caused by either negative expectations of success, negative self-evaluation, or diversion of attentional focus (Burton, 1990). It is characterised by worry, negative self-talk and imagery, and loss of attention. Somatic anxiety is the physiological or affective component related directly to autonomic arousal which may be manifested in a range of physiological responses including clammy hands, muscular tension and rapid heart rate. Important for both coach and athlete when managing the arousal-performance relationship is a multidimensional perspective (Martens et al, 1990). The athlete, regarded as a processor of information within a cognitive approach to sport psychology (Straub & Williams, 1984) is potentially vulnerable to differential effects on aspects of the information-processing system when under the stress of competition (Jones, 1990). The aim of good mental training is to harmonise the mental and training/competing states. It may take several months to half a year to master control over arousal. Coping skills must be rehearsed and practised under simulated conditions to maximise their efficiency. These techniques should not be carried out without specialist training and objective measurement. Imagery, audio and video tapes are only part of any procedure. This said, mental training is not to be overestimated as it is only part of the overall psychological preparation.

■ Performance management

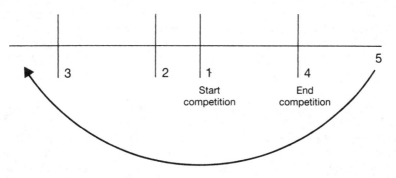

Fig. 56 *The stages of time of competition*
(1)   start conditions – the starting mental state of the athlete (minutes and seconds prior to the start)
(2)   short pre-start conditions – short-term pre-start mental state (minutes, hours)
(3)   long pre-start conditions – long-term pre-start mental state (weeks, days, hours)
(1–4)   competitive conditions – competitive mental state
(4–5)   post-competitive conditions – post-competitive mental state

The ability to understand and manage the stages of time of competition optimises the conditions which are under the control of the athlete. Each stage should be carefully analysed so that coach and athlete can manipulate existing variables. In no single stage should the athlete feel loss of control or uneasy with how things are going. Of particular importance is the handling of the post-competitive mental state (5) as this stage influences long pre-start conditions (3). This determines the actions of the coach following defeat and success to ensure that the athlete is able to re-enter at the pre-competition stage in a comfortable mental state. Care of the athlete is personality related, however sensitivity on the part of the coach following competition is more likely to contribute to the athlete's recovery from one competition and thereby assist his

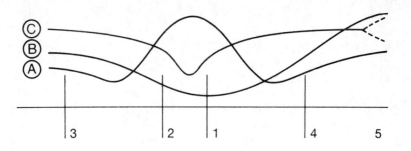

Fig. 57 *Arousal A: the arousal is too high in the short pre-start conditions. Thereafter, during the competition, the arousal falls due to its premature intensity prior to competition, leaving Athlete A feeling flat and drained; Arousal B: this profile represents low arousal in training, such as when there is little effort on the part of the athlete (long pre-start conditions). It slowly rises but optimal arousal is only reached following the competition. A poor performance for Athlete B; Arousal C: falls in the short pre-start conditions, rising in competition to a facilitating level. This demonstrates the correct timing and level according to the arousal level of the finished effort for Athlete C*

preparation for the next. Arousal can be depicted along the stages of time of competition. A simplified approach highlights the profiles of three athletes, A, B and C, in fig. 57.

Each athlete is, of course, different and will display a unique arousal pattern. However, it is a basic responsibility to explore the varied conditions under which the athlete will perform well or badly so that the accompanying skills and coping strategies can be learned. The day of the competition should not bring unexpected conditions, only a mixture of familiar experiences, or at least ones which the athlete can relate to. Post-competitive conditions are closely associated with the finishing arousal and effort of the athlete. Reactions may include euphoria or depression as these are part of the motivational cluster associated with the new training phase. Immediate post-game input should be neutral, free of value-judgements. Performance management is an integral part of coaching methodology.

Personality of the athlete

Given that personality is determined by an individual's characteristics, each person is unique. Hollander's (1971) notion of personality divides it into three separate but related levels: the psychological core, typical responses, and role-related behaviours. The psychological core, internal and most consistent in nature, includes the individual's self-concept, central attitudes, values and motives. As the deepest component of the personality, it represents the 'real you' (Weinberg & Gould, 1995). Typical responses, represented by the way in which an individual responds to an environmental situation, will give an indication of the individual's psychological core. If an athlete consistently avoids social situations, it is likely that he is introverted. Role-related behaviour is engaged in to fit the individual's perception of the environment. As the environment or perception changes, so too does the behaviour. This aspect of the personality structure is most superficial and changeable. The parent-coach can often have difficulty with the coexistence of both roles. Despite the fact that various methods have been designed to measure personality, such as rating scales, questionnaires and unstructured projective tests, including the Athletic Motivation Inventory (AMI), (Tutko & Richards, 1971, 1972); Cattell (16PF) Personality Factor Questionnaire, (1965); the Eysenck Personality Inventory (EPI), (1968); and the Minnesota Multiphasic Personality Inventory (MMPI), (in Cox, 1990), it is highly unlikely that a cause-and-effect relationship exists between a personality trait and athletic performance. This is also partly attributable to methodological concerns.

Personality differences between athletic females and non-athletic females exist. The female athlete has been shown to differ from the normative (non-athlete) female but to share personality traits with her counterpart, the male athlete and the normative male, such as assertiveness, achievement orientation, dominance, self-sufficiency, intelligence and reservation. Fencing, ice hockey, track and lacrosse demonstrated low personality variation, suggesting the viability of specific personality profiles in different sports (Williams, 1980). Elite sport lends itself to personality profiling. The coach must treat all athlete's as individuals, recognising that an exceptional talent may differ from the norm. However, knowledge of an individual's personality traits is not a predictor device.

Some researchers have turned their attention to how the situation and the environment affect the individual's behaviour (Bandura, 1977). According to the situational approach, environmental influences determine the way an individual behaves. A timid individual may play an extremely assertive game of soccer, the game situation necessitating the behavioral change. Despite the fact that the situation can certainly influence behaviour, it cannot accurately predict behaviour (Weinberg & Gould, 1995).

Superficial inventories cannot penetrate the personality. North American and British approaches have made extensive use of such inventories, whereas Soviet approaches have been inclined to use experimental methods, trying to establish and record objective data associated with the nervous activity of the subjects under observation (Vanek & Hosek, 1974). The coach, using personal experience, time spent with the athlete, and combining such factors with esteem and self-esteem scales, can make a fairly accurate assessment. It is better to construct an athlete profile over a period of time using simple observation techniques to get to know the athlete in different situations.

■ Relationship between athlete and coach

Initially, the athlete must adjust to the disposition of the coach given that the coach is stable and the athlete transitory. The coach has an approach consisting of systems and styles with which to influence the athlete directly and indirectly. Therefore the athlete should maintain self-direction, where the coach will identify with the athlete's personality and establish areas for reinforcement. A flexible structure is used by the coach throughout his operations – adapting to changing development needs of the athlete.

The science of coaching as a body of knowledge must be constantly innovative. The coach has a responsibility to continue his own learning by reading, listening, and attending workshops, clinics and courses. Only by thinking and reflecting on his work, and by integrating the supporting disciplines such as sport psychology, nutrition, physiology and bio-mechanics, can the coach continue to develop the discipline and his position within it. Murray (1995) notes that it is the synthesis of sport science information which produces the shift from multidisciplinary to interdisciplinary activity. Specialists can then provide a supporting network which informs, reinforces and enhances the operations of the coach-athlete partnership, reducing the possibilities of contradictory conclusions. Coaching methodology is, as a consequence, extended, broadening the scope for decision-making. The coach should learn to lead and co-ordinate the work of the support team, optimising individual input within a context specific to the athlete's needs. Within professional sport, such support should not be financed in accordance with session input, but should reinforce the partnership with specialist and coach by linking payment with performance outcome. Martina Navratilova maintained such a support team of 8 or 9 specialists including two sport psychologists, one handling training motivation, and the other tournament motivation, given that she felt it difficult to be constantly motivated. Communication occurring in two dimensions is therefore fundamental to performance support, coach and specialist, and specialist and athlete. The coach should be informed of discussions, for example, between psychologist and athlete, where the psychologist is respectful of confidential information. Unethical activities on the part of the sport psychologist include betrayal of trust and overestimation of abilities as a psychologist. The sport psychologist will work in different ways, observing, assessing, and testing players where results inform coaching activity and performance preparation, or again, as a consultant with both coach and athlete, giving psychological guidance. The number of people operating around the coach can either contribute to coaching aims or conflict with them. Overinvolvement should be avoided by strategically planning support with clearly identified roles.

The art of coaching is the experimental learning from value-judgements made on a trial and error basis. The coach records daily input so that decisions can be reflected upon in terms of the related outcomes.

Socially sensitive individuals are more able to progressively accumulate and develop the art of coaching. The centrality of the people business cannot be substituted by any other factor such as supporting technology. Technology should not detract from the creativity of the coach but only play a facilitative role rather than replace value-judgements. At the disposal of the coach is a complex system of metacommunication, where the tone of the voice, a certain look, or small signal can provide the athlete with very clear information. The coach does not need to use too many words but should also find a variety of metacommunicative methods. Short instructions are best suited prior to and during events. Following defeat there should only be instruction on immediate activities such as showering or refreshments. The coach will also be in an emotional state and should not risk anything said which may be difficult to recover from. Post-match/event analysis is more objective after a good nights sleep! In addition, a good performer never needs to be told when he has performed badly. The coach should not be interested in scoring points at this time.

Full team/squad meetings should be democratically executed, a formal and open route which the athlete can use without fear of recriminations. The athlete should be an active participant in the planning of his own destiny and be able to accept responsibility for under achievement or other problems because he has continuing personal involvement. The range of coaching styles can be used to reinforce different messages; a decision taken at such a meeting must be adhered to, thereby introducing a directive coaching style which the team associate with necessary discipline within a just environment. Coaching and supporting styles encourage the player to contribute to his own development, inviting constructive athlete input. End of season team meetings provide the opportunity to fully evaluate results with the benefit of hindsight, where responsibility for errors can be attributed providing useful information for the planning of post-season screening and guiding the pre-season training structure. In-between meetings occur in light of flexible adjustments to the coaching or performance programme and should follow a similar pattern. Consistency on the part of the coach creates a force on which the athletes can rely. Meeting procedures will allow the attending parties to focus on the relevant issues rather than be distracted by the order of the day. Language should also be grammatically uniform: it is not acceptable to say 'we won' and 'you lost'. If periods of success have the coach referring to 'we' and 'our', periods of adversity should also adopt the plural. Players subjected to coach inconsistency will begin to doubt the sincerity of the coach before losing trust completely.

■ Image and self-image of the athlete

Self-image is the result of self-reflection. The starting point comes with dealing with failure – 'why did I fail?' The point of failure is analysed giving the athlete the opportunity to compensate for practical aspects revealed in the analysis. If the self-image of the athlete is a positive one, where the athlete feels good about himself, he will comfortably identify with the goal and related activities in a confident manner. The athlete must accept himself regardless of any result at a competition. A non-achieved goal is not apparently as devastating as a failure. The coach observing the attributions selected by the athlete can evaluate the perceptions of cause and effect displayed. It makes sense for the athlete to attribute failure to an unstable cause, such as luck or lane draw, as this implies that the result may not be repeated. If, on the other hand, the athlete attributes the failure to a stable cause, such as lack of necessary skill, then this is in part predicting future failure (Weiner, 1985). The coach can encourage the athlete to attribute failure to causes such as lack of commitment, using unstable causes which the athlete can change next time. The converse relationship thus advises the athlete to attribute success to an internal, stable cause, such as ability, resulting in increased confidence.

Image is the product of the commercial sphere. The media creates and develops an image compatible with product advertising. A positive image is not the same as a positive self-image; self-image is more important for dealing with success and coping with failure. A winner must know himself and be comfortable pursuing his aims.

■ Cohesion

A most important task of the coach is to create a certain cohesive element allowing sufficient integration to polarise group members. Considerable research within the 1970s and 1980s reveals equivocal results as to the effects of cohesion; some studies of teams clearly demonstrate that greater levels of cohesion lead to success (Carron, 1982; Carron & Ball, 1977), whilst others report performance success with lesser levels of cohesion (Landers & Leuschen, 1974; Lenk, 1969). In the 1990s we are still investigating the determinants of cohesion in sport groups and teams, with the aim of identifying aspects within the control of the coach to enhance training and competition conditions (Murray, unpublished thesis). A sociological perspective identifies a group as more than a collection of individuals, in that individuals working together towards a common goal are much more effective than if they were to work independently of one another. Cohesion has been linked with certain factors fundamental to group development, such as increased communication, productivity, satisfaction, behavioural change, persistence, conformity and attendance (Carron, Widmeyer & Brawley, 1985). Within this context cohesion is seen to contribute to the development of the team, its maintenance and to the accomplishment of group goals. Certainly there exists a potential team-synergy which raises performance.

Cohesion acts as a uniting force influenced by both external and internal factors. Where pressure exists from other teams, the group will be more resistant, although excessive pressure can break the spirit of the group; for example, in times of intense emotion associated with failure, individuals may seek to look after themselves. Low external pressure will not serve to increase team cohesion. Conditions should be anticipated, allowing appropriate preparation. Inter-team conflict need not relate to a negative scenario. As the sport environment evolves so too does the range of potential differences, such as between team member and opponent, player and manager or athlete and coach. Inter-group differences can be used to resolve conflict if the method used to resolve the differences follows a pattern of integration; to bring together the various points of view without diluting respective principles nor merely achieving a short-term compromise. A satisfactory conclusion for those involved is more demanding intellectually than simply adhering to a decision made unilaterally. This type of approach will maintain consistent variables crucial to a team's operating efficiency. Constructive cohesion is a state in which team polarisation may or may not take place but which facilitates performance (Murray, 1996). Synergistic properties are associated with cohesive teams.

The application of cohesion within the sport environment has met with many problems due to the predominance of a unidimensional approach. However Carron et al (1985) produced the Group Environment Questionnaire (GEQ), presenting cohesion as a multidimensional construct comprising of individual and group aspects, each of which has task and social orientation. Some members of the team may be more interested in the task at hand and therefore integrate well together during a set practice or a game, whereas others may be attracted to the group for social reasons and find that they integrate better if allowed social opportunities with other team members. Each cohesiveness construct is assumed to be related through the interaction of task and social orientations as perceived by the group. The coach can obtain a measure of the cohesion level within a team or squad setting, indicating the orientation of the team players.

There are other team-cohesion questionnaires such as the Sports Cohesiveness Questionnaire (SCQ) as developed by Martens and Peterson (1971), Gruber and Gray's (1981, 1982) Team Cohesiveness Questionnaire (TCQ), and the Sport Cohesion Instrument (SCI) developed by Yukelson, Weinberg and Jackson (1983, 1984). This information will help the coach rate the importance of social events in terms of the well-being of the group, and design the training structure and environment in light of player requirements. The team-cohesion instrument should reflect the interests of both the coach and the athlete, and therefore the selection should be made carefully and in consultation with a sport psychologist. Coaches of individual sports can also benefit from an understanding of the cohesion profile of individual athletes given that there are many aspects to training. A training component, for example a speed or plyometric session, may be optimised in terms of training with a partner, within a squad or in the presence of the coach. Each athlete will train best in relation to a facilitating cohesive element which supports the athlete's personal motivations. For the coach to be comfortable in the knowledge that a custom-designed programme is fully serving the needs of the athlete, he should appreciate the conditions under which the athlete operates best.

■ Age and gender

Coaching behaviour also takes into account the specific age range of athletes. Prior to puberty, girls and boys need little differentiation in activities designed to give children confidence. A mother-figure among pre-school age children provides an input compatible with the child's level of development. Thereafter with the school age group the coach can be more demanding, not only supporting and encouraging but also introducing a father-figure into the family. Following puberty, girls are more sensitive and should be coached in a warmer, more friendly manner giving confidence. The coach can develop their competitiveness according to individual personality. With junior boys, a stronger handling is advisable. No matter what role the coach is fulfilling, mother role, father role, or full coaching role, he can introduce and implement basic psychological preparation. Performance enhancement through this channel will then be a natural progression within the athletic lifecycle.

Whilst there is empirical evidence to suggest that males do not attribute a win or a loss to a specific cause any more than females do, (Cox, 1990), coaches have almost certainly experienced other scenarios. Despite the fact that sport psychology literature does not reveal a consistent difference between the causal attributions of men and women, there is evidence to show that males are more likely to attribute their successes internally than females (Ickes and Layden, 1978). The coach to the female athlete should encourage the athlete to consider poor performance in terms of unstable characteristics such as effort and luck. Olympic volleyball player Peppler (1977) commented on the fact that male players participating in her volleyball clinics could be repeatedly beaten but were ready to try again showing complete confidence. External attribution should be practised so that failure is viewed as a passing result not adversely affecting self-confidence or self-esteem. The athlete does not always attribute performance outcome in a logical manner, such as when using an ego-enhancing strategy, attributing all successes to internal causes, or when using an ego-protecting strategy attributing all failures to external causes. There is obviously a danger if another party is constantly blamed for failure. Therefore the coach has to maintain a balance between enhancing the athlete's self-esteem, ensuring protection at vulnerable times such as following a defeat, and also maintaining a realistic perspective of actual performance.

At the beginning of the athlete's career, the aim of the coach should be to prepare a fully independent individual. Professional athleticism demands appropriately directed education from which the athlete can grow and develop. This leads to a self-educated athlete with knowledge of appropriate support sport sciences, and lifestyle, performance and medical management. Each coaching style: directing, coaching, supporting and counselling, enhances athletic, intellectual and motor abilities as the athlete has the opportunity to learn, reinforce, practice and implement skills within modified and, later, realistic situations.

■ **Selection**

Talent scouts can ensure that no child misses the chance to develop a natural talent or attribute. Children can be gradually introduced to competition through simple competition structures such as class v class and school v school, then moving on to national and international competition. Consequently, young gifted talent may be identified. Where the child can enter a sport (depending on the accepted system operating in the country), his subsequent participation remains his decision and that of his parents. The UK tolerates a club-driven system and tends to regard specialist training schools as rather extreme. However, it makes a lot of sense to observe young athletes and thereafter select them for a sport depending on their specific somatotype and displayed tendencies, effectively reducing the occurrences of disappointments at a later stage and giving the child the chance to move on to another sport which shares a similar core training preparation. The incidents of lost or mishandled talent are frequent and not something of the past. The youngster finishing with artistic gymnastics can make a very useful transition to athletics, particularly with the addition of more jumping events for women. Team sports such as volleyball also require gymnastic attributes. It is up to the coach to use his vision to provide the orientation for the young athlete. An integrated coaching network where core skills are imparted would ensure that every child has a basic preparation appropriate for a variety of sports increasing the young athlete's choice and access to sport in general. Non-residential academies of sport can provide an ideal base for a balanced approach to the preparation and care of the young athlete – the opportunity to enjoy specialist coaching and the normality of the home environment. One sport's loss should simply be another sport's gain. This situation is greatly preferable to losing the child to sport altogether.

■ **Summary**

There are no fixed ingredients to success, but the coach can teach the athlete to be aware of every possible ethical performance indicator and facilitator. Good organisation of each psychological preparatory step, from the management of coaching staff and integration with the sport science support team, to the actual movement of the athlete on the day of the competition, is vital. Accompanying administrators should also be carefully selected, goal-orientated and trained for the event conditions. Constant communication providing the extended support team with necessary information will create a positively controlled environment. The coach and team are there to help the athlete. Every step towards competition preparation is a step towards victory.

11
Technical training

Motor learning

Every individual has a need of movement, whether this is the fundamental requirement of the movement of inner organs or the movement of the muscles. Body movement may be either inborn, or acquired, although the exact determination cannot be identified. Accepted movements are certainly attributable to society, and are cultivated to form developed patterns of behaviour according to social politeness. General aims of education through physical activities are to let the participant understand that regular systematic movement is both a part and philosophy of life, and that sport is a school for life.

A range of conditions contribute to individual orientation. Differences between people are determined by factors such as cultural, political, and socio-economic backgrounds. National characteristics will also play a determining role in differentiating individuals. Conditions therefore contribute to differences between people; inter-individual differences distinguish one individual from another, whereas intra-individual differences occur within a person according to the situation, for example the athlete under stressful conditions. The athlete must be viewed as a unique entity, where individual personality is accounted for. Those involved in sport are advised to implant and nurture the need of motion throughout the entire lifecycle whilst acknowledging individual difference.

Motion, aptitudes and ability

An ability is a stable characteristic or trait, inborn and unaffected by practice and rehearsal. An aptitude on the other hand, can be developed or lost. Given this, the coach can assist the athlete through the development of aptitudes central to movement technique, and ultimately performance. To do so using motor learning theory in practical technique training, the coach emphasises first the sensory part of reactions or responses and, second, complete awareness and control over what is going on. Every sport has sensory aspects such as concentration on listening for the gun prior to a sprint start. The coach can take time to reinforce the sensory aspect of a particular technique or part of a technique, and environmental conditions. The tennis coach can emphasise the different sounds from the racquet where the player must identify the type of shot played; the blindfolded ice hockey player should be able to comment on the speed of the puck; the rugby player may rehearse the feeling of a specific movement to optimise use of information. Different sensory information is therefore available to facilitate 'reading' performance.

Development of sensory perception is accompanied by knowledge of what is going on in the body. As a result a total awareness and control of co-ordination and balance will become automated. The circus juggler must carry out different hand activities and simultaneously co-ordinate each independently whilst maintaining balance. The athlete must therefore learn to anticipate requirements. Feedforward, information sent ahead in time to prepare for following sensory feedback, has been shown through research on visual perception to advantage the performer (Gallistel, 1980). A copy of the motor (efferent) command sent to the eye muscles is, in addition, sent to a location in the brain; the visual perception system is in this way informed about the imminent movement of the eye. Schmidt (1988) notes that this 'efference copy' mechanism may indeed exert similar parallel control over the movement of the limbs as well. Evarts (1973) reported neurological evidence indicating that sensory information which is to be received by the muscles, is also sent to locations in the brain. Thus the aim of such activities may be to inform the sensory system and to prepare it for reception of feedback.

To develop sensory perception and necessary awareness, modified activities and games can be used to create a rich reservoir for understanding and perfecting techniques. The ballet dancer rehearsing movements before a mirror is educating the body in an entire movement range, teaching it through pre-determined sequences and acquiring more knowledge of what is involved. The athlete must consciously make himself aware of responses and reaction thereby accumulating movement information.

It is evident then that this movement must be harmoniously controlled, a function carried out by the pyramid and extra-pyramid cells coming from the sub-cortex and connecting every part of the brain responsible for movement. Co-operation between pyramid and extra-pyramid nerves is very subjective where potential influences include feelings and emotions. A lack of co-ordination results in a certain mental state, expressed by a movement error during performance. Each small dis-coordinated activity contributes to failure. Thus the aspect of self-control under a range of conditions faced by the athlete should be rehearsed where the athlete is to maintain a performance-facilitating equilibrium.

■ Feedback and knowledge of results

The coach regularly provides the performer with feedback regarding athletic movement. Feedback is information from the environment which informs the athlete about performance efficiency during and/or following the movement. Feedback can be further classified into intrinsic feedback, which provides a basis for movement evaluation, and extrinsic feedback, information produced to augment intrinsic feedback. Both are of great importance to the athlete wishing to develop his performance. However, the value of feedback would be severely limited without a dimension of external feedback known as knowledge of results (KR). KR, a verbal form of feedback, provides the performer with information which compares the actual performance with the intended goal. The athlete can use this information to improve performance. Another function of KR is that of motivation. The athlete's knowledge of results can motivate further performance improvement. Goals must be established for KR to be effective and meaningful to the athlete. A result without a pre-determined goal offers little value. Clearly videos and videographics are valuable tools in providing KR.

■ The learning concept

The concept of learning as a process of conditioned responses has now been superseded by a more complex model of events. This model might be represented as illustrated in figure 58a which is based on Bernstein's depiction of learning as a type of self-regulating system. Although the terminology differs from that used in Bernstein's (1957) picture of things, Anochin (1967) and associates explained the underlying theory of learning a technique along similar lines (fig. 58b). This theory is so frequently referred to in literature on technique training, that Anochin's explanation is briefly outlined thus: incoming information is supplied by two types of afferent.

(1)   The situation afferent embraces all environmental stimuli and consequently includes stimuli both relevant and irrelevant via the sensory organs (proprioceptors). Recollected stimuli may also be included. This area of afference causes an integration of the nervous processes which precede the causal afferent.
(2)   The causal afferent is the 'reading' of the situation afferent and selection of the relevant from the irrelevant.

This collective afference is referred to as the *afferent synthesis* and it concludes with the intention to act. Such intention is given expression by the *effector* apparatus. When afferent synthesis ends and action is effected, a specific afferent apparatus is formed which is called the *action acceptor*. This compares the afferent synthesis (the plan of action) with the completed action on which information is brought back via situation and causal afferents. If there is agreement, the cycle is complete. If not, new reactions are formed as the difference between planned and achieved action is assessed, and corrections made as the effector apparatus modifies the original action until agreement is reached.

In cybernetics, this concept of reafference is referred to as back-coupling or feedback. Principal types of reafferent may be classified as follows.

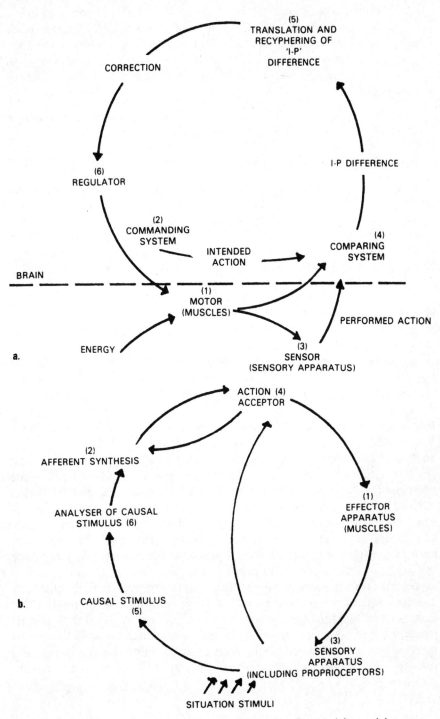

Fig. 58 *Events in the learning process (a) based on Bernstein's model; (b) based on Anochin's model (Numbered to help comparison)*

(1)   Kinaesthetic afferents, which are represented by proprioception.

(2)   Resultant afferents, which comprise all afferent characteristics which relate to the result of the completed action. However, all new actions arise from previous actions and those new actions will in turn form the basis for future actions. Hence Anochin's (1967) subdivision of resultant afferents:

- **episodic** reafferent, which provides information on intermediate actions
- **final** reafferent, which provides information on the final execution of the original plan of action.

The suggested existence of an afferent synthesis confirms the importance of factors such as training environment, motivation and a complete understanding of a given technique by the coach, while the action acceptor emphasises the importance of previous experience and a complete understanding of a given technique by the athlete. It rests with the coach to ensure that such factors are carefully assessed if technical training is to be efficient.

■ Senses and the afferent syntheses

Although we traditionally recognise five senses: visual, auditory, taste, smell, and touch, thirty such sensor receptions exist. Internal and external proprioreceptors register signals which form a complex support system often underutilised by the performer in sport. Visual stimuli often lead the sensory complex, however, other sensations affect the performer such as the feel of the weight and size of the ball used by the footballer or basketball player, or the smell of the chalk on asymmetric bars. Established Soviet and Czech coaching methodologies have long made successful use of sport-specific leading senses within the sensory complex. This is known as the afferent synthesis (see p. 156) providing the performer with permanent information prior to, during and following performance. The motor learning of an activity includes an appropriate breakdown of the skill, identifying and reinforcing the afferent synthesis. For example, a breakdown of high jump technique (Dick, 1993) can easily include the appropriate development of the leading analyser which will of course be athlete-determined (table 22).

During the movement series the leading senses are dynamically changed according to the demands of the movements of the body. If for instance the high jumper fails to clear the bar, knocking it off with the left lower leg, then the afferent synthesis will automatically facilitate greater attention to the awareness of the activity of the left lower leg in the next attempt. The performer is informed through this mechanism at every moment.

Table 22 *Model technique analysis sheet for the Fosbury Flop* (adapted from work by G. Tidow)

FOSBURY FLOP	PHASE	REFERENCE	CRITERION	LEADING ANALYSER SENSORY REINFORCEMENT	ASSESSMENT

	I Approach PENULTI-MATE STRIDE	A 1 foot plant
		     2 body/trunk
		     3 arms
		B 4 front supp.
		BC 5 supp. knee
		B 6 rear arm
		C 7 arms
			ball contact/curved path
			inclination/slight forward lean
			counter arm swing
			heel lead
			yielding
			held back
			parallel/behind trunk
				Visual as look for spot above the bar;
				Kinaesthetic as feel high knees to penultimate stride.	

	II Approach LAST STRIDE	D 8 trunk 9 supp. leg DF 10 take-off leg E 11 arms F 12 body/trunk F 13 foot plant EF 14 free leg	upright horizontal pushing action fast & active plant/pre-tension/'long' starting double swing inclination/backward lean 'through' the bar/optimal take-off pos bending/forward-upward movement	*Kinaesthetic* as feel tall; *Auditory* as hear foot plant; signal then to initiate upward push; *Kinaesthetic* as feel arms then lean.	
	III TAKE-OFF	FG 15 take-off leg FH 16 arms FH 17 free leg GH 18 free knee H 19 arms H 20 shoulders H 21 body	minimal & passive yielding active double arm swing active knee drive 'opening'/block in horizontal pos. blocked/bent lifted/horizontal vertical/parallel to upright	*Kinaesthetic* as feel arm swing & knee drive.	
	IV RISING OPENING	I 22 head I 23 outside arm IK 24 body IK 25 arms IK 26 free leg K 27 back K 28 head	view; along the bar 'leading' longitudinal axis rotation 'opening' lowering parallel to bar backward movement	*Visual* as spot over the bar; *Kinaesthetic* as feel body opening; feel rising.	
	V LAYOUT	KL 29 arms L 30 hips L 31 legs L 32 back L 33 head L 34 longit. axis	extended/'diving action' hyperextended/elevated bent/directed downwards 'arched' thrown back rectangular to bar	*Kinaesthetic* awareness of back & hips; exaggerate arched feeling.	
	VI RECOVERY	LM 35 pelvis M 36 head/trunk M 37 hips M 38 legs M 39 arms	active lowering 're-active' countermovement active bending synchronous active knee extension bending	*Kinaesthetic* acknowledgement of lowering of pelvis; *Visual* as see clearance of legs.	
	VII PREPARA-TION FOR LANDING	NO 40 head NO 41 hips NO 42 arms NO 43 body NO 44 legs	raised bent/blocked spreading in 'L-position' extended/directed upwards	*Kinaesthetic* with raised head; maintain 'L' shape feeling.	

In a competitive situation emotions can block the awareness of the afferent synthesis. Given this likelihood, the athlete should take the opportunity to engage an appropriate mental training technique. Similarly, following error, the athlete can make use of a compatible technique such as successful imagery or relaxation. Team and individual sports competitors use a range of mental training techniques reasonably successfully. The coach can ensure that the athlete/player has the opportunity to undertake such training with a specialist input. Useful mental training methods are integrated with technical training, optimising training conditions for the athlete. The athlete must be able to analyse the afferent synthesis so that he can read the appropriate sense and use it for anticipatory purposes. Beginners do not have this sense and so may find themselves stretched. For example, the young soccer player may pass the ball behind an oncoming team-mate. Anticipation together with the process of cognition gives the prediction and prognosis of events. It is sensible for the coach to include this type of training within the planning of competitive conditions.

The creativity of the coach will determine the effectiveness of such specialised input. Selected attention to specific performance components requires a thorough analysis of the movement by the coach, aided by video analysis, videographics or photo sequences, etc. demonstrating the movement of the limbs and/or entire body. Joint angles and the synchronisation of joint movements using the recorded locations of the limbs provides objective movement measurement. Electromyographic (EMG) recordings also record the movement in a muscle by establishing the electrical activity associated with the contraction of muscles specific to a response. The weak signal within the targeted muscle is amplified and then stored on a polygraph recorder for later analysis. Such a procedure can also be used to identify any associated signals when using imagery.

Internal imagery is primarily kinaesthetic in nature as the athlete feels himself performing whilst 'seeing out' from within his own body. External imagery is considered to be visual as the athlete pretends to watch himself perform from the outside. Internal (kinaesthetic) imagery has been proven a superior method given that it results in actual subliminal muscle activity in the muscles associated with the imagined actions (Mahoney & Avener, 1977). Both internal and external imagery skills should be developed.

Without doubt, one of the most powerful and effective technological aids in development of technique and technical application through imagery will come through the interactive potential of virtual reality.

With the need to develop the leading sensory channel, and the dynamic change of leading channels, a variety of practices should be designed. Approaching the hanging ball from different directions will assist the footballer with the skill of heading; the rugby team warming up for the game can increase the kinaesthetic feeling for the ball by passing the ball around the body and on to the next person in a circular formation, altering the activity whilst standing on one foot; the tennis player maintaining a bouncing tennis ball on the racquet whilst keeping a balloon off the ground with his foot couples sensory awareness with the attention required for a specific activity.

The kinaesthetic sense is often regarded as the dark sense as it is difficult to know what is sensed by the muscular apparatus. However, appropriate skill breakdown where the sensory complex is managed and reinforced will enable the performer to exert control over this automatic process. The actual breakdown and integrated series of practices, as with the high jumper, will help the athlete learn control at a conscious level. This type of sensory training shadows the athlete through his skill development. At the initial stages of games learning, activities for children involving throwing a variety of suitable objects such as soft miniature items and balls will introduce sensory awareness. Likewise an élite javelin thrower can benefit from increased kinaesthetic awareness of the hand by changing the throwing implement with emphasis on good technical form. Where every activity has a specific complexity of afferent synthesis, both coach and athlete can explore training opportunities to reinforce appropriate sensory perception. Patience is required as motor learning is not directly observable. However, practice and subsequent learning is relatively permanent; the athlete following such input will change in some way whether it be in how an activity is viewed or approached.

▪ Learning

Learning is a process involving the acquiring of increased skill capability. A series of internal processes associated with practice or experience will influence this capability for skilled behaviour, resulting in relatively permanent change. An individual will learn from the participation itself within an appropriate situation, and from the breakdown of skill. Whole and part approaches should be combined. To optimise later skill automaticity, part-skill practices should shape the first learning conditions. A learning ceiling is presumed when some success is experienced by a performer, however there is evidence to suggest that further practice brings about continued skill enhancement due to 'overlearning' (Schmidt, 1988), as opposed to learning beyond the original learning goal. Given the possibility of further improvements in performance, the learning design should facilitate adequate opportunity:

part skill – whole/modified
part skill – whole/less modified
part skill – whole/realistic situation
part skill – whole/game situation

Basic skills should be mastered sequentially to arrive at precise task performance. Whether premier division football, first division rugby or NBA basketball, fundamental errors are apparent particularly during emotive periods of the game; related consequences including breakdown in discipline, increased likelihood of distraction, and inability to attend to situationally-appropriate information can be reduced given thorough learning.

Associated with this notion is that of effort. As an athlete learns a motor skill, the subsequent execution of that skill requires less effort (Kahneman, 1973) leaving the athlete freer to attend to game/event specific information. Learning should allow the athlete processing and movement efficiency. Every life activity is directed by a high level of automisation of the basic elements of sensory and motor control. Given that the athlete must be able to concentrate on a range of game/event induced aspects if performance is to be successful, information processing should not be overloaded. Automaticity infers that skills do indeed become more automatic thus interfering less with other tasks. Learning occurring in the overlearning phase reduces attentional load and, according to Schneider and Fisk (1983), allows more accurate secondary task performance. Such improvement can perhaps be attributed to less interference from the main task.

■ Standard situation learning

The part-whole system must respect the most frequently occurring situations in the game/event and, taking advantage of existing technology, analyse each situation. Statistical analysis reveals such standard situations, which will then direct the central content of the whole learning to be automated by the athlete. It is the same for the co-acting athlete from an individual sport as it is for the interacting athlete within a team sport. Practice variation is vital. The athlete must become a sports-literate individual, able to read internal and external cues which enhance the execution of performance activities.

▌ Aims of technical training

The general aims of technical training are as follows.

(1) To direct the athlete's learning and perfect the most efficient technique(s) relative to a given sport. This demands that the coach has a complete understanding of the sport and its particular technical demands, of the athlete's present capabilities and his potential development, of techniques used by other athletes who are enjoying success, of teaching and developmental methods, and so on. In short, the coach must establish a sound technical or biomechanical model, based on athlete and sport, towards which the coach must direct the athlete.

(2) To direct the athlete towards a stable performance of the learned technique. This implies a progressive 'opening' of the situation in which the athlete must perform the given technique. One might visualise an initial stage in the process where all conditions for learning are perfect and totally without distraction. A final stage might also be visualised where, irrespective of the bombardment of distracting factors and within biological limits, the performance of a given technique is as perfectly reproduced as if the situation was without interference. Environmental interference may come from wind and weather, apparatus, altitude, spectators or other athletes.

(3) A further aim might be considered for sports where the athlete is forced to make a rapid selection of correct technique from a reservoir of many. The coach must direct learning of this capacity. Thus, it is not only the techniques themselves that separate the weight lifter from the football player, but also the total nature of the competitions in which their techniques must be perfectly executed.

■ Classification of technique

Attempts have been made to classify technique. The three classifications are determined by the nature of technique: single or multiple; and the performance/competition situation: constant or variable. These classifications are listed opposite.

(1) Sports where a single technique determines the performance, and which are based on a constant technical model, where the structure of competition is relatively constant. This includes most track and field events, swimming, bowling, shooting, archery, etc. Any variation within the structure of competition is restricted to factors such as weather, competition surfaces, facilities and equipment, etc.

(2) Sports where a multiplicity of techniques determine the total performance, and where the structure of competition is relatively constant. Within each sport there exists a similarity of technical model between certain techniques, but each technique is identifiably quite separate. Constancy of technical performance is made possible by the structure of competition and the conscious differentiation of techniques. Into this category will come artistic gymnastics, dance, figure skating, diving, etc.

(3) Sports where a multiplicity of techniques may be demanded of a rapidly changing competition structure. Athletes here must select appropriate techniques to meet the changing demands of competition but must also master each technique in the 'reservoir' at the athlete's disposal. Into this category come all team sports, combat sports, sports where there are exchanges with an opponent (such as racquet games) and sports where environmental demands other than the opponent, (e.g. weather, terrain), necessitate rapid and/or accurate selection of the most expedient technique (sailing, climbing, golf, canoeing, etc.).

The development of technical training must follow a different course for each classification.

Class 1
• Develop the technique in a closed situation (e.g. without environmental or competitive interference) as a 'performance'.
• Introduce a progressively open situation (e.g. more variables) while maintaining the 'performance' approach.
• Introduce a progressive intensity of competition.
• The general progression is from performing a technique to applying the technique in competition. In some cases the latter demands greater application of strength, speed, etc., (e.g. long jumps) while in others, accuracy of performance is essential (e.g. shooting).

Class 2
• Develop each technique separately and in an order which permits the learning of each to proceed without the interference of the other.
• Again, the situation for learning each technique must be closed.
• The situation is now opened through the use of other equipment, different facilities, etc. It may also be opened through a combination of techniques in movement sequences, etc.
• This progression may be pursued throughout the athlete's future development as new techniques are introduced and new permutations and combinations of these techniques are advanced.

• Introduce a progressive intensity of competition.
• Here the progression develops accuracy of reproduction in performance of techniques.

Class 3
• Develop each technique separately in a closed situation and in an order which permits no mutual interference.
• The situation is opened primarily by applying the technique in a changing situation (e.g. active opposition, varying climbs, sets, etc.).
• The athlete must also be exposed to technical adjustments necessitated by varying playing conditions, weather, etc. A more complex opening is where one of several techniques may be chosen by the athlete in the face of active opposition or varying terrain.
• Introduce a progressive intensity of competition or climb, etc.
• Here the progression is from learning and developing each technique to learning to select the correct technique for given competition demands.

Technique may also be classified by considering the aim of each technique. On this basis, Dyatchkov (1967) offered the following classifications.

(1) Sports where the aim of technique is to express intensive strength of brief duration within the ideal technical model, such as sprints, jumps, throws, weight lifting.
(2) Sports where the aim is endurance development with an optimal expression of strength. This embraces middle and long distance running, skiing, rowing, swimming, cycling.
(3) Sports where the aim of technique is development of those physical abilities which permit accuracy of performance of movements within a prescribed programme. This includes gymnastics, trampolining, figure skating, diving.
(4) Sports where the aim is the solution of those complex problems associated with interplay of athletes and/or environment, i.e. team games, combat sports, racquet games.

Despite these attempts to classify technique, certain activities may fall within several categories. However, the aim of classification is primarily to establish the planned technical development of an athlete. Consequently it is sufficient that the coach identifies the specific aim of technique for an athlete in a given sport. Having done so, it then rests with the coach's knowledge of anatomy, biomechanics, physiology, rules of the given sport, experience within that sport, the status of the athlete, and so on, to formulate a plan of technical development.

■ Learning technique
In general terms, it would appear that the learning process follows the pattern indicated in table 23. However, it will be recognised that the athlete arriving at stage 1, equipped with many (if not all) of the basic components of the total technique to be learned and with a sound back-

ground of general conditioning, is better prepared to advance through the stages than the athlete with little experience or conditioning to call upon. Returning to the concept of the learning process, one might suggest that it is in the interest of the athlete to be exposed to an education of basic movement components in pursuit of providing a more sophisticated action acceptor. Physical education appears to have focused emphasis on increasing the scope of a child's 'movement experience'. If such experience moves from the general and extends along a specific avenue of activity, it seems logical to anticipate the natural evolution of 'fundamental components'. From these fundamental components, highly specialised techniques may develop (fig. 59). The concept of fundamental components, and the development of exercises based on them, has been used in gymnastics in the German Democratic Republic (GDR) and it would appear that the concept could be applied to other sports.

Table 23 *Outline of learning stages in the acquisition of techniques*

stage or phase	morphological/ functional	regulative/ neural	teaching/coaching methods and conditions
1. Irradiation of stimulation processes	First concept of movement is learned, followed by an attitude to its learning.		Previously acquired related knowledge plus general total concept of action influence this stage.
2. Irradiation of stimulation processes	First ability to perform action and first acquisition of the action i.e. the basic form of the action is performed.	There is a generalisation of motor reactions together with muscle tensions and unnecessary movement, brought about by irradiation of stimuli to neighbouring areas of the cerebral cortex.	Teaching objective is to produce an accurate basic action and eliminate unnecessary movements, etc. Demonstration and film accompanied by verbal instruction (simple) is indicated. Training must be concentrated but too frequent repetition within a training unit will fatigue the beginner and impede learning.
3. Concentration through development of inhibitory processes.	Correction, refinement and differentiation. Finer co-ordination of movement.	Concentration of focus of cerebral cortex processes. Movement is accepted more fully into the consciousness and in greater detail. Individual phases of movement become stabilised. Proprioceptors begin to take a leading role.	Detailed learning of the movement is now worked on. Methods based on kinaesthesis (the feel of the movement) are used. Intervals between training units can now be increased, as can the number of repetitions within each unit.

Table 23 *(continued)*

stage or phase	morphological/ functional	regulative/ neural	teaching/coaching methods and conditions
4. Stabilisation and Automisation	High degree of precision in performing the action in a closed situation.	Complete harmony of neural processes where proprioceptors and cerebral cortex eliminate interference due to unnecessary movement; and rapid adjustment to changing conditions allows performance of a perfect action.	Stabilise action and perfect technical detail. Training is designed to eliminate variables and give opportunity for 'perfect' execution of the action.
5. Stabilisation and Automisation	Precision in performing the action in an open (more variable) situation.		Progressive development of physical capacities (e.g. strength, elastic strength, speed, etc.) necessary for long-term development in performance.

Establishing exercises based on components demands a detailed knowledge of the original technique used. Each of these exercises must have the greatest possible range of application in techniques within its sphere, yet the essence of the component must not be destroyed by further breakdown or modification of parts. This suggests the possibility of derivatives. Derivatives of the first degree coincide with the essential parts of the component, whilst derivatives of the second degree are characterised by comprising only some of the essential parts of the component. It will be appreciated, then, that the role of these components in the GDR research was in two parts.

(1) *The integrating role* (establishing the complete technical model from the components),
(2) *The differentiating role* (establishing stability of the technical model by ensuring an ability to clearly separate one technique from another, correct movement from wrong movement, and so on). From this, and similar work, some important points emerge:

- when the first component learned is one that unites as many parts as possible of the final technique, learning time is reduced
- learning time for differentiation is also reduced by this approach
- the use of first degree derivatives does not demand stability of the component, but second degree derivatives must not be introduced until the component is stable, otherwise there will be negative interference.

Each component must be constantly related to the whole technique. This is most important where the derivative is of the second degree, or where the derivative of the first degree contains a limited range of essential

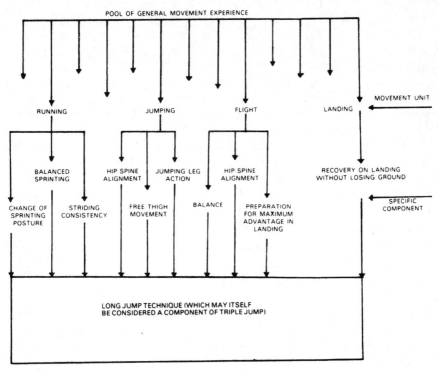

Fig. 59 *The development of specific technique via fundamental components*

parts. Harre has noted (1973) that athletes who learned derivatives of the first and second degree, by conscious acquisition of fundamental exercise, and who were made to differentiate consciously, proved, when learning new movements, to be more capable of distinguishing the details of the movement and performing them with accuracy. A progressive development in ability was noted with the increasing mastery of varying exercises.

The athlete must be offered the benefit of expert guidance during the learning of technique. Consequently the practice of providing instruction for beginner-athletes via novice coaches might be the basis of a poor technical education which will make itself evident at a later date in faulty technique.

■ Faults and corrections

Without the assistance of sophisticated equipment, the coach offers instruction based upon the comparison of a 'mental' technical model and what may be readily perceived. There are very obvious limitations to what *can* be perceived at any one time, so the coach relies mainly on experience of cause and effect. The immediately apparent problems are that coaches have varying amounts of experience and even with experience, cause and effect are not always easily identifiable. It is nevertheless essential to the athlete's development that accurate information is readily available when kinaesthetic impression and concept of movement are fresh in the athlete's mind. If there is no immediate feedback for the athlete, there is considerable risk of stabilisation of faults.

In order to provide immediate feedback to the athlete, the coach must consider use of polaroid photo-sequence cameras, video tape, film, kinographs, print-outs on force components, velocities, etc., photo-electric apparatus, computerised segmental analysis, and so on. Even if some of this equipment is not readily available for showing the athlete's own performance (e.g. video tape), it should still be possible to show the *correct* technique where the athlete is not matching the technical model (e.g. film, photo-sequences, demonstration, etc.). The efficiency of technique might be evaluated in one or several of the following broad categories of method.

(1)   As implied above, evaluating the athlete's technique against the technical model. This approach is used in many so-called 'skill tests', with the athlete 'scored' against norms. It is also used in comparative analysis of the athlete with another athlete known to be technically proficient, or of the athlete with a film of himself performing a technically proficient jump at some previous date and so on. Filming techniques, photo-sequence techniques, light-track photography techniques, or standard testing techniques may be applied to this type of evaluation.

(2)   Another type of method is the comparison of actual performance with theoretical performance. For example, a comparison of the height through which the athlete raises his centre of gravity with the height actually jumped in a high jump competition. This method may be extended to include comparison of performance with related criteria in standard tests.

Thus, the long jump athlete may compare competition long jump performance with, on the one hand, standing long jump, sargent jump, 30m sprinting speed, and so on, or, on the other hand, the horizontal velocity and parabola of flight of the athlete's centre of gravity. Again, filming techniques and a knowledge of related standard tests may be applied.

(3)   A third class of method evaluates a particular technique relative to its success or failure against opposition. Thus, technique is evaluated on the basis of training advantage in attack over defence or, conversely, in gaining advantage from defence over attack. It could be argued of course that, in this instance, tactics rather than technique are being evaluated in, for example, team games. Filming techniques are essential to this class of evaluation.

Despite detailed and expert planning, it is nevertheless possible for faults to arise. Before any attempt is made to correct such faults, the exact cause or causes must be determined. This is emphasised because, due to the fact that 'effect' is more readily recognised, the coach may occasionally reduce the effect of a fault, rather than eliminate the cause. It is also important to assess how well established the fault has become. Faults that come to light during the early stages of learning are less difficult to correct than those which have become stabilised to such an extent that they are almost a part of the athlete's technique. Possible causes of faults are listed below.

During learning

misinterpretation of kinaesthesis and/or poor motor ability

misunderstanding of concept of movement

negative interference from another technique

insufficient previous experience of components

interference of a poor learning environment (e.g. cold, poor equipment)

premature introduction of strength and/or speed in technique

lack of physical abilities required of technique (e.g. strength, mobility)

fear of injury

poor demonstration and/or explanation of technique

impropitious timing of technique training relative to athlete's growth and maturation

Well established

rational technique has not been learned

technique was not established before competitions were introduced

athlete has known the fault but has lacked either guidance for correction or knowledge of the correct movement

due to poor status of physical abilities in learning, compensating movements have been introduced

the technique is incompatible with the athlete's physical structure of levers

coach has been lacking in knowledge as the athlete has progressed. (A technique which has brought success at a lower level, may be inappropriate at a higher level)

poor training conditions

injury has caused compensatory movements

poorly organised training programme

Correction should always ensure the athlete's understanding of the technical model, the fault and the correction. This is vital because frequently athletes who are technically lacking in proficiency may produce superior performances and the novice may seek to follow *that* technique because it produces favourable results. Faults must be discovered and corrected early. To delay will stabilise the fault and possibly cause a stagnation in performance. Moreover, should the athlete 'grow with the fault' then any attempt at correction becomes more difficult. This is due to the basic inertia of an entrenched pattern and also because performance in general will fall below that recorded when the 'wrong' technique is used, thereby causing a loss of confidence in the process of developing a correct technique. Finally, the additional time required to correct a well established fault is hard to justify when the time should be directed towards improving an athlete's performance.

Correction may be pursued by contrasting faulty and correct technique via film or demonstration, guiding the correct action, encouraging the athlete to exaggerate the action, working on an individual faulty component, arranging that faulty performance is impossible, and practising the movement with, for example, the *other* leg or arm. The progressive replacement of a faulty technique with a correct technique appears to advance in four stages. The time span involved varies with the stability and nature of the fault.

Stage 1: the faulty technique asserts itself whenever concentration is lost. The correct technique is occasionally reproduced.

Stage 2: neither the faulty nor the correct techniques are strong enough to dominate, so there is frequently a confusing or mixing of techniques. The correct technique is reproduced more frequently.

Stage 3: there is a conscious differentiation, with the correct technique only occasionally lost, in fatigue, stress, etc.

Stage 4: complete stability of correct technique.

Opinions differ on the relative merits of massed and distributed practice as the athlete learns technique. Personal experience, in the absence of conclusive evidence, suggests an initial massing of practice until the whole activity can be put together, then a gradual separation of practice units.

■ General points on technical training units

It is impossible to be dogmatic in determining exact durations for technique training units because individual athletes vary not only in their capacity for concentration but also in their status of physical abilities. Several points might be made, however, as a basis for establishing suitable unit construction in technique training.

(1) Concentrated technique work should not go beyond 20 minutes without a break.

(2) The prospect of a long unit of technique work prepares the athlete for an extended distribution of effort. Consequently a prolonged unit must be divided into sub-sections, possibly with each section having a separate emphasis.

(3) Reduction of fatigue improves motivation, not only within the session but from day to day. Thus, within a training workout a technique training unit must come before a conditioning unit and a 'technical day' should not be preceded by a heavy 'conditioning day'.

(4) A compromise must be effected between maintaining the excited state of the neuromuscular system and allowing recovery from a previous effort. This will be individually arrived at. It would appear that during recovery from technical training there is a perseveration of neural processes. This may be because when intense external stimulation ceases, internal consolidation occurs. It has also been suggested that organisms are refractory to (resist) early repetition of an act.

(5)   During recovery there may be a tendency for incorrect associations to be 'forgotten' faster than correct ones. This could be due to the non-existence of positive reinforcements.

(6)   In technical development, unit construction should be so arranged that all practices are related to the given technique, unless the objective of the unit is to develop the ability to differentiate techniques, select appropriate techniques, put together a sequence of techniques, etc. Practices may be related by similarity of content, technique, principles, etc. It should be appreciated that these practices are techniques or sports in themselves and are not to be confused with components.

(7)   Only one technical point should be considered at any one time.

(8)   Adapt sport to athlete before adapting athlete to sport. This principle should be followed unless adapting the sport creates a wrong basis for development. Thus, hurdles are reduced in height and spacing, and 'mini' ball games are developed.

(9)   Approximately 80% of what is learned is from visual stimuli, so correct demonstration or a well explained film is more appropriate than words alone.

(10)   It is important to note that the novice athlete must be given expert technical instruction when being introduced to sport. Conversely, the novice coach must not be used as teacher of the novice athlete.

(11)   'Repetition is the mother of learning.' The athlete must know the correct technique(s) to repeat and be fit enough to perform sufficient repetitions without fatigue-induced compensations creeping in.

(12)   The progressions of adding endurance, resistance or speed to development of technique can only be introduced within the limits of keeping the technical model intact. To continue technique work without an intact technical model, can lead to 'chronic' rather than 'acute' technical errors.

(13)   When technique breaks down, it is essential that 'rebuilding' is done at a slower overall speed. The speed should be such that the athlete can feel the correct sequence of individual body segment contribution to the technique.

(14)   Because concentration and freedom of movement are fundamental to learning technique, conditions must be favourable. A warm, windless environment without interfering variables such as noise or distracting movements must be available. However, once the technical model is well established, the athlete must learn to keep technique intact in a climate where hostile variables increase in number and degree.

(15)   There appears to be little difference in the methods used in teaching techniques to both women and men. However, there can be variance in the techniques of men and women – even in the same discipline.

(16)   Children may not be equipped to learn techniques used by mature élite performers. It is the basic technical model which the young athlete learns, and not some sophisticated elaboration of that model.

█ Summary

Fundamental to the athlete's long-term development is the learning of sound technique. The coach directs such learning and works towards stability of technique through technical training. The classification of technique determines its course of development but, broadly speaking, coaching method is geared to various learning stages. An interpretation of cybernetic theory affords an explanation of the concept of learning. Within the framework of this concept the coach will identify the role of fundamental components, the need for accurate identification and speedy correction of faults, and the importance of providing the beginner athlete with the best available technical expertise.

12
Psychological changes and the growing child

The coach should be aware of the various stages of development through which the child must progress towards adulthood. The age divisions which follow are offered as guidelines and their appropriateness will vary according to individual rates of development, male/female differences, the differential effect elicited by society, and a host of other variables too numerous to list.

General patterns

Early primary school (5–7 years of age)
By the age of 5 the child has developed a wide range of abilities and skills and individual differences are already apparent. Whilst heredity plays a major role in this individuality, the seeds from which many psychological functions and characteristics of the developing personality have grown (and will grow) are to be found in the many forms of play which constitute the major activity of the child through the early primary school years. He is emotional, thinks graphically, seems to live in a world of half fantasy and half reality, has mastered a wide vocabulary and its use, and thinks rapidly in short, intense bursts which is a mark of mental agility rather than a lack of ability to concentrate. The roles he adopts in play are drawn most accurately from his immediate social environment and, towards the end of this period in primary school, relationships with other children become more stable.

During these formative years, the importance of play must be stressed in the introduction of sport because it is through play that the child develops. His imagination must be stimulated, with success attainable. Above all, activities must be intrinsically enjoyable. Award schemes (and variations) are extremely valuable at this stage for they offer a framework within which it is possible to shape the pupil's behaviour.

Finally, it is worth noting that psychological characteristics developed by the age of 5 may be dampened by the imposition of school discipline at that age. In most other cultures, school is postponed at least one year. It becomes clear then that the play concept must be the key to maintaining the impetus of developing in a broadening social world, as represented by the school. A guided play approach achieves better results when learning motor skills than does free play. The teacher plays an important part in the child's life at this time. Possibly the coach could

173

come to fulfil a parallel role in terms of an early introduction of the child to coaching in certain sports (e.g. gymnastics).

Primary–secondary school bridge (8–11/13 years of age)

This period may be described as a gentle shift from naive realism to critical realism. At the beginning of this period, the child is acquiring knowledge of the world without understanding relationships nor trying to see what lies behind reality. Nevertheless, he concentrates on the detail of his environment and can be analytical in perception, memory and thought. His power of concentration is still unstable, so the teacher or coach should avoid lengthy explanations. Variety both in content and method are prerequisites to successful instruction. Throughout this period, the child often requires guidance in the stabilising of social relationships and experimentation in group situations should be encouraged and closely observed.

As the period progresses, the child becomes capable of concentrating on specific tasks for longer periods of time and begins to seek logical connections and generalisations. As intellectual development progresses so does his play. Early play experiences (before 5 years of age) are to gain mastery over his environment and, having achieved this, past successes are reenacted in a symbolic manner as play develops towards the formality of the game situation. The trend, then, is away from imagination and towards logical thinking. Also worth noting is that children towards the end of this period will have a well developed ability to memorise.

This period also marks the separation of the sexes in that acceleration towards maturity is greater in girls. One consequence of this is that interests become extremely varied between the sexes. Emotions, while well balanced and optimistic early in this period, can begin to shift towards a less carefree profile. Consequently at the end of this period the child has completely altered physically, intellectually, socially and emotionally. Most children will already have entered the period of adolescence.

Mid-secondary or early leaving (11/13–16 years of age)

The start of this period is a whirlwind of change in every characteristic mentioned earlier. Learning becomes an intellectual exercise and productive activity assumes a major role. More social opportunity is now available and relationships within the family unit assume a different form. Social and physiological changes result in emotional imbalance and instability of mood. The young person's uncritical self-assurance is replaced by a fluctuation between esteem and doubt as he gradually pieces together a concept of himself from the collective impression he has of how others see him. This situation is a crucial factor in formation of attitudes which the young athlete in this age range will have towards participation in sport. For example, how he sees himself in the eyes of his peers may influence whether or not he will continue his commitment to pursuit of competitive advantage.

This phase over, the adolescent moves to the final phase in this period. The agitation and disharmony of the first phase gives way to inner assurance which is linked with a visible increase in social capacity. Hopefully the society in which he grows will not only make high demands of him, but will grant him the right to, and every possibility for, an all-round development of personality and, in particular, progressive situations demanding responsibility. Intellectual development reaches a near-adult level and his attitudes are consciously critical and searching in pursuit of independence of opinion and judgement. The teacher and coach must bear in mind this developmental continuum if the child is to grow within the social framework of the 'club' in particular, and the sport of his choice, in general. Throughout his development, the sport should be adapted to the child before the child is taught how to adapt to the sport. The spirit, not the letter, of both constitutive and reguiative rules and regulations should be applied to afford an attractive and flexible framework within which the child will be attracted to express himself. Gradually, by careful planning of his programme of sports education, the 'official rules' will replace this flexible framework without prejudicing his interest, enthusiasm or enjoyment.

As the adolescent moves towards the 17–22 year age group, the personality fills out around those basic characteristics evolved up to this period. More and more, however, that personality will seek to stamp itself upon the society about it, and our society (i.e. sport) must learn to accommodate rather than adapt it.

Motor learning characteristics

Early primary school (5–7 years of age)
The period of development probably begins around 3–4 years of age when a few basic forms of movement are at his disposal. He can crawl, walk, pull, swing, climb, clamber, jump down, run, throw from standing, jump low heights and short distances, and can both catch and kick a ball. Already a preference to left or right is evident. In the course of development, all these forms of movement are improved in quality and their repetition seems endless. The first combined movements (rather than movements in sequence) can be seen, i.e. running and jumping, high throwing and catching, running and throwing, running and slinging, running over low barriers in balance, jumping onto objects, running to swing on a rope, and so on. Consequently by the end of this period it is possible to carry out all-round exercise with plenty of variety and intensity of movement.

For many reasons, little is known of the development of physical abilities (e.g. strength) in this age group. However, it has been shown that speed of movement is only very slightly developed and does not reach more significant values until 9–10 years of age (e.g. up to 8 years of age, reaction time is in excess of 0.5 seconds). Also, as far as can be assessed, strength and agility are not well developed at this stage. On the other hand, mobility and aerobic endurance are well developed towards the end of this period. The explanation of the former lies in the elasticity of the movement apparatus and the looseness of joints whilst the latter is well developed due to the varied and active play activity. At this stage, we must employ a general approach to improve strength by using body weight and apparatus together with light resistances such as medicine balls and sling balls, as well as to improve the co-ordination of movement at speed. The introduction of many skills is quite practicable at this stage and the following may be borne in mind:

- these youngsters have a powerful but uncontrolled and non-directed joy in movement
- they can concentrate for very short spells
- they are undeveloped in their direction of effort
- they are limited in their capacity for motor learning
- they have a weak retention for what has been learned
- group consciousness is limited and exercising individually or in very small groups is recommended.

Primary–secondary school bridge (8–11/13 years of age)
This is without doubt the most important period in the progress of motor ability. It is that phase of development in which already familiar forms of movement are vastly improved and many new ones learned and stabilised, often without instruction. This is well demonstrated in activities such as roller skating, ice skating and cycling. New movement patterns are frequently mastered at the first attempt, following suitable demonstrations, concise explanation and one or two trials and accurate corrections. This period has been termed 'the age of specific achievement' or 'the child's best age for learning'. Almost all measures of physical achievement have their greatest rate of improvement at this stage, with speed, agility and aerobic endurance showing the most outstanding rises. Mobility, however, will decline shortly after this period begins and considerable work must be done to improve upon, or even maintain, the levels already acquired.

During these years, the youngster may develop a keen interest in sport, an enthusiasm for learning sport skills, a love of activity, an uninhibited attitude in the learning situation, and an increasing ability to embrace the value of learning athletic skills. Everything, then, is on the side of the educator, for the youngster wants and has the ability to learn, and enjoys an activity and its related practices. There is a longing for achievement and for challenge. Consequently, training loading can already be quite high provided the principle of gradual progression to sub-maximal load-ings (80–90%) has been strictly followed. Particular caution is urged in speed endurance and strength training. The former is known to be amongst the most severe stresses of athlete training and would certainly seem inadvisable at this stage. In addition it is debatable whether the youngster is well equipped to tolerate lactic-anaerobic stressors. Strength training is not advisable on the grounds of an unconsolidated skeletal structure to which only sub-maximal work should be offered as a load. With initiative and intelligent use of equipment and apparatus, the youngster should find sufficient resistance in the handling of his body weight. Certainly there is no justification at this stage for loading the spine by taking weights on the shoulders. Leg work is best done by other means and time would be better spent exercising the spine's own muscular apparatus.

Mid-secondary or early leaving (11/13–16 years of age)

Almost all physical ability statistics continue to show improvement through the traumatic phase of puberty (fig. 60). The neuromotor system should now have achieved full capacity and be able to offer a store of movement from which more and more complex permutations and combinations can be produced. From now on development will mean the increasing sophistication of technique, despite interference of environmental variables. In other words, the athlete now learns by instruction and experience to reproduce perfect movement despite wind, rain, temperature, opposition tactics, and so on. However, in the early years of this period, problems may arise in the shifting relationships of limb proportions. Such problems, should they occur, will affect co-ordinative ability, harmony of movement, ability to learn new skills, and motor adaptability. Agility suffers under these circumstances. The problems will manifest themselves in a temporary lack of performance stability, particularly where movement patterns were not learned in the 8–11/13 year old stage. This again underlines the importance of that stage and it is suggested that when such problems arise, no new skills be introduced but that work be done on the improvement and consolidation of known skills. It would be wrong, for example, to start working on hitch-kick, but right to spend time on stride-jump, in long jump, if this flight technique had been used up to this point.

Gradually, the youngster concludes the period of pubescence and slides gently into adolescence, which takes him towards adulthood and the relatively conclusive appearance of all physical and motor characteristics. A second opportunity now exists to introduce new patterns of movements, and progress towards sophistication mentioned earlier begins. Harre (1973) summarises this period as one of 'harmonisation, increased individualisation, relative stabilisation, and sex differentiation'.

With the relative conclusion of physical growth, untrained youngsters gradually reach their individual best achievements. This is illustrated in figure 60, which shows that girls mature at 15–16 years of age in contrast with boys at 18–20 years of age. Strength, elastic strength and endurance capacities are all highly trainable during this period and will continue to be so for several years. On the other hand, speed improvements become more difficult unless speed has been temporarily stagnated due to habitually low levels of stimulus (e.g. running with slower athletes, running solo, or running on slow tracks, etc.).

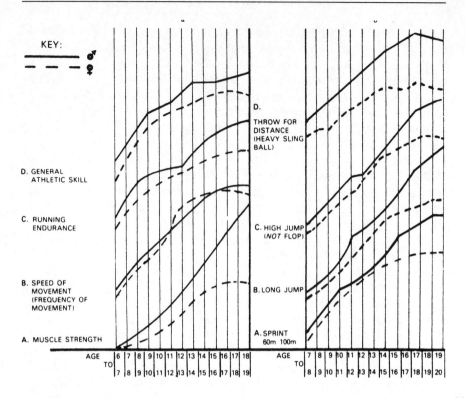

Fig. 60 *(a) Non-parametric representation of development, specific to age, of some physical characteristics* (from Smedley, Farfel, Jokl and Winter, 1959); *(b) Non-parametric representation of development, specific to age, of some basic athletic events* (from Peters, Stemmler and Janeff, 1959)

Summary

The coach clearly has a role to play in contributing to the education of the growing child. This brief outline of psychological and motor learning characteristics provides a basis for planning this contribution. Development of play constitutes an essential vehicle of total development and the concept of a progression from informal individual play through group games to the formality of organised sport, and serves as a framework within which the coach will develop the child's ability to express himself. The most critical period of technical development is suggested as 8–11 years of age (girls) and 8–13 years of age (boys). Sound technical expertise interpreted through play must be available in these years.

Summary of part 3

The coach works to improve the efficiency of energy production and of energy expression. At a simplistic level, this means getting the right fuel to the engine and making sure the engine can use it. But athletes are adaptable and creative and, unlike engines, become involved in their own development. The coach must, then, understand and be able to apply not just the 'technical business' but the 'people business'. *Both* are essential for the coach to be effective. So the coach must have a sound working knowledge of education and self-education in developing the athlete towards an independence in delivering a quality performance whether in an individual sport or a team sport and whether in a contributory role or a co-operative role within a team. The coach should understand the learning process, from the specific components which are moulded into a whole in developing an athlete's particular technique(s), through to the climate of emotional arousal, motivational environment, tentative maps of personality, and psycho-regulative phenomena which make every coach-athlete contact period far more unique than generic.

∎ References for part 3

Allport, G. W. (1961) *Pattern and Growth in Personality*. Holt, Rinehart & Winston, New York

Allport, G. W. (1937) *Personality*. Holt, Rinehart & Winston, New York

Allport, G. W., Vernon, P. E. and Lindzey, G. (1951) *A Study of Value: A Scale for Measuring the Dominant Interests in Personality*. Houghton & Mifflin, Boston

Anochin, D. K. (1967) *Das Funktionelle System Ais Grundlage Der Physiologischen Architektur Des Verhaltensaktes*. Veb Gustav Fischer Verlag, Jena

Apter, M. J. (1982) The experience of motivation. In *The Theory of Psychological Reversals*. Academic Press, London

Arkes, H. R. & Garske, J. P. (1982) *Psychological Theories of Motivation*. 2nd Edn. Brooks/Cole Publishing Company, Monterey, CA

Bandura, A. (1977) Self-efficacy: Toward a unifying theory of behaviourial change. *Psychological Review*, 84, pp191–215

Beggs, A. W. D. (1993) Goal setting in sport. In *Stress and Performance in Sport*, Jones, G. J. & Hardy, L. (eds.). Wiley, Chichester

Bernstein, N. A. (1957) *The Coordination and Regulation of Movements*. Pergamon Press, London

Biddle, S. J. H. (1995) Exercise motivation across the life span. In *European Perspectives on Exercise and Sport Psychology*, Biddle, S. J. H. (ed). Human Kinetics

Boutcher, S. H. (1993) The role of performance routines in sport. In *Stress and Performance in Sport*, Jones, G. J. & Hardy, L. (eds). Wiley, Chichester

Burton, D. (1990) Multimodal stress management in sport: current status and future directions. In *Stress and Performance in Sport*, Jones, G. J. and Hardy, L. (eds). Wiley, Chichester

Carron, A. V. & Ball, J. R. (1977) Cause and effect characteristics of cohesiveness and participation motivation in intercollegiate ice hockey. *International Review of Sport Sociology*, 12, pp49–60

Carron, A. V., Widmeyer, W. N. & Brawley, L. R. (1985) The development of an instrument to assess cohesion in sport teams: the Group Environment Questionnaire. *Journal of Sport Psychology*, 7, pp244–267

Cattell, R. B. (1965) *The Scientific Analysis of Personality*. Penguin, Baltimore

Cohen, F. and Lazarus, R. S. (1979) Coping with serious illness. In *Health Psychology*, G. S. Stone, F. Cohen and N. E. Adler (eds.). Freeman, San Francisco

Cox, R. H. (1990) *Sport Psychology. Concepts and Applications*. 2nd Edn. Wm. C. Brown

Davidson, R. J. and Schwartz, G. E. (1976) The psychobiology of relaxation and related states: a multi-process theory. In *Behavioral Control and Modification of Physiological Activity,* D. Mostofsky (ed.). Prentice Hall, Englewood Cliffs, NJ

Dick, F. (1992) *Winning – Motivation for Business, Sport and Life*. Abingdon, London

Dick, F. W. (1993) *High Jump*. British Athletic Federation. Birmingham

Dick, F. W. (1995) *Players Guide*. West Hartlepool Rugby Football Club

Doherty, J. K. (1963) *Modern Track and Field: Promotion, History and Methods*. Bailey & Swinfen, London

Dyatchkov, N. V. (1967) *Soversenstsvovanie Techniceskogo Masterstva Sportsmenov*. Fiskultura i Sport, Moscow

Evarts, E. V. (1973) Motor cortex reflexes associated with learned movement. *Science*, 179, pp501–503

Eysenck, H. J. & Eysenck, S. B. G. (1968) *Eysenck Personality Inventory Manual*. University of London Press, London

Freud, S. (1931) Libidinal Types, (1959) In *Sigmund Freud: Collected Papers Vol 5*, Strachey, J. (ed). Basic Books, New York

Fromm, E. (1947) *Man For Himself*. Holt, Rinehart & Winston, New York

Fromm, E. (1941) *Escape from Freedom*. Holt, Rinehart & Winston, New York

Fuoss, D. E. and Troppman, R. J. (1991) *Effective Coaching: A psychological approach*. Wiley, New York

Gallistel, C. R. (1980) *The Organisation of Action*. Erlbaum, Hillsdale, NJ

Gould, D. & Krane, V. (1992) The arousal-athletic performance relationship: Current status and future directions. In *Advances in Sport Psychology*, T. Horn (ed.), pp. 119–141. Human Kinetics, Champaign, IL

Gruber, J. J. & Gray, G. R. (1981) Factor patterns of variables influencing cohesiveness at various levels of basketball competition. *Research Quarterly for Exercise and Sport*, 52 pp 19–30

Gruber, J. J. & Gray, G. R. (1982) Responses to forces influencing cohesion as a function of player status and level of male varsity basketball competition. *Research Quarterly for Exercise and Sport*, 53, pp27–36

Harre, D. (1973) *Trainingslehre*. Sportverlag, Berlin

Harris, D. V., & Harris, B. L. (1984) *The Athlete's Guide to Sport Psychology: Mental skills for physical people*. Leisure Press, New York

Hollander, E. P. (1971) *Principles and Methods of Social Psychology*. Oxford University Press, New York

Huber, V. L. (1985) Effects of task difficulty goal setting, and strategy on performance of a heuristic task. *Journal of Applied Psychology*, 70, pp492–504

Ickes, W. J. & Layden, M. A. (1978) Attributional styles. In *New Directions in Attribution Research*, Vol. 2., J. H. Harvey, W. J. Ickes & R. Kidd (eds.), Erlbaum, Hillsdale, N. J.

Jacobson, E. (1929) *Progressive Relaxation*. University of Chicago Press, Chicago

Jones G. J. (1990) A cognitive perspective on the process underlying the relationship between stress and performance in sport. In *Stress and Performance in Sport*, Jones, G. J. and Hardy, L. (eds). Wiley, Chichester

Krech, D. & Crutchfield, R. S. (1962) *Elements of Psychology*. Alfred A. Knopf, New York

Landers, D. and Leuschen, G. (1974) Team performance outcome and cohesiveness of competitive co-acting groups. *International Review of Sport Sociology*, 2, pp57–69

Lenk, N. (1969) Top performance despite internal conflicts: An antithesis to a functionalistic proposition. In *Sport, Culture and Society: A reader on the sociology of sport*, J. W. Loy and G. S. Kenyon (eds), pp393–397. Macmillan, New York

Mahoney, M. J. & Avener, M. (1977) Psychology of the elite athlete: An exploratory study. *Cognitive Therapy and Research*, 1, pp135–141

Martens, R., Burton, D., Vealey, R. S., Bump, L. A. and Smith, D. E. (1990) The competitive state anxiety inventory-2 (CSAI2). In *Competitive Anxiety in Sport*, R. Martens, R. S. Vealey and D. Burton (eds). Human Kinetics, Champaign, IL

Martens, R. & Peterson, J. A. (1971) Group cohesiveness as a determinant of success and member satisfaction in team performance. *International Review of Sport Sociology*, 6, pp49–61

Maslow, A. H. (1954) *Motivation and Personality*. Harper & Row, New York

McClelland, D. C., Atkinson, J. W., Clark, R. W., & Lowell, E. L. (1953) *The Achievement Motive*. Appleton-Century-Crofts, New York

Munn, N. K. (1951) *Psychology–The Fundamentals of Human Adjustment*. 2nd Edn. Harrap & Co Ltd, London

Murray, P. F. (1996) *Cohesion, a perspective from operationalised coaching in co-acting and interacting sports*. Educational Research in 1995, Working Papers in Education. University of Wolverhampton

Murray, P. F. (1995) Integrated sport science support strategy: IS4. *BASES Newsletter, The British Association of Sport and Exercise Sciences*, 5, 2

Nideffer, R. M. (1985) *Athlete's Guide to Mental Training*. Human Kinetics, Champaign, IL

Orlick, T. (1986) *Psyching for Sport, Mental Training for Athletes*. Leisure Press, Champaign, IL

Pavlov, I. P. (1957) *I Rilfessi Condizionatti*. Einaudi, Torino

Peppler, M. (1977) *Inside Volleyball for Women*. Contemporary Books, Chicago

Schmidt, R. A. (1988) *Motor Control and Learning. A behavioural emphasis.* 2nd Edn. Human Kinetics

Schneider, W. & Fisk, A. D. (1983) Attention theory and mechanisms for skilled performance. In *Memory and Control of Action*, R. A. Magill (ed.), pp 119–143. North-Holland, Amsterdam

Schultz, J. H. & Luthe, W. (1959) *Autogenic Training: A psychophysiological approach to psychotherapy*. Grune and Stratton, New York

Selye, H. (1956) *The Stress of Life*. McGraw-Hill, New York

Singer, R. N. (1968) *Motor Learning and Human Performance*. Macmillan, New York

Straub, W. F. and Williams, J. M. (1984) Cognitive sport psychology: historical contemporary and future issues. In *Cognitive Sport Psychology*, W. F. Straub and J. N. Williams, (eds). Sport Science Associates, Lansing, New York

Tutko, T. A. & Richards, J. W. (1971) *Psychology of Coaching*. Allyn and Bacon, Boston

Vanek, M. & Cratty, B. J. (1970) *Psychology and the Superior Athlete*. MacMillan Co., Toronto

Vanek, M. (1967) *La structure de la preparation psychologique du sportif*. Atti. Simp. Int. Med. Psicosom. Sp., SIMP, Roma

Vanek, M. & Hosek, V. (1974) *Studie osobnosti ve sportu.* (Personality study in sport). Charles University, Prague

Vanek, M., Hosek, V. & Man, F. (1982) *Formovani vkkonove motivace.* (Forming of achievement motivation). Charles University, Prague

Weiner, B. (1985) An attributional theory of achievement motivation and emotion. *Psychological Review*, 92, pp548–573

Weinberg, R. S. & Gould, D. (1995) *Foundations of sport and exercise psychology.* Human Kinetics, Champaign

Williams, J. M. (1980) Personality characteristics of the successful female athlete. In W. F. Straub (ed.), *Sport psychology: An analysis of athlete behaviour* (2nd ed.). Ithaca, NY: Movement Publications

Yukelson, D., Weinberg, R. & Jackson, A. (1984) A multidimensional group cohesion instrument for intercollegiate basketball teams. *Journal of Sports Psychology*, 6 (1), pp103–117.

Bibliography

Alderman, R. B. (1974) *Psychological Behaviour in Sport.* W. B. Saunders, Philadelphia

Alderson, G. J. K. & Tyldesley, D. A. (1976) *British Proceedings of Sports Psychology.* F.E.P.S.A.C. Congress 1975, Leeds

Blanz, F., Kalliokoski, A., Suonperä, M. & Tomperi, K. (1973) *Urheiluvalmennuksen Psykologiaa*, S.V.U.K., Helsinki

Collective Authors (1974) *Beitrage Zur Sportspsychologie.* 2nd Edn. Sportverlag, Berlin

Collective Authors (1964) *The Seven Ages of Man.* New Society Reader, London

Gavreluk, V. & Korobkov, A. (March 1970) Psychological preparation of athletes. *Track Technique*, No 39. Los Altos, California

Kane, J. G. (1972) *Psychological Aspects of Physical Education and Sport.* Routledge & Kegan Paul, London

Knapp, B. (1967) *Skill in Sport.* Routledge & Kegan Paul, London

Loy, J. W. & Kenyon, G. S. (1969) *Sport, Culture and Society.* MacMillan Co., New York

McClelland, D. C. & Steele, R. S. (1973) *Human Motivation: A Book of Readings.* General Learning Press, New Jersey

Ogilvie, B. & Tutko, T. (1966) *Problem Athletes and How to Handle Them.* Pelham Books, London

Railo, W. S. (1970) *Iddretpsykologi.* Norges Idrettsforbund, Oslo

Robb, M. D. (1972) *The Dynamics of Motor-Skill Acquisition.* Prentice-Hall, New Jersey

Salminies, P. (1975) *Psychological Effects of Intensive Training.* Sport and Development of Youth, S.V.U.L., Helsinki

Whiting, H. T. A. (1975) *Readings in Sports Psychology.* Lepus Books, London

Whiting, H. T. A. (1975) *Concepts in Skill Learning.* Lepus Books, London

Wickstrom, R. L. (1970) *Fundamental Motor Patterns.* Lea & Febiger, Philadelphia

Wilson, J. R. (1972) *The Mind.* 3rd Edn. Time-Life International (Nederland) N.V., Amsterdam

Part 4

The language of training theory

In parts 1, 2 and 3, relevant aspects of the sports-related sciences have been reviewed. Parts 4 and 5 seek to draw together the practical implications of this review and, by considering these against a backcloth of practical experience, to apply them to the development of the athlete.

One of the greatest problems in studying training theory is the diversity of terminology. The most obvious examples of this are in the area of fitness and its components. In part 4, a framework of definition and explanation is set out to establish a sound basis in this aspect of training theory. The concept of *fitness* is examined as it applies to all lifestyles. The major components of fitness, seen here as *strength, speed, endurance, mobility*, and their derivatives, are brought into focus in separate chapters. An understanding of these components is fundamental to the construction of training programmes specific to athlete and discipline.

The final chapter of part 4 deals with *evaluation*, a process critical to the ordered progression of training and, consequently, of fitness.

13
Fitness

Fitness may be defined as the successful adaptation to the stressors of one's lifestyle. A scientifically based and systematic training programme is fundamental to the athlete's fitness. Training provides the athlete with the basic means to adapt to his particular stressors through controlled exercise. Training theory may supplement the coach's practical knowledge to help him formulate a balanced training programme. The principles of training which apply in designing fitness programmes apply equally to élite performers, recreational performers, developing performers and those whose lives are not oriented towards sport or physical recreation.

The general picture

If a fitness programme is to be relevant, three questions must be answered. What is the lifestyle of the person involved? Is that person fit for that lifestyle? How can that person become more fit, or maintain present fitness levels?

To answer the first question one must list the stressors of the lifestyle: work, social, family, leisure pursuits, and so on. The list becomes more complex when such factors as ambition and anxiety are taken into account. Without a detailed answer to the first question, it is impossible to consider the second. The evaluation is seldom easy, because not all stressors are obvious. Issues become confused as there is temptation to focus only on those factors which can readily produce the effects of stress-related problems. The fact that a person appears to have the measure of his cumulative stressor climate, as determined, say, by a favourable testosterone:cortisone ratio, should not be interpreted as meaning that one may dismiss the relevance of any component stressor within that climate. Each stressor must be listed – and the athlete's status relative to that stressor evaluated before addressing the final question of how to ensure that the athlete remains in control, or can regain control.

One's lifestyle might be thought of as a 3-lane motorway along which a person travels through life. There is overall purpose for the journey variously determined by religious beliefs or philosophies of life. Each lane represents a broad avenue of progression: one's occupation or means of earning; one's social and family responsibilities; and the avenue of one's personal expression or creativity. Each person is continually on the move along the 'motorway', meeting the demands of pursuing objectives in any or all of the lanes at any time. There are many possible stressors in pursuit of these objectives.

■ Occupation

Most occupations have their own in-built set of stressors. On starting a new occupation, one is more aware of what they are. The majority are soon accommodated as routine is established and they consequently represent a low-level package of stressors. However, crises have to be managed, personal emotions must be suppressed despite provocation, and routine must be pursued despite peaks and troughs of general health and instability in the non-working environment.

■ Family and social

Home and social situations also have their own stressor profile. Family bereavement not only represents an immense immediate stressor of emotional trauma, but also the shock waves can last months, or even years, putting health at risk. Moving house is also a most stressful experience as its disorientation drains reserves of physical and emotional energy. Other states of transition can have high potential as stressors. They include shifting from school to university or school to employment; from childhood through adolescence; from a stable to an unstable relationship; from employment to unemployment; from having children at home to having them leave; and from a comfortable economic scenario to one where there is seldom enough to meet the round of bills.

■ Personal expression

Because performance is competitive, sport is a total expression of an athlete's complex profile of competence and motivation, and pursuit of achievement represents a considerable range of stressors. They include the physical demands on the organism when training to develop those conditioning characteristics relevant to a given sport. These are represented in figure 61. As the athlete progresses through a year plan, the effects of physical stressors vary according to how the athlete's conditioning status matches the specific demands of cumulative training loads. The range of stressors also includes those associated with varied fortunes in pursuit of high ambition, especially when sport is 'occupation'!

Running across these three broad areas of stressor is that which we will call destructive living habits. These include such things as smoking, drinking, poor eating, lack of sleep, insufficient regeneration or recreation and so on. The total complex of the stressor environment is then, substantial, and is unique to a given person.

Each person may be located somewhere along a fitness continuum. Fitness may be broadly categorised per decade of age:

at 15–25 fitness may mean the pursuit of competitive advantage
26–35 keeping weight in check
36–45 avoiding coronary disease
46–55 keeping pace with the 35–45 year olds
56+ holding a pace that lets you enjoy life.

Using these definitions, one may maintain fitness for each age group by the following practices.

15–25 years of age

Even if one is not committed to becoming a 'sports star', these years could be vital in establishing a pattern of physical recreation. Sports centres, sports clubs, sports councils and governing bodies of sport will be able to advise on where and when one may participate in sport and recreation at one's own level. Regular exercise is the best form of preventive medicine against fitness and health problems in the following years.

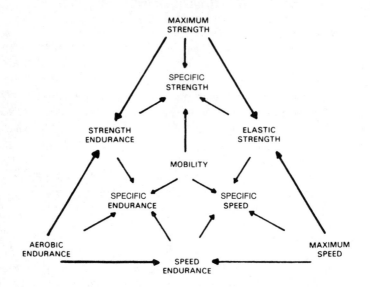

Fig. 61 *Schematic representation of the relationship of basic fitness characteristics and their involvement in the specific fitness required of individual disciplines*

26–35 years of age

Problems in this age group find their origins in the previous decade. Difficulties in weight control are derived from indiscriminate eating and lack of exercise. By reducing the daily calorific intake, weight will be lost but muscle tone will not improve. Only exercise will improve muscle tone, but it must be aimed at the appropriate muscles. Exercises fall mainly in the strength endurance, heart endurance and mobility areas. However if one is pursuing continued involvement in sport, all the characteristics mentioned for the previous decade will be developed at and to an appropriate level. Regular aerobic exercise is a *vital* form of preventive medicine to introduce in this age group.

36–45 years of age

The accumulation of stressors may lead to the possibility of a heart attack in this period (fig. 26, p. 72). If people in this age group have done very little exercise, they may have one or several of the following problems:

- overweight, which puts an extra load on the heart and is unattractive
- poor muscle tone, which endangers joints in sudden exertion (especially the back). It also leads to postural problems
- joint stiffness, which limits movement in the joints and consequently discourages exercise
- poor condition of the oxygen transporting system. This leads to breathlessness in even slight exertion, is related to coronary problems, and generally discourages active recreation.

Twenty years or so of inactivity will make it very difficult and even dangerous to launch into vigorous exercise now! The best policy is to start by improving the oxygen transporting system, then move on to muscle tone and then the joints. This, combined with dietary control, will reduce weight. As a result new life will be put into these years with the physical, social and mental benefits of physical recreation.

46–55 years of age
Many problems of the last decade still exist here and the exercise programme should be similar to that of the above age group. Oxygen transport may be improved by jogging, walking and swimming. Muscle tone improvement can come through strength endurance work, and mobility through exercise with or without apparatus.

56+ years of age
Major emphasis is now on efficiency of the oxygen transporting system, with a continuation of gentle mobility work. Strength is not a factor to be emphasised and any work in this area should be very light indeed.

Basic principles in training

The principles, or 'laws of training', of specificity, overload and reversibility are basic to the theory and practice of physical development, but will be more fully appreciated when related to the basic physical characteristics (see p. 189).

Specificity
Adaptation is specific to a stressor and the effect of a stressor is specific to an individual athlete. The importance of this should become apparent if we consider two athletes (a), and a training unit (b).

a) John: best 200m = 22.0 seconds; Angus: best 200m = 23.0 seconds
b) Unit = 6 x 200m in 24.0 seconds with 90 seconds recovery

Should this unit have the same effect on each athlete? The answer is of course *no*, and how would you evaluate the effect anyway?

Overload
It is necessary to provide a progressive heightening of the stressor to oblige the body to seek a higher status of adaptation. Progressive height-

ening, then, is the problem. Does the athlete become stronger by performing the same exercise more times, or by making the exercise harder and performing it the same number of times? Progressive heightening may be in terms of extent (e.g. more kilometres, repetitions, etc.), or in terms of intensity (e.g. more kilograms, faster runs), or in terms of density (e.g. shorter intervals of rest between exercises, repetitions, sets, units – 2–3 units per day), and so on. With so many variables, what changes will make the most significant contribution to the athlete's fitness for his event?

Reversibility

When intensity, extent or density is reduced, the degree of adaptation brought about by the training loads will gradually weaken. Strength losses are faster than mobility losses. Status improvements brought about by special methods over a short term are lost quicker than those brought about by 'slower' methods over a long term. Yet there are occasions when loads are reduced deliberately in special preparation for a major competition. The coach must decide the extent to which such training should be cut back and for how long.

▎Effect of training

Training might be considered as having three levels of effect.

(1) Immediate: the immediate effect of training is the body's reactions to the stressor of the training stimulus. They include increased heart rate, perspiration, increased blood lactate, heightened endocrine system involvement and fatigue.'
(2) Residual: the residual effect of training is what might be considered as the body's recovery and preparation response. The recovery response is seen in a raised general metabolism for some time after exercise is concluded. During this time the body's resting state is restored with the waste products of energy expenditure removed, and other stressor related effects gradually eliminated. The preparation response is seen in the heightened level of adaptation to future training stimuli. Having been stressed by a training stimulus, the body organizes itself to ensure that next time it will not be 'stressed' so much by the same stimulus! Put another way, this effect of training ensures that the body is prepared for a greater training stimulus next time.
(3) Cumulative: the cumulative effect of training is the body's progressive adaptation through the preparation response. This is what is measured in fitness monitoring tests over a period of months or even years.

The effect of training will be considered again in chapter 21.

Basic physical characteristics

The interpretation of specificity is clear when one considers the type of fitness required for a given lifestyle. Whereas the athlete works to increase fitness towards some level of excellence, the non-athlete may work to compensate for the damage his lifestyle is causing. Thus, the lorry driver slumped at his wheel uses few abdominal or back muscles and should therefore attempt to improve muscle tone in these areas.

The definition of overload chosen by the coach depends upon the particular physical characteristics that need to be developed.

Strength: overload is increasing the load (in weight) itself.
Strength endurance: overload is working with a load, which makes some demand on strength, and increasing the number of repetitions of the exercise.
Heart endurance: overload is increasing the amount of time that the person can continue a steady rate of work which makes very low demands on strength.
Speed endurance: overload is increasing the number of repetitions of an exercise per unit of time in the presence of endurance factors.
Speed: overload is simply performing a given task faster.
Elastic strength: overload is the increasing of a load while the speed of movement is maintained.
Mobility: overload is taking a joint action past its present limit.

Reversibility interpreted for the non-athlete or athlete will give an indication of how much exercise is required each week to maintain a reasonable degree of fitness. It is believed that a minimum of 2–3 units per week is necessary for the non-athlete, while the athlete is often involved in 2–3 units of training per day. The minimum will be used by the majority of non-athletes, e.g. day 1: jogging and mobility exercises, day 2: circuit training and jogging, day 3: some form of physical recreation. On the other hand, it would be ideal if some form of physical activity and regeneration training became part of daily routine.

Points on fitness and training

The following are some general points on fitness and training for both the athlete and non-athlete.

(1) Before beginning any exercise programme, both athlete and non-athlete should have a full medical check-up. It is good practice to make this the start of regular annual check-ups. Some medical conditions may suggest a modified programme.
(2) Children will not damage a healthy heart by exercising – quite the opposite. When children are tired they stop!
(3) Nor is there an upper age limit for exercise. The right exercise programme supported by relevant medical advice will keep the heart and muscles healthy to provide and use energy required to enjoy one's lifestyle.

(4) The starting focus of all exercise programmes is low intensity training to develop heart endurance – i.e. aerobic activity.

(5) Stiffness following exercise is natural – and not serious. Sharp pain rather than discomfort during the next bout of exercise may be cause for alarm. It might be due to slight muscle strain and rest followed by low intensity exercise and gentle stretching – or a prescribed rehabilitation programme should return things to normal. If the pain persists a physiotherapist must be consulted.

(6) Too much training does not shorten life, but too little may. It cannot be said that training will necessarily lengthen life, but it will help make one's 'allotted span' more enjoyable.

(7) There is no such thing as 'overtraining'. Physical, mental or emotional 'burn-out', is due to the cumulative effect of *all* the stressors in one's life. Rather than compromise the training programme, the overall picture must be reviewed with objectives and tasks prioritised to create 'space' for adaptation to take place.

(8) Women are able to train as hard as men. Following pregnancy, women's training load capacity increases and competitive performance in most cases improves above that of the accepted normal progression curve. Women may train hard throughout the menstrual cycle. However, in the 2–3 days prior to menstruation high intensity elastic strength work (i.e. jumping routines) which focus sudden high loads on the hips/lower back should not take the athlete towards fatigue. The sacro-iliac joint is less stable at this point in the cycle and can be strained.

(9) People do not 'go to fat' when they finish serious training. The fact is that their appetites often stay high while their energy expenditure is now low, and, consequently, weight increases. Such athletes should maintain a programme of lighter training as part of their personal fitness programme and review eating habits. This approach will also help maintain general muscle tone.

(10) Training does not make people 'muscle-bound'. This is an obscure expression which reflects the fact that certain types of strength training will considerably increase the size of muscles – for example in body building. This will only happen if this is the objective of training and specific diets or exercise are pursued to this end. Normal exercise programmes do not have this effect. In fact, by reducing fat around the muscle, and improving muscle tone, a more attractive definition of the limbs will result.

(11) Exercise machines are sound and safe for non-athletes to use provided their use is properly explained by a qualified instructor.

(12) For personal safety, neither athlete nor non-athlete should work alone with loose weights or exercise machines.

(13) Isometrics should not be used indiscriminately, especially by 35 year olds and over. They *may* overload the heart.

(14) Because fitness is specific, so also are fitness programmes. The objectives of each phase of a training programme should be clearly defined and the programme planned to meet those objectives.

(15) Personal fitness programmes, whether for athlete or non-athlete, must on the one hand set out details of physical activity and regeneration, and on the other, afford advice from fitness related areas such as nutrition, sports psychology and sports medicine – relevant to the individuals needs.

(16) No fitness programme can be seriously considered without a definite time commitment on the part of the person for whom the programme is designed.

Summary

The meaning of fitness is specific to a given athlete. Against the background of a fitness to tolerate the stressors of day to day living, the athlete seeks to develop a fitness specific to the demands of his sport. It must be borne in mind that just as the demands of each sport are diverse, so are the day to day lives of the athletes. If the athlete becomes 'unfit' for life outside sport, due to an inability to adapt to its stressors, then there will certainly be an overlap into sport and his capacity for developing fitness for his sport will be impaired. The coach must view the development of fitness as unique to athlete and situation, and consequently the totality of the athlete's life must be taken into account in identifying his 'uniqueness'.

14
Theory and practice of strength development

Strength

Strength, or the ability to express force, is a basic physical characteristic that determines performance efficiency in sport. Each sport varies in its strength requirements and, in the interest of specificity, we should examine its relationship to speed and endurance.

There are three main classifications of strength, namely maximum strength, elastic strength and strength endurance. The last two are most pertinent to sport in general, but maximum strength does have its place in some sports (e.g. weight lifting) and is clearly a component of elastic strength and strength endurance. When designing the strength portion of an athlete's personal fitness programme it is specific to athlete and sport/discipline. It will draw variously, then, on these three main classifications of strength (figure 61, page 186).

Maximum strength

Maximum strength (gross strength) is defined as the greatest force the neuromuscular system is capable of exerting in a single maximum voluntary contraction. Consequently it will determine performance in those sports where great resistance has to be overcome or controlled (e.g. weight lifting). 'Controlled' means here that the muscles may be required to remain in a state of static contraction (isometric) at maximum or near maximum static strength demands. It is possible to combine demands for maximum strength with a high speed of contraction (e.g. in hammer and shot put) or with high demands on endurance (e.g. rowing). The smaller the resistance to be overcome, the less the involvement of maximum strength. Accelerating the body from rest (sprinting) or propelling the body from the ground (jumps) means a greater resistance must be overcome than maintaining uniform motion, as in medium and long endurance sports. However, figure 62 helps to bring this concept of maximum strength involvement into perspective.

Elastic strength

The ability of the neuromuscular system to overcome resistance with a high speed of contraction is defined as elastic strength (power, fast strength). The neuromuscular system accepts and expels rapid loading at high velocity through the co-ordination of reflexes and elastic and contractile components of muscle. The adjective 'elastic' is very appro-

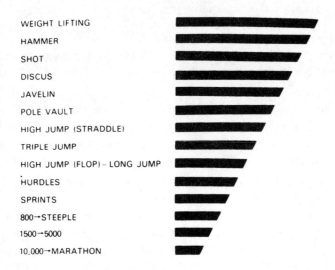

Fig. 62 *Schematic representation of maximum strength contribution to various athletic events* (adapted from Harre, 1973)

priate and a key to avoiding confusion between 'speed of contraction' or 'strength of contraction'. Although this mechanism involves both, it is their complex co-ordination and the involvement of reflexes and elastic components that defines it as a most specific area of strength. Elastic strength determines performance in all of the so-called 'explosive' sports, i.e. jumping, throwing, sprinting, striking, etc.

■ Strength endurance
This is the capacity of all or part of the organism to maintain strength expression through fatigue. It is characterised by a relatively high application of strength, together with mental and physical perseverance. Age-old tests of 'strength', such as maximum press-ups or holding a weight at arm's length for as long as possible, are in fact tests of strength endurance. It determines performance principally when considerable resistance is to be overcome for a fairly long period of time. Thus in rowing, swimming, cross-country skiing and track events between 60 seconds and 8 minutes duration, one would expect to find strength endurance a critical factor. This may explain the relationship in track and field athletics between hill running and 800m improvement demonstrated by Viru, Urgenstein and Pisuke (1972).

■ Absolute and relative strength
In sports where maximum strength is the principal component (fig. 62), body weight and performance are closely correlated. In other words, heavy athletes can, in absolute terms, achieve greater strength expression than lighter athletes. The maximum force that an athlete can express, irrespective of body weight, is therefore referred to as absolute strength.

On the other hand, the maximum force that an athlete can express in relation to body weight is known as relative strength. This is of obvious importance to athletes who must move their own body weight in, for instance, jumps and gymnastics. It is calculated by dividing absolute strength by the athlete's own body weight, and reduction in body weight will increase relative strength.

Shot-put athlete (male) weighs 100kg : leg press (90° knee) = 300kg
Therefore relative strength = 3.0kg/kg body wt.
Long jump athlete (female) weighs 60kg : leg press (90° knee) = 200kg
Therefore relative strength = 3.3kg/kg body wt.

Absolute leg press strength favours the putter, but relative leg press strength favours the jumper.

In some sports it is important for an athlete to have high absolute and relative strength. For example, in rugby union, a prop forward must have high absolute strength and body weight in the scrum, but must also be fast over short distances and have the level of endurance necessary to positively influence the pace of the game. This would suggest that relative strength must be high. Strength training for such a player should then reflect the fitness requirement of all aspects of his 'total' game. A similar situation exists for rugby league, Australian rules, NFL, Gaelic football etc.

■ Additional strength parameters

Interest in strength development in academic institutions has produced further parameters defined in the first instance by specific measurement criteria. Tidow listed several following the Freiburg 'Symposium on Strength' (1983). They include:

Parameter	Area of Definition
Absolute Strength	Electric-stimulation–maximum value, computer tomography of muscle cross-section.
Maximum Strength	Maximum voluntary contraction against an eccentric loading (150% maximum isometric).
Strength Deficit	Difference between maximum strength (as measured above), and isometric maximum strength (in %).
Strength Maximum	This is the maximum load which can be lifted.
Explosive Strength	Maximum rate of strength increase per unit of time (isometric/dynamic).
Starting Strength	Strength score achieved 30 milliseconds after start of contraction.

The athlete's status relative to such parameters may be used as a guide to the review of training programmes on the basis that such parameters are considered usable as indices of specific strength relative to the athlete's discipline or phase of training.

■ **External resistance and the athlete's ability to express force**

The athlete expresses force (or strength) through the body's lever system by converting chemical to kinetic energy and by neuromuscular co-ordination. In all physical activity, the athlete expresses this force against external force (or resistance). Resistance may take the shape of weights, throwing implements, water, air, the athlete's own body weight, momentum, and so on. Sometimes the athlete's ability to exert force is referred to as internal force, as opposed to the external force of the resistance. The relationship between the two is critical because it determines different classes of muscular activity (see chapter 6). These classes are apparent in the components of individual sports techniques. In the interest of specificity, exercises must develop efficiency of appropriate muscular activity in those muscle groups involved in specific joint actions. This means identifying the muscular activity and the actions. Is the muscular activity elastic strength, strength endurance etc? Is the action postural/synergic, protagonist etc?

■ **Static (or isometric) muscular activity**

This is frequently, but mistakenly, thought of only as maximum force of contraction. Measurements of isometric strength have perpetuated this belief, with tensionmeter and dynamometer tests being used to evaluate maximum strength in a specific area of joint action. However, the ability to balance on one foot, to maintain an upright posture, to counter the hammer's pull in the turns, or to hold a vertical alignment of shoulder/hip at long jump take-off, are all examples of static contraction.

During static muscular activity the force expressed by the athlete equals the force expressed by the resistance. In other words, the greater the resistance, the greater the strength required by the athlete to maintain the relationship between levers at a given joint. This implies that the athlete has sufficient reserves of strength to do this, which in turn implies an ultimate maximum for that athlete in a given joint action. When the resistance exceeds this maximum the muscular activity is no longer isometric, but a type of eccentric activity.

The range of isometric strength expression is obviously very great, yet the need for discrete neuromuscular adjustment to hold levers in critical alignment is essential to a successful performance in technical sports. Consequently, training should embrace work to develop specific isometric efficiency, e.g. in step-ups for young athletes where a medicine ball is held out by the athlete to develop the postural-isometric role of the extensor muscles of the spine. Weakness in muscles which act to maintain posture or which are synergists can increase the possibility of technical errors or injury. Whether an athlete is beginner or élite, the training programme must include work for development of these muscles. For example, standing on one leg and simply swinging the other leg forwards and backwards, then across in front of the standing leg and high to side, then 'drawing a figure of 8 out to the side' etc., helps develop those muscles supporting the foot, ankle, knee and hip of the standing leg.

■ Dynamic muscular activity

Dynamic muscular activity can be sub-divided into concentric and eccentric.

Concentric muscular activity

Joint movement will take place when the force expressed by the athlete does not equal that imposed by the resistance. In concentric work, the athlete is expressing more force than the resistance and consequently the muscle shortens to pull the levers it connects towards each other. Individual muscles, or groups of muscles, can be developed by resistance training which corresponds to this type of activity. Biceps curls, for instance, will develop the flexors of the elbow. This type of activity is very common in sport, but developing the ability to perform with greater strength will not necessarily lead to improved performance. The co-ordination and role of each joint action must be considered in its entirety and the whole must be developed.

Eccentric muscular activity

Elastic concept: like concentric activity, this results from a disparity between force expressed by the athlete and force represented by resistance. It operates at two quite different levels. First, the resistance may be less than the maximum strength which the athlete *can* express. This will occur when lowering a weight to the floor, or accepting body momentum as the athlete moves into the basic discus throw position, or with each landing/take-off in triple jump. The need to develop the athlete's ability to perform such muscular activity has given rise to training methods such as jump decathlons, Verhoshansky's (1971) depth jumps, Endemann's (1975) weights jacket work from boxes with throwers, and the Bulgarian system of mixing concentric work with eccentric work. This might also be referred to as elastic eccentric work (plyometrics).

Plastic concept: the second level is where the resistance imposed is greater than the athlete's maximum isometric strength. Here, the athlete can only attempt to control a losing struggle with the resistance. Because loading effect is maximum throughout the whole range of movement in this type of activity, the tone or quality of muscular contraction is constant and is referred to as *isotonic*. It is not technically correct to so describe all muscle activity where movement takes place, as the load effect alters along the range in a given joint action. The 'isokinetic' devices developed in the late 1960s allowed muscular activity to be more truly isotonic than other exercise methods at that time. Exercise employing this type of loading is used in progressive physiotherapy units, both to develop strength through a period of post injury or post surgery rehabilitation, and to measure strength throughout the full range of a given joint action. This may be referred to as *plastic* eccentric work and such exercise should be performed under supervision.

Strength relative to movement

Figure 63 schematically represents a biceps curl. If X units of strength are required to move from position A, more units of force must be employed to maintain movement with the increased resistance at B (note the increased length of the load arm). In moving towards C, however, the load arm diminishes and consequently so does the resistance. The movement will now be faster if the same number of units are used.

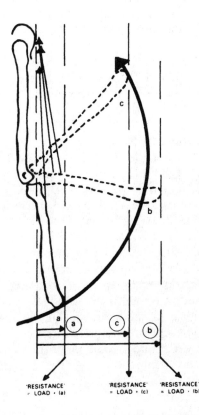

Fig. 63 *The change of 'resistance' at different points in the range of movement of flexion at the elbow*

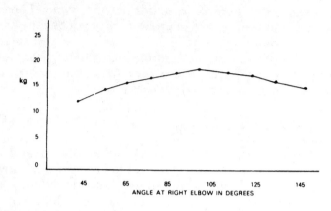

Fig. 64   *Kinetic strength measured at different joint angles for flexion at right elbow (schoolgirl aged 13)*

This variation implies that once initial inertia is overcome, the 'value' of the resistance will be less effective in the development of strength elsewhere in the range. In other words, only the beginning of the movement will be overloaded. Ideally, each point in the range of movement should be offered a similar overload, which could be assessed from graphs such as that in figure 64. However, isolating specific parts of the range may well interfere with the natural pattern of acceleration associated with movements through the full range.

■ Auxotonic muscular activity

Auxotonic activity is the particular neuromuscular pattern associated with a given sports technique. It involves the complex programming of static and/or dynamic activity at different joints, the control of muscle contraction against muscle relaxation, and the movement-specific speed that is both absolute in terms of the whole movement and relative in terms of synchronisation of different joint actions. In other words, it is a specific pattern dictating which levers are used, and how, when, and where they are used. To develop various strength requirements the athlete must load the various actions in accordance with that pattern. Consequently, orthodox weight training exercises can only contribute to improved performance in the sports technique if regularly channelled through special exercises and competition specific exercises. Auxotonic activity must be clearly understood in order to differentiate between general, specific and competition specific exercise, and to develop relevant practices.

▌ Development of strength

Development of this physical ability, like all others, must obey the three laws of training – specificity, overload and reversibility (see chapter 13). The athlete's strength requirement for a given sport, although specific to the sport and his status relative to that sport's demands, will in almost every case cover a range of strength classifications and sub-classifications. All sports bring something to the 'party' of strength development and, therefore, strength training. But that 'something' must be carefully interpreted and synthesised to meet the specific needs of a given athlete in a given sport. In particular, weight lifting units must be considered in this light.

■ Strength development training

From the discussion of theory, it should be evident that for each sports technique there will be a selection of exercises for the development of relevant strength. In a list of these exercises, broad classification would group exercises as *general*, *special* and *competition specific*. These terms are used throughout discussion of physical development and strength training, and may be described as follows.

General exercises

These exercises do not relate closely to specific technical models in sport. They must, however, provide the foundation upon which the more specific training for strength and technique are built. For this reason they have a greater share of an athlete's training load in his or her early development years and in the first 4–12 weeks of the annual cycle at all levels of development. They are used primarily:

- to ensure that the athlete does not develop disproportionately, i.e. by using a general conditioning circuit where all parts of the body are systematically exercised. Overuse injuries may be reduced by incorporating such sessions
- to offer a high level of active recovery, i.e. using general exercises during the competitive season where a total but light loading is of physiological benefit
- to establish a broad basis of general strength on which to build higher levels of specific strength. For example, the strength of the back muscles may limit loading in hip/knee extension work, therefore the back must be exercised
- to develop maximum strength in those muscles which are broadly related to the sport, i.e. in the use of power-cleans for jumpers. Here muscle areas involved in the events are developed, but not according to the time/force pattern implied by the sports techniques themselves
- to provide that level of strength in postural/synergist muscles which allows those muscles involved in the major joint actions of a given technique to operate optimally
- to afford a basis for athletes to perform more specific exercise. For example, exercises to develop foot speed in tennis requires that the player is generally strong enough in the foot/ankle/calf to perform the exercises required.

These exercises may involve whole body movement as in cleans, or single joint movement as in biceps curls. Where whole body movement is involved then other aspects of physiological adaptation are also affected, e.g. oxygen transporting system.

Special exercises (related)

Special exercises relate to the specifics of *joint action* or *muscle dynamics* involved in the techniques of the athlete's sport. These exercises take components of the sport's technique and develop them according to the type of strength required. Whereas general exercise for the discus thrower may be bench press, or dumb-bell flying, special exercises might include slinging a medicine ball 'explosively' from kneeling with hips extended. A wide selection of such exercises is absolutely vital in an athlete's development.

Technically it may be desirable to employ sophisticated methods of electromyography to determine which special exercises are most suitable in terms of their relationship to a particular technique. Ivanova (1967) has examined these possibilities in a comprehensive comparison of the activity of muscles in rowing with special strength exercises. For example, if one considers muscle activity of the quadriceps in rowing as 100%, full squats scored 420%, whereas standing long jump scored 258%.

Competition specific exercises (specific)

These strength exercises are essentially whole technique exercises, but the movement may be given added resistance. Throwing with heavier hammers, training for rugby or football with a weighted jacket, sprinting from blocks in harness, playing tennis with a weighted racket, running with ankle weights and so on, reproduce the movement and relevant speed patterns. Only the absolute speed of movement is decreased. However, one important word of caution is if the resistance causes extraneous compensatory movements in the body, then the correct movement pattern will suffer. Athletes should work on a varied resistance unit when doing such work so as to avoid the development of wrong patterns of movement.

■ Development of strength for static muscular activity

It is now well established that in strength training the principal type of training used should correspond to the type of contraction used in a given technique. It follows then that isometric or static methods are employed in the development of static or isometric muscle activity. It does *not* follow that isometric exercise will develop eccentric or concentric activity but some improvement can be expected as table 24 illustrates.

Table 24 *Isometric- and concentric-type contraction training compared* (adapted from Brunner 1967)

	static strength increase	dynamic strength increase
isometric-type training	15.1%	11.5%
concentric-type training	9.2%	18.1%

Isometric activity mainly occurs in the maintenance of posture and such conditioning may be developed in special or competition specific exercises where whole or part of the technique is loaded isometrically. Functional isometric exercise may also contribute at this level. These isometric exercises are executed at various points throughout the range of movement involved in technique, the theory being that the strengthening effect throughout the range is achieved by 'irradiation'. However, isometric training methods, as advanced by Hettinger and Muller (1953), have a limited application to sport. Their value will almost certainly be with sports requiring great maximum strength and, even then, their use must be supplemented by dynamic work.

Finally, muscle groups should be trained in their postural or synergist roles. Leg swinging routines target the postural or synergist functions of the supporting leg. The postural role of the muscles of the spine is rehearsed by being supported face down on a bench only to the hips: holding the upper body horizontal, move the weighted arms forward, down, side (crucifix), down back (towards legs), down. This movement is repeated several times obliging the muscles of the spine to retain postural alignment whilst adjusting to changing eccentric forces.

■ Development of strength for dynamic muscular activity

This is the most frequently used type of exercise in the development of strength in sport. Variations of loading intensity, extent or density will dictate the relative contributions to maximum, elastic, or endurance strength. Even if absolute speed of movement is reduced, the relative speed variations within the movement should reproduce as closely as possible that of the particular action at a particular joint when it is incorporated in a given technique. Consequently, attempting to develop an efficient hurdle trail leg recovery or tennis forehand against elastic resistance is not advised. When elastic is stretched the resistance increases, thus decelerating the lever in a joint action. This does not happen in the actual event. Working against a pulley resistance, or throwing heavier implements, would allow a scaled-down pattern of acceleration closer to the pattern of the event.

Kusnezov (1975) suggests that, whether or not technique action is dynamic or static, occasional units which include the other will aid development in the principal action, especially in general exercises for strength development. This may be related to the concept of active recovery.

■ Development of strength by eccentric activity

Resistance can be greater than the maximum strength which the athlete can express. When this is the case there will be very distinct gains in maximum strength because the system will be overloaded throughout and the stimulus will be of long duration (Gundlach, 1968). Strength in all three types of muscle activity will increase by this method. Where the resistance is less than the maximum strength of the athlete, considerable strength gains can be expected in those aspects of technique where eccentric activity is followed by concentric. Various types of rebound, loaded rebound and depth jumps fall into this category.

■ Development of strength by ballistic activity

Ballistic activity refers to that type of exercise where there is rapid exchange between eccentric and concentric contraction. Skipping, hopping, rebound jumping, catching and returning medicine balls, and jump press-ups are all examples of this. The term 'plyometrics' was coined in the United States to cover this sort of training. Although it has become most closely associated with 'special exercises', it has now increased its contribution within the 'general exercises' programme. Verhoshansky (1971) first introduced depth jumping within a systematic progression of strength training. His emphasis was at 'general' rather than 'special' training – with a view to a more effective maximum strength programme. His exercises were based on the body's momentum loading the legs.

Kusnetsov carried this further by considering how to similarly load the arms by catching and returning heavy weights on a sloping ramp. His work then progressed to the use of machines such as pendulums where athletes were swung at walls and were obliged to 'kick' off the wall with either legs or arms. Once into the use of technology to provide a level of loading not previously available, he postulated that if machines could oblige athletes to express strength faster, by recruiting elastic and reflex mechanisms, then human potential would break new ground. In the year of his death (1986) he was working on a machine which would react to pressure by 'kicking back' faster than the athlete's muscles were eccentrically contracting – forcing the neuromuscular system to 'learn' to move through the eccentric-concentric exchange even faster. In many sports, improved performance depends on expressing sound technique with greater force at greater speed. The most difficult aspect of this is co-ordinating that greater force at greater speed. There is little doubt that it is related to elastic strength but it also involves that sophistication of technique where the existing synchronisation of a specific neuromuscular pattern is challenged. In many cases this leads to reduction in performance as the new timings are learned.

■ Development of maximum strength

The optimal stimulus for the development of maximum strength is related to the following factors:

- the intensity of the stimulus relative to the maximum strength of the athlete. (This may be interpreted as a recruitment of maximum available motor units.)
- the duration of that stimulus
- the frequency of recruitment of maximum available motor units.

Loading to create such a stimulus will be that which will allow exercise to be performed once only. This load is referred to as maximum or 100%, for a particular exercise. Such intensity, however, cannot be considered acceptable in the following cases.

(1) Where the athlete has an unstable technique when performing the exercise. Here, the athlete must work with many repetitions of lighter loads until technique is stabilised. The possibility of injury is therefore very slight. However, should these lighter loads be repeated to the point of fatigue in training units, the load will again tend, in effect, to approach maximum, bringing associated problems. As a guide, the number of repetitions should not take an athlete to the point where exercise technique deteriorates.

(2) Where the athlete has not quite reached maturity and the muscle/bone/joint system is not yet completely stabilised. To work an athlete to maximum under these circumstances may interfere with muscle/bone connections and disturb the complex integrity of a system of joints. The contractile force potential of the big muscle groups would be completely out of sympathy with the development of bone, joint, and the juncture of tendon and bone. This is especially relevant where loads are taken on the shoulders while attempting maximum loading of the knee and hip extensors, thus placing the lumbar spine and sacro-iliac region at risk.

(3) Where maximum strength development is not relevant to the sports technique.

In terms of the training unit then, where maximum strength development is sought, optimal effects will result from working over several sets at an intensity which allows the exercise to be performed 1–5 times, i.e. 85–100% maximum (table 33, p. 273). Recovery periods of up to 5 minutes between sets are almost essential to avoid cumulative fatigue.

Where isometric training methods are being used, and the load may be varied, contractions against 80–100% maximum, held for periods of 9–12 seconds, should be used for advanced athletes, while intensities of 60–80% held for 6–9 seconds seems adequate for the novice. Using a lighter loading and repeating an exercise to the point of fatigue will also improve strength, but to a limited extent as such work moves into the area of endurance training. For the young athlete, this type of work over many exercises will establish a sound general basis of strength.

Eccentric work with loads in excess of maximum isometric strength will also develop maximum concentric strength. Specific intensities are not available from most research authorities, but personal experimentation suggests that loadings from 105–175% of the maximum concentric load can be used over specific ranges of movement. If, for example, an athlete's half squat was 100kg, the eccentric load will range from 105kg to 175kg. To achieve this the staggered sets, as advanced by Lay (1970), are used, but in reverse. Safety must be emphasised here and pins *must* be able to accept the load at the bottom end of the exercise.

The isokinetic machines while offering a considerable duration and maximum intensity of contraction, may interfere with the natural patterns of acceleration–deceleration in the muscle. On the other hand, where there is less emphasis on acceleration–deceleration in the muscle due to specific demands of a sport, this method offers considerable advantage. The case for inclusion in the programme will be stronger then, for rowers, swimmers and cross-country skiers, than for hurdlers or tennis players.

Several strength development systems focus on mixing the strength training stimuli. This is programmed at the inter-unit and intra-unit levels. For example, inter-unit mixing may take the form of alternating 3–5 x 5 x 85% with 3–5 x 10 x 65% with one day rest between. Intra-unit mixing may take the form of 'sandwiching' 5 x 85%; 10 x 65%; 5 x 85%; 10 x 65%. Again, the intra-unit mixing may, in order to provide a very rapid acceleration of maximum strength levels, mix 'orthodox' weights loadings with elastic or plyometric loadings. An example of this would be 5 x 85% ½ squat; 5 x 5 hurdle rebounds; 5 x 85% squat; 5 x 5 hurdle rebounds. This latter example is applied on a base of several weeks of 'orthodox' strength training units, or inter-unit alternation of intensities as suggested above. When applied it is usually for no more than 3 weeks.

Electronic stimulation of muscle to develop strength is a further option, but there is varied opinion on its application to elastic strength – specific activity.

Finally, it has been suggested that just as there is some optimal frequency of stimulus within a training unit, there is also an optimal interval of recovery between units where maximum strength is being developed. This interval is variously set at 36–48 hours for natural recovery to take place. This said, by varying the 'target areas' on alternate days, maximum strength units can be worked on daily, e.g. day 1, 3, 5, upper body, day 2, 4, 6, lower body.

■ Development of elastic strength

Broadly speaking, elastic strength can be developed by improving maximum strength and/or speed of coordinated muscle contraction. The problem lies in effecting an optimal compromise of development that can be translated to the sports technique. This is a problem because if the athlete works with a heavy loading then both strength and speed of contraction will develop for that specific exercise. However, there is not necessarily an increase in the speed of muscle contraction in the sports technique where loading is much less. On the other hand, if loading is very light there will be an improvement in speed of working against that load provided that load is within a certain range – variously stated at 5–20%. If outside this range, compensatory movements interfere with technical precision, so a programme which varies the intensity and consequently the speed of movement is recommended. It is therefore suggested that maximum strength work and light resisted special exercises must be used within each microcycle (see chapter 21) if specific elastic strength is to be developed. Moreover, within units for maximum strength, a lower intensity set or sets should be included in the exercise regimes. Experimental programmes have been tried to develop maximum strength first over several months, then followed by a training programme to develop speed. However, this attempted development of elastic strength in series has far less value than if both areas of development are advanced 'in parallel'.

In terms of training units the intensity of stimulus should be around 75% maximum, using 4–6 sets of 6–10 repetitions. As with maximum strength work, up to 5 minutes rest should be allowed between sets. Using this particular format, Harre (1973) and associates believe both maximum and elastic strength can be advanced at the same time. If maximum strength work is being done with training units, then elastic strength supplementary work is proposed by Harre (1973) at loadings of 30–50% maximum. Personal experimentation has shown increases in both elastic and maximum strength by alternating loads of 55–60% with 85–100%.

Strength training for the development of elastic strength, where relative strength is critical, should not be accompanied by muscle hypertrophy and consequent increase in body weight. According to Bührle (1971) hypertrophy is optimal where loadings of 65–80% maximum are repeated 6–10 times in 3–4 sets or more. Body builders have been known to work 6 sets of 12 repetitions at 60–65%. This work is not recommended for athletes requiring increased relative strength. Harre (1973) suggests that preference be given to working in specific movements with body parts weighted at 3–5% body weight in total, as used by gymnasts (wrist weights, jackets): 'The high muscle tension necessary for an increase of strength, is thus generated by the "explosively" quick muscle contraction.'

Without doubt the greatest single contribution to improved elastic strength is via balistic/plyometric routines which focus on related and specific exercises. Such work is with body weight, limb weights, weighted jackets using varied weight, light resistances such as medicine balls, logs, sand sacks and gymnastic equipment. It can take 1–2 hours of fairly concentrated work, but with sufficient recovery periods to ensure that fatigue does not take the 'elasticity' out of the athlete's movements. It is this repeated 'elastic' neuromuscular control of impact which provides the training effect. However, for the long bones and joints this may set the scene for damage. The extent of loading must, then, be carefully controlled to avoid fatigue.

■ Development of strength endurance

It is quite clear that an athlete with maximum strength of 200kg in one exercise, will repeat the exercise with greater comfort at 50kg than the athlete who has maximum strength of 100kg. Also, if two athletes have the maximum strength of 200kg the athlete with a well developed oxygen transporting system will endure more repetitions at 50kg than the athlete with poor oxygen transport status. However, the exact relationship between these poles and the characteristic of strength endurance is not clear. It would appear that the foundations of training in strength endurance lie in the ability to perform the highest possible number of repetitions against a loading which is greater than that normally experienced in the event. Moreover, according to Saziorski (1971), maximum strength ceases to be a critical factor if the strength requirement is less than 30% of maximum. While at the other end, according to Astrand (1970), oxygen transport efficiency is a necessary precursor of the anaerobic development required for development of strength endurance (see chapter 5).

A complex form of training appears to be the key, with resisted exercises preferably of the competition specific or special variety being employed. Thus, the athlete may run in snow, sand, uphill, in plough, in surf, or dragging a sled, whilst the oarsman may row pulling a drag and the swimmer may likewise swim pulling a resistance. Where general exercises are employed, circuit-type training is used and repetitions of approximately 50–75% of maximum, with a loading of 40–60% maximum and optimal recovery between, seems a sound rule of thumb.

■ Unit construction for strength development

A detailed account of unit construction was presented in six articles by Lay in Athletics Weekly 1969/70, which examined simple sets, super sets, pyramids, circuits and so on. The detail of these systems is beyond the scope of this book but, for reference, figure 65 suggests a relationship between intensity and extent.

■ Microcycle construction

In designing the strength training detail of microcycles/macrocycles, a coach must have a feeling for the situation summarised by figure 66. Each athlete has his specific development requirement with the 'specific strength' demands of a given sport, event or even position within a team. For example, in rugby the specific strength demands of a prop forward are not the same as those of a wing threequarter. So the detail of strength training units must reflect this. But more than this, any given microcycle is put together to meet not one but several training objectives and very careful value-judgement must be applied to ensure that each objective is constructively pursued without compromising progress of the others. In short, strength training units cannot be seen in isolation.

Moreover, the practical implications of developing and monitoring strength are rather greater when applied to athletes who have relatively long competition seasons, e.g. soccer, rugby, hockey; where double periodised years are pursued; or where the nature of the sport and related lifestyle includes several irregularly spread tournaments throughout the year e.g. tennis, squash, golf and to a certain extent Formula 1.

Of course, such variations in relationship of preparation and competition periods also influence development of other areas of conditioning such as endurance – but the greatest problems are in the strength programme.

General strength development will focus on an all-round balanced increase in the area of maximum strength, strength of synergists, stabiliser groups, compensatory work, and therapy or rehabilitation according to the demands of the sport/event and needs of the athlete.

Related and specific strength will focus on the specific joint actions and muscle dynamics required for the sport, it's techniques and it's competition framework and detail. It is the developmental bias implied by this kind of work which makes it essential that a general strength programme is spread, albeit with shifting overall load priority, throughout the year.

To construct an individual athlete's strength training microcycles then, the coach must know:

- the general all-round strength balance of the athlete
- maximum strength demands of the sport and the athlete's status in this area
- related/specific strength demands of the sport and the athlete's status in this area, e.g. a sprinter requires: starting strength via harness running; sprinting strike strength via skip drills; sprinting stride strength via bounding; sprinting arms strength via speed ball routines.

■ Evaluation of strength status

There is a wide variety of tests to evaluate strength, but not all are relevant to the assessment of strength for a sport. Selection must take into account the specific quality to be measured. If eccentric, concentric or isometric muscular activity is being measured then it is logical that any testing procedure should involve that activity. If the strength is maximum, elastic or endurance then, again, the testing procedure should measure that type of strength. The testing procedure must be valid, reliable and objective and, furthermore, must be validated against performance, or some test, in a given technique. If possible the testing procedure should involve the dynamics of movement typical of the event (table 25).

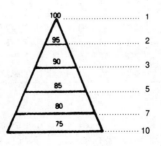

Fig. 65 *Pyramid relating intensity and extent of loading, suggested by Bührle in 'Die Lehre Der Leichtathletic' – 26.1.71. He suggested maximum strength depends upon (a) Cross-sectional areas of muscle (reps. of 6–10); (b) Intra-muscular co-ordination (reps. of 1–3); (c) Inter-muscular co-ordination (Technique and Standard of Performance). (Modified – Dick/Arbeit, 1996)*

Table 25 *Suggested approaches to evaluation of strength characteristics*

strength characteristic	static test	dynamic test
Maximum strength	Dynamometers Tensionmeters	Maximum load lifted in a given exercise. Harre (1973) suggests adding 75% athlete's body weight to the weight on the barbell, if body weight is also raised, as in squats.
Elastic strength		Standing long jump: vertical jump: vertical jump on landing from a set height: jump series over given distance against time: sprints from blocks over 10–20m.
Endurance strength	Timed maintenance of given position	Maximum repetitions of a given exercise within a specific period of time: timed resisted run over given course etc.

This said, it has become common practice to create specific strength controls. These controls are designed to monitor status of that type of strength which the coach associates either with progress at a particular phase in the training year or with level of preparation for optimal performance. So, for a long jumper in mid-preparation phase, a control might be standing long jump – whereas in early competition season it might be distance covered in 10 bounds against the time taken.

This approach has been applied by the former Soviet Union sprint coaches in linking target 100m times to particular jumps tests, as shown in the table below.

Table 26 *Bounding controls*

target time	standing long (m)	jump reach (cm)	3 bounds* (m)	5 bounds* (m)	10 bounds* (m)
10.20–10.65	2.90–3.20	76–85	9.20–10.00	15.90–17.10	29.50–39.50
10.70–11.10	2.70–3.00	68–77	8.50–9.10	14.60–15.60	27.00–37.00
11.20–11.70	2.60–2.90	60–69	7.90–8.50	14.00–15.00	25.00–35.00
11.80–12.20	2.50–2.80	53–61	7.50–8.10	13.40–14.40	23.00–33.00
12.30–12.70	2.40–2.70	46–54	7.20–7.80	12.80–13.80	21.00–31.00
12.80–13.20	2.30–2.60	39–47	6.80–7.40	12.20–13.20	19.00–29.00

*From standing.

Figure 66 is offered by way of a summary of muscular strength and its various forms expressed to meet the demands of individual sports. Development of strength to meet these demands is a unique blend of general and specific strength training programmed according to the athlete's status relative to these demands; the time available to train; and the quality of the training environment.

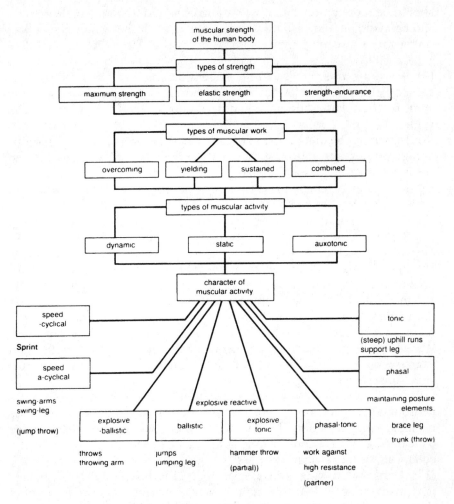

Fig. 66 *Summary of different forms of muscular strength*

In concluding this topic on strength development, table 27 provides a summary of suggested training loads.

■ Notes on strength training

(1) Emphasis in strength training is obviously on development of specific contractile properties. It is essential that mobility and stretching work is also included to ensure that a full range of movement is possible in all joint actions and that normal growth and development may proceed naturally.

(2) In young athletes and novices it is advisable that a broad basis of general strength training is used, involving medium intensity over sets of 8–10 repetitions.

(3) In strength training for women, whilst strength objectives, training load extent, intensity and frequency can be as for men, progression

should be more gradual and over a longer period. (Note: female athletes should avoid jumping activities or any exercise which puts sudden impact on the sacro-iliac joint in the 2–3 days pre-menstruation period – see note 8 page 190.)

(4) In young and novice athletes considerable attention in training should be directed at development of those muscles which stabilise the spine on the pelvis (abdominal and back muscles) and the rotators of the spine.

(5) Maximum training must maintain a natural balance of protagonist: antagonist strength ratio, e.g. building up the quadriceps and neglecting the hamstrings creates an imbalance.

(6) Maximum strength programmes must not be attempted when an athlete is already fatigued or has not warmed up.

(7) Passive mobility work must *never* follow maximum strength training.

(8) Activity should cease whenever sharp pain is experienced in the exercising muscles.

(9) In pursuing a maximum strength programme for a particular joint action, there should be variety in the exercises used. This not only enhances the strength development process but contributes to a healthy motivational climate. For example, although squat work might be the focus of exercise for developing the quadriceps and hip extensor, it should be interrupted and augmented from time to time with such exercises as leg press, hack lifts, front squat, knee extensions, step ups, slide squat, single leg squats etc.

(10) In all strength work, the range limits should be determined by neuromuscular control – *not* by the body's skeletal structure. For example in squat work, the 'full squat' limit should be as deep as the controlled eccentric contraction of the quadriceps will allow – *not* the collapsing of thighs against calves.

(11) Until the growing athlete has stabilised in bone/joint development, it is inadvisable to load the spine when exercising. As a rule, weights should not be taken on the shoulders until 16 or 17 years of age, unless the athlete has an extensive background of general strength work which has systematically developed the musculature supporting the spine.

(12) When loads are taken on the shoulders, strain is placed on the spine. The spine *must* therefore be kept straight, with no exaggerated lumbar curve nor rounding of the shoulders as either will put the joint complex of the spine at a serious mechanical disadvantage and consequently risk of serious injury could be considerable.

(13) All related/specific exercises with resistance must be well schooled from a technique point of view and kept close to the timings/accelerations of the technical models required by the athlete's sport or event. This implies learning with lighter loads, and fairly tight supervision through early progressions.

(14) Exhausting anaerobic endurance work should not follow maximum or elastic strength work, as this will create a climate for connective tissue injury.

(**15**) The general progression of strength should take the following shape:

- circuit training focused on all joint complexes for a balance of strength
- stage training using the same exercises as circuit training
- stage training using resistances such as weighted jackets; wrist/ankle weights; weight belts; medicine balls; sand sacks etc.*
- weight training based on multiple repetitions (up to 12) on foundation of sound technique*
- progressive loading weight training with periodic tests for maxima*
- special programme mixing intensities inter- and intra-unit
- special programmes using machines and/or electronic stimulation etc.* (Note: not all athletes will be suited to this area of progression.)
* parallel development of specific strength.

(**16**) Women's strength training programmes should be continued, if at a slightly lower extent, throughout the competition season. This is not so necessary with men.

(**17**) There is a time lag between achievement of new best results in control tests for strength, be that general or specific, and best performance in the athlete's sport. The time lag will vary according to the strength characteristic measured and the athlete involved. Coaches should be aware of this and plan the phasing of strength training and introduction of competition accordingly.

(**18**) In those sports where there is high maximum strength dependence, a strength unit is often introduced the day before competition. The theory behind this practice is that the neuromuscular system will remain in a state of high excitation for 24 hours after such a unit. The key is to avoid units where strength training is in pursuit of maximum values, or where the athlete is fatigued by the unit.

(**19**) Elastic strength units require a longer period of recovery than orthodox concentric strength work with weights etc. Consequently, it is *not* advisable to include elastic strength units in the 3–4 days before competition.

(**20**) Each exercise or movement requires an adjustment of balance to stabilise body parts. Strength training programmes must, then, include a variety of exercise and movement through the equipment and methods used, as much as through the combinations of training ratios and structures of loading. Strength training machines, orthodox weight training equipment, medicine balls, water resistance, partner work, heavier sport – specific implements, weights jackets, etc. *all* have their place somewhere in the athlete's year-round programme.

(**21**) In team games, the specific strength requirement of players varies according to the demands of their respective positions. For example, in rugby union, the strength programme for props differs from second row or back row, etc.

Table 27 Loading and strength training

objective	intensity of training load	repetitions in each set	sets in each unit	training system	recovery between sets	time holding isometric contraction	evaluation procedures	(possible event app.) probable event app.
Development of maximum strength in events where single expression of maximum strength is required.	Concentric 85%→100% Eccentric *105%→175%	1→5	A 5→8 N 2→4	Simple sets Super sets Stagger sets Pyramids-5 x 85% →1 x 100% Mixed sets (ecc-conc-isom)	4→5 mins	A 9→12 secs 80%–100% N 6→9 secs 60%–80%	Max lift dynamometer	eg weight lifting shot discus hammer javelin (jumps) rugby front 5
Development of maximum strength in events where multiple expression of maximum strength is required.	70%→85%	5→10	2→5	Simple sets Super sets Pyramids-8 x 75% ‹→6 x 80% ‹→5 x 85%	2→4 mins		Max lift dynamometer	eg (circle throws) javelin high, triple, long sprints hurdles, rowing
Development of elastic strength where work is also done in other units for maximum strength.	30%→50% or 55%→65% or 3%–5% body weight resistance exercises involving whole technique (eg gymnastics, jumping, etc.) or related plyometrics specific & special strength exercises	6→10 5→8 6→10 5→10	4→6 4→6 3→5 3→5	Simple sets Super sets Pyramid by intensity only. 10 x 30%: 10 x 40%: 10 x 50%: 10 x 55%: 10 x 60%: 10 x 65%. Performed as stage training Performed as stage training	3→5 mins		Standing long, triple, vert. jump etc.	All explosive sports

*Advanced athlete only

Table 27 (continued)

objective	intensity of training load	repetitions in each set	sets in each unit	training system	recovery between sets	time holding isometric contraction	evaluation procedures	(possible event app.) probable event app.
Development of elastic *and* maximum strength simultaneously.	a 75% or b 3%–5% body weight resistance exercises involving whole technique or c Alternating between 85% and elastic/ plyometric equivalent	6→10; 5 (x 85%) 6–10 (x plyometric)	4→6	Simple sets Super sets; Performed as stage training	3→5 mins; 3→5 mins		Standing long, triple, vert. jump	All explosive sports eg hockey rugby soccer
Development of a basic strength or strength endurance for all events.	30%→40%	25%–50% Max	4→6	Simple sets circuit	Optimal		Max repetitions Max holding time etc.	General for all sports especially young or novice athlete
Development of strength endurance in those events with high demands for it.	40%→60% loading the basic technique (eg hill running, swimming, rowing dragging resistance etc.)	50%→75% Max according to activity	3→5	Circuit training	30→45 secs	Not isom. but controlled lifts with 30%–50% max eg 6 secs flex. Performed as stage training		eg rowing wrestling swimming cross-country skiing ice-hockey steeplechase

Summary

Broadly speaking, the athlete develops strength to make available a greater potential force of energy expression. This force may be used against external resistance in pursuit of performance objectives where speed, strength, endurance and mobility are variously, and separately, the criteria of success. The role of strength for a muscle group assumes a unique character according to the technical demands of a sport. This role ranges from dynamic to static and from relative to absolute in pursuit of specific performance objectives. Methods used in development of strength reflect the demands of these objectives.

15
Theory and practice of speed development

Speed in sport

Speed in training theory defines the capacity of moving a limb or part of the body's lever system or the whole body with the greatest possible velocity. Maximum value of such movements would be without loading. Thus, the discus thrower's arm will have greatest velocity in the throwing phase if no discus is held and velocity would be reduced as the implement's weight is increased relative to the athlete's absolute strength.

Speed is measured in metres per second, as, for example, in quantifying the value for speed of moving one part of the body's lever system relative to another; the forward speed of the body in sprinting or at point of take-off in jumping; and the velocity of implements and balls at release or on being struck. The time taken to achieve a certain task may also be considered a measure of the athlete's speed. So controls for sprinting speed might be time taken to sprint 30m. Or again, the number of repetitions of a task within a short period of time might be considered an index of speed. For example, the number of repetition runs in a shuttle run over 5m in 20 seconds. Measuring equipment includes stop watches, photo-electric cells coupled to print-out devices, cinematographic techniques based on film speed, force plates, and so on.

Speed is a determining factor in the explosive sports (e.g. sprints, jumps and most field sports), while in the endurance events its role as a determining factor appears to reduce with increased distance. It is also a determining factor where speed of response is the difference between scoring points or losing points (e.g. combat sports); or where such response will gain competitive advantage on the one hand and protect life on the other (e.g. motor sports). As with the characteristic of strength, the relative contribution of speed to each sport varies according to the demands of the sport, the bio-type of the athlete and the specific techniques practised by the athlete. Consequently, the distribution of speed training units and the nature and number of practices are extremely varied.

Speed may be a determining factor directly, as in, for example, reacting to the starter's pistol, or indirectly, as, for example, in the development of kinetic energy in jumping. The difference between direct and indirect is that, with the former maximum velocity is sought, whereas with the latter some optimum velocity is required to permit maximum expression of relevant strength. It is therefore important to bear in mind that speed

215

increases may not necessarily lead to improved performance. The pattern of speed and acceleration of relative movements must be synchronised so that each part of the lever system can make an optimal force contribution. For example, there would be no point in making the discus arm so fast that it began to make its contribution before the legs and trunk, nor would it benefit the long jumper to have so much horizontal speed at the board that there was insufficient time for the take-off leg to express the strength required for vertical lift. Speed development is, then, very much a matter of learning how to use it.

∎ Speed development

∎ Speed in practice
There are seven areas in sports performance where training will enhance speed.

(1) Reaction to a signal, as for example in the sprinter's reaction to the gun, or the tennis player's reaction in volleying.

(2) Capacity to accelerate: this is of particular importance to those athletes who must beat opponents across the ground or who must quickly reach a particular point on the court/pitch to execute a technique.

(3) Capacity to rapidly adjust balance following execution of one technique in order to prepare to execute another. This applies to every games situation.

(4) Achievement of maximum speed: the athlete here is executing a given technique as fast as he is capable of without breakdown of that technique's effectiveness. Often speed is mistakenly thought of as an entity in itself. It is not. It is a sophistication of technique, where all demands of the technique are performed at the highest speed consistent with the general synchronised framework.

(5) Capacity to maintain maximum speed once it is reached. This also is a co-ordination issue, not an endurance issue, and is seen, for example, in sports where an athlete such as Bailey can maintain his maximum speed of 12.05m/sec for only 20m. This is not followed as one might expect by a gradual loss of speed for the balance of the race. Rather there is a breakdown of co-ordination for 10m (Bailey – 11.76m/sec) before a gradual deceleration will commence through to the finish.

(6) Capacity to limit the effect of endurance factors on speed: the rate at which fuel reaches the working muscles and waste products are removed, eventually represents a limiting factor to producing the high intensity muscle contraction and quality co-ordination necessary to maintain maximum or near maximum speed.

(7) Capacity to choose correct action options: in many sports, the difference between success and failure is the speed at which the correct action option is chosen by a player or players to solve a problem posed by the opposition; and a problem is then set for the opposition. The better the opposition or higher the level of competition, the less time a player has to make those choices.

The development of speed is dependent on several factors, the main ones being:

(1) Innervation (fig. 36, p. 91): a high frequency of alternation between stimulation and inhibition of neurones, and an accurate selection and regulation of motor units, makes it possible to achieve a high frequency of movement and/or speed of movement, married to an optimal expression or deployment of strength. This is the fundamental ability to move limbs at maximum velocity.

(2) Elasticity (fig. 38, p. 93): the capacity to capitalise on muscle tone via the elastic component of muscle has relevance to those sports demanding high starting acceleration (as in sprints and most field sports) or 'rapid strike' (as in sprinting and jumping). The precise mechanisms involved are not clear but there appears to be a complex co-ordination of motor units, reflexes, elastic component and the ability to contract muscle at high speed. The characteristic is, however, identifiable and has been referred to in sports jargon as 'bounce'. Elasticity is related to relative strength and elastic strength.

(3) Biochemistry: speed would appear to rely specifically on the energy supplies within muscle, i.e. alactic anaerobic pathway (see chapter 6), and on the speed of its mobilisation. Short duration maximum intensity work appears to be the training stimulus for development of this area.

(4) Muscle relaxability: the ability of the muscle to relax and to allow stretch in speed exercises is fundamental to perfect technique and to a high frequency of movement. Harre (1973) has said 'If these qualities are insufficiently developed, the required range of movement cannot be achieved in the course of the movement, particularly at the points of reversal of movement, the synergists have to overcome too great a resistance'. Training which obliges the athlete to relax all muscles not directly involved with a given series of joint actions, even in fatigue, is of the utmost importance. Mobility work is also clearly indicated.

(5) Willpower: the athlete must concentrate on maximum voluntary effort to achieve maximum speed. However, unlike the weight lifter who has a quantified target as the focus of his concentration, the athlete has nothing more to go on than physical sensation, comparison with another athlete, and the evidence of a stop watch. Human error may occur with the latter, so the coach must ensure that all possible information on speeds and times is given to the athlete. Moreover, to provide a suitable stimulus or target, speed work may be performed in groups, using handicaps, races, etc.

(6) Action acceptor: many situations, especially in combat sports and field games, etc., demand rapid selection of relevant cues and the technical ability to do so accurately will influence speed of movement or reaction.

(7) Environment: warm climate, altitude, footwear, running surface, low air resistance, clothing which enhances aerodynamics, or anything which may oblige an athlete to learn how to move faster will assist speed development.

■ Training for speed development

Speed development for track events has been extensively documented and will provide useful general knowledge of the practice of speed development for other sports.

Intensity

The intensity of training loads for speed development commence around 75% maximum. Here, the athlete is learning, at relatively high intensity, those adjustments necessary to maintain the pace or rhythm of a technique whilst 'timing' is put under pressure. Gradually, the athlete moves towards 100%. However, progression demands that the athlete attempts to surpass existing speed limits. Rehearsal of technique at intensities which break new ground is clearly not possible in great volume for reasons ranging from mental concentration through to energy production. It is for this reason that measures are taken to facilitate the learning process such as training athletes at altitude; pulling the athlete on an elastic rope or pulley system; reducing the weight of implements; reducing the time scales for making choices of action; in fact anything which requires a speed beyond the existing 100%.

Just as with strength training practices, the athlete must have mastery of technique before seeking to progress execution of technique at speed. The sequence of development is:

- develop a level of general conditioning which permits learning a sound basic technique
- learn a sound basic technique
- develop a level of specific conditioning which permits progressive sophistication of technique
- develop technique at speed.

Technical components should be learned and stabilised at slower speeds. Nevertheless, from the outset the athlete should be encouraged to consolidate technique by accelerating the level of intensity. This is necessary because the transfer of technique learned at a slow speed to the demands of maximum speed is usually very complex. To this end, practices are used in sprinting where the athlete runs a distance of, say, 75m, concentrates on the perfection of running action for 40m and then raises the speed of running for 35m. Or a technical component, such as those rehearsed in sprinting drills, is worked for 25m and then the athlete gradually accelerates to near maximum intensity over the next 50m. A hurdler strides over 3 hurdles with 5–7 strides between, then sprints over 3 hurdles with the normal 3-stride pattern. A tennis player brings the speed of service down to that which allows him to place the ball accurately in the service court, and to 'feel' the synchronization of each element in the technique. The idea is to relate to the timing of the technique as a basis for development; *then* to progress pace but within the constraints of sound technique. Finally the athlete masters that level of speed which permits him to select a given pace within his range, and which is sufficient to overcome the challenge of his opposition.

No fatigue should be evident in speed training because it is essential for the nervous system to be in a state of optimal excitement. Consequently speed training will follow immediately upon relevant warm-up. Endurance or strengthening work may follow, but never precede, speed training.

Extent

A relationship exists between intensity and extent of loading. If the athlete is working at maximum intensity, the extent of loading cannot be great. On the other hand, it is necessary for the athlete to rehearse a technique frequently at high intensity, if new levels of speed are to be stabilised. The following points may serve as a useful guideline to making decisions on extent.

(1) Techniques can be repeated in high volume *and* high intensity only if presented in small 'learning packages'. This ensures the highest speed of execution *and* recovery periods which permit athletes time to consolidate neuromuscular memory patterns. So a large number of sets with small numbers of repetitions of very high intensity would be most suitable.

(2) In sprint training the minimum distance to develop acceleration is that which allows the athlete to achieve near maximum speed. For most athletes this is around 30–40m. However, in other sports there are constraints imposed by the confines of the playing area. In some sports, then, the athlete must learn to achieve maximum acceleration over a very short distance (5–10m) and 'arrive' at the conclusion of such a burst of speed, prepared to select and execute a high precision technique. Soccer, tennis, and basketball are examples of such sports.

(3) Where maximum speed is being practised, a limiting factor to effective rehearsal can be the exhausting process of accelerating to maximum speed. For example, in long jump and in games where passing must be practised at the highest speed, the athletes must lift their pace from being stationary to the pace required. This is very tiring. To overcome the problem, some athletes practise from longer rolling starts or with the assistance of downhill starts. This means that although the athlete will look to distances of 10–30m to practise maximum speed itself, it may be necessary to have 40–60m roll-in to reach that speed.

(4) Optimal values can only be determined by individual testing on how long maximum speed can be held. The initial problem is, of course, to achieve maximum speed. It has already been pointed out that Bailey could only maintain his maximum speed for 20m. Co-ordination and concentration are the keys to extending this distance, but it is unlikely that it will reach 30m or further without the assistance offered by altitude, following wind etc., and then over distances of 25–40m.

(5) In sprinting, most athletes require 5–6 seconds to achieve maximum speed. This suggests that distances of 50–60m are required to develop the linking of initial acceleration and the 'pick up' to maximum speed.

Density

Recovery periods between runs at maximum speed must be long enough to restore working capacity, but short enough to maintain excitement of the nervous system and optimal body temperature. Given a reasonably warm climate, the interval between each run should be 4–6 minutes, which creates problems for athletes living in countries with long cold winters.

In the interest of gaining optimum advantage from each run, it might be advisable to allow this interval and to 'warm-up' before each run. Sets should again be used with, say, 3–4 runs per set and 2–3 sets per unit.

Units

The total number of runs per unit, as indicated above, should lie between 6 and 12, although individual variations exist. The number of units per weekly microcycle (microcycles, macrocycles and units are explained in chapter 21) will vary throughout the year, but at least one unit per microcycle must be included in phase 1 of the annual cycle (see p. 224) with 2–3 in phase 2, and 2–4 in phase 3, irrespective of the sport. With endurance sports, speed work will range in intensity from maximum to racing pace and unit distribution will vary according to racing distance, phase of the year and the athlete concerned.

Activities other than running

Throwing: speed in throwing can be developed by using lighter implements. Insufficient research data is available to provide detailed information, but the following points may serve as guidelines.

(1) If the implement is too light there is the risk of injury and disruption of the normal motor patterns of technique. Choosing implements approximately 5–10% lighter is a recommended basis from which to work. It is recommended also that the athlete works with the normal implement in the same unit, possibly on a 'set for set' basis. This mix can be extended to include specific strength work with implements heavier than the normal implement.

(2) Rebounding work or plyometrics should be considered as speed related training. Work in this area may effect a faster transition from yielding to the power of approach, shift or turn, to overcoming the load of impetus when moving levers (legs, hips) through the throw. This is particularly so for javelin, where increased speed of approach will place a considerably greater load on both legs. It is as if the athlete must concentrate on 'bouncing' out of the entry into the throw, rather than accepting the momentum of approach or shift. The danger is that to 'accept' is often to 'cushion' and this decreases speed and the elastic use of kinetic energy.

(3) Speed should only be pursued within the limits dictated by the athlete's technical ability. The fundamentals of technique must be not be abandoned for speed.

Jumping: the development of speed in jumping should be considered in two parts: development of approach speed (e.g. sprinting), and development of ability to use kinetic energy of increased approach speed. The previous discussion of sprinting speed should be applied to the development of approach speed, bearing in mind that the approach run must be consistent, even with advances in speed. The problem of using this increased speed is best solved by learning the new motor pattern of a faster passage over the take-off foot, and then progressing to the application of strength at this increased speed. The high energy cost of acceleration means that flat-out approach runs from scratch are inadvisable. The areas of practice that should be explored are:

- downhill approach to take-off
- fast 'touch-off' take-offs
- rolling start approaches
- pole plant in sand following the above (landing area placed over long jump-pit – pole vault)
- faster high jump approach onto extended landing area
- increasing the speed of non-jumping limb movements relative to the jumping limb.

Ultimately, the ability to use the kinetic energy of the approach is strength-related and consideration must be given to elastic strength work, rebound work, and depth jumping. *Relative* strength rather than *absolute* strength is critical.

■ The speed barrier

Saziorski (1971) suggests that a 'speed barrier' can arise if the young athlete trains exclusively on sprint exercises, or if the advanced athlete neglects the use of special exercises for the development of elastic strength. Osolin (1952) tends to agree by stating that due to establishing a 'kinetic (motor) stereotype' by working at maximum intensity (e.g. training with the same group at all times) the development of speed may be made more difficult, or even prevented. However, he offers a note of optimism by suggesting that practices such as 'forced speed' (e.g. catapulting the athlete with use of an elastic rope), or 'assisted speed' (e.g. altitude sprinting, downhill runs, or wind assisted runs), or lighter implements, or increased competition demands, etc., will break an athlete's existing speed barrier.

Upton and Radford (1975) appear to support this and explain 'The benefits of teaching methods which stress fast limb movements and the sensation of speed (e.g. by towing) may well result from improvement of neuronal programs, increased motoneuron excitability and more synchronous firing of motoneurons'. This observation highlights an often neglected cause for speed barriers – the failure to involve efficient 'neuronal programs . . . and more synchronous firing of motoneurons'. The introduction of sprint drills to the conditioning programme may be an attempt to establish motor unit programming. In fact, Ballreich (1975) goes as far as stating that '. . . sprinting for top level sprinters can probably best be improved by developing its technical (coordination) rather than its conditioning (power) component'.

■ Endurance and speed training

The basis of competition specific speed endurance appears to lie in a certain measure of aerobic endurance developed by suitable loading. Although the absolute extent of this loading is low in the endurance programme of an endurance athlete, the relative extent can be high and may reach 90% in phase 1 of the preparatory period. Williams (1974) has suggested that this type of training improves aerobic capacity and glycogen concentration in red muscle fibres. This has a positive effect not only on speed endurance, but also on the capacity to recover after loadings of sub-maximum and maximum intensity. Thus, the athlete will be able to attempt *more* repetitions at the maximum and near-maximum intensities of speed training.

Once a foundation for the development of aerobic endurance has been established, the athlete must be exposed to competition specific loadings similar to those of competition conditions. This work will be introduced in phase 2 and continued in phase 3. Broadly speaking, units for the development of competition speed endurance may be listed as follows.

(1) Repetition runs at sub-maximum to near maximum intensity. Long recovery periods are necessary between runs of near maximum intensity to ensure that quality is maintained, while shorter intervals are required where runs are of sub-maximum intensity. Sets of runs with 2–4 minutes between runs are recommended, but these will of necessity be short sets (e.g. 2–4 runs) to maintain quality. Between sets, longer intervals of 10–15 minutes should be introduced and it is recommended that at least half of this interval is active.
(2) Stress loading at maximum or near maximum intensity (for the distance used) over distances between ⅔ x and 2 x the racing distance.
(3) Stress loading at maximum racing speed over stretches of up to 10%–20% longer than the racing distance.
(4) Varied speed runs where the tempo or intensity varies in the course of the run, e.g. 150m of 50m acceleration, 50m hold, 50m acceleration.
(5) High repetition, short distance sprints (30–60m) where maintaining maximum striding rate is emphasised, e.g. 6 x 6 x 40m – incomplete recovery in sets.
(6) Competitions.

A microcycle of 2–3 units per week should be used in phase 2, but 1–2 units per microcycle will be adequate as the competition density assumes an endurance training role of its own.

Speed endurance practices for sports other than pure sprinting are poorly documented, but the endurance factor must be borne in mind. Five sets of top class tennis frequently exceed 5 hours (McEnroe–Becker, Davis Cup 1987, 6 hours 38 minutes); vault and high jump competitions can last over six hours; qualifying throws/jumps may be separated by 60 minutes; athletes declining to jump may cause an athlete to have several jumps/vaults in rapid succession; a qualifying contest and final in one day can necessitate 9 throws/jumps at maximum intensity; field games last from 60–90 minutes; boxing (professional) may last 75 minutes; sailing lasts hours, etc. In Formula 1 races, the heart rate of drivers is, for approximately 90 minutes, in the range of 175–185 beats per minute. These factors may mean speed endurance and strength endurance work for all sports where there is a demand for speed in the presence of fatigue. For example in throwing:

- rapid succession throws with normal implements being fed to the athlete (full throws, isolated action and standing throws)
- rapid succession throws with medicine balls or lighter implements, as above
- single throws separated by 15–60 minutes, etc
- track workouts followed by throws
- maximum repetition simulation throws per 30 seconds, etc.

Or in jumping:

- rapid succession short approach jumps
- rapid succession 'step-down' jumps (e.g. 21 stride, 17 stride, 13 stride, 9 stride) with walk-back recovery
- speed bounding/hopping, etc., over 30m
- jumping circuits over 400m (50m bound, etc.)
- single jumps/vaults separated by 15–60 minutes, etc
- fast agility work on ropes, bars, etc., for simulated work on the pole.

Or in games:

- rapid succession strokes in tennis/squash
- continuous pressure passing/lay up practice in basketball
- unopposed non-stop rugby/soccer/hockey
- high speed games without breaks at altitude
- conditioning work followed by continuous speed work under pressure.

■ Attitude and speed training

In the intensely interactive world of team games, combat sports, racquet games, etc., in order for speed of individual or team performance to be delivered instinctively under the pressure of competition, it must be repeatedly rehearsed in training. Successful performance is not only due to speed of movement across the ground and speed of choosing correct action options, but also speed of thought and interpretation of situations. Just as a typist thinks in 'phrases' rather than 'letters and words', these players must think and act in 'action phrases'. A player giving or passing the ball to a colleague must be thinking about, and moving immediately to, a position to support the person receiving the ball. This means having this attitude in even simple practice situations. Without doubt it contributes immensely to the rhythm and speed at which a given team will play in competition.

■ The annual cycle

The annual cycle may be split into three definite phases for training purposes. Phase 1 will increase the extent of loading to prepare the athlete for phase 2 and an increase in the intensity of loading. Phase 3, the final phase of the year, will develop and stabilise competition performance. A detailed account of this 'periodisation' will be found in chapter 19.

Phase 1 (preparation)

Training should be aimed at developing aerobic endurance, elastic strength, mobility and technical efficiency.

Both general and special training methods are used, i.e. general: games, fartlek; special: bounding, drills. The intensity of runs in technique sessions must be varied, but at all times the relaxation, rhythm and range must be maintained. Should pursuit of power or increased stride frequency cause the athlete's technique to deteriorate, the intensity must be reduced until compatible with the athlete's technical level. In technique sports, the athlete must concentrate on the course of the movement and *not on expression of strength*, and finally, acceleration work should be used.

Phase 2 (adaptation)

Training must now use mainly special methods for the development of speed, speed endurance and elastic strength. Sub-maximum and maximum intensity must be introduced more and more frequently as the speed development factors are pulled together (see p. 216: speed development). Considerable emphasis must now be laid on extensive warm-up and warm-down, with specific mobility (passive and active) included in the former.

Phase 3 (application)

Competition density/frequency must now be geared to the individual athlete. Elastic strength, active recovery and lower intensity units must be interpolated, and maximum intensity work for speed may be used in 2–4 units per microcycle.

Sub-maximum intensity and maximum intensity work for speed endurance must be included with thoughtful evaluation of competition frequency.

In long season sports such as tennis, soccer, rugby etc., due to the fact that there is limited time to build a strong foundation to the conditioning programme, it is necessary to work on endurance, strength, speed and competitive sharpness throughout the competition phase. This means that preparation, adaptation, and application have to be built into very short microcycles of 4 day – 7 day – 10 day etc. duration.

■ Risk of injury

To introduce detailed exercises, such as drills, would overburden this text; these are to be found in specific sports literature elsewhere.

Speed work, in reaching for maximum limits of force expression, range of movement, frequency of movement, and so on, exposes the athlete to immense injury risk, and it seems appropriate to include the following advice from Harre: 'Speed loadings put maximum demands on the muscles, sinews and ligaments. The potential for injury is relatively high. Main causes are local overloading, lack of versatility, stress-loading in too cold a state or in a state of fatigue, or inadequate ability of the muscles to relax as a result of insufficient direct preparation (warming-up) for the demands of speed. Therefore careful preparation in training before competition is an essential for any speed performance. In addition, demands for speed at maximum intensity in the early morning hours should be avoided. At the earliest approach of pain or cramp in the muscle, the loading is to be discontinued. In cool weather, suitable clothing (track suit) is essential. Finally, the most extensive use should be made of relaxing exercises and massage. The rubbing into the skin of strong embrocations to improve circulation should only be done with medical approval.'

■ Summary

Speed of whole body movement, or of individual joint actions, is a decisive factor of successful performance in many sports. While speed is frequently the product of a co-ordinated sequence of strength expression of joint actions, the development of speed is not synonymous with the development of strength. In speed-dependent sports, it is important that speed of technical performance is introduced early. However, this must not compromise the basic technical model. Speed is considered under the heading of 'conditioning training' in many programmes, due to the possible combination of speed with strength, endurance and/or mobility. However it may equally be considered as a sophisticated extension of technical training. Practices for development of speed are specific to the technical demands of a sport. Such demands vary according to the involvement of strength, endurance and mobility, the synchronised use of varied speed of joint action, and the requirement for optimum or maximum speed.

16
Theory and practice of endurance development

Training methods

It has already been suggested that a scientifically based and systematic programme of training is fundamental to the pursuit of high level performance in sport. Of all sports, the endurance events of track and field and swimming are the best documented in these terms. Certain types of exercise *increase* certain bodily functions, while others *decrease* them (table 19, p. 127). Williams illustrated at the 1974 Meadowbank Convention that the effect of training is directly related to the duration and intensity of training load. The purpose here is not, however, to labour the 'scientific bases' but to examine the type of training included in the systematic programme. Various references to physiological measures are more in the nature of comment than detailed argument.

All training methods for the development of endurance can be divided into three groups: duration, repetition, and competition and testing methods (fig. 67).

Duration

Continuous method: this is running at a steady pace or intensity where the heart rate lies between 130 and 160 beats per minute. The duration of such running will be over 30 minutes for the young athlete and from 60–120 minutes for the mature. Improvement in VO_2 maximum (aerobic capacity) is achieved here via long-term loading under aerobic conditions. This method is recommended especially for the long distance endurance athlete.

Alternating pace method: this is long duration running, with the speed of successive stretches alternating according to a plan. At the simplest level, one might have a slow pace (HR = 130–150 beats/minute) for 1.0km alternating with a fast pace (HR = 170–180 beats/minute) for 0.5km. The forced entry into anaerobic work and consequent oxygen debt demands repayment within the next 1.0km and this situation acts as a strong stimulus for the improvement of VO_2 maximum. This method is used extensively both by middle and long distance athletes.

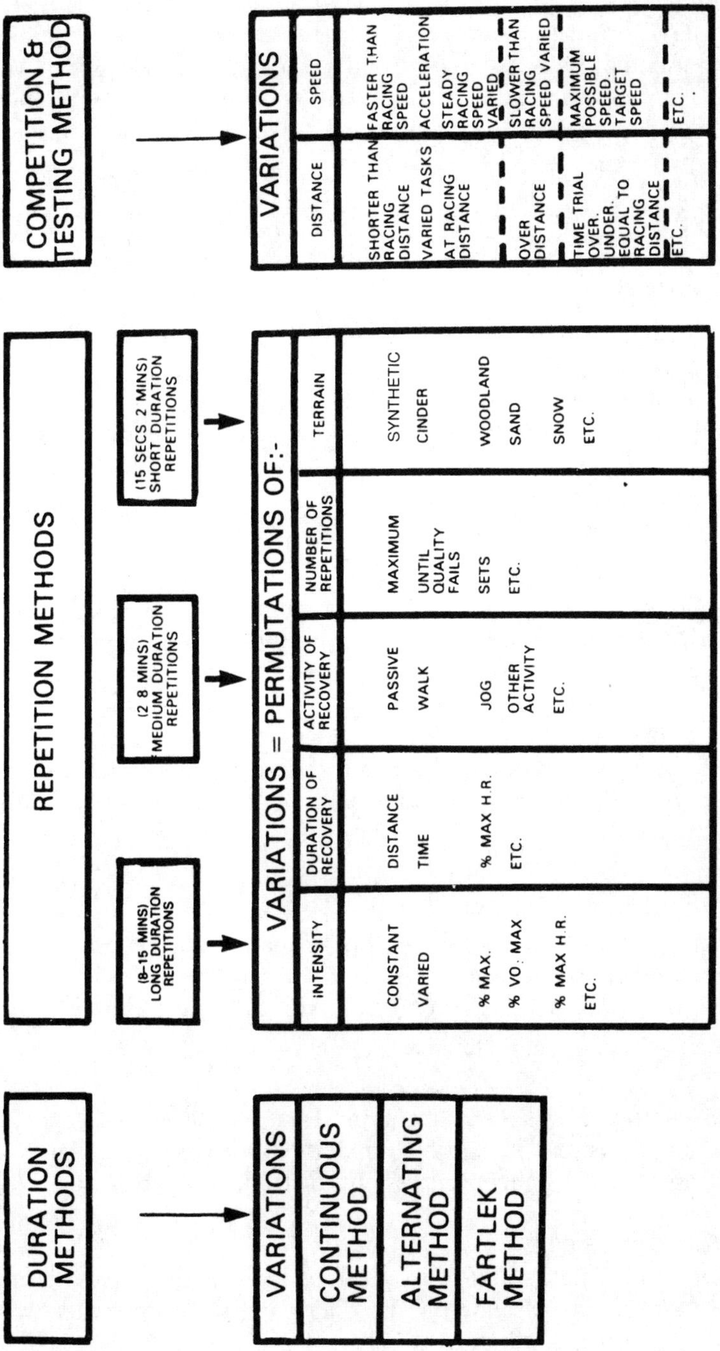

Fig. 67 Summary of endurance training methods (adapted from Harre, 1973)

DURATION METHODS

VARIATIONS
CONTINUOUS METHOD
ALTERNATING METHOD
FARTLEK METHOD

REPETITION METHODS

(8-15 MINS) LONG DURATION REPETITIONS

(2 8 MINS) MEDIUM DURATION REPETITIONS

(15 SECS 2 MINS) SHORT DURATION REPETITIONS

VARIATIONS = PERMUTATIONS OF:-

INTENSITY	DURATION OF RECOVERY	ACTIVITY OF RECOVERY	NUMBER OF REPETITIONS	TERRAIN
CONSTANT	DISTANCE	PASSIVE	MAXIMUM	SYNTHETIC
VARIED	TIME	WALK	UNTIL QUALITY FAILS	CINDER
% MAX.	% MAX H.R.	JOG	SETS	WOODLAND
% VO. MAX	ETC.	OTHER ACTIVITY	ETC.	SAND
% MAX H.R.		ETC.		SNOW
ETC.				ETC.

COMPETITION & TESTING METHOD

VARIATIONS

DISTANCE	SPEED
SHORTER THAN RACING DISTANCE	FASTER THAN RACING SPEED
VARIED TASKS AT RACING DISTANCE	ACCELERATION
	STEADY RACING SPEED
	VARIED
OVER DISTANCE	SLOWER THAN RACING SPEED VARIED
TIME TRIAL OVER. UNDER. EQUAL TO RACING DISTANCE	MAXIMUM POSSIBLE SPEED. TARGET SPEED
ETC.	ETC.

Fartlek: this is running with varying intensity according to the requirements of the athlete and the dictates of terrain. The athlete will use a terrain which undulates and makes varying demands upon him (e.g. hills, woodland, plough, sand). Like the alternating pace method, anaerobic periods provide a strong stimulus for the improvement of VO_2 maximum. In addition, the demands of terrain stimulate strength endurance development and proprioceptive balance adjustment of ankle, knee and hip.

■ Repetition

These methods offer a wide variety of possible training effects, due to the number of variables.

(1) Duration of the training run (distance *or* time: classified as short, medium, long).
(2) Duration of the recovery period (distance *or* time).
(3) Intensity of the training run (m, seconds, % VO_2 maximum, speed, etc.).
(4) Number of repetitions and sets.
(5) Activity of recovery (walking, jogging, passive).
(6) Terrain for training (uphill, track, sand, surf, etc.).

Training is geared to the type of endurance required for a given sport and the difference in effect of adjusting these variables is quite startling. For example, the following are worth noting.

Interval training

This is training for the rapid development of aerobic endurance and has proved successful. Returning to the variables, interval training might look like the following.

(1) 200m.
(2) 200m.
(3) Intensity sufficient to raise HR to approximately 180 beats/minute.
(4) Progressive increase in repetitions.
(5) Jogging for 90 seconds – returning HR to approximately 120 beats/minute.
(6) Track.

This session is known in sports jargon as slow–fast 200s, and makes a more rapid improvement in aerobic capacity compared with duration methods (long steady distance), but its effects are lost quicker.

Speed endurance training

This develops the athlete's ability to produce high quality performance despite the by-products of anaerobesis. There are an infinite variety of units for this objective and their value may only be truly assessed by studying their place in a training plan. For example, in the month of August, a girl running 4 x 200m in 27 seconds with 30 seconds recovery may have progressed in intensity and density, but regressed in extent from a unit performed in January of 10 x 200m in 30 seconds with 75 seconds recovery. Of all types of track training, the control of these units is the most difficult, and coaches tend to use past experience as the main key for adjustment. Broadly speaking, the following general rules apply.

(1) Increase the total extent (number) of repetitions (e.g. 4 x 200m → 12 x 200m).

(2) Using a given recovery time, standardise an intensity of run over the training distance (each run aims at a given time, e.g. 12 x 200m in 34 seconds with 75 seconds recovery).

(3) Gradually increase intensity (make runs faster, e.g.12 x 200m in 34 seconds → 30 seconds with 75 seconds recovery).

(4) Reduce the total extent (number) of repetitions (e.g. 12 x 200m in 30 seconds with 75 seconds recovery → 2 x 4 x 200m in 27 seconds with 75 seconds recovery and 15–20 minutes between sets).

(5) Gradually increase density (shorten the recovery, e.g. 2 x 4 x 200m in 27 seconds with 75 seconds → 30 seconds recovery).

This type of work seeks to maintain quality and striding rate, and work sets are often used. If the times for repetitions fall off in the course of the unit, the training is moving towards strength endurance rather than speed endurance. Consequently, all progression must guarantee the maintenance of quality. It should be noted that within a unit, varying pace may be used in separate sets – hence units such as 'step-downs'. For example:

> 3 x 300m in 48 seconds with 100m jog recovery in 60 seconds
> (jog 100m in 60 seconds between sets)
> 3 x 300m in 45 seconds with 100m jog recovery in 60 seconds
> (jog 100m in 60 seconds between sets)
> 3 x 300m in 42 seconds with 100m jog recovery in 60 seconds

Or again, varying distances may be incorporated with varying pace within a unit. For example, the following comprises one set of a 3-set unit, with 100m jog between sets and repetitions:

> 600m in 108 seconds
> 400m in 68 seconds
> 300m in 48 seconds
> 200m in 30 seconds
> 100m in 14 seconds

These two unit variations are means of educating the athlete in pace judgement *and* in the physiological demands of pace change. Speed endurance training, in making complex demands upon the athlete in terms of energy provision, co-ordination, and strength, creates a stimulus for the complex adaptation required of middle distance athletes.

Strength endurance training

This is training to develop the athlete's ability to apply force in the climate of lactic anaerobesis. Quality demands are reduced and replaced simply by the task of completing the training unit. Recovery periods are normally very strict and, although the intensity of the run is seldom monitored, the athlete must run as hard as possible. Thus we have units such as:

circuit training
2 x 4 x 100m 'back to back' (30 seconds recovery)
2 x 5 x 80m 'turnabout' (shuttle running)
6 x 150m hill run (jog recovery 90 seconds)
5 x 80m sand dune climb (walk down recovery)
6 x 200m in surf (passive 3-minute recovery)
4 x 200m Skip B (high knee and clawing action; passive 3-minute recovery)
resisted performance of a given activity in the climate of endurance factors, i.e. 6 x 50m swimming and towing a drag, 8 x 500m rowing and towing a drag.

Strength endurance training causes considerable wear and tear in the athlete's organism and it is possible that a saturation of microcycles with units of this type would cause a loss of mental and physical resilience. However, these units help the athlete to keep going when lactate is high and, although annual training plans vary, such units may be best inserted between phases 1 and 2, and/or late in phase 2 (see chapter 15).

■ Competition and testing
Without doubt, competition and testing methods are the best stimulus to develop specific endurance qualities. This is especially so if the actual competition duration is used for this purpose. Embraced by this type of endurance training method could be:

• time trials at distances equal to, less than, or in excess of the racing distance
• specific task runs where the athlete must reach a certain point in a given time, then meet the demands of a maximum intensity finish (e.g. 600m where the athlete must reach 400m in 60 seconds, then sprint to finish)
• standard training units where the athlete attempts to perform a given unit prior to being tested for various items significant to a bioprofile
• competitions themselves, e.g. indoor, cross-country, etc. It is also possible to give an athlete a specific task within a competition – say in 1 mile, to reach the bell in 3 minutes 3 seconds – then break 4 minutes for the final mile time
• maintenance of high rate of execution and accuracy of a given technique in the climate of endurance factors.

However, the intention here is not to advocate one method over another since each method and variation brings about psychological, physiological and biomechanical reactions. It is not sufficient to rely on one choice for the optimal development of the specific endurance capacities in a given athlete. Perhaps this point is best illustrated by referring to the study undertaken by Viru, Urgenstein and Pisuke 1972 (fig. 68). They trained 9 groups of students using different training units. The difference in training effect was quite marked. For example, (1) interval training increased heart volume, while duration methods (continuous/fartlek) were more effective in increasing the oxygen carrying capacity of the blood than interval training; and (2) the greatest improvement in 800m performance was noted in the hill-run group (15°) and least improvement was noted in the complex method group. They concluded that no single method provided development of the total organism, and suggested that to use one method only may ultimately impair performance. Only by the skilful integration of the principal training methods, and their variations, will the required level of adaptation be approached, let alone achieved.

The training plan for an athlete must be dictated by:

- the competition demands of the sport
- the individual athlete's training status
- the stage of development of the athlete (age, sex, anatomy, physiology, etc.)
- the long- and short-term objectives of training
- the limitations of the training environment
- the demands of the non-athletic environment
- the athlete's own personality.

The competition demands of the sport

One school of thought holds that since there appears to be a percentage breakdown between the energy pathways in different sports, as shown in table 28, then training should be similarly divided. Another school of thought holds that the sport should be evaluated on its demands relative to short-, medium- and long-term endurance, as well as speed and strength endurance.

Table 28 Aerobic v anaerobic contribution to energy requirement according to distance run

distance in m	aerobic	anaerobic
200	5%	95%
400	17%	83%
800	34%	66%
1500	50%	50%
5000	80%	20%
10000	90%	10%
Marathon	98%	2%

Short-term endurance: the endurance required for covering efforts of 45 seconds to 2 minutes duration. Obviously, a high percentage of anaerobic involvement exists in such efforts. Speed endurance and strength endurance status is critical to short-term endurance.

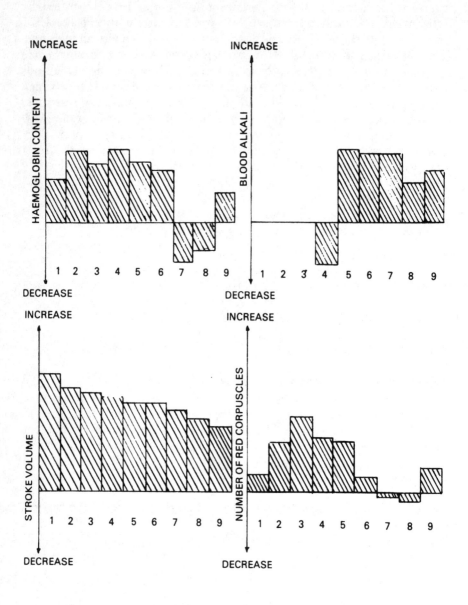

Fig. 68 *Effects of certain training programmes on selected physiological parameters (adapted from work by Viru, Urgenstein and Pisuke, USSR, 1972) (1) Sets of 4–5 runs with 1½–2 mins recovery; 7–10 mins between sets. e.g. 3 x 4 x 150m (75%); (2) Complex training involving various sessions; (3) Long steady distance; (4) Fartlek; (5) 2–5 flat out runs – full recovery; (6) Interval sprints (40–50m sprint/jog); (7) Hill runs up 15° gradient; (8) Intensive interval runs 100–200m at 80%–90% with 1–3 mins recovery until quality drops; (9) Extensive interval runs – such as slow/fast 200m*

Medium-term endurance: the endurance required for efforts of 2 minutes to 8 minutes duration. Again, anaerobic processes are involved, but an apparent steady state has been achieved. Strength endurance and speed endurance determine medium-term endurance efficiency since a relatively high resistance, represented by the amount of force which the athlete must apply, must be expressed at a relatively high frequency over the whole period. Although present world times fall outside this range, steeplechase may be considered as having *very* high medium-term endurance demands.

Long-term endurance: the endurance required for efforts in excess of 8 minutes duration and during which time there is no essential decrease in speed. The performance depends almost exclusively on aerobic efficiency. As the time increases, so the aerobic role becomes more exclusive. This type of endurance should be considered as virtually synonymous with aerobic endurance/heart endurance, etc.

Speed endurance: the endurance required to resist fatigue due to loading at sub-maximum and maximum intensity (approx. 85–100% maximum intensity), and predominantly anaerobic production of energy. It is essential in sports demanding this type of endurance that speed is not reduced due to fatigue or innervation inhibition.

Strength endurance: the endurance required to continuously express relatively high strength efficiency when anaerobic by-products are accumulating. This is related not only to the alkali-acid imbalance in working muscle, the result of which painfully terminates activity, but also to the psychological aspects of willpower and the ability to tolerate pain.

The schematic relationship of these different endurance capacities is represented in figure 69.

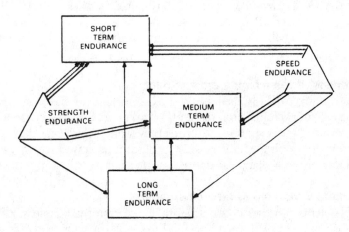

Fig. 69 *Inter-relationship of various areas of endurance*

Yet another school of thought holds that *all* endurance events are founded upon an extensive base of aerobic efficiency – so much so that approximately 67% of the training year is devoted to duration methods and their derivatives, and approximately 20% of the training year to the specific demands of a given endurance sport, as well as 13% to competition. Whatever basis is used for assessing endurance requirements, serious consideration must be given to such assessment because requirements vary for all sports.

The individual athlete's training status
This may be judged by bioprofiles, haematological analyses, VO_2 maximum tests, etc., and by personal best performances at commencement of training, how long the athlete can run at a predetermined speed (e.g. 20 seconds/100m), and standard training programme (e.g. the athlete runs 5 x 500m at a speed of 90 seconds/500m with a fixed recovery period). Before and after each repetition, and the total training programme, heart rate and lactate measures are taken.

The stage of development of the athlete
According to Williams (1974) (see also chapter 9) the exposure of pre-pubertal athletes to units consistent with anaerobic development is inadvisable. Also, training for general development of endurance must be stressed with emphasis on long stretches at a low intensity, rather than interval methods predominating. Methods which tax strength or strength/speed endurance in the young athlete are not recommended.

Long/short term objectives of training
The athlete will have some ultimate goal in mind as a supreme *raison d'être* for training. This may be an Olympic final, a world record, etc. However, he will also have landmarks that must be reached en route. This may be a particular level of performance, a victory at a National Championship, etc. Programmes will therefore be constructed to meet the various goals, each leading towards the ultimate and never being ends in themselves.

Limitations of the training environment
The proximity of hills, beaches, plough, surf, ideal stadia, basic stadia, gymnasia, sports halls, etc., must all be taken into account, together with their training value potential. Not every athlete has access to the ideal complex of training facilities so a programme may have to be created imaginatively in a situation that is not ideal.

Demands of the non-athletic environment
The problems of other commitments, e.g. to family, business, education, social scene, cultural pursuits, and so on, must be solved with the assistance of athlete, coach, and a carefully constructed plan.

The athlete's own personality

According to Harre (1973) (see also chapter 10), duration methods encourage development of buoyancy and elasticity of mind. Buoyant behaviour 'includes all those volitional controlling qualities of personality that help to overcome inward and external difficulties and problems, by a consistency in readiness to make an effort of will'. On the other hand, he suggested that interval training develops that form of control which he refers to as 'impetus of will'. By this he means a fluctuating, varying nature. He goes on to point out that only in consideration of specific demands can buoyancy and impetus of will have a positive or negative value, and that they can be present as integrated behaviour patterns in an athlete.

Working from strength v compensatory work

There are two poles of opinion when attending to the specific needs of an endurance athlete. The first looks to building a programme based on the athlete's strength, and by so doing gradually make ground on his weakness. The other looks to focusing on the weakness, and building a compensatory programme. This method is founded on the belief that the athlete's strengths need little work to maintain a high level, and the weaknesses can therefore be afforded more time – and brought up to the same level as the strengths. To give an example, if an athlete can run 200m in 23.00 secs, and 800m in 2 minutes, it is clear that endurance should be worked on. The 'working from strength' coach will build his programme around repetition work over 100m, 200m, and 300m, gradually introducing longer repetitions and long runs. The 'compensatory' coach will look to longer endurance work and longer repetitions from the outset. Working from strength fits better into Harre's idea of building programmes according to the athlete's personality. Moreover, at a most fundamental level, it ensures that the athlete enjoys a positive motivational profile through a period of hard work.

Examples of endurance training plans

But what of the plan itself? It would appear that whatever it might be, it must fall into one of two categories: the Lydiard method or the Complex method. The former has now appeared in many forms and varieties, for example that used by Kari Sinkkonen with the Finnish distance athletes in 1975 (fig. 70), or any of the African systems. The latter has new varieties every day!

Every athlete and coach evolves a different interpretation, but for the sake of illustration, figure 71 includes a variation on the model (referred to as 'the Oregon method') used by Bill Bowerman of the University of Oregon.

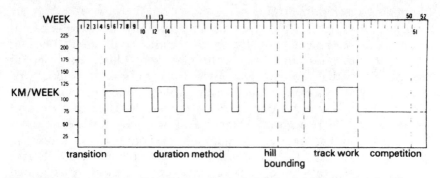

Fig. 70 *Interpretation of Lydiard method of planning endurance training* (from Sinkkonen, 1975)

■ Altitude training in practice

Training at altitude has become a regular feature in the annual cycle of preparing athletes for major championships. The following notes are a distillation of the experience of Bulgarian, Romanian, and former Soviet Union and German Democratic Republic coaches in using altitude training camps.

(1) Training at altitude for young athletes (17–19 years) is only recommended if these athletes have already achieved a very high level of training.
(2) Only athletes who can train with a full load should go to altitude. They must, therefore, be healthy. Altitude exacerbates infections and dental problems, so a complete health check is required before athletes can attend an altitude camp.
(3) Athletes should have a trial period at altitude outside the competition season before using it as final preparation for a major championship. This affords the opportunity to learn what suits a given athlete.
(4) The minimum period for altitude training should be 21 days.
(5) Athletes should be tested under normal sea level conditions to establish different speeds for endurance training at altitude. For example, this will indicate the point at which activity changes from aerobic to aerobic/anaerobic. Once this information is recorded (in metres/sec) subtract 0.20–0.30 metres/sec and these are the speeds for use at altitude. For example: 4.70 metres/sec – sea level = 4.40–4.50 metres/sec – altitude.
(6) Young athletes should work primarily on:
• steady running at low–medium intensity, 30 mins–60 mins
• sprint training over distances which *do not* go into lactic anaerobic work
• general conditioning training.
(7) Because there is a feeling of euphoria after some days of training at altitude, athletes often feel motivated to push too hard in training. Coaches *must* apply a friendly discipline and carefully supervise all training to ensure that altitude will not have a negative effect. Interval work should permit recovery to midway between steady resting and maximum heart rate. Steady runs should be resting heart rate plus 65%–70% heart rate range.

(8) In the first three days at altitude, athletes should keep things at the intermittent walk/jog level to allow gentle adaptation. This is *essential* for first time trainers at altitude, but even established altitude trainers should have two days like this. At the end of the training period, days 19, 20 and 21 should be at a reduced training level.

The pattern should be:

days 1–3/4	acclimatisation, e.g. instead of 2 x 60m runs – 4 x 30m runs.
days 3/4–18	hard training – normal programme but gentler progression; longer recoveries, etc. (bearing in mind note 5).
days 19–21	assimilation and recovery – lower intensity and extent.

(9) Athletes dehydrate readily at altitude so *must* take extra funds (2.5 litres water per day minimum including electrolyte replacement). Athletes also require a higher intake of carbohydrate. Iron and water soluble vitamin supplementation is also advised.

(10) After the end of altitude training athletes may feel unwell and although tired will have difficulty sleeping. These first 2–3 days back at sea level, training loads should be lower. After this period the athlete will feel much better and performance capacity increases.

(11) Athletes may however record an exceptional performance within 3–4 days of returning to sea level (but this is an individual matter!). Then performance goes down for about 7 days – to be followed by a return to high performance from the 10th, 11th, or 12th day which can continue for about 4 weeks. 85%–90% of all experienced altitude trainers produce their *best* results after 3–4 days and after 18–24 days.

(12) Ultraviolet radiation is more intense at altitude. Sun creams/blocks and sunglasses should be worn.

(13) Warm clothing should be taken for evenings and for immediate post-training.

(14) An extra 1–2 hours sleep should feature in the training period at altitude.

(15) The most used altitude facilities are as listed below in table 29. 2000–2200 metres is generally agreed as the best training altitude.

Table 29 *Altitude training venues*

	venue	country	altitude (m)
1	Belmeken	Bulgaria	2000
2	Tzahkadzor	Armenia	1970
3	Font Romeau	France	1895
4	St. Moritz	Switzerland	1820
5	Sestriere	Italy	2035
6	Pyatra Arsa	Romania	1950
7	Issyk-Kull	Kirgizia	1600
8	Zetersfeld (Linz)	Austria	1950

Table 29 *Altitude training venues (continued)*

	venue	country	altitude (m)
9	Addis Ababa	Ethiopia	2400
10	Nairobi	Kenya	1840
11	Ifran	Morocco	1820
12	Kunming	China	1895
13	Mexico City	Mexico	2200
14	Toluca	Mexico	2700
15	Colorado Springs	USA	2194
16	Keystone	USA	2835
17	Flagstaff	USA	2300
18	Bogota	Colombia	2500
19	Boulder	USA	2000
20	La Paz	Bolivia	3100
21	Quito	Ecuador	2218
22	Davos	Switzerland	1560
23	Pontresina	Switzerland	1900
24	Crans Montana	Switzerland	1500
25	Kaprun	Austria	1800
26	Zilvretsha	Austria	1800
27	Medeo	Kazakstan	1691
28	Kesenoy-Am	Russia	2000
29	Pzhevalsk	Kirgizia	1800
30	Tamga	Kirgizia	1700

■ Endurance sports and the female athlete

Although strength and structural disadvantage are critical factors in the lower performance ability of women in endurance sports (compared with men), Wagner (1976) maintains that the most important factor is the poorer status of aerobic capacity. Keul (1973), in demonstrating that there is no difference between men and women in anaerobic capacity, appears to endorse this. Wagner (1976) further suggests that an increased emphasis on aerobic training, coupled with an increased number of training units per week, may explain the rapid improvements since 1975 in women's middle distance events in track and field athletics.

PACE FOR THE MONTH   62 sec/400m: NEXT MONTH 61 sec/400m

	WEEK 1	WEEK 2	WEEK 3	WEEK 4
SUNDAY	20 miles continuous			
MONDAY	8 x 400m: 62: jog 400m	10 x 400m: 62: jog 200m	8 x 400m: 62: jog 100m	10 x 400m: 62: jog 100m
TUESDAY	10 miles alternating 800m jog between sets	(as before)	(as before)	(as before)
WEDNESDAY	2 x 5 x 300m: 46.5: jog 300m	3 x 4 x 300m: 46.5: jog 200m	4 x 3 x 300m: 46.5: jog 100m	5 x 3 x 300m: 46.5: jog 100m
THURSDAY	Fartlek – 60 mins			
FRIDAY	10 miles continuous			
SATURDAY	Competition – Training/Cross Country/Time Trials/Indoors/Etc.			

Fig. 71 *Interpretation of complex method of planning endurance training*

Summary

The preparation of endurance training plans and their progressive units (from the wide range of training practices) is a most interesting and rewarding exercise for the coach. Our well documented knowledge of related physiology offers an excellent framework within which to apply training units consistent with the laws of specificity, overload and reversibility. Thus, with insight, the coach may accurately evaluate the endurance demands of sports (ranging from the marathon to ice hockey) and create a training programme geared to adapting the athlete's physiology to meet these demands.

The female athlete must have aerobic training emphasised in her training plan. Nevertheless, the coach should be aware that it is not sufficient to compensate for weaknesses and that he should build upon strengths when planning training.

17
Theory and practice of mobility development

Mobility classification

Mobility is the capacity to perform joint actions through a wide range of movement. In sport, it should be considered in the light of an optimum application of strength throughout a range of movement appropriate to the demands of a given technique. Mobility is measured in degrees, radians or centimetres. Passive values are greater than active values and the reduction of the active-passive difference is often used as a criterion of achievement. There are three distinct varieties of mobility: active, passive and kinetic.

Active mobility: the capacity to effect movement by contraction of those muscles which naturally cause the movement. In figure 72, the athlete is flexing the femur on the pelvis by contraction of the hip flexors. In this instance, the neuromuscular pattern provides stimulation of the hip flexors (protagonists) to contract, and inhibition of the hip extensors (antagonists). The relaxed hip extensors are consequently 'stretched'. This represents the classical reciprocal inhibition.

Passive mobility: that movement which is effected by expression of external force on the joint action (e.g. apparatus, the weight of the body, a partner). In figure 73, the femur is being flexed on the pelvis by the combined effects of body weight and resistance of the wall bars. In this instance, the neuromuscular pattern stimulates neither the hip flexors nor hip extensors to contract. There is a variant of passive mobility which merits special mention here. This involves inhibition of reflex contraction in the antagonist muscles. This is referred to more in terms of training method than a sub-classification of mobility, as 'Proprioceptive Neuromuscular Facilitation' (PNF method).

Kinetic mobility: that movement which is effected due to momentum of one or other or both of the levers involved. In figure 74, the femur has been flexed on the pelvis by the momentum of its swing. In this instance, the neuromuscular pattern provides stimulation of the hip flexors (protagonists) to contract forcefully, and inhibition of the hip extensors (antagonists). However, as the movement reaches the limit of extensibility of the hip extensors, the muscle spindle reflex mechanism may initiate a reflex contraction of the 'overstretched' hip extensors. Consequently, this type of mobility presents the possibility of muscle damage, not only when it is applied as a means of developing mobility in general, but also when it is applied as an essential feature of technique. Kinetic mobility is also known as 'ballistic mobility' and 'bouncing mobility' and has also been covered by the umbrella title of 'dynamic mobility' (discussed below).

Fig. 72   *Examples of active mobility exercise*

■ Factors influencing mobility
(1) The elasticity of muscle and tendon of those muscles being stretched (but note that increased strength of a muscle does not reduce its extension capacity).
(2) The elasticity of ligaments supporting the joint involved. This presents one of many coaching dilemmas. The ligaments provide joint stability but the characteristic to be developed is joint mobility. Ligaments

Fig. 73   *Example of passive mobility exercise*

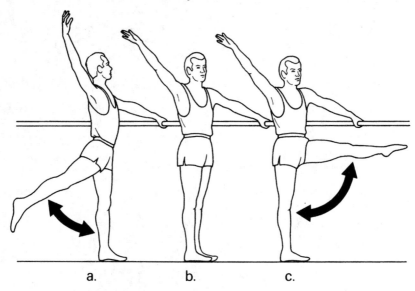

a.   b.   c.

Fig. 74   *Example of kinetic mobility exercise*

do not display any apparent elasticity but, given extensive exposure to stretch, may be extended to a new length. This, while providing increased mobility, reduces the stability of the joint. Consequently, great care must be taken to ensure that those muscles which cross the joint are strong enough to provide some compensatory stability to protect it from injury.

(3) The structural barriers of any muscle hypertrophy, or any skin and tissue folds which prevent freedom of joint range (e.g. 'spare tyres' – in hip flexion).

(4) Structural barriers of joint construction and bone.

(5) The strength of the protagonist in active and kinetic mobility.

(6) The capacity of the neuromuscular system to inhibit the antagonists (those muscles being stretched).

(7) The degree of technical mastery of the movement concerned, especially if the movement is one of several which comprise a sports technique.

Table 30 *Alterations in mobility under different conditions* from Osolin (1952)

conditions	time	result in mm
After night's sleep	8.00	−15
" " "	12.00	+35
10 mins with body exposed at 10°C	12.00	−36
10 mins in warm bath at 40°C	12.00	+78
After 20 mins loosening up	12.00	+89
After tiring training	12.00	−35

(8) The athlete's internal and external environment (table 30).

(9) The effect of recent injury in the muscles or joints concerned, or of fibrous adhesion of an old injury which has caused the athlete to be restricted in a given movement for a considerable period.

(10) The restrictions of inappropriate clothing.

(11) The athlete's age and stage of development. After the age of approximately 8 years, mobility will gradually reduce. Mobility training is therefore essential to the athlete.

(12) Structural adaptation to occupational postures (e.g. stooping over a machine, studying in a cramped position) or muscle habits may reduce free movement in certain joints.

■ Role of mobility

Mobility is fundamental to efficient performance of any action, both in nature and degree. Poor mobility development will present the athlete with several problems.

(1) The learning of sports techniques is difficult and in some cases impossible. This prevents the athlete from successful participation in certain sports. Moreover, the coach may believe an athlete's inability to perform a given technique is due to poor motor learning, lack of strength, etc., when in fact the problem may be quite simply that the athlete has insufficient mobility to assume a requested position.

(2) There exists the very real problem of injury due to muscle, tendon or ligament strain. For instance, when the athlete attempts to exceed his mobility range, there can be strain of other muscles and tendons which are employed to compensate for poor mobility in a given range, or strain of ligaments which become excessively loaded when restricted range of movement demands extraneous compensatory and balance adjustments.

(3) The development of other characteristics (e.g. strength and speed), or their effective application in technique, may be retarded. Ultimately, in terms of results and execution, this will lead to poor technical performance.

(4) The range of movement through which force may be applied (e.g. throws, golf swing, tennis strokes, stride length, etc.) is reduced and consequently the total performance is impaired.

(5) If the quality of a given movement is reduced due to lack of mobility, that movement cannot contribute fully as a component of more complex

or similar movements. Thus the total movement potential of the athlete is reduced.

(6) A lack of mobility in any joint action imposes an extra workload and tension on those muscles compensating for this deficiency. The result is more rapid tiring and a reduction of performance capacity.

The net result of all of the above is that a lack of mobility reduces the athlete's 'sphere of influence' in game situations, and his adaptability and technical efficiency of sports performance. Moreover, it increases the athlete's risk of sudden injury and unnecessary cumulative strain of muscle, tendon and ligament. A lack of mobility, then, has far reaching effects. The athlete must develop and maintain a level of general mobility to gain maximum advantage from training, freedom from the risk of injury, and attainment of a certain level of specific mobility, in order to meet the demands of technique.

▌Mobility training

Training to develop mobility must also obey the laws of specificity, overload and reversibility.

Specificity: training must focus on a particular joint action and the active, passive or kinetic nature of the mobility required in that joint action. 'Specific', here, refers to athlete, joint action and technical demand.

Overload: range of movement will not be maintained unless the existing limit is reached regularly, nor will it be improved unless that limit is exceeded. For instance:

- active mobility exercise is acceptable for maintaining a range of movement, provided strength of the protagonists is not lost. It has only limited value for developing mobility and implies increased strength of the protagonists and work in the end position, i.e. at the existing limit of the range of movement
- passive mobility exercise, given appropriate external force, will maintain or increase the range of movement
- kinetic mobility exercise makes its greatest contribution by relating mobility achieved through active or passive exercise, to the dynamics of a sports technique. However, as a carefully supervised type of exercise, it may also improve mobility.

Reversibility: mobility status is lost more slowly on cessation of regular specific training than other characteristics. Nevertheless it is gradually lost so the athlete should include mobility training either as an introduction to a unit, or as a unit in its own right.

▪ Mobility unit construction

There are virtually thousands of mobility exercises to choose from but, for the guidance of coaches, a summary of points relative to mobility unit construction is included here. Obviously, the coach must understand the specific joint actions to be mastered by the athlete and, as always before selecting training units, the laws of specificity, overload, and reversibility must be obeyed. The following order of events should also be observed.

(1) Raise body temperature by jogging, striding, and gentle warm-up exercises in 1 or 2 track suits, preferably in a warm environment.
(2) Active and slow, sustained exercises for each joint action.
(3) Passive exercises with partner, apparatus, body weight, etc.
(4) Kinetic exercises and combined strength/mobility exercises (advanced athletes only).
(5) Work on specific movements involved in the relevant 'whole' movements.

Mobility work should *always* precede other training and *never* be practised in a state of fatigue (following strength or endurance training, etc.) unless gentle active mobility is used. Like all training, mobility must be carefully supervised while the athlete learns training discipline (e.g. no experimentation, no interference with other athletes, no lazy 'compromised' movements, etc.).

Especially with the young athlete, *all* joint actions must be afforded mobility training as the basis upon which specific mobility training will develop. With the advanced athlete, general mobility training holds high priority in phase 1 of the annual cycle and should be included (possibly in warm-up for other training units) throughout the year. Highly specific mobility is for advanced athletes only. However, all levels of athlete require a complementary development of strength, but in separate training units. The advanced athlete may combine mobility and strength work in kinetic mobility exercises, but this work should be supervised and never taken to the point of fatigue.

Sets of exercises should comprise 10–15 repetitions, since only after several repetitions is there any visible increase in range of movement. The recovery period between sets must not be long enough to permit temperature reduction. It may also be active (walking, jogging, general stretching) or passive (relaxing in warmth). When active or passive mobility exercise is used in training units, the end position of stretch should be maintained for 6–10 secs in each repetition. Several authorities recommend daily or twice daily units of mobility training. Personal experience suggests that general and/or specific mobility work as part of warm-up for daily training units, supplemented by separate units within the microcycle where mobility is trained exclusively, is sufficient for athletes in the majority of sports. Exceptions are sports such as gymnastics, where daily mobility units are essential.

PNF method would be used at stage 4 in the training unit. It must be used with care, and partners should be mature, responsible persons, trained in application of the method. The athlete's partner slowly forces the relevant limb to the existing comfort limit of a range of movement. When the athlete feels discomfort, the movement stops and the partner then offers a resistance so that the athlete can perform an isometric contraction against the original direction of movement. This is held for 6–10 seconds. Athlete and partner rest for 30 seconds then repeat the exercise 3–6 times. An extension of this method, referred to as 3 PIC requires the athlete to contract the protagonist muscles for 3–6 seconds immediately following the isometric contraction. The partner then recommences the cycle of forced stretch, isometric contraction against the direction of stretch, and active contraction *with* the direction of stretch. The cycle is repeated 3–4 times before resting for 30 seconds and going through the exercise again. The total number of repetitions of the exercise is 3–6.

■ Mobility derivatives

Fleishman (1964) distinguishes between 'extent flexibility', which is defined here as mobility, and 'dynamic flexibility' which is an ability to perform repeated contraction and stretching of muscle. This derivative of mobility appears to embrace innervation, as previously discussed, and kinetic mobility. Thus, dynamic flexibility may be more accurately thought of as a specific 'functional' or 'applied' mobility. That the derivative exists is beyond doubt but, because it is dependent upon the degree of specific technical competence, it apparently belongs to a class of characteristics which is removed, as it were, from the fundamental characteristics. It is impossible to list all of those characteristics presently believed to be in the 'removed' category. This is not so much because of its length, but because of a frustrating lack of standard definitions.

▌ Summary

Basic to a development of the technical model, or models demanded of a sport, is a wide range of movement in all joint actions. A limited range of joint action compromises movement potential for the interpretation of technique, and the range through which force is applied is a critical factor in determining the nature and degree of force expression. The structure of joints, elasticity of soft tissues, and neuromuscular co-ordination are significant. The most important factors determining active, passive or kinetic mobility are specific exercise, joint structure, elasticity of soft tissue surrounding joints, neuromuscular co-ordination, and temperature.

18
Evaluation in sport

Training programmes must be planned to meet the stressors of the athlete's lifestyle and chosen sport. The coach must firstly evaluate the demands of the sport, then the athlete's capacity to adapt to these demands. A programme of training may then be planned to improve that capacity.

It is beyond the scope of this book to deal with the complex subject of evaluation in detail. However, a general guide to evaluation in sport may be helpful and it should be emphasised that evaluation is essential to the athlete's progress, as the coach applies the cycle: PLAN–DO–REVIEW.

Status classification

The primary objective of applying testing procedures is to establish the athlete's status in the parameters measured. The classification of possible parameters is as follows.

GENERAL PARAMETERS	EXAMPLE
Anthropometric measures	Height, lean body mass
Physical capacities	Strength, mobility
Physiological capacities	VO_2 maximum, blood pressure
Psychological capacities	Personality
Technical abilities (neuromotor)	McCloy's general motor ability
SPECIFIC PARAMETERS	
Sports performance	Personal bests
Tactical abilities	Tactical solution to specific situations
Technical performance	Shooting accuracy
The general parameters specific to specific sports	ECG during training or competition
Jumping strength	Bosco test

Due to the 'chicken and egg' relationship of athlete and environment, factors known to influence athletic performance must also be evaluated. Classification of environmental factors might be:
- finance – financial assistance for sports equipment
- nutrition – dietary supplements, calorie intake, smoking
- occupation – student, labourer, mother
- social – family, institution, religion
- support – physiotherapy
- training – equipment, facilities.

Mass longitudinal screening techniques, or bioprofiles, assess the athlete's status in all quantifiable parameters and environmental factors relevant to athletic performance. Such information, married to the athlete's training programme over many years, may benefit the athlete if an exchange of information can be established between coach and researchers.

The measurement of status is a simple statement of fact. The next step is to evaluate these facts by comparing current results of a given test with the athlete's previous performance, with relevant norms or standards, and with other athletes. Thus, a girl athlete's VO_2 maximum, say on 15th March 1989, may be 59ml/kg/m, while on 15th September 1988 it was 55ml/kg/m, and on 15th March 1988 it was 56ml/kg/m. She runs 800m and 1500m for which the Swedish norms are 52–58ml/kg/m. Her team-mate training for the same event recorded 57.5ml/kg/m on 15th March 1988 and 56ml/kg/m on 15th September 1988. The coach, equipped with this information, can make any of the above three comparisons.

Having done this, the evaluation may help the coach reach important conclusions or decisions in several areas. Measurement and evaluation may be used as detailed below.

(1) **To assess the athlete's aptitude for a given sport:** testing procedures are not yet sufficiently sophisticated to assess this quality with scientific precision. However, indices of aptitude may be derived from the collective evaluation of the following:

- the status of the athlete's performance of the given technique/sport, with respect to existing norms according to age, sex, etc
- the athlete's status in those capacities characteristic of the given sport (physiological, physical, anthropometric, etc.)
- the speed at which the athlete improves performance during the period of instruction
- the ability to reproduce consistently good performance (stability).

Clearly, the most important condition for diagnosing aptitude, is regular participation in the sport concerned.

(2) **To plan the athlete's developmental programme:** only by exposing the athlete to a comprehensive battery of tests and comparing the athlete's status with norms according to chronological age, developmental age, sex, etc., in a given sport, will the coach be fully equipped to set out a plan for the athlete's development. The general scanning concept represented by the bioprofile system discussed above should be applied here.

(3) **To assess the effect of training systems on performance:** here, the athlete's status in those parameters which are to be developed by the training system (e.g. strength, aerobic endurance), is compared with performance in the sport. The results are also compared with previous results in the same testing situation. The contribution of the athlete's status in each parameter to the performance is thereby assessed.

(4) **To assess the efficacy of training systems in developing specific parameters:** as the athlete works to develop strength, speed, etc., via various specific training units, the athlete's status in these parameters must be constantly monitored. Evaluation of results will allow any necessary adjustment of loading within each training unit.

(5) **To establish homogeneous groupings for training:** it is reasonable to group athletes according to physical capacities such as speed, strength, endurance, and so on. Evaluation will enable the coach to form those groups to the best advantage of their members.

(6) **To access knowledge of a given sport:** the athlete must understand tactics, rules, training principles, and so on. Although it is not commonplace to test the athlete's command of this knowledge, it is important and may be seen as part of the training process.

(7) **To establish the characteristics demanded of a given sport:** a detailed study of biomechanics, physiology, psychology, etc., provides some insight into the demands of a given sport. However, by evaluating the status of successful athletes in physical, physiological, and other parameters, a more substantial link between athlete and sport can be established.

Tests are not ends in themselves, but a means of evaluating an athlete's status. In short, testing procedures assist the coach in understanding the athlete's training status and its development, and in making training programmes more efficient.

■ Notes on tests and testing

The coach must conduct testing sessions with care. Every testing procedure must be valid (testing what it purports to test), reliable (consistency of reproduction), and objective (consistency of result, irrespective of tester). The following points may help to achieve these aims.

(1) A test should measure only one capacity/ability/factor.

(2) Unless technique is being assessed, the tests should not require technical competence on the part of the athlete.

(3) There is little purpose in duplicating tests within the same unit (i.e. testing the same parameter with different tests) unless the purpose of the session is to validate new methods of testing.

(4) Each athlete in the test situation must understand exactly what is required, what is to be measured, and why. At conclusion, the results should be interpreted for the athlete.

(5) The method of conducting the test (e.g. administration, organisation, environmental requirements) should be standardised. (A set of simple instructions will help to standardise procedure on subsequent sessions.) The standardisation of procedure should be as strict as possible (e.g. constant venue, temperature, time of day, day of menstrual cycle (girls), degree of motivation, tester, previous nutrition, time allowed for warm-up, nature of equipment, etc.).

(6) The venue, score cards, equipment, etc., should be prepared in advance of the tests.

(7) The coach will find some knowledge of statistics, mathematics, and presentation of data (e.g. graphs) very useful.
(8) The complete evaluation process involves physiologists, physiotherapists, general practitioners, psychologists, the coach and, in some cases, parents, other coaches and athletes. The sum evaluation by this 'team' should be documented and filed, but a record of tests conducted by the coach may also be kept in the athlete's training diary.

Summary

Evaluation is an essential ingredient of modern coaching methods. By assessing the demands of each sport, and the status of the athlete relative to these demands, the specific progressive programme of training may be constructed for that athlete. This is achieved by applying knowledge gained from an ongoing system of evaluation. The well designed system aids in selection of sports most suited to the athlete's abilities, in planning training most suited to his needs, and in monitoring the contribution of training to the progression of his fitness for a specific sport.

Summary of part 4

The interpretation of fitness for an individual is unique to his lifestyle. For the non-athlete it should be understood that lifestyle in the teens influences that in the twenties and this, in turn, influences that in the thirties, and so on. A well balanced daily routine which includes physical activity might be seen as a basis for a healthy life and should be established early on. Physical activity will range from walking and jogging, each of which requires little or no equipment, to those aspects of physical recreation which are practised in recreation or sports centres or which require specialist facilities, as in skiing and sailing.

For the athlete, part of his lifestyle is pursuit of competitive advantage and fitness must therefore be developed accordingly. On the sound basis of general strength, endurance, and mobility, technical efficiency is developed and progressed towards the specific requirements of physical and physiological status demanded of a given sport. The broad direction of development is from general to specific, as well as from a basic technical model (or models) towards expressing that model with greater strength and speed, sometimes in the climate of endurance factors where there are such facets of a particular sport. Against the constant backcloth of a well managed training and non-training environment, the final sophistication of development is a mature competitive attitude which permits sound performance in progressively variable situations.

Perhaps the most demanding problem for the coach is arriving at the most appropriate training plan for the development of physical and physiological status. The relative contributions of strength, speed, mobility, endurance (and their derivatives) may in most instances be established with the intelligent use of evaluation procedures.

Nevertheless, the coach requires the full measure of his artistry to create an individually oriented programme from the expanding areas of related theory and practice.

References for part 4

Astrand, P. O. & Rodahl, K. (1970) *Textbook of Work Physiology*. McGraw-Hill, Toronto

Ballreich, R. (1975) *A Model for Estimating the Influence of Stride Length and Stride Frequency on the Time in Sprinting Events*. Proceedings of the VIth International Congress of Biomechanics, Jyväskylä, Finland

Brunner, J. A. (1967) Untersuchungen über Statisches (Isometrisches) und Dynamisches (Isotonisches) Muskelwaining. *Körperererziehung No. 5*, Switzerland

Bührle, M. (Jan 1971) *Prinzipen des Krafttrainings*. Die Lehre Der Leichtathletik

Dyatchkov, V. M. (1969) High jumping. *Track Technique*, No. 36

Endemann, F. (1975) *Learning Practices in Throws*. VIth Coaches' Convention Report

Fleishman, I. E. (1964) *The Structure and Measurement of Physical Fitness*. Prentice-Hall, New Jersey

Gundlach, H. (1968) Zur Trainierberkeit Der Kraft–Und Schnellkeitsfahigkeiten Im Prozess Der Korperlichen Vervollkommnug. In *Theorie Und Praxis Der Korperkultur 17*, Beiheft, Teil 11, S., 167

Harre, D. (1973) *Trainingslehre*. Sportverlag, Berlin

Hettinger, T. & Muller, E. A. (1953) Muskelleistung Und Muskeltraining. *Arbeitsphysiologie, 15*, 111–126

Ivanova, L. S. (1967) *u.a.: Die Korperliche Vorbereitung Der Sportler Hoherer Leistungsklassen*. Entwicklung Der Kraft. (Fiziceskaja Podgotovka Sportsmenok Wyssych Razrjadov. Razvitie Silyl), Fiskultura i Sport, Moscow, Ubersetzung An Der DHfK Unveroffenlicht

Jäger, K. & Oelschlägel, G. (1974) *Kleine Trainingslehre*. 2nd Edn. Sportverlag, Berlin

Karvonen, M. J., Kentala, E. & Mustala, O. (1957) The effect of training on heart rate. *Annales Medicinae Experimentalis et Biologae Fenniae, Vol 35*

Keul, J. (1973) *Limiting Factors of Physical Performance*. Thieme, Stuttgart

Kusnetov, V. V. (1975) *Kraftvorbereitung–Theoretische Grundlagen Der Muskelkraftenwicklung*. 2nd Edn. Sportverlag, Berlin

Lay, P. Fundamentals of weight training. *Athletics Weekly* (13th Dec 1969, 10th Jan, 7th Feb, 28th Feb, 11th Apr, 16th May 1970)

Murase, Y., Hoshikawa, T., Yasuda, N., Ikegami, Y. & Matsui, H. (1975) *A Study of Analysis of the Changes in Progressive Speed of 100m from the Points of View of Anaerobic Energy Output and Running Patterns*. Proceedings of Vth International Congress of Biomechanics, Jyväskylä, Finland

Osolin, N. G. (1952) *Das Training Des Leichtathleten*. Sportverlag, Berlin

Osolin, N. G. (Jan 1973) Speed endurance. *Modern Athlete and Coach, Vol 11, No 1*

Pahud, J. F. & Gobbeler, C. (1986) *Training at Altitude: General Principles and Personal Experience*. New Studies in Athletics, September 1986, Rome

Pohlitz, L. (1986) *Practical experiences of altitude training with female middle distance runners*. Leichtathletik. Berlin 25, vol. 3

Saziorski, W. M. (1971) Die Korperlichen Eigenschaften Des Sportlers. In *Theorie Und Praxis Der Korperkultur*. Beiheft 2

Sinkkonen, K. (1975) *The Programming of Distance Running*. Paper to E.L.L.V., Congress, Budapest

Upton, A. R. M. & Radford, P. F. (1975) *Trends in Speed of Alternated Limb Movement During Development and Amongst Elite Sprinters*. Proceedings of Vth International Congress of Biomechanics, Jyväskylä, Finland

Verhoshansky, J. W. (1971) Grundlagen Des Speziellen Krafttrainings Im Sport. In *Theorie Und Praxis Der Korperkultur*

Viru, A. A., Urgenstein, Y. U. & Pisuke, A. P. (1972) Influence of training methods on endurance. *Track Technique*, No 47

Wagner, P. (1976) *Male-Female Differences in Middle Distance Training and Competitions*. VIIth Coaches' Convention Technical Report

Williams, C. (1974) *Special Forms and Effects of Endurance Training*. Vth Coaches' Convention Report

Bibliography

Arthur, R. (May 1973) What swimmers can teach to runners. *Modern Athlete and Coach, Vol 1*, No 3

Clarke, H. H. (1967) *Application of Measurement to Health and Physical Education*. 4th Edn. Prentice-Hall, New Jersey

Counsilman, J. G. (1970) *The Science of Swimming*. Pelham Books Ltd., London

Hettinger, T. H. (July 1975) Muscle trainability of men and women. *Modern Athlete and Coach, Vol 13*, No 4

Hogg, J. M. (1972) *Land Conditioning for Competitive Swimming*. E. P. Publishing Ltd, Wakefield

Jensen, C. R. & Fisher, A. G. (1972) *Scientific Basis of Athletic Conditioning*. Lea & Febiger, Philadelphia

Jesse, J. P. (July 1976) Young athletes and weight training. *Modern Athlete and Coach, Vol 14*, No 1

Kendrick, D. (May 1975) Activity and ageing. *New Behaviour, Vol 1*, No 6

Koslov, V. (July 1970) Application of maximum power in throwing. *Modern Athlete and Coach, Vol 8*, No 4

Margaria, R. (1976) *Biomechanics and Energetics of Muscular Exercise*. Clarendon Press, Oxford

Petrovski, V. & Verhoshansky, J. (1975) Aspects of sprint training. *Modern Athlete and Coach, Vol 13*, No 4

Pickering, R. J. (1968) *Strength Training for Athletics*. 2nd Edn. B.A.A.B. Instructional Booklet, London

Polunin, A. (1994) *Training in Middle and High Mountains*. EACA Workshop Paper, Belmekan

Schmolinsky, G. (1974) *Leichtathletik*. 7th Edn. Sportverlag, Berlin

Schon, R. (1994) *Recommendations Based on Experience of Altitude Training with Young Athletes*. EACA Workshop Paper, Belmekan

Shephard, R. J. (1969) *Endurance Training*. University of Toronto Press

Skaset, H. B. (1970) *Trainingslaere*. Norges Idrettsforbund, Oslo

Taylor, A. W. (1972) *Training–Scientific Basis and Application*. Charles C. Thomas, Illinois

Whitehead, N. (1988) *Conditioning for Sport*. A & C Black, London

Part 5

Planning the programme

Without knowing your destination, you cannot plan your journey. Your destination in sport is the competition objective or goal. It might be to win a league competition, a cup tournament, an Olympic medal, a place in the National Championships, a qualifying performance for team selection, or a lifetime best performance in a particular competition. It must be realistic and must be agreed between coach and athlete. Your journey is the preparation programme planned to help reach the objective or goal; it is quantifiable and has a timescale.

The structure of that plan, and its details must, however, be sufficiently flexible to move and adapt to the dynamics of athlete, coach and situation. The destination is not a terminus, but a milestone. The programme must be capable of adjustment on the way to that milestone, and for progressing beyond it.

We must, however, start with some kind of 'route map'. The division of the training year into periods of varying duration, characterised by their progressive contribution to reaching the 'destination', is such a 'route map'.

For athletics, it grew from such origins as:

Period 1 Autumn and Winter Training for and competing
in winter field games
Period 2 Spring Training for athletics
Period 3 Summer Lighter training and
competing in athletics

to:

Period 1 Winter training
Period 2 Pre-competition training
Period 3 Competition training
to current systems of periodisation.

This evolution of how the year is planned might be thought of as a progressive shift towards considering training as a cyclical year-round process, which is part of a total development of training and performance over several years.

In part 5, in order to explain the underlying principles of designing a year-round programme, it is expedient to illustrate the process with reference mainly to a summer season sport – athletics. Here, the preparation portion of the year is long – and the competition portion(s) short. This makes things very simple. However, in long competition season sports such as winter games (e.g. soccer, rugby, hockey, lacrosse, basketball), or year-round racquet games (i.e. tennis, squash, badminton), life is rather more complicated and both preparation/conditioning and competition objectives must be pursued simultaneously on the foundation of a very brief (1–2 month) preparation/conditioning base.

Part 5 sets out the athletics training year and, where relevant, reference is made to application of training principles in practice in long season/year-round sports.

19
Periodising the year

Periodisation may be described as an organised division of the training year in pursuit of three basic objectives:

- to prepare the athlete for achievement of an optimal improvement in performance
- to prepare the athlete for a definite climax to the competition season
- to prepare the athlete for the main competitions associated with that climax.

Occasionally, annual objectives are not embraced by the three stated. These may be considered under two separate headings:

- to aid recovery from injury, illness or a particularly stressful training year
- to prepare the athlete for meeting the above objectives in subsequent years, by increasing special training status, stabilising technique or performance, and so on, over the period of one or more years.

Special programmes are required to meet the last two objectives and, although they are not dealt with in detail here, the terminology and broad principles of programme construction still apply.

Modern theory of periodisation was originally advanced by L. P. Matveyev (USSR), in 1965, as an updating of work which he first introduced in 1962. From early ideas of preparing an athlete for a competitive programme distributed throughout a season, he looked towards a specific competition climax or peak (e.g. National Championships, Olympic Games, etc.), for which not only training periods, but also a selected competition programme was a totality of preparation. Matveyev suggested that the year be divided into three periods: preparation, competition, and transition. The first two periods he divided further, and these will be referred to here as *phases* (fig. 75). A closer look at these phases will help identify their individual character.

Preparation period

Phase 1
This is the longest phase in the annual cycle and should occupy one third of that cycle. Thus, in the single periodised year (fig. 76), it occupies 4 months while in the double periodised year (fig. 76 and text) it occupies

MONTH	OCT	NOV	DEC	JAN	FEB	MAR	APR	MAY	JUN	JUL	AUG	SEPTEMBER
PERIOD	← PREPARATION ————————→							← COMPETITION —			→←	TRANSITION→
PHASE					II		III		IV		V	VI

Fig. 75 *The division of the training year will obviously be influenced by the 'competition calendar'. The division shown here was used by USSR in preparation for Munich—where athletes used a 'single periodised year' (from Osolin and Markov, 1972)*

	NOV	DEC	JAN	FEB	MAR	APR	MAY	JUN	JUL	AUG	SEP	OCT
DOUBLE	I	II			III,			II,	III,	IV	V	VI
SINGLE		I					III		IV	V		VI

Fig. 76 *Single and double periodised years*

2–2½ months, to be reintroduced after the first competition period (3_1) for a further 1½–2 months.

The main aim is to increase the athlete's ability to accept a high intensity (quality) of loading in phase 2 by increasing extent (quantity) of loading during phase 1. The high volume of work involved necessitates a very gradual increase in intensity during this phase, but this increase is essential to progress in phase 2 and to the stabilisation of performance in the competition period. Training is more general in nature, and during this phase the athlete is working at the endurance end of his event development. However, in the interest of continuous development of performance, it is also necessary to pursue special event training and competition specific training. A mixed programme is required, which must take into account the particular event and the athlete's stage of development when establishing a ratio of general:special:competition specific training. It may be useful to describe these broad areas of training.

General training: this is training for the whole organism. A basic all-round programme is usual and, above all, the establishment of a sound basis of aerobic fitness, and a certain minimum status in the foundation of fitness for a specific sport (e.g. mobility and strength for jumps, goal-keeping, diving, etc.).

Special training (or 'related' training): this is training to perfect the individual components of sports techniques and specific fitness, e.g. work with heavier implements (throws), technique work with resistances (gymnastics, swimming), drills (games), bounding, hill running, under/over distance work (endurance sprints/middle distance).

Competition specific training (or 'specific' training): this is training where technique is completely rehearsed and, more specifically, in the competition situation. This area varies from a shade of special training to actual competitions, embracing technique, tactics, etc. It plays a much smaller part in the total extent of training than the other two.

At the risk of being over repetitive, *all three areas* are covered throughout the year, but their contribution will vary from phase to phase. At the end of phase 1, the basic components of fitness for a specific event must have reached the level necessary to ensure a planned increase in performance. Tests may be used to check this. For example, a long jumper working towards 8.00 m from a 20-stride approach should jump 7.00 m from 10 strides.

This phase might be viewed as 'training to train'.

Phase 2

This phase, according to Matveyev (1965), lasts 2 months when single periodisation is used and 1 month plus 2 weeks in double periodisation. However, it is possible to stretch this to 2 or 3 months, and 1 month plus 1 month respectively, if the annual cycle is extended slightly beyond 52 weeks. There are many advantages to such stretching, but most important is that the increase of load intensity will be gentler. There is no doubt, however, that this is the hardest working phase in the year.

Phase 2 runs directly into the competition period. Its aims are to unite the component parts or foundations of training into a harmonious whole (e.g. training moves from workshop to assembly line). While the character of this phase is that of specialisation, the areas of training in the first phase are continued. The training ratio decreases in the general area and, while the total extent of work remains the same or is gently reduced, the intensity of loading in special and competition specific training increases sharply. Technique must be schooled and stabilised as the athlete learns to use increased strength, speed, etc. It is absolutely essential that technical development and development of strength, speed, and so forth, are advanced together. A season can be completely lost if they are 'out of step'.

Towards the end of this phase, the athlete must be exposed to more open competition situations such as wind, rain, noise, morning, floodlights, etc. Should training progress successfully, the young athlete will (according to Harre (1973)) improve on previous best performance after three competitions. The experienced athlete should at least equal his previous best. It would appear from personal observation that if the young athlete is within 2.5% of his best performance in a technical event after three competitions (spaced over 2–4 weeks), it is reasonable to assume that progress is 'on schedule'. By increasing load intensity, particularly via competitions, he will improve performance still further. If no improvements follow, it is frequently a result of the intensity having been raised too rapidly in the second phase, or the extent of competition loading being too great, or the total extent of loading at the end of the preparation period having been excessively reduced.

This phase might be viewed as 'training to compete'.

Competition period

Phase 3

The main task of this phase of the competition period is to develop and stabilise competition performance as fully as possible (see also chapter 24). The athlete will then be able to produce optimal performance in key competitions. The blending of new levels of specific sport or event fitness, which has been developed throughout the preparation period, must be continued in order to produce high level performance. Moreover, these new levels of fitness must be maintained via competition specific loadings and competitions themselves. Consequently, the loadings in this area are increased, while those in the general and special areas are reduced. The total extent of training is therefore decreased as the intensity rises. The reduction of extent is very steep where sports demand maximum or elastic strength or speed (e.g. jumps, throws, weight lifting, games), but only slight in endurance sports in the interest of maintaining aerobic fitness. General training should be seen primarily as a means of active recovery in the non-endurance sports.

It is important not to neglect the status of basic fitness components such as strength, speed, mobility, etc., in favour of technical development. Strength losses, for example, can be considerable, even over 2–3 weeks and such losses, if continued, will be reflected in performance. Consequently, the strength programme has its place in the competition period (fig. 77).

The frequency of competitions depends on the individual athlete's capacity for the emotional and physical stress of competition loading. It is very difficult to establish ideal numbers of competitions and this topic is discussed more fully below. At one end of the scale, a man might feel that two major marathons in one year is acceptable but, at the other, a 13 year old may be happy to spend all year competing twice a week in several sports.

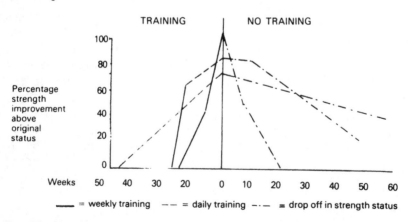

Fig. 77 *An outline of work conducted by Hettinger, illustrating not only different effects of daily and weekly training, but how strength training loses its effect once stopped* (from Hettinger, 1968)

Competition frequency and the amount of competition specific loading determine development of performance in the competition period. An optimal balance can only be arrived at individually, but, once known, the athlete can expect to record best performances 6–8 weeks from the start of this phase (i.e. phase 3 single periodisation, and phases 3_1 and 3_2 double periodisation). Thus, after 3 competitions (4–6 weeks from start of phase 3), the athlete will be within 2.5% of lifetime best and by 6–8 weeks will have improved upon lifetime best. Trials and qualifying competitions, and most of the main contests for young athletes, should therefore fall within phase 3 (single) and Phase 3_2 (double).

This phase might be viewed as 'competing to learn'.

Phase 4

If competition is to continue beyond phases 3 and 3_2, it is advisable to introduce a phase of 4–6 weeks in which the proportion of competition specific training is reduced, competitions are eliminated, and general and special training are increased. The value of general training should be noted here, as it serves an important role in active recovery from the emotional and physical stresses of competition.

If the athlete has *not* been brought to peak performance in the previous 6–8 weeks, a longer period may be necessary, and phase 4 may be omitted and the training ratio left unchanged. If the athlete *has* achieved peak performance, phase 4 aids recovery, protects from injury, and prepares for phase 5. The latter is most important in a major season (e.g. Olympic Games) as this phase will be seen as a special preparation period.

This phase might be viewed as 'training to win'.

Phase 5

Again, by evolving an optimal blend of competitions and competition specific training, further improvement in performance may be expected within 3–4 weeks. Ideally, the major event of the athletic calendar will fall within this phase (Olympic Games, National Championships, etc.).

This phase might be viewed as 'competing to win'.

▌ Transition period

Phase 6

Just as restful sleep must follow a hard day's work, so a period of regeneration must follow a hard year's training and competition. This period of regeneration must bring the athlete to commencement of the next training year totally prepared for training; from positive motivational profile through to fully 'recharged energy batteries'.

If the season has been 'low key', little wear and tear on the organism might be expected and, following a medical and physiotherapy check-up, the athlete will go straight into preparation period after phase 5. This would mean a rapid increase in extent of training, and a drop in intensity. If on the other hand the season has been 'high key', 3–6 weeks active recovery must precede the next preparation period. The athlete should not start the new preparation period without a full recovery from the previous competition season, otherwise the effect of future loading will be extremely limited, adaptation problems will quickly arise, a risk of injury will occur, and the disappointment of poor progress in training may have effects reaching into the next competition period.

The transition period sees the gentle reduction of all loadings, with general training assuming the leading role in the training ratio. While technical schooling may be introduced, the emphasis should be on physical and emotional relaxation involving leisure pursuits. On no account should this period be passive.

Finally, a quote from Harre (1973): 'Naturally, the athlete must maintain a way of life in-keeping with athletic standards.'

This phase might be viewed as 'recharging to train'.

Year-round adaptations

In broad terms, it is possible to establish a 'competition' period which constitutes priority competitions, and another 'preparation' period where there are no competitions or very low priority ones. For example, soccer's competition period in the UK commences mid-August and concludes mid-May. This leaves approximately 12 weeks for the preparation period during which the regeneration objectives of phase 6 and the objectives of phases 2 and 4 are pursued. The loose guide to training unit distribution here is general:related:specific – 50%:30%:20%. Through the competition season it is a matter of ensuring that microcycles of 7 days, variously having one or two or even three competitions, are designed to regenerate; to produce competition sharpness; and to maintain general:related:specific conditioning status. A possible unit distribution to achieve this would be 20%:30%:50% bearing in mind that competitions themselves are included in the 50% specific.

This said the programme should be sufficiently flexible to return to the preparation period distribution should the opportunity arise. In rugby union in the UK, such an opportunity is afforded by the mid-winter league break. In international tennis, players must create blocks of time to regenerate and build a conditioning base by prioritising their tournaments through what can amount to a twelve month 'season'!

Summary

Periodisation is an organised division of the training year in pursuit of basic objectives of training. The divisions are, in the first instance, those of preparation, competition and transition. These are referred to as *periods*, which are further sub-divided into phases. Phases 1, 2 and 4 are planned according to specific objectives of preparation, while phases 3 and 5 are planned in pursuit of specific objectives of competition. Phase 6 coincides with the transition period.

20
Variations in periodisation

Although a full period cycle is usually twelve months, 2–4 years (or even more) may be considered a total cycle of preparation and competition for an Olympic Games or World Championship. Here, a close examination is made of a twelve month cycle, in the knowledge that it is a cycle upon which others may be built, and which may itself be built upon work done in previous years.

Setting out the time scale

The start of the competition period(s) is dictated by (1) the number of competitions necessary for the athlete to reach and stabilise best performance, (2) the dates of the major competition and main competitions, (3) the recovery period required by the athlete between competitions, and (4) the period required for preparation for the major competition (this period must take into account possible acclimatisation to a new environment – time adjustment in East–West shift, altitude adjustment, etc.) These conditions are worth further explanation.

(1) **Number of necessary competitions.** Although Harre (1973) suggested 6–8 weeks, other authorities have advanced 6–10 weeks as a reasonable range of time for athletes to reach and stabilise their best performances in phase 3. Harre's (1973) suggestion is more acceptable for phase 3_2 if double periodised. Some athletes commence the competition period with low key non-pressure competitions which are virtually an extension of training time trials. These constitute a type of 'competition control', reintroducing the disciplines of competition warm-up and reporting procedures. Moreover, irrespective of the athlete's level of performance, he has an opportunity to 'get the adrenaline moving' without the stressors of pressure which will come later in the season. Once this stage is completed, the athlete then decides with his coach the venues, levels of competition, and frequency of competition which are required to produce his best performance, his springboard for the main business of the season.

The coach should be aware of the influence which early good performances by opponents have on an athlete. The season's objectives *and* the week by week objectives must be understood by athlete and coach. The athlete's early season performances should not be so far adrift from those of the opposition that the athlete feels pressure. Consequently, coaches should introduce the athlete to competitions *only* when the athlete is ready and only when the objective is understood and attainable.

(2) **Dates of competitions**. The important qualifying rounds should be found in the latter 2–4 weeks of the suggested range, thus giving up to 6 weeks of preparatory contests and up to 4 weeks of main contests. The major competitions will be, as it were, the 'fixed point' of the season. Thus, if the athlete views the National Championships as the major competition, phases 3 or 3_2 and 4 are worked from that date. The coach has the problem of providing the relevant phase 3 (3_2) levels of competition for the athlete over the time span dictated by the National Championships date. On the other hand, the major competition may be an Olympic Games. It would then be in the interest of the Olympic athletes for trials and competitions, designed to produce qualifying marks, to be time-tabled for a relevant phase 3 or 3_2. Moreover, as Olympic Games and other major championships constitute a tournament rather than one-off competitions, the athlete must be afforded the opportunity to rehearse the sequence of qualifying rounds/heats and finals in the period leading up to the final selection dates or in the course of the final selection dates.

(3) **Recovery period**. This will vary from athlete to athlete according to event, age, experience and standard of competitions. The young athlete, whose ability to produce performances near the limit of his capacity is as yet undeveloped, will compete very regularly – as often as twice to three times per week in inter-club, intra-club, league or open meetings, etc. Although competitions are meaningful to such an athlete, times, distances and heights are a long way from being an ultimate expression of ability. On mounting the club/district/regional/national/international record ladder, however, the athlete begins to take a more serious view of success and failure. With this change of approach from 'playing' to commitment, both physical *and* psychological stressors mean more time to prepare for and recover from competitions. It is not unusual, then, to find an athlete at this stage competing only once a week, or every other week. Again, the idea might be extended so that there are only 2 or 3 competitions in the season (specific competition climaxes or peaks), while a few other competitions are entered to test fitness or for practice.

Matveyev (1965) suggests that in explosive sports, where the technical component is high (e.g. field events, tennis, gymnastics, team games), several peaks may be pursued. However, where the technical component is lower (e.g. sprints, hurdles), three peaks per season at most can be worked for. This argument can only be defended if, by 'peak', we consider a block of time rather than a particular time on a particular day. On this basis, it is suggested that most athletes cannot sustain maximum performance levels beyond 21 days, and even then such performances are not being repeated at high frequency within these 21 days. The main problem here is as much a psychological/emotional one as it is physiological/physical. Clear understanding and application of the concept of regeneration is essential to ensuring that peak 'blocks of time' can be repeated not only within a given season, but also over several seasons.

In endurance events, where complex training has been used, only two peaks can be expected. The first of these peaks might be considered a 'performance peak' where the athlete pursues a performance objective such as a record, or a performance control on which to base achievement targets for the main competition focus. The second is a 'competition peak' where the athlete builds on what has been achieved in pursuit of the first peak through tournament planning and tactics, to reach for success in the season's major championships. Endurance athletes using the Lydiard method normally aim for one peak in the season. This peak embraces pursuit both of performance and competition objectives and is sustained over a period of up to 6 weeks during which time competitions are judiciously spaced to have both objectives coincide with the major championships.

It is clear that the process of planning an athlete's season up to a selection date is unique to a given athlete. Ideally, the programme of local, area, national and international competitions made available to athletes is such that the athlete can select those competitions which best suit his programme of preparation. This means that athletes must occasionally make value-judgements on whether or not to compete on occasions which have high priority for those organizing the competitions, but low priority for the athlete. The objectives of periodising the year were set out at the start of chapter 19. The athlete's value-judgements must be made within the framework of these objectives if he is to produce optimal performance at the major championships.

(4) **Preparation period.** This period is really phases 4 and 5 looked upon as a whole, with phase 4 lasting 4–6 weeks and phase 5 lasting 3–4 weeks. The content of phase 4 will, of course, be altered considerably from that described above in that it represents a specific programme of preparation for a specific competition. For the young and developing athlete, there seems little justification for imposing a rigid structure of competition in the competition period. For the mature national and international athlete, however, it is essential.

Top level athletes cannot be expected to produce maximum performance on every outing. To avoid pressure to do so they may choose not to compete against key opposition. In commercially oriented sport, the pressure is great to meet various contractual obligations. Decisions must be made early when planning the year's programme to strike a balance which will avoid compromise to the pursuit of performance and competition objectives, yet will satisfy the sport's commercial sector. When an athlete is preparing to meet the best in the world, both preparation and competition represent intense mental and physical efforts and cannot be entered into at short intervals. Failure to accept this will lead to an athlete 'burning himself out', and can set the scene for falling short at the major championships.

According to Harre (1973) the total process of the main competition period spans 12 weeks. Personal experience suggests that this can be 16 weeks in a single periodised year. Young and developing athletes should not go beyond 12 weeks; developing athletes may reach 16 weeks due to the more general nature of their training; and top level athletes will operate between 10 and 16 according to how they have periodised the year, and how they may have organised the progression of competitions and the competition peaks within the season. Several countries arrange their fixture lists in such a way that a periodised competition season may be followed, e.g. the German soccer season.

Before leaving this general look at the phasing of the competition period, comparative study of Olympic performances in Mexico and Munich is worth comment. Kruger (1973) found that those following Matveyev periodisation of the summer improved significantly (0.5 level), compared with nations who did not. If the Belgians and Finns were excluded, significance was at the 0.1 level! This study had one or two limitations in that it had information on the athlete's main event alone, and on competition results only, but no knowledge of competition conditions. Moreover, Matveyev periodisation *should* show Matveyev results! Nevertheless, within these limitations, the value of this approach to periodisation seems considerable. The ability of an athlete to peak at the right time must be considered a possible cause of such significant results.

▌ Single and double periodisation

Several attempts have been made to accelerate performance improvement by establishing two competition seasons. The concept of two competition seasons is referred to as double periodisation, while one competition season is single periodisation. The double periodised year has been successfully applied to swimming and track and field. Matveyev (1965) has demonstrated that by this method it is possible to achieve a greater increase per year in those events where maximum and elastic strength are key characteristics (table 31).

Table 31 *Percentage annual improvement in performance comparing double and single periodisation from Matveyev, 1965 Die Periodisierung, Des Sportlicher Trainings—Fiskultura i Sport—Moscow*

event	double periodisation	single periodisation
100m	1.55%	0.96%
Long jump	1.46%	1.35%
High jump	5.05%	2.40%
Shot	3.85%	2.58%
Discus	3.87%	3.11%

Matveyev's explanation is that the more rapid sequence of competition periods prevents an undue fall-off of competition performance and contributes to the stabilisation of technical performance. By stabilisation it is presumed he is referring to the continued integration of technique and conditioning of one keeping in step with the other. However, this implies a certain status in technical development. It should be emphasised, then, that where long periods of consolidation and development are needed (e.g. basic strength, speed, etc.), and in technique as in the young and developing athlete, double periodisation does not have a strong case. To sub-divide the year into short periods of preparation will only result in incomplete mastery of technique, unstable performance, and a reduced rate of development in the foundations of fitness. The stressor of competition in these circumstances will exaggerate those faults which accompany the pursuit of immediate wins, as opposed to an ultimate optimal improvement in performance. This said, any discussion of single or double periodised years should assume that the athlete has a training maturity of several seasons. The young and developing athlete should therefore use any second season as an adjunct to training rather than a deliberate competition climax (e.g. other games, cross-country, etc.).

Since one is dealing with mature athletes, the main competition period is long both for single and double periodisation. This period is sub-divided for both systems into phases 3, 4, 5 or 3_2, 4, 5. So the fundamental difference between single and double periodisation, then, is the existence of a second season. Despite Matveyev's evidence to support the double season, it is not without its antagonists. However, their criticisms are more requests for caution than rejections, and should be noted.

■ Implications for the long season sports

Simply playing a team game, as opposed to an individual sport, does not make players different in their capacity to produce peak performance. It becomes essential, then, for team managers in sports such as rugby, ice hockey, basketball etc. to establish some form of rotation of players to avoid burn-out of all first team players at the same time! Of course the first team will be critical to achieving success in big competitions, but these must be prioritised and individual player preparation plans should be woven round the prioritised competition dates. If players are also to be able to peak for international team duties, these dates must be included in the prioritised list.

So many peaks, by definition, means a well planned regeneration pro-gramme and the cyclic reintroduction of general and related training units. In those sports with high and multiple technical demands and conditioning demands, there is a year round requirement for technical and conditioning work. Cycles of general:related:specific work cannot be compromised to meet the demands of ranking systems. Short-term objectives *must* be consistent with long-term objectives, and not ends in themselves.

▌ Summary

A double competition season provides a greater potential for increase in annual performance. The advantage gained by expanding the time available for competition opportunity must be weighed against the loss to preparation time. Consequently, when applying double periodisation, careful thought must be given to the phasing of the preparation period within the annual cycle. Moreover, in the athlete's competitive 'life', sound judgement is required in the distribution of double periodised years.

21
Units, microcycles and macrocycles

The world of 'schedules and sessions' is now examined, although these expressions are losing their popularity. Consequently some of the expressions used here may be new and it may therefore be useful to define them.

The training unit

The training unit is a single practice session in pursuit of a training objective. For example, the objective may be to develop sprinting speed so the unit might then be 3 x 4 x 30 m rolling start sprints, 4 minutes between repetitions, 7–10 minutes between sets. The objective may be development of aerobic endurance so the unit might be a 20 km steady run, or the objective might be active recovery so the unit could be 20–30 minutes squash, and so on.

An athlete's visit to a training venue may in fact allow him or her to work on one or several training units. For instance, a female basketball player may work through three units in one visit to the gym. At 13.00 hours she begins the first unit (mobility exercises) to develop mobility. At 14.00 hours she practises shooting drills to develop accuracy. At 15.00 hours she begins the third unit of 6 x 200m sprints in 29 seconds to develop speed endurance, with 3, 2, 1, 3 and 2 minutes recovery in between. On the other hand, an evening or lunchtime session may only allow time for 1 unit. So, simply referring to both situations (i.e. 3 units in one day, and 1 unit in one day) as two 'sessions' might cause confusion. This would certainly be the case if one were discussing the number of units per week. To say 'six sessions per week' might mean anything from 6 to 18 units!

The microcycle

The microcycle is a group of units organised in such a way that optimal training value can be obtained from each unit. Moreover, the microcycle may be repeated several times in pursuit of overall objectives of a phase or period.

It is expedient to plan microcycles for a period of one week (table 32) as this helps to fit training units into the general framework of social routine. However, it is clear that for many younger athletes the unit ratio of work to rest, even on a 1 unit per day basis, can lose its training value at 6:1.

Table 32 *Phase 1 microcycle of a male discus thrower*

day	objective	unit	*demand
Sunday	general conditioning and mobility	fartlek and woodland conditioning circuit	medium
Monday	elastic and maximum strength	maximum and sub-maximum weights	high
Tuesday	special development	throws in weighted jacket with heavy implements	medium-high
Wednesday	elastic strength	combined sub-maximum weights and jumps	high
Thursday	maximum strength	maximum weights	very high
Friday	general throwing	other throws, jumps, hurdles, special exercises	medium
Saturday	technique development and strength testing	throws and tests	high

*Note varying demands of each unit. Classification was made according to athlete's own impressions in working through programme.

A regular cycle of 3:1 may suit this athlete's development better, but the training cycle will fall out of synchronisation with the calendar cycle of one week. If this caused problems, the units might be rearranged. For example, one unit on Saturday, two on Sunday, none Monday, one each on Tuesday, Wednesday and Thursday, and none on Friday. Naturally, the units on Sunday would require careful selection. The ratio of the number of training units:the number of recovery units within a microcycle is the inter-unit training ratio.

Several points are worth noting on the construction of a microcycle.

(**1**) The profile of extent of loading and intensity of loading must be given careful consideration (fig. 78). This profile is often referred to as 'the structure of loading'. Both extent and intensity of loading will be dealt with in greater detail in chapter 22.

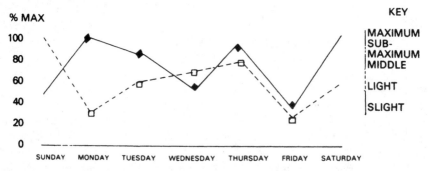

Fig. 78 *Alterations in intensity:extent ratio in the course of a microcycle in Phase II. The subject is a female long jumper, and the scale of intensity (maximum, sub-maximum, etc.) is read against percentage of maximum (vertical scale). The scale of intensity is as suggested by Carl when he advanced the concept as 'spheres of intensity' for weight lifting (from Carl, 1967)*

(2) The demands made on the athlete vary in individual training units in terms of the intra-unit training ratio. This is the relationship of stimulus:recovery within a unit. Thus, the training load represented by each unit has anything from a very high to a slight demand upon the athlete. The athlete must not be exposed to very high demands upon his system in successive units (table 32). Although assessments of demand are mainly subjective on the part of the athlete, the observant coach should read the effect of units upon the athlete with whom he is working. Athlete and coach share responsibility for value-judgements on the effect of training, and apply their collective input to programme planning as a consequence.

(3) Each unit is in pursuit of a specific objective and should vary within a day, and from day to day. Programme planning should then have not only an inbuilt variety of general, special and competition specific units according to athlete, sport and place of training, but also variations in unit detail in pursuit of a specific objective. Notwithstanding the need for variety, athletes also require a sense of routine in the programme. The values here range from a basis for comparison to monitor progress, through to the 'comfort' of an established microcycle design. Part of the coach's art is to arrange microcycles in such a way that variety is a key feature within a flexible framework of routine.

(4) In order to avoid overexertion, the interval between two training units should be long enough to allow the athlete to recover sufficiently to gain maximum training effect from the next unit.

(5) Recovery is accelerated if units of active recovery, or 'regeneration' units are introduced into the microcycle (see chapter 23).

(6) When training units with different objectives and varying demands follow each other, it may not be necessary to await complete recovery. This is the case when different systems are being stressed. According to Craig (1973), this also protects the athlete from 'overuse' types of injury.

(7) Microcycles also permit concentration on one particular objective in individual units, allowing some optimal period of time when the athlete can be exposed to the desired stimulus. This helps adaptation to develop in a particular area. Poor organisation may bring conflicting objectives into badly grouped units (e.g. when speed loading and endurance loading are brought together *some* contribution is made to speed and endurance, but the maximal development of either is impossible). Similarly, when an athlete rushes intervals between repetitions of set pieces in games, development of technique is impaired and very little contribution to speed or endurance is made.

(8) Microcycles reduce monotony in training despite high frequency of training units. Failure to use these cycles may mean a standard session or variation on a session being used *ad nauseam*, the result of which would

be a stereotyped reaction to the exercise stimulus and an ultimate stagnation of performance.

(9) Demands on speed or elastic strength or maximum strength should be carried out on days of optimal capacity and never following days of high demand, especially if this involves lactic–anaerobic endurance training. A similar rule will apply when several units are being worked in the course of one day. So the following order of events should be pursued:

Several units in 1 day:

- warm-up and/or mobility
- neuromuscular work (e.g. technique, speed, elastic strength, maximum strength)
- energy systems work (all endurance – heart, speed, strength)
- aerobic warm-down.

From day to day:

- aerobic/general/recovery
- neuromuscular
- anaerobic endurance.

In the maximum strength events the day to day pattern alters by intensity and/or exercises.

(10) As a rule, more than 24 hours are required to recover from very high loadings which will, of course, include competitions. Consequently the loading in the competition period must be so placed that the competition can be carried out in the phase of accentuated capacity (or overcompensation) brought about by optimal loading 1½ to 3 days beforehand (figs. 79 and 80).

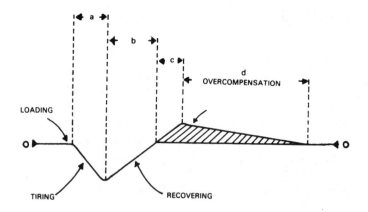

Fig. 79 *Cycle of overcompensation* (from Yakovlev, 1967). *a–d represent periods of time; o represents original status of capacity being trained*

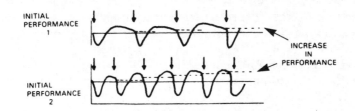

Fig. 80 *This illustrates the cumulative effects of training. Since the period of overcompensation, or improved performance, gradually diminishes, there is less increase in performance with longer intervals (1) than with shorter intervals (2). The optimal improvement in performance is achieved when the new loading is presented at the highest point in the overcompensation phase* (from Harre, 1973)

■ Adaptable microcycles

For some sports, there are occasions where microcycle design cannot be fixed for any length of time. For example, where players are 'on the road' in constant national or international travel, changing time zones, training and competition venues; or where what happens in terms of tournament progression dictates subsequent training time, availability and location. This is very much the situation for the full-time professional athlete or player.

In these cases, against the background of the foregoing points on microcycle construction, and on the understanding that there is a sound conditioning base, the following notes may help meet the player's or athlete's training needs.

(1) In the main, try to follow a cyclic pattern of adaptation; application; regeneration; through training units, with full recovery between units. Extent and intensity of loading in adaptation units should be low to medium, while loading in application units should be low to medium in extent, but high to very high in intensity.
(2) Create for the athlete/player a selection of those microcycle structures which may be called for, given certain situations. For example there should be a structure provided for 1, 2, 3, 4, or 5 days training opportunity. Where there are more days, either the basic microcycle for that phase in the year, or a special training camp microcycle will apply.
(3) Provide a selection of training units from which the athlete will choose the best suited to a given training situation. For example, a player's training microcycle has 'aerobic run' as a unit. The selection on the programme is either 45 minutes easy run (heart rate 155–165) **or** 30 minutes hard fartlek on undulating terrain (heart rate should vary between 140 and 180) **or** 30 minutes steady water jogging (heart rate 155–165) **or** steady mountain bike ride for 75 minutes (heart rate 150–160) **or** 20 x interval runs using diagonal of a soccer pitch for the fast run (heart rate 180), jogging on side line (heart rate 170–180 during 2 minutes); (heart rate returns to 130–140 in 60 seconds).

If the player is in a hotel in the centre of a city which has a swimming pool, the player is able to water jog. The next day, the player may travel at mid-day and will not arrive at his destination until late at night. The training unit for that day is 'general strength' for which the selection on the programme is either personal weight training programme (60 minutes) **or** personal strength machine programme (45 minutes) **or** personal body circuit (30 minutes).

Time and limited equipment suggest the latter programme. In other words, the coach must prepare a series of options in advance.

(4) Encourage the player/athlete to keep a record of what is done so that this information can be considered in designing the next basic microcycle.

(5) Regeneration units should also be on the basis of a selection to choose from. The player/athlete will, then, develop an involvement in establishing his area of training as part of a lifestyle which can become stressful. Regeneration units are very important inclusions in the 'adaptable microcycle' as a contribution to stress management.

■ Macrocycles & mesocycles/phases

The macrocycle, and smaller mesocycle, is the sum of all units required to bring the status of training to that level required to meet the macrocycle objectives. However, it might also be said that macrocycles exist due to the characteristic progress of intensity and extent of loading, and are required to make the rhythmic changes from long periods of high average loading, to shorter periods of reduced loading. They are obviously closely regulated by the competition period but extend over 4–6 weeks during the preparation period. Very careful consideration must be given to extending duration of the macrocycle beyond 6 weeks as there is a danger of dulling the athlete's motivation and response to training loads.

The shape of loading in the preparation period arises from the basic principle that within each macrocycle an increase in extent of loading is achieved, then the intensity in each unit is raised. The Oregon method of endurance training classically demonstrates this principle. Ter-Ovanesyan (1965) describes extension of the principle to competition preparation, where, over a 5-week period the total extent of loadings were increased over weeks 1–3, and then reduced while intensity continued to increase to the week of competition.

In preparing a macrocycle, the coach must have the following information:

- the number of units of training available in the macrocycle. For example, in the months of November/December, the athlete may be able to programme 9 units per week – approximately 70 units in total
- the % distribution of general, special and competition specific training
- the inter-unit training ratio
- the structure of loading for the macrocycle
- the structure of loading and intra-unit training ratio relevant to each type of training

- the manner of increasing extent and intensity within the macrocycle
- the athlete's evaluation of the effects of training at unit, microcycle and macrocycle levels.

Table 33 *Possible breakdown of units for a 17 year old girl sprinter – phase 1*

training area	classification	% units
aerobic endurance	general	11
speed endurance	special	11
strength endurance	general	11
speed	competition specific	5.5
elastic strength	special	11
maximum strength	special	5.5
mobility	general	11
sprint technique	competition specific	11
active recovery	general	23

For example, in table 33 we have a suggested breakdown of units for a 17 year old girl sprinter in phase 1. This represents 10 units per week for 5 weeks. In each microcycle of 1 week, the athlete has a programme as set out below:

Saturday	2	Wednesday	1
Sunday	2	Thursday	2
Monday	1	Friday	0
Tuesday	2		

The next step will be to detail the unit objective of each unit indicated on the weekly microcycle, over all five weeks of the macrocycle. This might be done as shown in table 34. Obviously, the final interpretation of the percentages is flexible, but they have been kept, in the main, close to the original suggestion.

Table 34 *Approximate distribution of training objectives against the suggested percentages*

day		week 1	week 2	week 3	week 4	week 5
Saturday	A	sprint tech	sprint tech	sprint tech	sprint tech	sprint tech
	B	aerobic	aerobic	aerobic	aerobic	aerobic
Sunday	A	max strength	elastic str	max strength	elastic str	max strength
	B	speed/endur	speed/endur	speed/endur	speed/endur	speed/endu
Monday	A	active recov	active recov	active recov	active recov	active recov
Tuesday	A	speed	sprint tech	speed	sprint tech	speed
	B	mobility	mobility	mobility	mobility	mobility
Wednesday	A	active recov	active recov	active recov	active recov	active recov
Thursday	A	elastic str	elastic str	elastic str	elastic str	elastic str
	B	strength end	strength end	strength end	strength end	strength end
Friday		0	0	0	0	0

Next, the detail of each training unit in terms of number of repetitions, sets, distances, intervals, kilos, exercises, etc., would be listed. Finally, the progression of extent and intensity would be established. For example, numbers of repetitions and/or sets will be increased in weeks 1–3, while in weeks 4–5 repetitions and sets will return to those of week 1, but runs will be faster, loads heavier, or intervals shorter.

As a guide to training ratios, table 35 is offered as suggested percentages on which to work for track and field. It will be noted that columns are headed G (general), S (special) and C (competition specific). Osolin and Markov (1972) suggest statistics for the three periods and their figures have been used in compiling the percentages listed here.

Table 35 % distribution of general (G), special (S), and competition specific (C) training units according to the phase of the periodised year

	I			II			III			IV			V			VI		
beginners and developing athletes	G	S	C	G	S	C	G	S	C	G	S	C	G	S	C	G	S	C
10–14 yrs	70	10	20	60	20	20	50	20	30	60	20	20	50	20	30	80	10	10
15–17 yrs	60	20	20	50	25	25	50	20	30	50	25	25	50	20	30	70	20	10
18–19 yrs	50	25	25	40	25	35	25	25	50	45	30	25	15	25	60	75	15	10
novice seniors	50	25	25	40	25	35	25	25	50	45	30	25	25	25	50	75	15	10
experienced athletes																		
sprints, long and triple	25	55	20	15	60	25	10	55	35	25	55	20	10	60	30	80	10	10
middle distance and walkers	20	75	5	20	70	10	10	70	20	10	85	5	10	80	10	55	40	5
long distance and marathon	10	85	5	10	85	5	5	90	5	10	85	5	5	90	5	45	50	5
hurdles, high, pole vault	35	35	30	25	35	40	10	40	50	20	40	40	10	40	50	80	10	10
throws	25	35	40	15	45	40	10	40	50	20	40	40	10	40	50	80	10	10

Percentage of training units

■ Summary

The pattern of the training plan should be seen in relation to that of all other natural phenomena. Just as the seasons follow a cycle, and our various physiological systems follow the laws of chronobiology, so training must follow a cyclical pattern. The broad areas of the cycle may be summarised as preparation, adaptation, application, and recuperation. The areas are reflected at all levels from unit to annual cycle to the athlete's competitive 'life'. To progress the athlete's pursuit of competitive advantage, training units that represent specific structures of loadings are organised for optimal effect by applying correct training ratios into microcycles. These are repeated with progressions to form mesocycles and macrocycles, the largest 'units' of the phase. By careful emphasis on distribution of general, special, and competition specific training, the phases are structured to meet objectives relative to progression through the periods of the annual cycle. Finally, each annual cycle has a unique character in terms of its contribution to the athlete's ultimate sporting objective.

22
Adaptation to loading

Adaptation is the raising of the athlete's functioning capacity due to external loading and/or adjustment to specific environmental conditions. Both physical and psychological adaptation must be seen as one process. For example, it will have been noted by coaches that training not only raises the athlete's status of strength, speed, etc., but also affects the athlete's ability to 'dig deeper' into reserves of performance.

Definition

Training offers the athlete external loading and it is quite obvious that there is a relationship between loading and adaptation. The three laws of training (specificity, overload and reversibility) qualify and quantify loading. However, while these laws are fairly explicit, there are some points which should be emphasised.

(1) A high extent of load without the necessary minimum intensity fails to produce adaptation just as much as high intensity with too little extent.

(2) The more the amounts of loading approach an optimal value relative to the athlete's capacity *at the moment of loading*, the more rapidly adaptation takes place. Conversely, the greater the departure from that value (either over- or underloading) the less the adaptation.

(3) If the demands of loading exceed the athlete's capacity, or if the structure of loading is wrong, then the athlete's capacity for adjustment will be impaired and performance will stagnate or even be reduced.

(4) The relationship between loading and recovery is critical and they should be seen as a whole (fig. 79, p. 270).

(5) While 'overcompensation' is quickly transformed to a higher level of performance in the young and developing athlete, this process takes weeks or months with the mature athlete. Each loading close to the optimum will leave behind it a trace of overcompensation, but for the mature athlete it is only due to the cumulative effect of training that improvements come at intervals, and not necessarily regular intervals. Matveyev (1965) refers to this as 'delayed transformation': '(it) prevents the continuous flow of information on the effect of loading on training

275

that is necessary for the optimal regulation of the training process'. Progressive adaptation is not therefore easily apparent and only the results of competition or tests at the end of phase 2 or at the start of phase 3 show whether or not loading has been effective. Periodic checks and test procedures geared to accurate prediction are therefore vital throughout phases 1 and 2. It is feasible that the introduction of phase 3_2, in double periodisation, may provide a most relevant testing procedure.

(6) Loading must be systematically and progressively increased. Loadings that remain unchanged are more easily overcome in time and cause less disruption of the body's systems, but their effect diminishes until they simply maintain a stationary state of adaptation.

(7) The rate at which capacity reduces on reduction or cessation of loading is critical to the athlete. Illness, travel during the competition season, examinations, injury etc., all imply disruption of the systematic increase of loadings. Moreover, during the competition season, loadings are frequently reduced in extent (and even intensity by some coaches). Again, this represents a break in continuity of the adaptation process. The more recent the level of adaptation, the more quickly it will be affected by reduced loading. Long periods of gradual development are therefore indicated. Lengthy transitional periods without training loading are to be avoided and, if the interval between training units is too long, the effect of loadings is lost. Finally, attention is drawn again to the relevance of a 'polyvalent' or mixed approach and to pursuing a changing training ratio throughout the year.

(8) Loadings of great extent and slight to medium intensity primarily develop endurance capacity. Those of less extent, but sub-maximum to maximum intensity, mainly develop maximum strength, elastic strength and speed. While this may be accurate for the mature athlete, the young and developing athlete is affected by loadings in a far more complex way. Consequently, as Harre has noted (1973), the bulk of his or her work which is low to middle intensity, also develops strength and speed, to a certain extent.

But what exactly do expressions like middle intensity mean? To arrive at an explanation, one must first examine the expression 'intensity'.

■ Intensity of loading
The intensity of loading is characterised by the strength of the stimulus, or by the concentration of work executed per unit of time within a series of stimuli. Intensity for endurance or speed is calculated according to the speed in m/second or the frequency of movement, e.g. cadence in sprinting. For strength exercises the amount of resistance is measured, and for jumping or throwing, the height or distance (loaded and/or unloaded) is used. Since intensity varies in exercise it is useful to distinguish between 'spheres of intensity', as Carl (1967) has called them.

In order to compare the loading of athletes, these spheres should be established with reference to a fixed point and should be clearly delineated. For exercises to develop maximum strength, speed, elastic strength, etc., the highest possible individual intensity of stimulation is taken as the point of reference, maximum loading being equal to 100% (tables 36 and 37).

A standard scale of intensity would be most useful. It would establish a basic frame of reference and help in the evaluation of training theory. It is, after all, at the comparative level that the real meaning of loading becomes apparent. For too long there has been no market place to exchange the various currencies in which each coach transacts the business of relating unit to athlete. Table 38 is offered as a basis for such an intensity scale.

Table 36 *Example of possible table for percentage intensity to be used for track running. The spheres of intensity are then derived from this. A problem arises where authorities offer varying spheres of intensity (see table 37)*

Best 150m					% of best time					
100	65	66.7	73	75	80	83	87.5	90	95	97
18.3	27.9	—	25.0	—	—	22.1	20.8	20.1	19.2	18.8
18.5	—	27.4	25.1	24.6	23.1	22.4	21.1	20.5	19.5	18.9
18.8	28.4	27.9	25.5	25.0	23.4	22.7	21.4	20.8	19.7	19.2
18.9	28.9	—	—	25.1	23.8	—	21.7	21.1	20.0	19.5
19.2	—	28.4	26.0	—	24.2	23.1	22.1	21.4	20.3	19.7
19.5	30.0	28.9	26.4	25.5	—	23.4	22.4	21.7	20.5	20.0
19.7	30.6	—	26.9	26.0	24.6	23.8	22.7	22.1	20.8	20.1
20.0	—	30.0	—	26.4	25.0	24.2	—	—	21.1	20.5
20.3	31.3	30.6	27.4	—	25.4	24.6	23.1	22.4	21.4	20.8
20.5	31.9	—	27.9	26.9	25.9	—	23.4	22.7	21.7	21.1
20.8	—	31.3	—	27.4	—	25.0	23.8	23.1	22.1	21.4
21.1	32.6	31.9	28.4	27.9	26.3	25.1	24.2	23.4	22.4	21.7
(Best 200m)										
20.0	30.7	29.4	27.3	26.6	25.0	24.0	22.7	22.2	21.0	20.6
20.2	31.2	30.3	27.7	27.0	25.3	24.3	22.9	22.4	21.2	20.8
20.4	—	30.7	—	—	—	24.6	23.2	22.7	21.5	21.0
20.6	31.7	—	28.1	27.3	25.6	—	23.5	22.9	21.7	21.2
20.8	32.2	31.2	28.5	27.7	25.9	25.0	23.8	23.2	21.9	21.5
21.0	—	31.7	28.9	28.1	26.3	25.3	24.0	—	22.2	21.7
21.2	32.7	—	—	—	26.6	25.6	24.3	23.5	22.4	21.9
21.5	33.3	32.2	29.4	28.5	27.0	25.9	24.6	23.8	22.7	22.2
21.7	—	32.7	29.9	28.9	—	26.3	—	24.0	22.9	22.4
21.9	33.8	—	30.3	29.4	27.3	—	25.0	24.3	23.2	22.7
22.2	—	33.3	—	—	27.7	26.6	25.3	24.6	—	22.9
22.4	34.4	33.8	30.7	29.8	28.1	27.0	25.6	25.0	23.5	23.2
22.7	35.0	—	31.2	30.3	28.5	27.3	25.9	25.3	23.8	23.5

Table 37 *Comparison of terms used in describing loading as % max. intensity*

Myer	designation of intensity	Carl*
	slight	30–50%
	light	50–70%
65–73%	middle	70–80%
75–83%	high	
87.5–97%	sub-maximum	80–90%
	maximum	90–100%

*Suggested spheres of intensity in weight training.

Table 38 *Suggested standard intensity scale*

scale of intensity	percentage of maximum
low	30%–49%
light	50%–64%
medium	65%–74%
high	75%–84%
sub-maximum	85%–94%
maximum	95%–100%

When training for endurance events, intensity is ideally evaluated against the best performances over the training distance, or against the average competition speed at the moment. However, in passing, it should be noted that since training at given intensities of VO_2 maximum have great relevance to the energy system involved, the measure of intensity may well be 'read' from the working heart rate and against the percentage of VO_2 maximum (table 13, p. 81). The extent of loading at certain percentages of maximum intensity should be recorded to help establish a pattern of relative intensity over a unit/microcycle/macrocycle, etc. A difference then exists between this, the relative intensity, and the highest intensity recorded in a particular unit, or cycle. In this case, the value is known as absolute intensity.

As indicated, intensity must be above a certain threshold level before adaptation results. For example, Hettinger and Müller (1953) suggest that isometric training with intensity less than 30% maximum produces no increase in maximum isometric strength, while Karvonen (1957) suggests training at 60% of the athlete's range of heart rate (resting-maximum) in order to increase maximum oxygen uptake. Training at intensity a little above the threshold, provided it is extensive, develops the physical ability in question slowly, continuously and to a high degree of stability. The basic ability to take loading is raised with this type of training. Training at the other end of the scale causes a rapid improvement of status, but adaptation is less stable and must be continuously stabilised by more comprehensive extensive loadings.

In the interest of stability of performance, especially in technical events with beginners, the intensity must be low enough to permit efficient execution of the technique in question. On the other hand, in those events demanding maximum and elastic strength, one must work through a particular extent of loading in the competition specific range of intensity in order to stabilise athletic technique corresponding to demands of competition.

■ Density in loading

The density or frequency of stimulus in loading is determined by the objective of the unit, the stimulus being controlled both by its intensity and duration. Knowing this, an optimal density can be established which will allow an evaluation of the number of consecutive occasions per unit when the athlete is exposed to the stimulus, and also the amount of time between these occasions. In pursuit of specificity of loading effect, numbers of repetitions and sets are married to the interval of time between them to create an optimal density. From these precepts, crude formulae have evolved for the development of specific endurance capacities (table 39).

In strength and speed work at sub-maximum to maximum intensities, 2–5 minutes are necessary between successive loadings.

Table 39   Suggested intra–unit training ratios according to endurance characteristic to be developed

characteristic	loading:recovery	intensity
heart endurance	continuous	light
heart endurance	2:1–1:1	high
speed endurance	1:3–1:6	sub-maximum

■ Duration of stimulus in loading

The duration of stimulus is the period of influence of a single stimulus, the distance covered in a repetition, or the total time to complete all loading in a unit. Just as there appear to be thresholds of intensity, so also for duration. Thus, Gundlach (1968) suggests at least 20–30% of maximum holding time is essential for the improvement of isometric strength. Endemann (1973) used this information in his 'auxotonic training' where resistances were consciously controlled in their speed of movement (e.g. 5 seconds lowering, 5 seconds raising bar in bench press). Hollmann (1962) determined that at least 30 minutes duration of stimulus was required at a given intensity for significant improvement in aerobic endurance. Moreover, it seems clear from figure 32, p. 87, that a minimum of 2 minutes duration at a relatively high intensity of stimulus is necessary to adapt the athlete to the acid base imbalance of competition in short and medium duration endurance disciplines. Obviously, the duration of work in maximum and elastic strength, mobility and speed development must not be so long that fatigue reduces the ability to perform efficiently.

Finally, in pursuit of strength endurance, the duration of loading must be such that considerable effort of will is required to complete the unit.

■ Extent of loading

The extent of loading is the sum of duration (time *or* distance) and the repetitions of all stimuli in a training unit. Consequently it will be expressed in kilometres in endurance training, in kilograms in strength training (the sum of loadings), and in the number of repetitions in strength endurance, etc. It is necessary, of course, to divide the extent of loadings into various spheres of intensity, or, if it is agreed, to divide the loadings according to the suggested scale in table 38.

The unit, then, is a complex of intensity, extent, duration and density of loading. For optimal value to be derived from each unit, no athlete should arrive at the start of one unit while still fatigued from the previous unit. A full understanding of the unit complex, and the effect each unit has upon the athlete, is essential to the coach. From here the microcycle begins to evolve with an understanding of what should constitute a unit of loading for an athlete and the frequency of exposure of the athlete to that unit.

Extent of training is therefore the sum total of hours, kilograms or kilometres of training, calculated from the cumulation of units and their frequency – the whole being expressed over a microcycle, macrocycle, phase, period, or indeed, annual cycle (fig. 81).

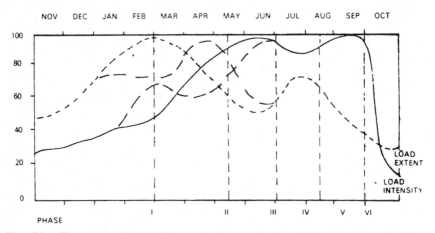

Fig. 81 *The suggested relationship between extent and intensity of loading in the annual cycle of single and double periodised years* (from Matveyev, 1965)

■ Progressive loading

'Progression of loading in pursuit of progression of performance improvement' might, in a nutshell, represent the whole purpose of training. From the above discussion of adaptation and loading, 'progression of loading' will be seen as greater extent, higher intensity, longer duration, greater density or increased frequency, or a combination of some or all of these. Loading must always bear a particular relationship to the athlete's present loading capacity. Consequently, no 'absolutes' can be given in terms of loading progression. However, as outlined below, certain general principles do operate to guide the coach when increasing loading.

(1) In technical and tactical training, loading is increased by imposing greater demands on the co-ordination required of a technique. This can be achieved by:

- demanding greater speed in execution
- requiring technical exactness in an endurance situation
- combining various elements of practice
- changing external conditions
- learning more complex technical variations
- offering competition pressure.

Not only do such practices develop technical efficiency, but they also develop specific physical capacities such as mobility and the ability to make rapid and correct adjustment when a loss of balance threatens technical precision.

(2) For endurance, strength, speed, elastic strength, etc., the structure of loading must be altered. The main problem here is to decide exactly the alteration of ratio of intensity and extent from macrocycle to macrocycle, or, for that matter, from athlete to athlete, in the whole range from the beginner to the professional. The problem does not end there, however, because great thought must be given to the question of which components (endurance, strength, etc.) should be stressed in the increase of loading. To say simply that this varies according to athlete and event, and that herein lies the art and mastery of coaching, is quite an indictment of coaches' progress in establishing firm training principles. It is true that to date the state of knowledge in this field is most unsatisfactory, yet it is equally true that the roots of such knowledge lie with coaches and athletes. However, until knowledge in this area becomes more specialised, it is clear that, in general, when the athlete's degree of adaptation has been raised, loading must then become more comprehensive and more intensive. This means that the athlete must be exposed to raised loadings *specific to all facets of his sport* and that such an increase is not one of extent, but of intensity. This generalisation must be applied to specific sports. Consequently the coach must evaluate both sport and athlete and be able to apply this information to improve the athlete's status of adaptation.

(3) For the beginner in sport, another general principle is 'Fit the sport to the athlete – then fit the athlete to the sport'. Once this introductory stage is past, these athletes will achieve more stable adaptation and, ultimately, a greater improvement in performance if intensity is raised cautiously and loading progression is primarily via more extensive training. According to Harre (1973), the progression is:

- raise the frequency of training (e.g. number of consecutive units, say from twice weekly to daily training)
- raise the extent of loading per training unit, while keeping frequency constant
- raise the density of loading within the training unit.

As a rule, it is not acceptable to the athlete to bring about these three stages simultaneously. At first an optimal frequency is sought and only when time is limited should the coach consider increasing the load.

(4) Analysis of individual athletes' training has shown that a linear gradual increase of loading is not as effective as increases by 'jumps' spaced at given intervals. It would appear that increasing loading in such jumps suddenly taxes the status of the athlete's capacities and 'disturbs the physical-psychological balance' (Harre, 1973). This then forces the athlete's total organism to establish new physical-psychological processes of regulation and adaptation. The most obvious examples of this are seen at the start of phase 1 where extent is advanced by jumps (compared with phases 4 and 6 of the previous cycle), thus affecting rapid strength endurance and aerobic status, and at the start of phase 3 where intensity is advanced due to severe competition specific loadings and is accompanied by rapid improvements in performance. The time interval between such jumps is, again, arrived at individually, but several coaches now tie these in with 23–28 day macrocycles. Chronobiology will almost certainly offer a great contribution to understanding such time intervals. Obviously, the athlete will require some time to adapt to the sudden increase in loading and stabilise his training level, but adaptation of processes and stability do not necessarily advance together.

(5) The next question is how much to increase loading with each jump, or from year to year. Again, there is little to use as a basis for absolutes, but Matveyev (1965) determined an increase of 20–50% in extent from one year to the next. This of course will vary from sport to sport and will depend on conditions and time available for training. The progressions then will grow from an educated appraisal by the coach of conditions and time, using a logical progression based upon the foregoing general principles. The hardest area of judgement for the coach is when to maintain rather than increase extent or intensity.

On the subject of increasing intensity, personal observation suggests a maximum increment of 5% per macrocycle where a particular unit or its derivative runs throughout a year. This policy is only altered for testing sessions, or when the very high intensity demanded of phases 3_1, 3, or 3_2 implies work to maximum (see below).

Repetition runs over 300m – female long jumper (100% taken as previous best):

Phase 1: 3 x 75% (4 min) → 5 x 75% (4 min)
     Test to establish new 100%
4 x 80% (4 min) → 5 x 80% (4 min)
     Test to establish new 100%

Phase 2: 4 x 85% (7.5 min) → 5 x 85% (7.5 min)
     Test to establish new 100%
3 x 90% (10 min)
     Test to establish new 100%

Phase 3: 2 x 90% (15 mins)
1–2 x 100% with full recovery
(figures in brackets are recovery times)

(6) Within training units, at the exercise level, there can be considerable confusion over the available avenues for progression. Quite simply, there are only three:

- perform the exercise more often (or for greater duration) (endurance factor)
- perform the exercise against increased resistance (strength factor)
- perform the exercise faster (speed factor).

Progression may only be considered when the athlete's performance of the exercise is technically sound. If the performance breaks down to a comfortable compromise, then clearly there is no basis for progression.

(7) It is important that the coach fully understands that the athlete experiences three separate effects of training. They are: the immediate effect; the residual effect; the cumulative effect. Each contributes to the pattern of events which have been represented in figures 79 and 80, and merits brief discussion here.

The immediate effect: this is the effect on the organism during application of the stimulus. Associated aspects are biochemistry of energy production, mobilisation of those aspects of physiology which permit the organism to support the activity, regulation of neuromuscular control of movement patterns, fatigue factors and so on.

The residual effect: once the stimulus is removed, the organism operates to bring about recovery from the immediate effect. This involves a heightened metabolic rate to repair damage and restore the status quo in those systems which have been stressed. This process, as is illustrated in figure 79, in fact overcompensates and makes it possible for the stimulus to be progressed.

The cumulative effect: as was indicated in figure 80, judiciously timed application of further stimuli during the period of overcompensation permits successive residual effects to be built upon, so that over a period of time, the athlete's status in pursuit of a specific training objective is considerably advanced.

The overall picture is illustrated in figure 82.

This is all very straightforward when the training objective is singular, for example in progressing leg strength through a weight training programme. The situation becomes more complex when several training objectives are being pursued. Figure 83 represents the weekly microcycle of a decathlete, and shows how pursuit of the stated objectives will proceed over a 6-week macrocycle. The proposed progressions for individual units are sound as they stand – but they may not be if the aggregate cumulative effect of all training units is such that the aggregate residual effect cannot reach the level of overcompensation. At this point the overall training load will damage rather than benefit the athlete. The importance of responsible interpretation by coach and athlete of the athlete's subjective evaluation of training effect is clearly highlighted here, and there must be a flexibility built into the programme for adjustment to progressions within the macrocycle. Clearly, progressions in pursuit of all objectives cannot proceed at the same rate.

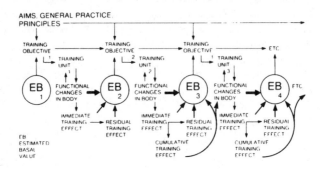

Fig. 82   *Summary of the effects of training*

▌ Summary

To conclude this discussion of adaptation to loading, the basic guiding principle should be:

- step 1 – preparation for training
- step 2 – training for competition.

Without doubt, the most rapid development of performance will come from high intensity competition specific loadings, but where these are used to too great an extent, they quickly wear out the physical and psychological potential of the athlete. The more thorough and extensive step 1, the longer will be the amount of time before such 'wearing out'. Nevertheless, there are occasions when the athlete appears to have gone 'stale' for reasons that are not always apparent. This phenomenon has critical implications for coach and athlete and may be examined in the following chapter.

The defining of optimal loading for an athlete is critical to progression of his fitness and maintenance of his health. It demands fine judgements on the part of the coach. The cycle of preparation, adaptation, and application must be followed at all levels. Without doubt, the most rapid development of performance will come from high intensity competition specific loadings, but where these are used to too great an extent they quickly wear out the physical and psychological potential of the athlete. This emphasises the importance of a thorough and extensive preparation part of the cycle and of viewing *stimulus plus recovery* as a total process.

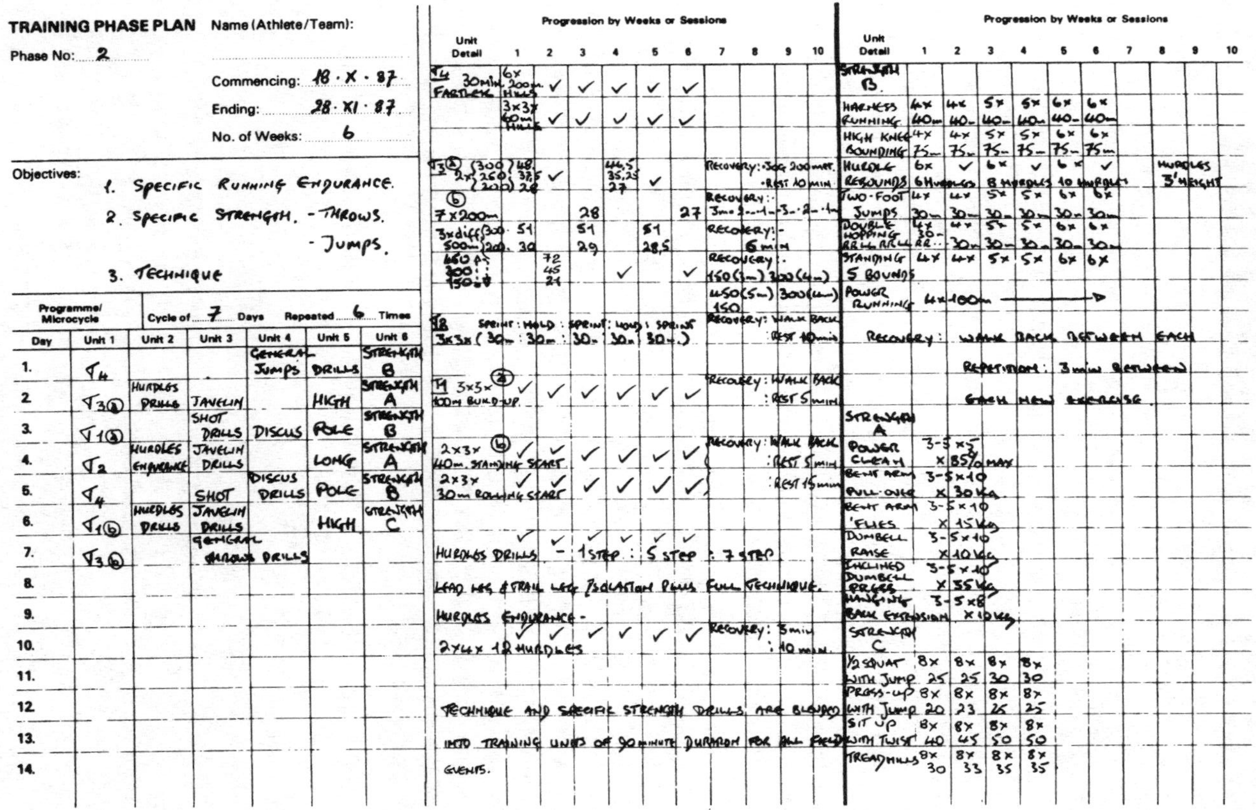
TRAINING PHASE PLAN Name (Athlete/Team):

Phase No: 2

Commencing: 18 · X · 87

Ending: 28 · XI · 87

No. of Weeks: 6

Objectives:
1. Specific Running Endurance.
2. Specific Strength. - Throws.
- Jumps.
3. Technique

Programme/Microcycle — Cycle of 7 Days Repeated 6 Times

Day	Unit 1	Unit 2	Unit 3	Unit 4	Unit 5	Unit 6
1.	∇4			General Jumps	Drills	Strength B
2.	∇3 ②	Hurdles Drills	Javelin		High	Strength A
3.	∇1 ③		Shot Drills	Discus	Pole	Strength B
4.	∇2	Hurdles Endurance	Javelin Drills		Long	Strength A
5.	∇4		Shot	Discus Drills	Pole	Strength B
6.	∇1 ⑥	Hurdles Drills	Javelin Drills		High	Strength C
7.	∇3 ⑥		General throws drills			
8.						
9.						
10.						
11.						
12.						
13.						
14.						

Progression by Weeks or Sessions

Unit Detail	1	2	3	4	5	6	7	8	9	10
∇4 30min Fartlek	6x 200m Hills	✓	✓	✓	✓	✓				
	3x3x 60m Hills	✓	✓	✓	✓	✓				
∇3 ② 2x (300 / 250 / 200)	48 / 37,5 / 28	✓		44,5 / 35,25 / 27	✓		Recovery: Jog 200 mtr. · Rest 10 min			
⑥ 7x200m			28			27	Recovery: 3min – 1 – 3 – 2 – 1			
3x diff (300 – 500m / 200)	51 / 30		51 / 29		51 / 28,5		Recovery: 6 min			
450 / 300 / 150		72 / 45 / 21		✓		✓	Recovery: 450 (5m) 300 (4m) 150 (3m) 300 (4m) 450 (5m) 150			
∇8 3x3x (30m : 30m : 30m : 30m : 30m) Sprint : Hold : Sprint : Hold : Sprint							Recovery: Walk Back · Rest 10 min			
∇1 3x3x ② 100m Build-up	✓	✓	✓	✓	✓	✓	Recovery: Walk Back : Rest 5 min			
2x3x ⑥ 40m Standing Start	✓	✓	✓	✓	✓	✓	Recovery: Walk Back : Rest 5 min			
2x3x 30m Rolling Start	✓	✓	✓	✓	✓	✓	: Rest 15 min			
Hurdles Drills	✓ -	✓ 1 step	✓ :	✓ 5 step	✓ :	✓ 7 step				
Lead leg & trail leg isolation plus full technique.										
Hurdles Endurance - 2x4x 12 hurdles	✓	✓	✓	✓	✓	✓	Recovery: 3 min : 10 min.			

Technique and specific strength drills are blended into training units of 90 minute duration for all field events.

Progression by Weeks or Sessions

Unit Detail	1	2	3	4	5	6	7	8	9	10
Strength B.										
Harness Running	4x 40m	4x 40m	5x 40m	5x 40m	6x 40m	6x 40m				
High Knee Bounding	4x 75m	4x 75m	5x 75m	5x 75m	6x 75m	6x 75m				
Hurdle Rebounds	6x 6 Hurdles	✓	6x 8 Hurdles	✓	6x 10 Hurdles	✓		Hurdles 3' Height		
Two-Foot Jumps	4x 30m	4x 30m	5x 30m	5x 30m	6x 30m	6x 30m				
Double Hopping RRLLRRLL	4x 30m	4x 30m	5x 30m	5x 30m	6x 30m	6x 30m				
Standing 5 Bounds	4x	4x	5x	5x	6x	6x				
Power Running	4x100m ——→									

Recovery: Walk back between each repetition : 3 min between each new exercise.

Unit Detail	1	2	3	4
Strength A				
Power Clean	3-5 x5 x 85% max			
Bent Arm Pull-Over	3-5 x10 x 30 kg			
Bent Arm 'Flies	3-5 x10 x 15 kg			
Dumbell Raise	3-5 x10 x 10 kg			
Inclined Dumbell Press	3-5 x10 x 35 kg			
Hanging Back Extension	3-5 x8 x 10 kg			
Strength C				
½ Squat with Jump	8x 25	8x 25	8x 30	8x 30
Press-up with Jump	8x 20	8x 23	8x 26	8x 25
Sit up with Twist	8x 40	8x 45	8x 50	8x 50
Treadmills	8x 30	8x 33	8x 35	8x 35

Fig. 83 *Example of a microcycle for a decathlete, and progression through a macrocycle*

23
Training v straining

Training is only one of several stressors that bombard the athlete each day. They include career studies, domestic life, social life, institution demands, and so on. Where the total load of these stressors is in-keeping with his level of adaptation to stress, training will progress normally and performance will improve. Fatigue induced by training should be overcome relatively quickly, depending on the nature of loading. But in any case, even after very heavy loadings, the initial value at rest is regained within 24–48 hours. This sort of fatigue is normal. The athlete will be ready to tackle normal physical and mental work after the training loads and should feel well rested and fully recovered the morning after.

On the other hand, the cumulative stressors may be too much for the athlete and this will be referred to as overstressing the athlete. Short of complete and regular bioprofiles on athletes, which demands access to physiological testing laboratories, the coach has very little with which to assess the contribution of training to the sum total of stressors. This said, in some countries it has become an accepted feature of the National Performance Programme that athletes will undergo periodic 'stress' monitoring to reduce the risks of overstressing the athlete. In Finland, at Vierumakki, athletes present themselves for such monitoring on the following basis:

Stress level	Chronic long-term training stress–disturbances at hormonal level.	Acute short-term training stress–disturbances in muscle membranes and in energy production.
Relevant measurement	Measuring the ratio of testosterone:cortisone levels in blood serum.	Measuring urea/creatinine/creatine-kinase concentration in blood serum.
Timing of measurement	4 times per year; twice during the main preparation phase, once during the competition preparation phase, once one month before the main competition.	During hard training microcycles (e.g. training camps) samples taken each morning.

Clues which the coach might pick on are shown in table 40.

Table 40 Symptoms of tiring after optimal and excessive loading

	optimal loading	excessive loading	recovery after excessive loading
Skin colour	flushed	very flushed	paleness for several days
Sweating	heavy sweat in upper body	sweating throughout body	night sweats
Co-ordination	slight loss of precision as unit proceeds	loss of precision, distressing confusion, increased reaction time	reduced precision from 24–48 hrs.
Concentration	reducing span of attention; reducing capacity to solve technical problems; reducing power of identifying irrelevant cues	inability to concentrate for even relatively short periods; forgets instructions	unable to correct technical errors for 24–48 hrs; unable to concentrate on academic work
General health	progressive muscular weakness, reduced efficiency	possible muscle and joint pain, light headedness and stomach upset. General feeling of malaise, even headaches	difficulty in sleeping; pulse remains higher than normal for up to 24 hrs; continued physical inefficiency and discomfort
Approach to training	desire for longer recoveries but eager to train	desire for complete rest; doubts on value of training; fear of further loading	disinclined to train next day; negative attitude to coach—perhaps even inventing excuses for avoiding training

Overstressing causes progressive fatigue. Capacity is not restored after training in this situation and will continue to deteriorate until the causes of overstressing are removed. If they are not, the athlete may become ill.

Israel (1963) points out that overstressing can produce either of two extremes of response: overexcitement of the system (overstimulation), or overdepression (overinhibition). He refers to the former as *basedovoid* overstressing and suggests that, within the training context, this occurs chiefly as a result of suddenly increasing the density of sub-maximum intensity loadings in the training programme, or of making the excessive demands on the power of concentration. He refers to the latter as *addisonoid* overstressing, and this is brought about by very comprehensive endurance programmes with persistent overemphasis in the extent of loading.

Whilst there is general agreement amongst coaches and training theorists with Israel's observations, these broad causes of overstressing are seldom the only cause. In fact they should be viewed more as major contributors to the syndrome. The fact is that the phenomenon of overstressing arises from the cumulative effect of many stressors – which leaves the individual exposed to a very small threshold of stress tolerance. Other stressors include the following.

(1) Principal faults in the training process: recovery is neglected (mistakes in the build-up of micro- and macrocycles, and inadequate use of general exercise sessions for recovery); demands increased too quickly so that adaptation cannot be consolidated; too rapid an increase of loading after forced breaks (injuries, illness); too great an extent of loadings of maximum and sub-maximum intensity; too high an intensity of duration loadings in endurance training; excessive and forced technical schooling in complicated courses of movement without adequate recovery; excess of competitions with maximum demands, combined with frequent disturbance of the daily routine and insufficient training; excessive bias of training methods and units; lack of trust in the coach; repeated setbacks as a result of coach setting sights too high; inability of athlete or coach to keep sport 'in perspective'.

(2) Factors reducing performance:

- lifestyle – inadequate sleep; irregular daily routine; dissolute conduct; use of alcohol and tobacco; excess of caffeine; distracting company; lack of free time or inability to relax; nutritional deficiencies (lack of vitamins); frequent necessity to adjust body weight; accepting more stressors when already at capacity
- environment – poor living conditions (overcrowding, etc.); excessive family duties and tensions; difficulties in personal relationships; dissatisfaction with career, studies, school; poor marks in school, studies, etc; conflict with attitudes inimical to sports (family, superiors); excess of stimuli (TV, cinema); temporary upsurge of anxiety (e.g. exams)
- health upsets – feverish colds; stomach or intestinal upsets; glandular

fever; chronic purulent illnesses (e.g. of tonsils, teeth, ovaries, sinuses); after effects of infectious illnesses (e.g. sore throats, lingering cough etc.); injury; neglected infections (e.g. athlete's foot, rashes etc.).

Management of the athlete's lifestyle outside the sporting context, whilst finally resting with the athlete, requires knowledge and skill in areas including time management; personal health and hygiene; control of inter-personal communication and relationships with people in social and business situations; and direction in pursuit of career. There is no single 'educator' here. Learning resources include parents, family, teachers, friends, and coaches. Because of this, it is often wrongly assumed that 'someone else' is taking care of such matters. The truth is that *all* of the athlete's potential 'educators' must accept responsibility for relevant input. Before anyone loads the athlete with yet another stressor, the existing stressor profile should be known, and help afforded in ensuring that the athlete's tolerance to stress is not overloaded.

Within the sporting context, there is much the coach can do in the area of preventing overstressing. With careful planning, means and methods to encourage recovery or regeneration can be included in the training programme. This will ensure that the aggregate effect of the training programme does not constitute a stressor which will tip the athlete into the overstress situation.

The means and methods may be considered at three levels: intra-unit, inter-unit and inter-micro/macrocycle.

Intra-unit (between repetitions and/or sets)
The period of time involved here is measured in seconds or minutes. During this period the athlete must recover to a level which permits the objective of the training unit to be met. For example, if the unit is interval training, the degree of recovery, monitored by noting heart rate, must allow the athlete's heart rate to fall to around the mid-point of the total range. If resting heart rate is 60 and maximum is 180, then the athlete's heart rate should be around 120–130 before he performs the next repetition.

If maximum quality of performance is required over a number of repetitions, say for speed, recovery must be complete between runs. A unit of 3 x 60m then, will require at least 10 minutes between repetitions.

If incomplete recovery is required to guarantee cumulative fatigue for development of anaerobic tolerance, time periods are chosen to ensure that the athlete can perform sufficient repetitions to guarantee a training effect. This effect may or may not require that the athlete maintains a minimum quality of performance in each repetition. If it does, then clearly the time periods are larger and the quality of performance is sub-maximum.

Recovery activities include:

- lying down
- walking
- jogging
- doing a related activity

- doing an unrelated activity
- massage
- changing footwear
- warming up.

Intra-unit recovery is, by definition, part of the training *load*. However, it may also be considered part of the stimulus in certain types of training. For example, in some special strength work, where the objective is to accelerate strength levels, instead of:

$$load = stimulus + recovery$$

it becomes

$$load = stimulus\ (1) + stimulus\ (2)$$

So, in leg work, the training unit might become:

$$stimulus\ 1–5 \times 85\%\ max\ ½\ squat$$
$$stimulus\ 2–5 \times rebounds\ over\ 8\ hurdles\ at\ 3ft.$$

Immediately on completing stimulus 2, the athlete starts again with stimulus 1. The total unit is 3–5 x (stimulus 1 + stimulus 2).

Inter-unit (between units on a given day or from day to day)

The period of time involved here is measured in hours or days. Few athletes outside the endurance group pursue the same training objectives in successive units. Having said this, many endurance athletes follow a pattern of 'hard unit' – 'easy unit' alternation. Inbuilt to most training programmes then, is a form of recovery from the *stressor of specific training loads*.

Coaches must learn to feel comfortable not only at including rest days and rest units in the microcycle, but also at introducing periods of up to several days recovery when necessary. The flexibility of programme design, as suggested in chapter 22 in connection with the aggregate cumulative effect of training, should allow for this.

Recovery activities include:

- special diets, lying down, sleeping, massage, jacuzzi, sauna, change of venue, work/study, going out to a show, watching TV, listening to music etc.
- doing another event/sport at recreational level, e.g. swimming, golf, cycling etc
- varying – the training objective; the level of athlete involvement in decision making; routine; between training and competition
- general activity units
- warm-up units
- 'feel good' sessions
- 'finding space' sessions
- relaxation units – dynamic/passive
- dance, aesthetic expression.

Although it seems commonsense to include such activities, both athletes and coaches can occasionally abandon commonsense under pressure. For example, it is not unknown for programmes to be made harder rather than easier when performance in training does not come up to expectation. For athletes who are achievement-oriented, lack of commitment or hard work is not an acceptable explanation for performance problems. It is more likely that the athlete has been over-committing and overworking, or that the work has been inappropriate. Whatever the explanation may be, the coach must ensure that units for recovery or regeneration not only appear in the programme, but are also carried through.

Inter-micro/macrocycle (normally at transition or regeneration phase)

The period of time involved here is measured in days or weeks, and suggests that such cycles/phases should be considered and introduced to the programme at the same time as the year plan itself is set out. This is not to say, of course, that given certain circumstances, such a phase may not be introduced in pursuit of a specific regenerative objective, at any time in the year.

The 'early planned' regeneration phase is normally between conclusion of the competition period and commencement of the introductory phase of the year plan. It should be planned in such a way that the athlete returns to training highly motivated and fully prepared to commit himself to the rigours and discipline of training. This is best achieved quite simply by taking a vacation. This suggests:

- a different climate
- different surroundings
- different routine
- different social environment
- different physical activities
- different diet
- different emotional and mental demands.

The 'introduced' regeneration phase is normally associated with recovery from crises. Unexpected and critical defeat; selection for a major championship; serious injury/illness; all represent possible crises which may require a regeneration phase to help bring things back into focus. However, it should be said that the crisis situation seldom arrives out of the blue. It can often be spotted early. Timely regeneration will help avoid the situation becoming virtually irretrievable.

The coach should be aware of the following.

(1) Psychological symptoms: increased irritability; obstinacy; increased argumentativeness; 'flying off the handle'; complaining about trivial things; defiance; anxiety; melancholy; avoidance of contact with coach and colleagues; oversensitivity to criticism; blaming everyone else for problems; increased indolence; fullness; 'imagining things'; depression; insecurity.

(2) Performance symptoms:

- techniques – increased incidence of disturbance in the basic technical model, e.g. reappearance of old faults; cramps; inhibitions; loss of confidence; disturbance in the rhythm and flow of the movement; reduced ability to differentiate between right and wrong movement
- condition – diminishing endurance, strength, speed; longer recovery times needed; loss of 'bounce' in training – becoming almost a 'slog'; loss of personal effervescence on and off track
- competitive qualities – reduced readiness for competition 'action'; fear of competition (or rather of losing); giving up under pressure; confusion in competition such as departure from competition plan or inability to respond correctly to the strategy of the opposition; easily demoralised; loss of belief in self and abilities; talks about lack of point in continuing the struggle; wants out!

(3) Somatic functional: sleeping difficulties; lack of appetite; loss of weight; 'addictive' eating; increase in weight; disturbance in digestive function; longer recovery of pulse to resting rate, increased resting heart rate; dizzy spells; night sweating; increased susceptibility to injury/infection; loss of vitality.

Should such symptoms arise, especially if there are several symptoms, the coach should:

- have the athlete check with his doctor
- put the athlete *immediately* on a regeneration programme.

Selection of components to be included in the regenerative programme vary according to whether the athlete's reaction is *basedovoid* or *addisonoid*. Israel identified examples of such variance and these have been divided into three sections.

Basedovoid

Diet: encourage the athlete to eat more; choose basic foods such as milk, vegetables, fruit; avoid spicy or greasy sauces/dressings; avoid coffee, tea and soft drinks containing caffeine; reduce protein consumption, especially red meat; take a concentrated course of vitamins, especially B complex, C and A; take small quantity of alcohol e.g. a glass of sherry prior to sleeping; take tonics and nutritional drinks which are approved by anti-doping bodies.

Physical therapy: swim outdoors; bathe in the evening for 15–20 minutes (at water temperature 33–37°C) with additives such as Radox, Badedas, extract of pine needles, hops, valerian, carbonic acid etc; take jacuzzis; in the morning, take cold shower followed by a brisk towelling; take soothing massage; do soothing slow pace aerobics/exercises to music with emphasis on slow stretching.

Climate: move to a quiet area e.g. forest or mountains; avoid intense ultra-violet radiation; live in moderate temperature of 18°C–24°C.

Addisonoid

Diet: encourage maintaining a strict 3 meals/day routine; increase protein intake e.g. meat, cheese, eggs, cereals; take a concentrated course of vitamins, especially B complex and C; avoid alcohol; take occasional caffeine based drinks with meals.

Physical therapy: take alternate hot/cold showers in the morning and in the evening; take saunas in the middle of high range of temperatures; take vigorous massage using hot rubbing lotions; do vigorous fast pace aerobics/exercises to music, with emphasis on elasticity.

Climate: move to a bracing climate – windy seaside location is ideal; look for moderate ultra-violet radiation; seaside in a warm climate allows benefits of hot sun and high temperatures to be alternated with plunges in the sea; live in moderate to high temperatures of 22°C–28°C.

Because several people may be involved in an athlete's development and lifestyle, they should all understand the complex business of over-stressing. Consequently, there should be some level of communication across what amounts to a 'team', to help establish that balance of stressors which will not harm the athlete.

▌ Summary

The effect of training may become negative if the athlete's lifestyle outside sport is poorly managed, so the total content of that lifestyle must be known. The coach must accept a responsibility to help ensure sound management in this direction, and also to develop an understanding of the unique aggregate of stressors represented by the athlete's lifestyle.

Both the structure of loading and the training ratio must be carefully planned if negative training effects are to be avoided. More specifically, the coach must ensure adequate recovery before the athlete is exposed to subsequent loadings. Means of accelerating recovery in normal training and in the event of possible overstressing, should be understood and applied.

Close observation of the athlete for early identification of symptoms of overstressing may help eliminate any serious damage to the athlete's fitness status in the long term.

24
Competition period

Competition

It must always be borne in mind that optimal performance can only be recorded in a competition. After all, there are no awards offered for world records in training! This point must be emphasised. The coach is preparing the athlete to improve his competition performance and therefore all training is in pursuit of this end. The concept of periodisation implies producing or reproducing the high-point of performance in a particular competition.

Training competitions

Bridging phases 2 and 3 is a 'grey area' where competition specific training is mainly composed of competitions themselves. These competitions have immense importance in the development of the athlete's training status and his competition performance. Moreover, they are a means of evaluating status and stability of performance. These competitions are seldom used to evaluate status relative to other athletes. Instead, they may evaluate the athlete's status relative to his own previous competition performance, or those at the same time last year, etc. It seems reasonable to refer to all such competitions as 'training competitions'. These may be simple competitions to assess training status, or progressively sophisticated in terms of objective (and frequently referred to as 'build-up competitions'). It is worth pointing out that these competitions may well include events other than the athlete's own. For example, a 400m hurdler may run 500m to assess speed endurance, or a breast stroke swimmer may swim medleys to assess strength endurance, and so on.

Principal competitions

Apart from these training competitions, one should also distinguish principal competitions. These competitions dictate the patterns of macrocycles in the competition period, just as the pattern of the complete annual cycle is dictated by the climax of the competition period. The macrocycles must be so arranged that the best possible performance can be produced in each principal competition. The principal competitions should be seen as including the 'main' and the 'major' competitions.

These main competitions are the final preparations for the major competition or the 'competition climax'. According to the nature of the sport, Matveyev (1965) believes two or more peaks (including the competition climax) are possible. However, from practical experience, it is most unusual for an athlete to produce more than four peaks even in the explosive sports where the technical component is high.

By way of summary of these points, the competition programme might be represented schematically as in figure 84.

Date	Level Event	Phase	Macrocycle Content	Macrocycle Objective
April 5		II	Progression into optimal competition frequency:	Rapid increase in competition performance. Training
12			loading extent reducing:	competition 'hardness'.
	(a) 200m: 110H: 4 x 100		training itself reduced but	Evaluation of technical
19			loading not yet at optimal	performance and training
	(a) LONG: TRIPLE: HIGH		intensity. Probably one	status. Stabilising
			macrocycle only.	competition performance:
26				putting together competition
	(a) LONG: 100m: 4 x 400			experience.
May 3				
10	(b) LONG: 100m			
			Emphasis on training:	Correction of technical
			correction of technical faults	faults:
17	(a) 200H: 200m		found in previous macrocycle:	preparation for III/III₂ based
	(b) 100m: LONG		intensity progressing steadily.	on above evaluations:
24	(a) 100m			commencement of main
31	(c) LONG: 4 x 100			competitions.
June 7			Main competitions with	Stabilsiing optimal
			gradual reduction of extent	competition performances.
14	(a) LONG: 100m: 4 x 400	III	as loading now moves to	Recording these in
		or	optimal intensity, but	main competitions.
		III₂	structure of loading is still	Collection of all relevant
21	(d) LONG: 4 x 100		inkeeping with event	data on behaviour in all
			requirements. There will be	competition situations.
28			several mesocycles here.	
	(a) 100m			
July 5	(c) LONG: 200m			
12	(d) LONG: 4 x 100			
	(a) 4 x 100: 4 x 400			
19			Period of special preparation.	Special preparation for
			Extent of loading rises for	major competitions
26	(b) 100m: 200m	IV	3 wks then decreases as	based on analysis of
			intensity reaches optimal—	III/III₂.
Aug. 2	(b) LONG		and highest in the annual	
			cycle. The whole of this phase	
9			is a complete macrocycle.	
16	(d) LONG			
23		V		
30				

Note: (a) Simple training, (b) build-up, (c) main competition, (d) peaks.

Fig. 84 *Possible distribution of competitions for an athlete whose main discipline is long jump. Note that from approximately April 12th–May 21st there is almost a 'grey area' where phases II and III are bridged*

■ Competition v training

But why should competitions have anything more to offer training than, say, a trial in a training session? In training, one can only simulate competition situations. In competition, the athlete, due to the experience of competition and its *emotional* demands, emerges more completely exhausted than in training. Consequently the stimulus for adaptation to high or maximum loading is more effective than that which can be reproduced in training. Just as important, however, is that competition is the most specific training that exists to master emotional excitement, and in such a way that it helps the athlete surpass present limits of performance. It is not unusual to hear of an athlete producing superb achievements in training, yet experiencing disasters in competition. He has failed to master himself in competition, reacting negatively to the insecurity it threatens. Once back in the quietness and security of the training situation, all is well again. Competition is the only means of adapting to the stressor of competition and to avoid its particular stress simply increases the stress potential of the next one.

In addition to this factor which validates competition as a training means, exposing the athlete to a wide variety of competition situations lessens the likelihood of him being confronted with the unfamiliar. Every competition has a character of its own, determined not only by the physical environment of stadium, wind, humidity, and so on, but also by the group of athletes involved. Athletes must be encouraged to seek out opposition, especially if the opposition is known to be better. By competing with the same opponents, a system of stereotyped, albeit efficient, reactions will evolve. Varied opposition and environment develops the capacity to adapt more readily to varying competition conditions.

■ Competition frequency

Frequency of competition is determined by athlete preference and relevant competition availability at one extreme, and the structure of sports competitions at the other. Weather conditions also play a part in the UK!

Time is needed for recovery from the physical and emotional stress of a main or build-up competition, and also to correct training deficiencies. Consequently, the 'build-up' and principal competitions will be 7–10 in number. Any additional competitions should be low key, at the level of 'simple training' status. Against this background, speed and elastic strength events in track and field can amount to 1 or 2 per week, while strength endurance and the longer track events can be separated by up to 14 days.

Occasionally there are instances where athletes saturate part of the competition season with a concentration of quality performances. In 1965, Ron Clarke raced 21 times in 56 days, lowering the 500m record twice, and the 10 mile record once. Moreover, in the month preceding this period, he set a world record for 3 miles; and three months after this period, in the space of 40 days he set world marks on three occasions: 3 miles/5000m, 3 miles, and 6 miles/10,000m. In 1980, Sebastian Coe established three world records again over a very brief time scale:

July 3	Oslo – 800m	1 min 42.33 sec.
July 17	Oslo – 1 mile	3 min 48.95 sec.
August 15	Zurich – 1500m	3 min 32.03 sec.

Only after several years preparation can such a programme be contemplated – and it certainly cannot be repeated over 2–3 successive years. At this level, the concept of using a year to regenerate is not uncommon. On the other hand, at the lower end of the scale, it has already been suggested that the young and developing athlete seems to be quite uninhibited in his appetite for competition. In fact, according to Thiess (1967), improvement in performance is directly proportional to competition frequency. He recommended, following the 1966 Spartakiad, 20–30 competitions in the period cycle leading up to the major competition.

Before moving on to competition preparation, and by way of summary, the following points should be noted:

- the athlete must compete as often as is necessary to achieve and stabilise a good competition performance
- the better opponent must *not* be avoided without good reason
- the athlete should only compete when he is physically and emotionally prepared for it
- too many competitions (especially when they are close together or involve considerable travel) not only interfere with training progression, but cause cumulative psychological fatigue
- competitions should be in ascending order of difficulty, building up towards a major competition with all competitions subordinate to it.

■ Long season sports

A team at the top of the F.A. Premier League may, due to the success of the club, have roughly 60 competitions in the course of approximately 270 days. Some of the players will also have international duties, and no allowance is made here for any replays. It still means, however, that for 75% of the year, players are potentially in line for one competition every 3½–4½ days!

In such cases, competition frequently becomes a central factor in maintaining a player's level of conditioning. It also, of course, saps the player's physical and emotional energies establishing a climate for the negative effects of stress.

Managers and coaches must, then, create a rotating cycle of development for *each* player, where regeneration is ensured and conditioning status is updated to give consistent high performance and motivation. It should not be injury or illness which determine when a player is rested, but value-judgements related to an individual player's conditioning and motivational status. A system of player rotation must be understood by players and coaches, and fitted into the year phase in a way which allows the club to meet team and player development objectives. For the non-competitive 25% of the year it becomes essential that all players build the greatest possible conditioning base *and* regenerate fully from the competition season, so that the 'player rotation' approach can be effected with minimal difference to team performance.

■ **Competition preparation**

Specific competition preparation assumes a given status of training in the athlete for a given sport. This understood, the coach must carefully prepare units, etc., leading up to the competition itself. The following points should be taken into account.

(1) The specific objective of the competition must be known by, and discussed with, the athlete. If it is not known, there is no means of evaluating success or failure, nor is there any distinct purpose to training. The objective may fall into one of two categories, or be a combination of both:

• competition with the athlete himself. These contests are to advance training status, improve performance, etc. Here, the opposition is used to aid pursuit of the objective
• competition with an opponent. These contests are to win a point for the club/country, qualify for the next round, eliminate opposition, win a title etc. Here the opposition is to be defeated.

(2) The opposition must be clearly identified and known to the athlete, as not all athletes in a contest may be opponents. Information on each opponent should include previous best performance, recent history of competition, and behaviour in competition (e.g. how series are strung together, favourite tactics, strengths and weaknesses etc.).

(3) It is difficult to adapt quickly to unfamiliar conditions (a strange surface, humidity, altitude, temperature, etc.). Where possible, training should involve similar conditions to those at the competition venue.

(4) The chronobiologist encourages the coach to understand the peak and trough of human performance in terms of body rhythms of daily and longer cycles. The athlete must be able to complete at specific times and the coach should make allowances for adjustments in body rhythms. For instance, if travel has meant an East/West time shift, the athlete should arrive at his destination with enough time to spare to 'reset' his body clock. If this is impossible, the athlete's normal day must be 'shifted' in training.

(5) The athlete should be educated towards complete independence and the capacity to act 'executively' in the competition situation, and must take his opposition seriously yet concentrate upon the task in hand. The athlete must *never* be afraid of opposition and certainly never be encouraged to avoid opponents equal, or superior, to himself. In fact, the athlete should be hungry for such opposition, looking forward to these encounters with a positive anticipation. After all, this level of opponent represents the highest stimulus to increased adaptation.

(6) Despite the athlete's physical and emotional concentration on the forthcoming competition, anxiety should be discouraged. The contest must not be seen as some kind of threatening monster. In the last few days, the coach should stimulate the athlete's belief in success, aid

relaxation via recreation and reading, avoid boredom by organising interesting but relaxing outings, and so on. Autogenic training, as formulated by Schultz (1956), or by the variation advanced by Machak (1964) may have something to offer in the control of 'pre-start reaction'. The athletes are originally 'trained' to relax by the coach, but eventually may induce the same state of relaxation themselves. On the other hand, post-hypnotic suggestion can be applied to only few athletes, though in general rather than specific ways. Hypnosis, of course, does not allow an athlete to adjust his behaviour to an unexpected situation that might occur in competition.

(7) Athletes naturally vary in their behaviour immediately prior to competition. Puni (1961) refers to this as 'pre-start reaction' and tabulated variations of this are shown in table 41. If the athlete shows start-fever, warm-up should be relaxed, while for those with start-apathy the warm-up should be vigorous and lively. According to Vanek and Cratty (1970), both extremes should benefit from autogenic training. Athletes also vary in their degree of sociability during warm-up, and over the last few days before a competition. A stronger feeling of security can sometimes come from being in a group, but this is not always the case.

(8) The younger athlete will especially benefit from observing other events prior to his own. The more mature athlete may learn something of the atmosphere of the stadium, the temperature, variations in wind, and so on. There is always the morale boost, of course, when witnessing a successful performance by a colleague. On the other hand, morale can slide with an early defeat. While this can be turned to advantage as a spur to other team members, the athletes who are yet to compete should not be exposed to the demoralising effect of discussing the defeat with the unfortunate athlete. There will be time for this after the day's competitions are over.

(9) It is the athlete's responsibility to check his personal equipment, but it is the coach's responsibility to ensure that the athlete knows the specific equipment required.

(10) In the construction of the special competition preparation cycle, the following should be noted:

- a decision must be made by the coach whether to programme for improved performance or stabilisation of existing performance level. There are times when to demand increased levels of intensity will 'burst the bubble'
- the athlete's own status, that of his opposition, and the competition environment must be evaluated
- microcycles must allow complete recovery between units
- any additional competition must not itself be a peak but rather a build-up. Errors here will deplete reserves of emotional and physical energy. At least one such competition should be at or near the venue of the

major competition, especially if the athlete must travel East/West, to altitude, to extreme humidity, etc

- the coach must develop the athlete's emotional focus and his appreciation of the need for complete preparation for the forthcoming contest. Too often an Olympic qualifying mark is reached, an athlete selected, and apathy follows. Or, again, a player who has gained international selection may lose his edge in the next game for his club. It is as if gaining selection was the major objective. Once targets have been reached, *new* targets must be set or qualifying targets should be higher than is necessary

Table 41 *Principal forms of pre-start reaction* from Harre (1973) according to Puni (1961)

state of readiness for competition	start-fever (nervous anticipation)	start-apathy (listlessness/inhibition)
All physiological processes proceed normally.	The athlete radiates great excitement; acute physiological changes (considerable increase in pulse rate, trembling in the limbs, feeling of weakness in lower extremities, etc.).	Listless, completely inhibited movements, yawning.
Slight excitement, enjoyable and rather impatient anticipation of the coming challenge, optimal power of concentration in complete control of own behaviour, radiating energy.	Great nervousness, un-controlled movements, forgetfulness, absent-mindedness, uncertainty of action, haste, un-necessary activity.	Limp, lazy, apathetic, anxious; low spirits; desire to 'cry-off' from competition, tired, 'sour', unable to get going.
The athlete enters into competition in a highly organised way and exactly according to plan, sees the way ahead clearly, masters the situation, all forces at his disposal are brought into use in a tactically correct way; the anticipated result is achieved or surpassed.	Athlete's activity is disturbed, partially dis-organised, he competes rashly, departs from his usual tactical line, loses the feeling for tempo, exhausts himself pre-maturely; movements are uncontrolled, accumulation of mis-takes in face of high technical demands; very cramped.	He does not compete energetically, willpower soon abates, the athlete is incapable of mobilising the strength he possesses, action does not flow; after competition he is not exhausted because all reactions were on a low level.

Table 42   *Observations for construction of specific cycle*

previous competition series	procedure in special preparation
Performance steadily improved, capacity for loading high.	Previous training microcycles continued, but recharging emphasised in first week. Moreover, extent of lower intensity training raised for first 2–3 weeks, then high intensity of competition specific loadings in final 2–3 weeks.
Not daily training, perhaps every other day or 2:1:3:1 etc., but very high intensity of loading in each unit. Performance reasonable but small increases.	Move to daily training at lower intensity. Extent is therefore high in general and special, but competition specific training should be low. Intensity is reduced for 2–3 weeks—then accelerated to very high—perhaps even returning to training every other day in last 2 weeks.
High competition frequency has interfered with total extent of training and normal progression. Perhaps no further improvements in performance, loadings of very high intensity.	Increase extent of general and special, but very low competition specific. Loadings roughly equal to late phase 2. Include 2–3 build-up competitions in last 2 weeks, i.e. highest intensity of competition specific loadings. This accompanied by all round increase in intensity, decrease in extent.
Poor or even regressive results in competition. Competition life is a struggle, yet training similar to last year.	Check with bioprofile and physiotherapist. If this gives the athlete an 'all-clear': for the experienced athlete, great increase in extent of all loading two weeks; then great increase in intensity as extent falls for 10–14 days; then high intensity competition specific over final week. 1–2 build-up competitions in final 10 days. For the inexperienced athlete, raise extent of general and specific loadings for two weeks to values of late phase 2; two build-up competitions in successive days, seven days prior to major competition—then high intensity competition specific final week. If athletes are found unfit by check-up then the value of proceeding to the major competition is in doubt.
Early performances excellent—then overstress symptoms appear as performances fall.	If this overstress is traced to the nature of loadings, the immediate objective is to restore stability of training status. High extent of general and physical recreation activities—with rising extent of special training in first 7–10 days. Once enthusiasm for more intensive loadings returns, hold medium extent of all loadings with gradually raised intensity for next 10–14 days—then inject a steep increase in intensity (especially in competition specific) up to competition. Value of build-up competition is limited. If overstress is due to other factors, trace source then proceed as above.

- the first week of the special cycle leading up to the major contest should emphasise general development, relaxation and the recharging of batteries before the concentrated four weeks of build-up are started. This will be interpreted variously according to the patterns of performance in the previous cycle
- no technical variations should be attempted
- a thorough check by a physiotherapist or sports medicine specialist should be sought in the first week of this five-week cycle
- rules and regulations specific to the forthcoming competition should be clearly understood by the athlete. Moreover, commands and instructions in a foreign language should be rehearsed, where applicable.

(11) While the content and composition of units and microcycles vary between individual athletes, some general observations may be of value to coaches and athletes (table 42).

On the day, only one person can bring the hours of work to a successful conclusion. The athlete's own will to co-ordinate all that has been learned and worked, and to express his own personality within the limitations imposed by the sport and the competition, is the most vital quality of the successful athlete.

When the competition is over, the athlete will have a post-event reaction. This will be coloured by whether or not the acknowledged objectives of the competition have been met. Those who have not met the objective need not be reminded of it! Those who have been successful need little encouragement to be aware of this! The coach should encourage a state of normality and relaxation for the rest of the day of competition. Certainly there must be no criticism unless the athlete has for some reason misinterpreted the result relative to the objective. *Any evaluation and planned modification of programme should be made the day after the competition at the latest.* Such evaluation and modification is part of the athlete's preparation for the next competition and must not be neglected.

▋Summary

It is in the competition period that the objectives of the periodised year are met. Each competition should be seen as fulfilling several roles. It serves as training for future competition, is a test situation for evaluation status, and is the *raison d'être* of training. The athlete's objectives in competition will vary and they must be identified prior to a given competition. The coach, in planning and distribution and frequency of competitions, and in identifying competition objectives, must have detailed knowledge of the competition programme available and the level of each competition. Only then can he bring the athlete to each competition prepared to meet the identified objectives.

Summary of part 5

When planning the athlete's annual training programme, the coach must have access to a considerable volume of information and also have the ability to interpret this in the light of current training theory. The structure of this programme begins to take its final shape during the transition period at the conclusion of the previous competition season. However, this is not to say that the programme is inflexible. The coach must appreciate the dynamic nature of his work and be prepared, where necessary, to make ready adjustment within the structure.

Information required by the coach is as follows.

(1) He should know the programme of competition available to the athlete and the precise nature of each competition.
(2) He should know how to plan the year to accommodate the best competition programme for the athlete's development.
(3) He should know the theoretical distribution of general, special and competition specific training in each phase of the year.
(4) He should know the number of training units and the training environment available to the athlete.
(5) He should know the relevant training practices, structures of loading and training ratios for development of specific fitness required of the athlete to meet his training objectives.
(6) He should know the principles of unit, microcycle, mesocycle and macrocycle construction, and their variations according to the phase of the annual cycle.
(7) He should know the status of the athlete relative to the demands of the event.

The final product should reflect the coach's interpretation of training theory and application of experience in a programme designed to meet the unique needs of an athlete in pursuit of competitive advantage.

The athlete's fundamental objective in sport is pursuit of competitive advantage. It represents a serious commitment of time and effort, but is nevertheless undertaken for the pleasure which that commitment brings. To be invited to direct the athlete's growth and development in sport is a great honour, to accept that invitation is to acknowledge an immense responsibility. The coach must known that his work with the athlete will provide a systematic progression towards his fundamental objective, whilst contributing to his total wellbeing. Such knowledge is born of an understanding of those areas of study which feed into the science of sport as outlined in parts 1, 2 and 3, and of an appreciation of how these relate to the athlete via training theory, as presented in parts 4 and 5. It is my belief that when the coach thoughtfully weaves this knowledge into the fabric of practical experience, the athlete must certainly achieve his fundamental objective. Moreover, the athlete's life in sport will be a purposeful and enjoyable experience which will add a lasting richness to his life outside sport.

References for part 5

Bauersfeld, M. & Voss, G. Neue wege im schnelligkeitsteaincing. Munster: Philippka 1992. In *Trainer Bibliotek, Vol. 28*

Bellotti, P. (March 1991) A few aspects of the theory and practice of speed development. In *New Studies in Athletics, Vol. 6*, No. 1

Bosco, C. Eine neue methodic zur eimschatzung und programmierung des trainings. In *Leistungssport*, Munster 22 (1992), No. 5, pp 21–28

Carl, G. (1967) *Gewichtheben*. Sportverlag, Berlin

Craig, T. (1973) *Analysis of Female Athletic Injury Frequency*. IVth Coaches' Convention Report

Dick, F. W. (1993) *Foundation of Jumps Development and Initial Conditioning*. Proceedings of E.A.C.A. Congress, Berlin

Donati, A. (March 1995) The development of stride length frequency in sprinting. In *New Studies in Athletics, Vol. 10*, No. 1

Endemann, F. (1973) *Throws Conditioning*. IVth Annual Coaches' Convention Report

Gundlach, H. (1968) Zur Trainierbarkeit der Kraft und Schnelligkeitsfahigkeiten Im Prozess der Korperlichen Vervollkommnung. In *Theorie Und Praxis Der Korperkultur 17*

Harre, D. (1973) *Trainingslehre*. Sportverlag, Berlin

Hettinger, T. (1968) *Isometric Muskelkrafttraining*. Thieme-Verlag, Stuttgart

Hettinger, T. & Müller, E. A. (1953) Muskelleistung und Muskeltraining. *Arbeitsphysiologie*, 15 111–126

Hollmann, N. & Venrath, H. (1962) Experimentelle Untersuchungen zur Bedeutung Eines Trainings Unterhalb Und Oberhalb Der Dauerbelastunsgrenze. In *W.u.a., 'Carl Diem Festschrift'*, Frankfurt

Israel, S. (1963) Das Akute Entlastungssyndrom. In *Theorie Und Praxis Der Korperkultur 12*

Karvonen, M. J., Kentala, E. & Mustala, O. (1957) The effects of training on heart rate. In *Annales Medicinae experimentalis et Biologae Fenniag, Vol. 35*

Kruger, A. (1973) Periodisation or peaking at the right time. *Track Technique*, December

Machak, M. (1964) Relaxacne–Aktivacni, Autoregulacni Zasah, Metoda Nacviku a Psychologicka Charackteristika. *Czechoslovakian Psychology, 3*

Matveyev, L. P. (1962) Die Dynamic Der Belastungun Im Sportlichen Training. In *Theorie Und Praxis Der Korperkultur 11*

Matveyev, L. P. (1966) *Periodisation of Sports Training*. Fiskultura i Sport

Osolin, N. G. & Markov, D. P. (1972) *Distribution of Training* (part translation from Russian). Lehka Atletika, Moscow

Puni, A. Z. (1961) *Abriss Der Sportspsychologie*. Sportverlag, Berlin

Schiffer, J. (September 1994) Overtraining. In *New Studies in Athletics, Vol. 9*, No. 3

Schmolinksy, G. (1974) Leichtathletic. 7th Edn. Sportverlag, Berlin

Schultz, H. H. (1956) *Das Autogene Training*. Konzentrative Selbstentspannung, Stuttgart

Sinkkonen, K. (1975) *The Programming of Distance Running*. Paper to E.L.L.V. Congress Budapest

Ter-Ovanesyan, I. (1965) 'Ter-Ovanesyan on the Long Jump', *Modern Athlete and Coach, Vol 4 No 4*. (Translation from Russian – Lehka Atletika, Moscow)

Thiess, G. (1967) Wettkampfhaufigkeit Im Nachwuchstraining. In *Theorie Und Praxis Der Korperkultur 16*

Vanek, M. & Cratty, B. J. (1970) *Psychology and the Superior Athlete*. MacMillan Co., Toronto

I have also received personal communications from Erkki Oikarrinen (Finland), Peter Tschiene (Germany), Helmar Hommel (Germany), Dr Ekkart Arbeit (Germany), and Elio Locatelli (Italy), and am grateful for their exchange of views.

Postscript

Putting the principles into practice

In providing the leadership an athlete needs for his development, coaches have applied one of three systems according to the situation.

Escort system: where a coach and athlete remain together from beginner stage to élite stage.

Transfer system: where an athlete moves from one coach to another according to the athlete's developmental needs. This is similar to progressing through school from infant teacher through to specialist teachers at high school, or lecturers/tutors at college/university.

Partnership/team system: where a number of coaches are responsible for an athlete's development within the same programme.

It should be clear from this book that an athlete's development needs may extend beyond those which a coach or team of coaches can meet. Consequently, the partnership system must now involve more support people. For example, an athlete may require input from a sports psychologist, a sports physiologist, a doctor, a physiotherapist, a sports biomechanist, a personal manager, a technical coach, a conditioning coach and so on. The number of support people and their level of competence and involvement is determined by the athlete's development needs. The athlete must not become the victim of his support team's limitations!

Providing such a quality of development support requires a special kind of co-ordination:

- to evaluate development needs
- to access relevant human resource
- to harmonise contribution.

The person delivering such a role in many instances may be the coach, but not necessarily. The role is best described as a 'development synthesiser', and the person responsible must synthesise each contribution to ensure that the athlete and all other support people can apply it to the athlete's development advantage. That person will be like an adapter for an electrical appliance, adapting a power source into a form that will make it possible for the appliance to operate.

It will be through the development of this role as a further sophistication of coaching that sports training principles and the sports sciences from which they are derived will be fully focused on meeting the athlete's development needs. Although it will require a high level of competence in the 'technical business' of performance, it will require an even higher level of competence in the 'people business'.

Index

abduction 6–7, 12–23
acclimatisation
  to altitude 81–2
  to temperature 104–6
acetylcholine 107
adaptation 260
addisonoid 288, 292–3
adduction 6–7, 12–23
adenosine diphosphate (ADP) 53, 61,
    84–96, 103, 110
adenosine triphosphate (ATP) 53, 61,
    84–96, 103, 110
adrenal cortex 115–6
adrenal medulla 117
adrenocorticotrophic hormone
    (ACTH) 111–2
aerobic energy pathways 85–8
afferent synthesis 156–61
age 151–2
amino acids 57–9
anaerobic energy pathways 84–5
androgen 116
angiotensin 109
ankle 22
annual cycle
  adaptation 224
  application 224
  preparation 224
anterio–posterior axis 4–5, 12, 15–16,
    18, 20, 22, 35
anti–diuretic hormone (ADH)
    99–100, 111
arousal 142–6
athlete
  and coach relationship 132, 147–9
  emotions 138–40
  image and self–image 149–50
  intellectual preparation 132–33
  nutritional intake 65–7
  personality 146–7, 235
axes 4–6

basal metabolism 102
basedovoid 288, 292
blood 69–75, 80, 97
  pressure 75–6, 122
  vessels 76
bone 8

calcitonin 114
carbohydrates 48–52
cartilage 12
children
  growth 27–33
  physiology 122–7
  psychology 173–8
cohesion 150–1
competition 294–302
  frequency 296–7
  nutrition 66–7
  preparation 298–302
  principal 294–5
  training 294
conduction 103
convection 103

disaccharides 49–50
discs (spine) 16–17

elbow 14–15
endurance
  altitude training 236–8
  and the female athlete 238
  development 226–36
  training methods 226–31
energy 36, 46–7, 84–92, 96
erythrocytes 69–71
escort system 305
esteem scales 134–6
evaluation 207–9, 247–50
evaporation 104
extension 6–7, 12–23

5–HT 109–10
fats 52–7
fatty acids 52–8
feedback 155–6
fingers 16
fitness 184–92
flexion 6, 12–23
fluid
   accumulation 99
   extracellular 98
   interstitial 98
   intracellular 98
   loss 99
follicle stimulating hormone
   (FSH) 113
foot 22–3
force 36

gender 151–2
glands
   adrenal 115–7
   parathyroid 114–5
   secreting 113–20
   thyroid 113–4
glucocorticoids 115–6
gravity 34–5, 40–1
growth 27–33
   and the child 27–33
   hormone 111
gut 79

heart 75, 80, 122–7
hip 19–20
histamine 107–8
homeostasis 97, 107, 121
hormones 30, 103, 107–12
   general 110–13
   local 107–10
hypothalamus 113

joint actions 6–7

kinins 109
knee 21

learning 154–62
   standard situation 162
   technique 164–7
leucocytes 71–2
ligaments 10
lipids 52–7

liver 79
loading
   adaptation to 275–85
   density 279
   duration of stimulus 279
   extent 280
   intensity 276–9
   progressive 280–4
long season sports 297
lower limbs 19–23
lungs 76–9
luteinising hormone 113
lymph 71–2, 99

machines 36
macrocycles 272–4
major monosaccharides 50
maximal oxygen uptake 80–1
menstruation 120, 125
microcycles 206–7, 267–72
   adaptable 271–2
mineralocorticoids 115–6
minerals 60–2
mobility 12
   classification 240–1
   development 240–6
   factors influencing 241–3
   shoulder 13
   role 243–4
   training 244–6
modelling 133–4
momentum 41–2
motion 34, 154–5
   laws of 40
motivation 136–8
motoneuron 88–93
motor learning 154–6
motor learning characteristics
   early primary school 175–6
   mid–secondary 177–8
   primary/secondary school 176–7
muscle 9–10, 80, 88–96, 102–3
   fibres 88–93, 95–6
muscular activity 102–3
   auxotonic 198
   dynamic 196–7
      concentric 196
      eccentric 196–7
   static/isometric 195–6

nutrition 46–68

oestradiol 119
ossification 30
ovary 119
oxygen debt 86
oxygen transport system 69–83, 86
oxytocin 111

pancreas 117
parathyroid hormone 114–5
partnership system 305
performance management 145–6
periodisation 255–66
    competition period 258–9
    preparation period 255–7
    single/double 264–5
    transition period 259–60
    variations in 261–6
periosteum 10
pituitary gland 110–13
plasma 73–4, 97
polysaccharides 50
progesterone 120
prolactin 113
prostaglandins 108–9
proteins 57–60
psychology 140–5, 173–8

radiation 103
rotation 6–7, 12–23

sarcomere 89–93
selection 153
self–esteem scales 134–6
senses 156–61
sensory motor training (SMT) 133–4
shoulder 12–14
skeletal development 30
skeleton 8
speed
    attitude 223–4
    barrier 221–2
    development 215–25
    endurance 222–3
spine 16–19
    shape 17
    movement 17–19
strength
    absolute 193–4
    development 192–214

elastic 192–3
endurance 193
maximum 192
parameters 194–5
relative 193–4
training 209–13
stress 122–7, 286–93
sugars
    simple 48, 50
    complex 48, 50–2
synovia 10

technical training 162–72
temperature regulation 101–6
    clothing 104
tendon 10
testes 118–9
tetrasaccharides 50
thrombocytes 72
thymus 118
thyrotrophin 113–4
thyroxine 113–4
tissues 79
training
    effect 189
    unit 267
training principles
    overload 187–9, 244
    reversibility 188–9, 244
    specificity 187,189, 244
transfer system 305
transverse axis 4–5, 12, 14–17, 20–2,
    35
trisaccharides 50

upper limbs 12–16

vertebrae 16–17
vertical axis 4–5, 12, 14–15, 19–22,
    35
vitamins 62–5
    fat soluble 64–5
    water soluble 62–4
VO_2 maximum 80–2, 122

warm–up 106
waste products 79–80, 104
wrist 15–16